MEDIEVAL
AND
RENAISSANCE
DRAMA
IN ENGLAND

Editorial Board

MEDIEVAL AND RENAISSANCE DRAMA IN ENGLAND

Volume 17

Editcd by

John Pitcher and S. P. Cerasano

Madison • Teaneck
Fairleigh Dickinson University Press

Associated University Presses
2010 Eastpark Boulevard
Cranbury, NJ 08512

The paper used in this publication meets the requirements of the American National Standard for Permanence of Paper for Printed Library Materials Z39.48-1984.

International Standard Book Number 0-8386-4032-X (vol. 17)
International Standard Serial Number 0731-3403

All editorial correspondence concerning *Medieval and Renaissance Drama in England* should be addressed to Professor S. P. Cerasano, Department of English, Colgate University, Hamilton, N.Y., 13346, USA (phone: 315–228–7262; fax: 315–228–7815). Orders and subscriptions should be directed to Associated University Presses, 2010 Eastpark Boulevard, Cranbury, New Jersey 08512.

Medieval and Renaissance Drama in England disclaims responsibility for statements, either of fact or opinion, made by contributors.

Leeds Barroll: Scholar, colleague, and friend

Contents

8   CONTENTS

Foreword

Leeds Barroll founded *Medieval and Renaissance Drama in England* twenty years ago. One of his aims was to publish a journal with enough space for everyone interested in the drama to have their say. Theatre historians would have a place as well as textual scholars, social historians, and students of plays in performance, early and modern. Texts of documents would be as welcome in *MaRDiE* as studies of the political foundations (or agenda) of this or that play.

It is now a proper time to thank Leeds for giving us *MaRDiE* and to thank him too for his many contributions to the study of Shakespeare, the drama, and royal and aristocratic patronage in early modern England. The contributors in this volume wish to honor Leeds with what they have discovered in the archives (a black African in an English lawsuit, a school for girls in Windsor, the provenance of the *Telltale*) or found out about individual lives and circumstances (the little-known "William Appowell, Priest" as well as Henslowe, Daniel, Lord Chancellor Egerton, and King James's taste in tapestries). The special interest Leeds has had in Shakespeare is reflected in this volume too, with studies of *King Lear* as well as its progenitor *King Leir,* of Desdemona's courage, and of Shakespeare's personal dealings with the Chamberlain's Men in 1598. The study of the English history play at the end of the sixteenth century is complemented by an account of the Rose Rage productions of Shakespeare's histories at the end of the twentieth century.

JOHN PITCHER
S. P. CERASANO

Contributors

John H. Astington is Professor of English and Director of the Graduate Centre for the Study of Drama at the University of Toronto. Since the 1970s much of his work has been on the history of the English theater before the Restoration, including royal patronage of the stage. His interests have coincided extensively with those of Leeds Barroll, from whose published work and private conversation he has drawn benefit and encouragement. Both the Shakespeare Association of America and *Medieval and Renaissance Drama in England* have supported his career significantly, and he is pleased to share in celebrating Professor Barroll's generous and energetic scholarly enterprise. John Astington's essay in this volume is dedicated with affection to a man distinguished not only by learning, but by wit, warmth, courtesy, and charm.

HERBERT BERRY is Professor of English Emeritus at the University of Saskatchewan. He has written articles and books about the so-called Shakespearean stage, relying often on the surviving documents of the sixtcenth and seventeenth centuries. His principal recent work is the section about playhouses in *English Professional Theatre, 1530–1660* (Cambridge: Cambridge University Press, 2000).

Herbert Berry has known Leeds Barroll for many years and has joined him in several academic projects. He has also contributed articles and reviews to Professor Barroll's journals.

ANNE JENNALIE COOK is Professor Emerita at Vanderbilt University. As her contribution to this volume makes clear, she has served as the Executive Director of the Shakespeare Association of America and enjoyed her close working relationship with Leeds for some years. Her best-known works are *Making a Match: Courtship in Shakespeare and His Society* (Princeton: Princeton University Press, 1991) and *The Privileged Playgoers of Shakespeare's London, 1576–1642* (Princeton: Princeton University Press, 1981).

S. P. CERASANO is the Edgar W. B. Fairchild Professor of Literature at Colgate University. Her most recent book is *The Routledge Literary Sourcebook on William Shakespeare's "Merchant of Venice"* (2004). Additionally, she served as the book review editor of *Medieval and Renaissance Drama in En-*

gland, under Leeds Barroll and John Pitcher, for over a decade. She writes: "Putting together this volume is but a partial thanks to Leeds Barroll for his unwavering guidance, wisdom, and friendship over what have now turned into many years."

RAPHAEL FALCO is Professor of English at the University of Maryland, Baltimore County. He has published *Conceived Presences: Literary Genealogy in Renaissance England* (Massachusetts, 1994) and *Charismatic Authority in Early Modern English Tragedy* (Johns Hopkins, 2000). At present he is completing a study tentatively called *Cultural Genealogy: The Institution of a Myth*.

R. A. FOAKES is Professor Emeritus at UCLA. In recent years he has edited *King Lear* for the Arden Shakespeare, Series 3. Additionally, he has published a second edition of *Henslowe's Diary* (Cambridge University Press, 2002), and a book entitled *Shakespeare and Violence* (Cambridge University Press, 2003).

Of Leeds Barroll, he writes: "Meeting Leeds many years ago was a unforgettable experience, not simply because of his remarkable bass voice that seems to come from deep inside him, but because of the immediate impact of his geniality, scholarship and charisma. I have learned, too, to appreciate his (and Susan's) kind hospitality and wonderful sense of enjoying life to the full. His record as a scholar and critic speaks for itself, but that is only half the story about someone who is also a sterling human being."

CHARLES R. FORKER is Professor of English Emeritus at Indiana University, Bloomington, and has published widely on Shakespeare, Marlowe, Webster, and other Renaissance dramatists. His most recent book is the Arden 3 edition of Shakespeare's *Richard II* (2002). An essay on Richard II's unstable identity (2001) appeared in *Renascence*, in addition to which articles are forthcoming in the *Shakespeare Yearbook* and the revised *Dictionary of National Biography*. Professors Forker and Barroll are professional associates and friends of long standing. Forker contributed a well-known discussion of Shakespeare's historical-pastoral to the first volume of *Shakespeare Studies* (1965), founded by Barroll, and since then has been a frequent contributor to it and its companion annual, *Medieval and Renaissance Drama in England*, both as essayist and reviewer.

JOAN OZARK HOLMER, Professor of English at Georgetown University, includes among her publications *The Merchant of Venice: Choice, Hazard and Consequence* (1995), as well as articles on Shakespeare, Marlowe, Nashe, Saviolo, Milton, Herrick, and others.

Of Leeds Barroll she says: "I will always be deeply grateful for how spontaneously and warmheartedly Leeds befriended me in my early years of research at the Folger Shakespeare Library and how his encouragement of my discoveries continues to uplift my endeavors. As a young scholar I could not have found a more nurturing supporter to help ground and guide my work in Renaissance studies. My first published essay on Shakespeare's *The Merchant of Venice* appeared in *Shakespeare Studies*, edited by Leeds, and he initiated my own editing experience, whetting my unfailing fascination with the wonders of *Romeo and Juliet*. For scholarly service and collegial collaboration, Leeds, like Shakespeare's Antony, knows no winter in his generosity."

GRACE IOPPOLO is the author of *Revising Shakespeare* (1991) and the forthcoming monograph *Dramatic Manuscripts, in the Age of Shakespeare, Jonson and Middleton* (2004). She is the editor of *Shakespeare Performed: Essays in Honor of R. A. Foakes* (2000) and co-editor, with Peter Beal, of *English Manuscript Studies: Manuscripts and their Makers in the English Renaissance, Volume 11* (2002). She has edited plays by Middleton and Shakespeare and has published numerous articles on the transmission of the early modern text. She is grateful for Leeds Barroll's generous support and mentorship over the years and misses eating burgers with him at Chadwick's in Washington, DC.

RICHARD J. KUHTA is the Librarian of the Folger Shakespeare Library. B.A., Swarthmore College; M.A., Shakespeare Institute, University of Birmingham (England); Dipl. Anglo-Irish Literature, Trinity College Dublin (Ireland); M.L.S., Columbia University. His research interests before the Folger bridged two worlds, Shakespeare (seventeenth-century Shakespearean Drollery) and the Irish Literary Renaissance (Cuala Press). Since 1994 his work has focused on the Shakespearean paintings of Henry Fuseli, and on the subject of provenance and ownership, in conjunction with the exhibition, *Thys Boke Is Myne* (Folger Shakespeare Library, 2002). He comments: "Meeting people like Leeds and Susan in 1994 assured me that a move from a small liberal arts campus to a research environment of international stature was clearly going to be a catalyst in my personal and professional life. I so admired what Leeds was doing for the Folger Institute, particularly with his "Researching the Renaissance" students, teaching young scholars how to open doors into the collection and how to think and work collaboratively. Leeds loves libraries, and knows how they work. So it was a great pleasure when our conversations about one shared passion, libraries, recently moved to another, chamber music, and continues apace.

WILLIAM B. LONG taught Elizabethan-Jacobean-Caroline drama at Washington University in St. Louis and at the City University of New York. He has published a number of articles exploring various aspects of English theatrical manuscripts surviving from the late sixteenth and early seventeenth centuries. Basic to these studies are his investigations of manuscript playbooks, which reveal much about how playing companies accomplished the transformation of the playwrights' words into live theater: how players used their stages, what they did to the playwrights' dialogue and stage directions, and what effect their actions had on the transmission of texts. Although regularly ignored by the editor of Shakespeare and his contemporaries, these manuscripts can be extremely helpful in attempting to determine the provenance of early printed texts.

Like Leeds Barroll, Dr. Long was a student of Gerald Eades Bentley at Princeton, who instilled not only a long-term commitment to the subject matter, but also a relentlessly rigorous insistence that facts be carefully tested and that conclusions, even tentative ones, be constructed with great caution. Central to this discipline were the assumptions that the arduous search for new information and the analysis of fragments of Elizabethan-Jacobean-Caroline theatrical archeology unquestionably warranted investing enormous amounts of time in studying and in instructing others.

When Leeds sought to found a journal concentrating on Medieval and non-Shakespearean Renaissance drama, his telephone call to Long, then Senior Editor in a scholarly publishing house, found an eager collaborator. Soon, *Medieval and Renaissance Drama in England* became a reality. From its inception, MaRDiE has concentrated on theater history and archeology and on the closely related study of manuscripts and early printed texts.

SCOTT MCMILLIN, Professor of English at Cornell University, has written *The Elizabethan Theatre and The Book of Sir Thomas More, Shakespeare in Performance: 1 Henry IV,* and (with Sally-Beth MacLean), *The Queen's Men and Their Plays,* which won the Sohmer-Hall Prize for the best piece of theater history in 1999. He has edited the quarto version of *Othello* for Cambridge University Press and the Norton Critical Edition of *Restoration and Eighteenth Century Comedy,* which includes *The Man of Mode, The Country Wife, The Rover, The Way of the World, The Conscious Lovers,* and *The School for Scandal.*

Of Leeds Barroll, he writes: "I first became aware of Leeds when we were both trying to get Gerald Eades Bentley to take us seriously as students at Princeton. I didn't know Leeds's name then—he was a graduate student, I an undergraduate, and Princeton allowed no intermingling of these groups—but there was a striking figure seen day and night on Level B of Firestone Library who came to stand for all graduate students in my view: that's what they look like, that's what they do, carry all those books around, and seem to enjoy it too! This was Leeds Barroll, I later learned.

Actually graduate students don't all look like Leeds, but I was right about the books and having to carry them day and night. Years later, when Leeds gave his amusing Presidential Address for the Shakespeare Association on one man's adventure with the personal computer, I remembered his armloads of books on Level B and wondered if the new technology had reduced the burden at all. But a decade later, at the Folger, there he was every day, books, books, books. One of the pleasures of my professional life was being on the editorial board of the Cornell University Press when Leeds's *Politics, Plague, and Shakespeare's Theatre* was offered to us, and seeing what a good book it was bound to be. I've been carrying it around lately myself, as the opening paragraphs of my contribution make clear. It's no burden at all."

JOHN PITCHER is a Fellow of St. John's College, Oxford. He has recently edited *Cymbeline* for the New Penguin Shakespeare and *The Winter's Tale* for the Arden Shakespeare, third series. He has served as Editor of *Medieval and Renaissance Drama in England* since 1995. His chief work for many years has been toward the multivolume Oxford edition of the Elizabethan poet, Samuel Daniel. This has involved detailed studies of Daniel's patrons, his circumstances at court, and intellectual and political contexts. Leeds Barroll has been an exemplary friend, adviser and supporter in this work. He writes: "Leeds knows a fabulous amount about the Elizabethan and Jacobean courts, knowledge which he shares with great generosity. He is shrewd about evidence, wise in his estimate of people(modern academics as well as Renaissance courtiers), and an erudite and civilized man. It is a honor to play a part in presenting this volume to him."

PATRICIA TATSPAUGH, who has held academic and administrative posts in the USA and administered study-abroad programs in the UK, writes about theater and about filmed versions of Shakespeare's plays. Her essays include the performance history of *The Winter's Tale*, in the New Variorum edition of the play, edited by Robert K. Turner and Virginia Haas (forthcoming), and "The Tragedies of Love" for *The Cambridge Companion to Shakespeare on Film*, edited by Russell Jackson (Cambridge, 2000). She is the author of *The Winter's Tale* for the series Shakespeare at Stratford (Thomson Learning, 2002).

She comments: "One of my earliest memories of Leeds is of a paper he gave in the 1970s at a dinner colloquium sponsored by the Folger Institute (or, as it was then the Folger Institute for Renaissance and Eighteenth-Century Studies). It was a gory affair—the paper, that is, for it included graphic details about the symptoms of the plague. Fortunately for this squeamish member of the audience, I soon learned that Leeds's interests range far beyond describing such things as hemmorhages, bruises, blisters, ulcers, and carbuncles. I value his friendship for his wise counsel, for his intellectual curiosity, and for long, relaxed meals in both Washington and London, where he does not dare mention the plague. For Leeds I have written an essay that has a few gory details."

GUSTAV UNGERER is professor emeritus of English Literature at the University of Bern. He is the author of *A Spaniard in Elizabethan England: The Correspondence of Antonio Pérez's Exile*. Two fields of investigation have stood out from the rest since his postgraduate days and retirement: cross-cultural interactions and marginalized persons in early modern England, reaching from Anglo-Spanish transcultural relations to Anglo-Moroccan bonds between Moroccan Jews and English merchants, prototypes of the Shylock/Antonio bond; from Antonio Pérez secretary of state to Philip II and Spain's most prominent Tacitean writer, an "epistolomaniac," who sensationally took refuge in Essex House (1593/95), flooding the Elizabethan court with Spanish and Latin epistles, to Jacques Francis, the first sub-Saharan African slave to be granted the status of a witness in an English lawsuit of 1548.

Professor Ungerer's acquaintance with Leeds goes back to 1983 when he accepted a paper on Sir Andrew Aguecheeck for publication. He writes: "Since then I have been privileged to share with Leeds a deep commitment to recovering historical realities. I feel heavily indebted to him for his constant encouragement of my research. Without his generous advice my papers on Mary Frith, Mary Newborough, and Morocco would never have been completed. Besides, both of us were born under the same astrological sign, Leeds almost within hailing distance of Bern, and we are both 'melomaniacs' in terms of musical culture."

LAETITIA YEANDLE is Curator of Manuscripts, Emerita, at the Folger Shakespeare Library. In addition to cataloging and reference work, she has taught courses in English Renaissance paleography for the Folger Institute. With Giles E. Dawson she compiled *Elizabethan Handwriting, 1500–1650* and, with Jean F. Preston, *English Handwriting, 1400–1650*. She edited the texts of the Tractates and Sermons for *The Folger Library Edition of The Works of Richard Hooker*, under the general editorship of W. Speed Hill, and, with R. S. Dunn, edited *The Journal of John Winthrop, 1630–1649* for the Massachusetts Historical Society. She writes: "Leeds Barroll has long been a friendly presence at the Folger Library, ever ready to assist anyone who asked his advice, whether a reader or staff member. His delight in his research has been contagious."

MEDIEVAL
AND
RENAISSANCE
DRAMA
IN ENGLAND

Leeds Barroll:
Scholar, Colleague, and Friend

J. Leeds Barroll III: A Tribute

ANN JENNALIE COOK

YOU never can tell what the future holds. When I embarked on a two-semester seminar in Shakespeare thirty-five years ago, I expected a major extension of my graduate study but not an encounter with a legendary figure. In 1968, though J. Leeds Barroll III had already established credentials sufficient to secure him an endowed professorship at Vanderbilt, he had barely begun the remarkable achievements that now make him so distinguished. Many others whose lives and careers he has touched or transformed might have written this essay in his honor, but no one else, I suspect, has known him in as many different capacities. Teacher, scholar, visionary, administrator, editor, colleague, mentor, friend. It has been my privilege to observe Leeds at first hand in all these capacities.

He might well have made his mark solely as an extraordinary teacher. In that long-ago seminar at Vanderbilt, he set up procedures that demonstrated not only his own enormous grasp of Shakespearean scholarship but also his high standards for professional competence. Each week we heard a brilliant, meticulously crafted lecture on some aspect of the field—biography, theater history, textual studies, bibliography, critical approaches, and other methodological matters in the first semester, with a sweep through the canon in the second semester. I still consult my notes sometimes, humbled yet profoundly grateful for the foundation Leeds Barroll provided us. One unique feature, which I subsequently incorporated into my own teaching, involved weekly assignments at random to two or three students who had to prepare a critical review of some essential work in Shakespearean scholarship related to the topic for the next session. Regardless of any other commitments for any other courses, we had to assess the work in an ungraded but formally written three-minute presentation (accompanied by a handout identifying three significant reviews of the book), delivered as if it were a paper at a professional meeting. Nowadays, when graduate students routinely show up at such meetings and submit papers for pre-PhD publication, this practice may seem commonplace. At the time, however, it provided a rare, realistic foretaste of the pressure to produce which haunts anyone with serious aspirations. After each presentation, the weekly victims received critiques of their performances by fellow students and by Leeds. We learned more than we realized, and though some despised the experience, I did not. More routinely, final papers and a rigorous final examination covering lectures and assigned readings completed each semester's work. That capacity to create precisely what a particular course should provide for its students has characterized Leeds's teaching, whether at the graduate or undergraduate level, within a university setting or at the Folger Institute, where he has served so ably.

As a Shakespeare scholar, few can match the contributions of Leeds Barroll. Earlier in his career, it seemed as if other significant professional projects might prevent the definitive publications that everyone who knew him well hoped he would produce. He seemed to have read and absorbed everything ever written by anybody else, always preferring the "hard" work of exhaustive research rather than the "soft" work of a trendy critical approach. For a while in the early seventies, it looked as if editing might claim his loyalties. He edited the Blackfriars *Hamlet* and *Othello*, directed the editions of fifteen other plays in the series, and also trained several fine editors, including Paul Werstine and John Andrews. *Artificial Persons* (1974) addressed a vital subject that had lingered in neglect since the old-fashioned criticism of A. C. Bradley, though it did not become the seminal work every scholar wishes to create. Nor did the equally solid, thought-provoking *Shakespearean Tragedy: Genre, Tradition, and Change in "Antony and Cleopatra"* (1983). Fortunately, the passage of time has allowed Leeds to publish the massively detailed *Politics, Plague, and Shakespeare's Theater: The Stuart Years* (1991) and *Anna of Denmark, Queen of England: A Cultural Biography* (2001). During the research process, articles and major lectures in prestigious venues have led readers and listeners through the political entanglements of Jacobean drama. Placing Shakespeare's company within a dense historical nexus while negotiating the complexities of theoretical historiography brings to fruition the sort of critical acumen it takes a lifetime to acquire. There is simply no one else presently in the field who could have written these major works of Shakespearean scholarship except Leeds Barroll. And there is more to come. He is preparing a companion volume on the plague for the Tudor years, as well as *Cultural Intertextualities and the Early Modern Reception of Public Drama*, which deals with the effects of audience awareness of rumor, news, and stories related to the Mongols, the Ottoman Empire, Russia, and Spain.

It is one thing to write a definitive book or a series of such books that establish a lasting reputation. It is quite another to transform one's profession. Yet I hope no one will ever forget that Leeds's vision has fundamentally altered the way Shakespeareans conduct their careers. By the time he had completed his doctorate at Princeton in 1956, he was already an unconventional figure. Few, like him, were already husbands and fathers; fewer still had come to graduate school after a stint at secondary school teaching. Those with the right degrees from the right universities and the right connections with established scholars could hope for prestigious, or at least promising, appointments. Such individuals could also expect preferential consideration of manuscripts, for the readership that determined publication rested in a tight circle of power exercised by prominent figures on the east and west coasts, as well as in England. Leeds thought that situation was wrong because it stifled talented thinkers and bolstered an already entrenched establishment. Amid a storm of criticism at his upstart presumption, he launched *Shakespeare Studies* from the wilderness of Cincinnati in 1965. The new publication had no arbitrary limits for articles, accepted work from known as well as unknown writers, and in its first few volumes featured a valuable assessment of "Significant Articles, Monographs, and Reviews" by the editor. It met with immediate success, though not many who now take for granted its status in the field understand the degree to which *Shakespeare Studies* revolutionized accepted protocols when it began.

Leeds next turned his attention to the wider community of Shakespeareans. At the first-ever World Shakespeare Congress of 1971 in Vancouver, the delegates endorsed a call for future global gatherings and for the establishment of new scholarly organizations. Only the Deutsche Shakespeare Gesellschaft (East and West branches at the time) and the Shakespeare Society of Japan then existed, and there were no comparable groups in any English-speaking country. While most people simply left Vancouver with fond memories, Leeds Barroll returned to the University of South Carolina with a vision. Using his own money, he paid for the legal incorporation of the Shakespeare Association of America, a name graciously vacated by Mary Hyde after an earlier SAA became defunct. (The older organization had founded *Shakespeare Quarterly* but turned over its publication to the Folger in 1972.) Many would have doomed the enterprise because of the rival centers of power based on both coasts as well as a general fragmentation among Shakespeareans. However, Leeds astutely persuaded G. E. Bentley to serve as President, then put together a board that included representatives from every part of the country. With the backing of his university, he issued a call to the first annual meeting of the SAA at Washington, DC, in 1973. A hundred attendees would have represented a triumph. Over two hundred showed up. The organization gathered strength through the next two meetings in Pasadena and New Haven, culminating in the 1976 World Congress of the International Shakespeare Association, an organization Leeds also helped to launch. Over the years some events, such as the annual lecture delivered by an esteemed senior scholar, were scrapped, while groups like the seminars and the workshops came in later under my auspices. Yet certain principles have prevailed: inclusiveness, experimentation, dialogue with theater professionals, and excellence regardless of perceived status.

After bringing to birth *Shakespeare Studies*, the SAA, and the ISA, Leeds Barroll might well have retired from translating vision into reality for the benefit of his profession. However, in 1984, responding to another scholarly need, he began the publication of *Medieval and Renaissance Drama in England*, in part to facilitate the flow of valuable research generated by the SAA's ongoing theater history seminars. Again, a major venue furthered work in the field, owing its origin to this remarkable man. His ability to perceive crucial areas that scholars ought to address is never merely theoretical. He advises graduate students to tackle significant thesis topics and urges colleagues to continue important projects they may have set aside. One need only imagine the bleakness of a scholarly world without *Shakespeare Studies, Medieval and Renaissance Drama in England*, the SAA, or the ISA to understand the magnitude of Leeds Barroll's contributions to us all.

As an editor and administrator in his own right, Leeds prefers to set policies and to conceive new schemes rather than handle the details. While stints in New Jersey's system of higher education and at the National Endowment for the Humanities introduced him to the hard, uncongenial limitations of politically driven organizations, in the scholarly realm he became an astute innovator, delegator, and negotiator. As a former Associate Editor of *Shakespeare Studies*, I enjoyed an astonishing degree of freedom at the pre-publication levels, but I always operated with an intense awareness of Leeds's exacting standards for *his* journal. Over the years, he groomed a series of skilled editorial assistants, such as Scott Colley, John Andrews, Barry Gaines, Paul Werstine, James Shapiro, John Pitcher, Susan Cerasano, and Susan Zimmerman. Moreover, he debuted a host of subsequently well-known scholars whose work first saw the dark of print in articles he accepted, my own included.

Yet in my judgment, it was not the publications so much as the organization Leeds founded that showed his generosity of spirit. In 1975, the SAA had committed to host the Bicentennial World Shakespeare Congress of 1976 at Washington, DC, in association with the fledgling ISA and the Folger Shakespeare Library. Set to leave the University of South Carolina for an NEH directorship, Leeds had to vacate his position as Executive Secretary of the SAA, since he could not administer the Endowment's grant for the Congress. At the annual meeting in New Haven, he persuaded the SAA trustees to appoint me as Interim Executive Secretary. Though I was only three years out of graduate school and had never organized a conference or managed a grant, he confidently assumed I could handle the challenges. And I did, with highly visible help from SAA President Maynard Mack and the Trustees, O. B. Hardison at the Folger, and Levi Fox at the Shakespeare Birthplace Trust. Invisibly, behind the scenes, Leeds gave me shrewd advice when necessary but more often simply offered assurance and approval. He never asked for or received the credit he fully deserved for the success of the Washington Congress. And he went on to propose a bylaws change that allowed me to continue in a position he had every right to resume. I have gone into some detail here because so few now remember precisely what personal sacrifices he made to hand over a position of leadership to someone else. Very quietly, he simply did what he thought best.

That kind of generosity also marked Leeds Barroll's career as an academic colleague. When we served together on the faculty at the University of South Carolina, he made it a point to set up cordial relationships with other members of the department, promoting their careers whenever he could. With the ear and the purse of a generous USC President, he had a Shakespeare Center that provided editing, speaking, and publishing opportunities for various colleagues, as well as for graduate students. Even among luminaries such as James Dickey, George Garrett, Morse Peckham, Matt Bruccoli, and James Meriwether, Leeds wielded extraordinary power. As Joe Katz wryly put it, "With a name like mine, you really have to work hard to establish a reputation, but look what you can do with a name like J. Leeds Barroll III." Thanks to his good offices, at least two talented professors left Vanderbilt, where they and Leeds had been underappreciated, for more congenial positions at South Carolina. Years later, he would arrange a similar change of scene for Lena Orlin, when she moved from the Folger to a faculty appointment at the University of Maryland Baltimore County, bringing with her the SAA offices. Such action might seem Machiavellian to his detractors, but it has won Leeds a cadre of fiercely loyal friends who sometimes marvel that he never asks for return favors and is routinely embarrassed by expressions of appreciation. Indeed, he may not be at all happy with this laudatory essay in his *festschrift*.

Nonetheless, faculty colleagues are not the only ones in his debt, for countless individuals in the profession have profited from his assistance and advice. Sometimes Leeds quietly suggests a place to publish an article, and not always in one of his own journals. At other times, he may set a confused graduate student on a productive path. He may find a spot on a panel for a promising new mind. From the earliest meetings of the SAA, he has brought young, unknown professionals to the podium. He takes a keen interest in the work of fellow researchers at the Folger, often pointing out sources that prove crucial for solving a problem or solidifying an argument. And as a mentor he has a marvelous way of cutting through distracting externals. At the end of my graduate work, when I was set to pick up a doctorate hard on the heels of a divorce, he said, "Just be sure you put all your academic records and all your publications in your own name. You don't want to screw up the bibliographies, and you don't want someone else to get credit for your work. Besides, how do you know how many husbands you'll marry?" I have been Ann Jennalie Cook ever since. It is impossible to know how many others have benefited from Leeds Barroll's wisdom and example. To the names already mentioned, surely dozens if not hundreds could be added.

Ironically, Leeds rarely strikes casual observers as benign or kindly. There is an inherent reserve, a detached dignity that protects him from tedious chatter or fawning adulation. He can sometimes seem aloof, even prickly to those who do not know him well. Behind such superficial appearances, however, his friends know him as a delightful, sensitive, perceptive, quixotic human being. He is deeply learned and deeply passionate about his work. He loves music and model trains. With the straightest, most serious face imaginable, he can be excruciatingly funny, as he was in his SAA presidential address, lamenting the speech he should have written had not his computer betrayed him. In his papers, brief comments of deadly wit occasionally punctuate some recounting of historical events, betraying Leeds's eye for the absurd. Because he zealously guards his family life from professional view, I will mention only that friends rejoice because his wife, Susan Zimmerman, provides him with the compatible companionship he has always deserved. She stands first among a large company who admire the abilities of Leeds Barroll, applaud his achievements, and appreciate his contributions to their own lives. We all hope he enjoys good research, good health, and good cheer for many years to come.

Leeds Barroll as Colleague and Teacher

RAPHAEL FALCO

MY landlady in Baltimore is a UMBC graduate in English. A returning student, she finished her degree a few years before I arrived at the university in 1993. Recently we were discussing her experiences at UMBC and ended up talking about the faculty. She was not bashful and quickly skewered several professors while praising others. Then she paused and changed her tone. "There was one fellow," she said quietly, "who commuted down each week from New York. He taught Shakespeare, but he seemed to know everything about everything." I knew instantly whom she meant. "Dr. Barroll," she murmured with satisfaction, as I tried to work out which of Leeds's many incarnations would have found him living in New York. "He was the best professor in the department. Taking his classes was a different experience altogether."

My landlady's conversation caught me off guard. Of course, I shouldn't have been surprised that Leeds had made such a strong impression on a student. He was after all a professor of English for more than forty years. Yet my own experience of him as a colleague seems to have crowded out the picture of him in the classroom, even though I remembered, with the prompting of my landlady's remarks, that Leeds had often offered a World Literature course because he thought our students needed the background—and even though, on thinking back, I remembered that he always had an eye out for the superior students. Still, to realize, after the fact of our dual participation in the daily life of the department, that Leeds so influenced his students (behind my back, as it were) was almost like discovering the guilty secret of a respectable maiden aunt.

I met Leeds under the worst possible conditions, engineered by our professional organization: a job interview in a cramped hotel room in New York. The room was cramped in part because the department couldn't afford a suite, and in part because stray faculty members had decided to sit in on the interview—"sit in" being a euphemism for "sprawl along the bed." Leeds had his own chair. I already knew the name J. Leeds Barroll but dutifully reviewed his books in preparation for the interview, although I didn't have the combination of shamelessness and rhetorical technique that it takes to praise an interviewer's work during the interview. And, in any case, Leeds was too canny an interviewer to allow the conversation to drift toward his own work. In fact, he drove me in that conversation deeper and deeper into an unadorned explanation of my scholarly plans. I can still remember his resonant baritone in that overheated hotel room. "And what will your third book be?" he asked mischievously. *Third* book! I'd only just finished a first, basically my dissertation. Nevertheless I airily described my plans for a third book and Leeds nodded his head with interest. Only the slight twinkle in his eye indicated that he knew what I probably didn't suspect at the time—that that so-called third book had about as much chance as Stephano's conspiracy.

In later years I came to recognize that twinkle in Leeds's eye as the sign of an exceptional intelligence more often than not amused by what passed before it. Leeds never parades his brains; he doesn't have to be the smartest person in the room, although he usually is. He allows his canniness and experience to blossom naturally. In ordinary conversation, in the course of committee work, in intensive strategizing sessions, Leeds would maintain the same even demeanor, leading always, but always from within. His leadership style was most evident in the way he thought the UMBC English department should function. Although he took his turn as chair (before my time), his abiding conviction was that, because we were a small department, the faculty members not involved in research should act as chairs, thus freeing the researchers to do their work. This system worked for quite some time, and thanks largely to Leeds's insistence on the primacy of research our department was able to attract a number of assistant professors with significant accomplishments. Similarly, still leading from within, Leeds guided the department chair in his negotiations with our provost and successfully brought the Shakespeare Association of America to UMBC.

This was the Leeds I knew in the English department—not the professor of students, but rather a guide and fellow traveler. Many an afternoon I'd wander down to his office at the end of the hall, clear a chair of books and mail (usually hopeful submissions for *Shakespeare Studies* or *MaRDiE*), and settle in for a talk. The content of our talks would vary, of course, but the form stayed more or less the same. It resembled the old inverted pyramid journalists liked to use. We began with all the facts in broad array at the top and worked our way down to a specific point of strategy. Often we were talking about a particular issue coming before the department at our next meeting and Leeds would tick off the votes, explaining almost clairvoyantly who would be for and who against, and why. I learned more about academic politics in those brief afternoon sessions than in ten years of department meetings, university committees, and dialogue with administrators. We didn't always win, Leeds and I, but we always knew why we lost. And perhaps that

was Leeds's best example to me in all departmental and university matters—to know why the other side is other.

But I don't wish to give the impression that we politicked for politicking's
sake. To the contrary, we had a preeminently tangible goal. With Leeds's
guidance, we were determined to transform the reputation of the UMBC English department both intramurally and in the profession at large. Leeds believed strongly that we should, and could, be known for our research. He not
only set an example of this belief by his own publications and his daunting
editorial responsibilities to two major journals, both of which he founded and
both of which were housed at UMBC. He also exerted a steady pressure on
the department to represent itself as research-driven, and, despite the lack of
a graduate program, to hire only scholars with ambitious research plans. The
success of Leeds's aims is evident now in our department, and not simply
in the work of professors whom Leeds himself had a hand in hiring. More
importantly, the generation of new professors hired by those of us who felt
Leeds's unyielding pressure has exceeded our earliest goals. They include
Lena Orlin, distinguished scholar and Executive Director of the Shakespeare
Association of America; and Christoph Irmscher, an internationally re-
nowned Americanist recently promoted directly from assistant to full professor, an unprecedented action at UMBC. As we continue to make new
appointments, the new generation of scholars automatically seeks to hire can-
didates with a scholarly agenda and to fulfill the ideal of a research-driven
department. They never look back, nor should they, and they little suspect
how much their work is the fruit of a seed planted and watered through many
a dry season by Leeds Barroll.

Leeds is gone from that office at the end of the hall now. His retirement a
few years ago left a hole in my afternoons and a feeling of disorientation
when I'd glance in his door and see the wrong person swiveling in his chair.
But the disorientation didn't last long, and I soon filled the afternoons. And
soon after that I realized why—the nickel dropped. Leeds had left me with
all a mentor can leave—with all, in fact, Mentor gave Telemachus. I no longer
needed him to understand my job, my responsibilities, my colleagues. The
sense of politics he'd revealed has become part of my operating knowledge.
The order of departmental values and professional ambitions remains a permanent part of my life—a mild yoke, as Milton says. All that's missing is
the deep baritone reminding me to laugh.

There is a danger in a reminiscence like this one of presenting the subject
as a figure of the past. Nothing could be further from the truth in Leeds's
case. Earlier I called Leeds a friend and fellow traveler. The fellow traveler
at UMBC might be gone, but the friend remains. Leeds, who paradoxically
has become even more active in the profession since his retirement, meets
me from time to time for lunch in Washington, DC. We talk on the telephone,

still strategizing a bit, and meet at conferences. He has become Scholar-in-Residence at the Folger Shakespeare Library, where he taught the masters research seminar for many years. Last year he published another book, on Queen Anne and the Stuart masque. And so on, and on. There is no evidence, in other words, that Leeds Barroll plans to drown his book any time soon.

Leeds Barroll, Scholar-in-Residence

RICHARD KUHTA

THE Folger Shakespeare Library is a small universe, but it is inhabited by
the best in the business of teaching and humanities scholarship in the early
modern period. It's a subset of the academic world, a microcosm of research
activity that occurs globally, and functions as a deceptively simple organism
whose primary ingredients are readers and collections. But the emphasis on
community and human exchange is what sets the institution apart from many
of its peers. Scholars are attracted to the Folger because of its remarkable
collections, but come back to participate in its programs, and look forward to
returning in order to resume conversations and renew friendships.

The degree to which libraries are successful in creating a supportive environment has a good deal to do with the way people are treated. That, in turn,
influences such things as whether readers return, how long they stay, and
whether they choose to participate in academic programs and the cultural life
of the institution. The stimulation and energy created by innovative programs
draws scholars from around the world. But why are scholars so eager to return, why do readers come forward so readily to lead seminars, encourage
their students to work at the Folger, become involved in exhibitions, assist
with conference preparations, or devote time to mentoring junior faculty? Library staff does much to set the tone of the environment, but the Folger
wouldn't be the place it is without the extraordinary goodwill of readers. The
difference I see between the Folger and many other institutions is the extent
to which readers are involved in shaping and influencing the life of the Library, and few have done more in recent decades than Leeds Barroll to make
the Folger a vibrant and welcoming place.

Leeds became a Folger reader in June 1956, the year he earned his Ph.D.
from Princeton. Since that time his sphere of activity at the Folger has
touched many lives and his accomplishments have earned him respect and
recognition. But it is the range of his activity that is so impressive. Leeds has
lead NEH summer institutes, directed Folger Institute seminars, twice given
the annual Shakespeare Birthday Lecture, been involved with the Center for
Shakespeare Studies from the beginning, and lectured in programs for the
Center of the History of British Political Thought. He has also participated
in programs for secondary school teachers, and worked five years in the Fol-

31

ger's High School Fellowship Program. Over the course of his distinguished career Leeds has touched all the bases at the Folger, and is currently one of the institution's Scholar-in-Residence.

Scholarship is a lonely business. It leads people into remote corners of collections around the world to work with difficult, and often obscure, material for extended periods of time. It can force people into themselves. To make it otherwise, to remove some of that isolation, has been one of the great achievements of Leeds's career. One student in Leeds's Folger Institute seminar, "Researching the Renaissance," observed,

> By having us articulate our research interests in a range of ways throughout the term . . . different forms of scholarly communication encouraged us to formulate ways of thinking about our own concerns that would interest and benefit others. I'm grateful for having had to do this because humanities research is often solitary, lonely work, and one can become ensconced in one's own limited world too easily. The précis critiques forced me to learn how to speak to others about their work in thoughtful ways. (1998)

Leeds's seminar was much more than an exercise in research methods, teaching others how to use the tools of the trade; it was an experience that brought participants out of themselves and humanized scholarship. "Researching the Renaissance" was about community, and in my view it was one of the Folger's most valuable seminars, superbly directed by Leeds throughout the 1990s. During this time, Leeds mentored dozens of students through the most difficult and lonely passages of their professional development. As he organized it, the seminar had at least three recurring components, each crucial for its success. First, he provided an expert introduction to the resources of the Folger, both standard and esoteric, tailored to individual needs and crafted in a way that allowed students to develop their own strategies for effective use. Secondly, Leeds counseled students individually and personally introduced them to distinguished scholars at the Library, helping young scholars build bridges to professional and personal relationships. Finally, Leeds turned dissertation students into their own support group, free of envy or competition, able to listen to and encourage each other. Leeds's work in this seminar was masterful.

Leeds has been instrumental in shaping the Folger Institute for nearly a quarter of a century. He joined the faculty at the University of Maryland Baltimore Campus in 1979, and a year later UMBC became a member of the Institute and named Leeds their faculty representative to its central executive committee. In Leeds's world, when you join you participate, and in fall of 1980 he set the example by directing his first seminar for the Folger Institute on "The Structure of Shakespearean Tragedy." In 1981, he followed with "Shakespeare's Milieu," and directed "Shakespeare and the Social Pressures of his Time" in 1985, all the while urging his best students to follow him to Washington. In 1989, Leeds directed an NEH summer humanities institute on "The Problem of an Intellectual History for Shakespeare's Age," a topic of enormous scope that signaled the agenda of the burgeoning Center of Shakespeare Studies. Typically, Leeds was pushing against the borders, and asked others to join him in exploring new territory. That experience set the model for inviting visiting faculty that distinguishes Institute programs to this day.

Leeds's ability to survey the profession and identify innovative topics for Institute programs was evident most recently in a conference he organized in 2002, "The Impact of the Ottoman Empire on Early Modern Europe." Typically, it broke new ground, initiated conversations across disciplines, and helped people and ideas connect. The Ottoman conference pushed the Folger into new, and to some, surprising, areas. It only worked because someone of Leeds's stature endorsed it and was able to assemble the right voices.

Leeds was one of the first people who held out his hand when I began my tenure as Librarian at the Folger in February 1994. He and Susan invited Candace and me to dinner that first Independence Day, when a group of us watched fireworks on the mall from their balcony and talked through the evening about life in Washington. It was a warm and generous welcome, and it made me feel the Folger Shakespeare Library was the place I wanted to be, and work, in order to be around such people. I still feel that way. I've never been in a place where there are so many talented, smart, unselfish people. Where people work together for the common good, where conversations aren't interrupted, where rank is immaterial in the Tea Room, where intellectual exchange isn't a battleground of egos, and where newcomers are so welcomed. In the face of what we know to be the norm in human life, those are the ingredients of a truly remarkable environment. But the unusual chemistry that brings people together at the Folger does not happen by accident. It is because of people like Leeds Barroll, who have spent a lifetime inviting others into the conversation, then listened to them.

Leeds is now a Scholar-in-Residence at the Folger; a distinction utterly fitting for someone who has been so devoted to making the Folger Shakespeare Library a center for advanced research and environment of goodwill. The values that Leeds embodies—intellectual integrity, service to community, academic rigor, and kindness—are essential to institutions devoted to supporting humanities scholarship. Leeds's career has taught us that.

These are observations gathered over the last ten years. Others have expressed similar views far longer. I quote from the opening paragraph of a two-page expression of gratitude from participants in the Folger Institute seminar, "The Structure of Shakespeare Tragedy" (1981):

we shared a remarkable educational experience. In his lectures, Dr. Leeds Barroll offered us the rare combination of both sound scholarship and stimulating interpretation. His critical standards were rigorous, yet he treated each of us with a generosity and respect that made the intellectual challenges enjoyable. We were a group with widely divergent backgrounds and interests who became friends and collaborators under his tutelage. He served as a model of what each of us should demand of ourselves as thinkers, scholars, and teachers.

Thank you, Leeds, for lifting us all a bit higher.

Articles

A Jacobean Ghost, and Other Stories

JOHN H. ASTINGTON

ONE of the most unusual events of the Jacobean court must have been the performance, in April or May of 1621, of an entertainment called *The History of Abraham*, shown in the presence of King James. What may have led, in a year that saw the mounting of such elegant and up-to-date material as *Pan's Anniversary*, *The Essex House Masque*, and *The Gypsies Metamorphosed*, to the revival of such a musty piece of medieval antiquity? Leeds Barroll has rightly pointed out that King James was not a particularly avid patron of theatrical entertainment, unlike his successor;[1] he was, however, genuinely interested in matters of religion, unlike his predecessor, so that some kind of drama which compared the achievements and reputation of a founding patriarch of biblical history favorably with those of the incumbent of the throne of the two kingdoms may have drawn some encouragement. On the other hand, at a time when religious war had already unseated the Bohemian king and queen, was about to break out again in France, and King James and his counselors were wooing both France and Spain to end the conflict in the Palatinate, any court event in which religious material was given political color would seem to have been very unwise and lacking in tact. Ambassadors noted such things in their dispatches. Further, and on the level of theatrical practicality, who in 1621 may have written such a play, and what company may have mounted it? Was it perhaps the product of courtly amateurs, and who may they have been? What evidence do we have, finally, that such an entertainment ever took place?

The opening sentence of my essay is written from the point of view of one who, if surprised, believes what he reads in standard volumes of information about early modern theater history. My starting point is Yoshiko Kawachi's calendar of *English Renaissance Drama 1558–1642*, published in 1986.[2] As is usual with such compilations, the listings given, including the item above, are drawn from other sources: in this case Kawachi cites G. E. Bentley's standard work of reference for the English theater between 1616 and 1642, *The Jacobean and Caroline Stage*.[3] With some persistence one finds in the index of that work, under the heading "ANONYMOUS," and placed alphabetically with other "histories of," one reference, to Bentley's "Annals of Theatrical Affairs" in the seventh volume, published in 1968.[4] There one discovers that

37

the original testimony to the existence of the "History of Abraham" (I quote Bentley's format) occurs within a declared account of the Treasurer of the Chamber, a royal official who traditionally paid wages to those performing services within the king's or queen's household. In April/May 1621 eight people spent four days preparing the Banqueting House at Whitehall for the king to see whatever the "History of Abraham" may have been; Bentley's contextual presentation of the reference once again leads any casual or even earnest inquirer to believe that it was a theatrical event, as he himself must have done. One also discovers a further reference to a still earlier scholarly source, the sixth in the series of the Malone Society's *Collections*, an edition of extracts from the annual manuscript accounts presented by the Treasurer of the Chamber to the Audit Office, and now preserved in the Public Record Office. This selection was edited by David Cook and F. P. Wilson, and published in 1962. The editors do not precisely give an account of their principles of extraction from the original manuscripts, though they describe the content and layout of the documents in considerable detail. Their book is organized in two parts, however: the first is "Payments to Players, Etc.," which seems a clear category, and gives transcriptions supported by useful notes. The second section, "Apparellings," is more schematic in layout, and gives less sense of the original context of the words on the manuscript page; it calls on more effort from the reader to work out its codes and abbreviations. Any scholar who has coped with the difficulties of similar manuscripts will be grateful for the digest, but also may wonder what he or she may be missing.

The yeomen, grooms, and ushers of the Jacobean royal household did all the preparatory work in setting up royal apartments for specific events, then clearing them again once such events were over. Whenever the monarch was present the royal state—dais, throne, hangings, and canopy—had to be constructed in advance in any chamber where it was not a usual fixture. Temporary seating, observation platforms, railings and barriers to control crowds, together with suitable decoration with hangings and upholstery, all might be required.[5] Such arrangements for theatrical occasions—plays, masques, acrobatic displays, and dancing—did not differ notably from those at which similarly large groups of people came together for a ceremonial occasion: the annual Maundy ceremonies before Easter, say, or the reception of new ambassadors from foreign states. In the annual account detailing the expenses of the preparatory work for these occasions individual jobs are frequently listed sequentially in no particular order of importance, and without punctuation. It is therefore easy to misread individual details, and to invent the causal from the casual.

The 1621 document, however, seems clear enough. John Gosnold, Gentleman Usher, with seven assistants received fees for making ready, over the course of four days, "the Banketting house wth the History of Abraham for the king to take view of them."[6] The final plural pronoun relating to the sin-

gular referent is no paradox, and should be a clear sign that we are not reading about a play. This "History of Abraham" was an artifact of a quite
different kind: it came in ten parts, and was among the most valuable of many
sets of tapestries in the royal collection. More remarkably, it survives today,
and is usually displayed in the Hall of Hampton Court palace. What King
James viewed in April 1621 can now be gazed on by the casual tourist. The
individual pieces are enormous: the panel showing the sacrifice of Isaac, for
example, measures sixteen feet high and twenty-six feet long.[7] Gosnold and
his seven men would have been working very hard to maneuver such heavy,
valuable fabrics safely into place. I shall shortly have more to say about the
tapestries and why the king was looking at them, but it is clear that they have
nothing in themselves to do with the history of drama or performance. There
are some significant points of comparison between the art of fabric design
and the art of drama, in the sixteenth century particularly, which this essay
will go on to explore, but within calendars of theatrical events the "History
of Abraham" has no place. A contextual slip by the Malone Society editors
forty years ago, and subsequent endorsement of its spurious authority, has
left a faint trail of confusion across the firmament of Jacobean court culture
as viewed from our early twenty-first century moment.

The original cultural meaning of the Abraham tapestries is to be understood in terms of King Henry VIII's deliberate pursuit of magnificence in
artistic patronage, as well as having a place within the iconography of his
religious policies. The tapestries were woven in Brussels in the early 1540s;
they had been received in the Great Wardrobe in 1544. Probably commissioned by officers of the English court in 1540 or so, the hangings are examples of the highest standards of design and finish of their time. The designers
were Bernaert van Orley and Pieter Coecke van Aelst; the panels are woven
in wool and silk with a great deal of metal thread, originally gold.[8] They can
be hung together only in very large chambers: the effect of their being seen
as an ensemble in such a setting is as impressive today as it was meant to be
in the mid-sixteenth century. If, until King Charles I began serious collecting,
the English court lacked for great paintings that might compare with those of
the Italian or French palaces of the élite, it was rich in woven pictorial fabric
of the sixteenth century. The enormous collection assembled by Henry, and
partly taken over from Cardinal Wolsey, defined the visual magnificence of
English court chambers. Dynamic and striking compositions executed in
terms of texture and soft, glowing color, accented with shimmering reflective
thread, lively and mobile in candlelight, and set within a variety of larger and
smaller spaces, characterized the interior environment of the court throughout the long reign of Elizabeth. If by 1600 such decoration was beginning to
look rather passé, it was still shown off with pride: the Swiss visitor Thomas
Platter, visiting Hampton Court in 1599, saw the Abraham tapestries, as well
as "The history of Lot on a golden tapestry," with other "histories"—of

Pompey, of Tobias, and of the murder of Julius Caesar.[9] The Old Testament pieces, he noted, were "thought to be the finest and most artistic in England, indeed the representations are immense in size."[10]

So the Abraham tapestry series was indeed old in 1621, but it had been famous in its time, and perhaps still held some special significance, depending on King James's judgment after his viewing. From soon after they were delivered to London from Brussels the tapestries were taken to decorate Hampton Court, and probably were not much moved before 1621. In the exhaustive inventory of the king's goods conducted in later 1547, after Henry's death, the Abraham tapestries, "Tenne peces of newe arras of thistorie of Abraham,"[11] were at Hampton, as they were fifty-two years later when Platter visited. They probably were not, as they are today, on permanent view in the hall, though they were certainly hung there for ceremonial occasions. When in 1649 and the years following the hundred-year-old tapestries might have been sold off, as was a great deal of the royal art collection, they received the very high valuation of £8,260 from the parliamentary assessors, and one potential buyer from France noted their excellent preservation, "n'ayant jamais servi que dans les jours de cérémonies."[12] In the event, they were chosen by Oliver Cromwell for his own use, and thus returned eventually to royal possession.

The ceremonial occasions at which they *were* on view no doubt included Christmas festivities at Hampton Court, including James's first Christmas as King of England, in 1603–04, the significance of which in terms of foreign policy has been recently pointed out by Leeds Barroll.[13] When the hall was transformed into a temporary theater, however, with "degrees" set against its side walls, the tapestries, valuable and treasured objects, were undoubtedly moved to their storeroom, or to the Great Chamber. The occasion for which they were being considered in 1621 was the procession and feast of the Knights of the Garter on St. George's Day, 23 April. The new Banqueting House was not entirely finished, but it must have been in a suitable state to proceed with its employment for a very important event of the court year.[14] The Polish ambassador witnessed the processions between the old buildings and the new, and visited the ceremonial dinner that marked the end of the ceremony, and which may have been held in the Banqueting House itself.[15] The Abraham tapestries were thus chosen to be part of one of the principal occasions of royal ceremony and display, in an impressive new stately setting; inappropriately so, according to John Chamberlain, who judged the new building to be "too faire and nothing sutable to the rest of the house."[16]

The St. George's Day events had been a significant part of court ceremonial since the preceding reign, and James took the symbolism of the Order of the Garter quite as seriously as had Elizabeth. Through the processions, particularly, with king, prince, and leading nobles dressed in the splendidly elaborate scarlet robes and white-plumed hats, the British court proclaimed i's magnificence, and its Protestant affinity; the badge of the Order, the George, symbolized the overthrow of papal evil by active Protestant virtue, and it was featured prominently in several portraits of the king and his chief nobles.[17] There is every indication that the building of the new Banqueting House, though its genesis was accidental, gave rise to a renewed program of royal image-making, and consequent patronage. Though it may be true that "Put simply, James did not lead an arts-centred life,"[18] he understood as readily as his Tudor predecessors the importance of the splendid and impressive accoutrements and ceremonies that should surround the symbolic center of state power. In 1621, apart from the difficulties of foreign diplomacy in the context of war, there was also the question of the marriage of the Prince of Wales to consider, and the status of the British court in the eyes of Spanish and French ambassadors was a particular priority.

Two royal portraits seem directly connected with the St. George's Day events of 1621, both made by relatively newly appointed court painters from the Netherlands. Paul van Somer's portrait of about 1620 seems to overcome court impatience at the slow progress of the new building, showing the standing James in full regalia—crown, robe, a collar with the George badge, and holding orb and scepter in extended arms and hands. Through the window behind him (that of the Great Chamber at Whitehall, presumably) we see Inigo Jones's classical masterpiece filling the background. James is shown as the upholder of traditional kingly magnificence, symbolized by the older Tudor chamber in which he stands, and as the creator of new splendor, particularly in the bay of the Banqueting House we see clearly through the open window to his right, as if raised magically by the power of his scepter, which points toward it.[19]

A splendid icon, it appears a rather old-fashioned picture when compared with the portrait painted by Daniel Mytens in 1621, possibly to commemorate St. George's Day, and the opening of the new Banqueting House. It shows a seated James, turned three-quarters left, dressed in the full regalia of the Knights of the Garter, and with his plumed hat set on a table behind him to the right. The rich, heavy robes contrast rather ironically with the tired, vulnerable man who wears them, whose hands droop limply over the arms of the throne, and whose eyes and set of mouth make him appear more quizzical and less commanding than Van Somer's king. It is almost a "backstage" portrait, showing the king resting before or after summoning the effort to walk with suitable processional dignity in the cumbersome clothing.[20] Apart from the psychological difference, however, Mytens's portrait celebrates the king's magnificence just as much as does Van Somer's, save that here the emphasis is solely on rich fabric as a sign of the monarch's place and power.

The "view" James was taking of the Abraham tapestries in the days before 23 April 1621 bespeaks the concern of someone in control of the effects he wishes to create. The tapestries, after all, were quite familiar to him, and he may himself have suggested that they be used; he was then given the opportunity to approve an impression he had anticipated. The old hangings set within the new hall might symbolize royal continuity in a fashion similar to the two styles of building in Van Somer's portrait: within King James's spacious and elegant building were set the richest tapestries of King Henry VIII. Their subject, the legend of a founding patriarch of a chosen people, blessed by God, extended the echoes of historical destiny back to the beginnings of time.

The tapestries may also have provided something of a model for a contemporary project, that of the Mortlake tapestry factories, founded with royal support, and beginning to operate between 1619 and 1622. "It is hardly a coincidence," writes Per Palme, "that King James's initiative in setting up the Mortlake factory was taken in the same year as the building of the Banqueting House was begun, and with it a general renewal of the State Apartments at Court, nor that we find much the same trusted servants, headed by Lionel Cranfield, moulding and framing both projects."[21]

Apart from their fame as superbly designed and executed works of fabric art, in what ways might the Abraham tapestries have been felt to be appropriate to the occasion? The Order of the Garter was chivalric, in part, but also religious. At Windsor the knights had, and have, their own chapel, and when ceremonies were held at Whitehall, as in 1621, the chapel there held the service that formed an important part of the day. One might think that the ideal designs for hangings to decorate such an event would have figured the legends of St. George, or some more directly related theme. After his accession as King Charles I, James's son remained committed to the Garter ceremonies, and became "the greatest Increaser of the Honour and Renown of this most Illustrious Order."[22] A 1638 project for a set of tapestries showing the Garter procession itself, based on designs by Van Dyck and to have been woven at Mortlake, survives only in an oil sketch by the artist on this subject.[23] Yet Charles used the Abraham tapestries at least once more, in 1635, for St. George's Day ceremonies at Whitehall.[24]

The subject of the hangings belonged to a tradition of exemplum that, though stronger in the sixteenth, was not dead in the seventeenth century. In his recent commentary on the Abraham group, Thomas P. Campbell explains their significance thus: "Much of the propaganda and official iconography generated by the Tudor court during the years of the Reformation was concerned to draw parallels between Henry [VIII] and the Old Testament patriarchs, in order to substantiate his newly defined role as head of the English church and, in effect, patriarch to his own people."[25] James, who would have been quite aware of this tradition, also saw himself as a founding figure, the first monarch of Great Britain; he saw his kingship consistently through a patriarchal model, and he saw political power as entirely involved with divine will. His own traditional Old Testament model was Solomon, who formed the paradigm of the sermon preached at James's funeral in 1625,[26] and who is alluded to in the iconography of Rubens's paintings, which were to become the permanent decoration within the Banqueting House.[27]

A further attraction of the Abraham tapestries to observers such as James was their inclusion of elaborate borders showing the personified virtues apparent in each scene within the entire history. I quote again from Campbell's commentary: "Taken as an ensemble, the border personifications invite the viewer to consider the narrative as a meditation on Abraham's secular and religious virtues . . . More generally they relate these qualities to the concepts of Fame and Honor [personifications that appear in the border of *Abraham Meeting Melchizedek*], which, according to the teachings of the *speculum principis* (mirror of princes), were the pinnacle of achievement for European rulers."[28] The tapestries' immediate sensory impressiveness is supported by a moral and intellectual scheme that strengthens their significance and coherence as a series. A sophisticated emblematic series of meanings is set before the viewer; the margins gloss the central picture rather as commentaries in contemporary Bibles expound the significances of the central text. The program of the entire series of woven pictures, as explained above by Campbell, is entirely in key with the ideals of the Order of the Garter. It is hard to imagine that James would have been dissatisfied by what he saw in the Banqueting House in 1621.

While the Chamber account tells us nothing directly about court theater, then, it unlocks a great deal about court sensibility in the closing years of James's reign, and about James's consistent policies, which other "histories" of that period—the dominance of Buckingham, for example—might ignore or obscure. In the next part of this essay I move away from the moment of 1621 to return to that of 1547, when the great inventory of King Henry's goods was made, and to consider both the contents and the phraseology of that list. The verbal formula that tricked the Malone Society editors into thinking that tapestries were a written fiction is "the History of": it occurs throughout the Henrician inventory, always meaning some kind of visual representation, and usually signifying a series of pictures which tell a story sequentially. The distinction between a single unified subject (the Judgment of Solomon, e.g.) and a history is apparent in the description of an item in the Wardrobe at Whitehall—not woven, in this instance, but painted: "Item a stayned cloth of Phebus ridinge in his carte in the ayre with thistorye of hym."[29] Predominant in this visual scheme, that is to say, was a representation of the sun chariot, with other parts of the Phoebus myth placed marginally around it. Histories might be thematic ("thistorye of the twelve moneths" on twelve distinct tapestries), sacred ("thistorye of thactes of thappostles"), on subjects from both Old and New Testaments, or pagan and classical ("vij peces of fine newe Tapsterie of the Historye of Vulcanus Mars and venus").[30] What was to become the standard English variant of the word "history" in the sense of the examples above is also apparent in the inventories, used in exactly the same way. At Greenwich, for example, there were hangings showing both "The Storye of king david" (five pieces) and "The Storye of youthe" (two pieces).[31] Both these "stories" were also given dramatic shape, the latter during the earlier part of the reign of King Henry VIII, and one would like to know if the tapestries showed figures similar to those in the play, and to what extent the two versions of the story may have conformed.

That "story" and "history" are interchangeable, indifferent terms is shown by a listing of three tapestries at Oatlands "of the Storye of Salamon," followed by that at the More of "vij peces of thistorie of Salamon" that had formerly belonged to Cardinal Wolsey.[32] I intend to pursue the history of one of these "diverse storyes"[33] in particular, but at this point it is worth considering how one kind of story—the biblical text in the first instance, to choose a popular source for visual "histories"—might influence another, and further, how the reception of a story, in either sense, might be influenced by knowledge of it in another form. Tudor and Stuart courtiers would have known their Bible from reading it, from hearing it read at divine service, and from seeing it around them on the walls. Religious imagery, both élite and popular, did not disappear with the break from Rome. Even Cromwell gazed at *The History of Abraham*. The significance of any biblical episode as read or heard might be mediated by its significance as a visual history, with a particular form and composition; it goes without saying that reception of pictorial stories was influenced by the observer's familiarity with them through reading and listening.

To take a particular example from a play that seems to have impressed King James, *The Merchant of Venice*.[34] In act one Shylock tells an exemplary story from what the royal inventory-makers called "Thistorie of Jacob."[35] The Tudor hangings, once belonging to Cardinal Wolsey, came in seven pieces, and presumably showed seven episodes from the book of Genesis. That told by Shylock is the selective stock-breeding practiced by Jacob on Laban's flocks (Genesis 30:25–43), a fairly obscure piece of scripture to modern ears, and known to most literate laypeople, I would guess, through its Shakespearean frame. As it happens, however, Shylock's tale of when "Jacob graz'd his uncle Laban's sheep" (1.1.71)[36] formed a consistent part of the iconography of the Jacob story as told in visual form in the Renaissance. A drawing from 1480–1500, after Hugo van der Goes, shows the "woolly breeders in the act" (1.1.83), as does an engraving made by Crispijn de Passe for his series *Liber Genesis*, published in 1612.[37] The "certain wands," usually not "stuck up," as Shylock has it (1.1.84–86), but more strictly set "in the gutters of the watering troughs" (Genesis 30:38), also are consistently shown in prints, the designs for which were also frequently used as models for tapestries, as well as mural painting, painted glass, plasterwork, and decorated pottery. A particularly striking Jacob tapestry, after a design by Bernaert van Orley, and hence comparable with the Abraham series, was made between 1528 and 1534, and today survives in Brussels. The foreground shows Jacob and Laban dividing the flock according to their agreement; in the center midground Jacob supervises the flocks drinking at the troughs—he holds the wands in his hands, and bends over the sheep to show them.[38]

Not only was Shakespeare's story well known in visual form—those who did not very often see tapestries might have access to it through the widespread formats of woodcut and engraved prints—but so was the moralized framework within which Shylock sets it. He wants to read it as endorsing thrift; Antonio objects that what Jacob did was merely a "venture," and impossible to achieve without "the hand of heaven" (1.1.89–93). Most interpretations favor Jacob, naturally, the hero of the piece, but verses attached to a print of the episode by Maarten de Vos of about 1581 interestingly see things in terms of everyday motivation: "Te vellet, Iacobe, Laban fraudare: sed ipse / Semet fraudatum comperit arte sua" (Laban wanted to cheat you, Jacob, but he found himself cheated by his own art).[39] The cheater cheated in a livestock deal has a broad comic appeal; reversal is also particularly apposite to *The Merchant of Venice*.

An audience of Shakespeare's time, in short, had a broad field of reference in which it could place Shylock and his story, probably including a variety of interpretations of Jacob and the sheep, as well as memories of the story told in visual form. I want to pursue the connection between visual art and drama by considering another Old Testament story, a consistent favorite for both graphic representations and those in the theater between the middle ages and the later seventeenth century. My focus is a lost play of 1567, mounted at the first purpose-built Elizabethan playing place of which we currently have knowledge, the Red Lion: it was called *The Story of Samson*.

Although no Samson play in English survives before that of Milton, published in 1671, and hardly intended for the commercial stage, the subject was popular across Europe as a whole, including the Spanish *Auto de Sanson* of about 1500, a *Story of Samson* mounted in Haarlem in 1550 by the Wijngaardranken society of rhetoric, of which the artist Maarten van Heemskerck was a member (and of whom I will have more to say below), and a play by Hans Sachs, *Tragedia der richter Simson*, of 1556.[40] In Shakespeare's lifetime there were at least two Samson plays staged in London: that specified above, and a play by the Admiral's Men at the Fortune in 1602, perhaps partly written by Samuel Rowley, and seen by the visiting Duke Philip Julius of Stettin-Pomerania on 14 September of that year.[41] Perhaps that play, or yet a third, is being alluded to in Middleton's *The Family of Love*, of about 1607, in which playgoers have seen "Sampson bear the town-gates on his neck from the lower to the upper stage";[42] in the context of satirical comedy such references cannot be taken too literally, although the episode itself, as I shall show, was a chief part of Samson's story, consistently represented in graphic form.

The story as told in the Bible, Judges 13–16, is not especially coherent, and its entire significance is open to exegesis and interpretation, which began in the New Testament. Milton concentrates on the end of the story, on Samson's failure and weakness, and his eventual redemption in the catastrophe, even if he has recently been accused by a modern reader of ethnic terrorism.[43] The austerity of *Samson Agonistes* is unlikely to have been matched in the Elizabethan plays of 1567 and 1602. Episodic adventure of a spectacular and violent nature was grist to the contemporary theatrical mill, and if an audience were promised *The Story of Samson* they would have expected the whole thing, not a meditative retrospect with the main fictional event off-stage. With what kind of resources, then, might the epic events of the Samson story have been managed, and how might the story on the stage, which combined verbal and visual narratives, have alluded to and reflected the story as told purely pictorially? If you could never bring in a wall, a narrative requirement in another story, what hope of a collapsing temple? Further, apart from its aspect as a crowd-pleaser and getpenny, why might the Samson story have been chosen as a dramatic subject, and have been staged quite when it was?

The popularity of Samson as a visual theme in the sixteenth century is apparent from the 1547 royal inventory; five distinct sets of tapestry, in various houses and palaces, told the story of Samson, one "havinge A border of the late Cardinalles Armes."[44] The last detail would suggest that Samson was as fully a Catholic worthy as he was Protestant; indeed in 1610 Cardinal Borghese, in Rome, was pursuing the commissioning of a large set of tapestries to be woven in Brussels, on the subject of the life of Samson.[45] The English court tapestries came in series of various sizes, from a single piece forty-eight feet long, on which "thistorye of Sampson" was presumably represented in consecutive vignettes, to a set of fifteen distinct pieces: both were at Greenwich in 1547.[46] A later inventory, produced at Kenilworth in 1588 following the Earl of Leicester's death, demonstrates that earlier Tudor taste persisted for at least another forty years. Leicester owned many hangings showing "stories," of Susanna, of Saul, of Jezebel, of David, of Abraham, and many others, including "Fyve peeces of the storie of Sampson, of oulde stuffe."[47]

As a legendary figure, Samson carried with him a long history of interpretation, from St. Paul onward.[48] In the Epistle to the Hebrews Samson is placed with Abraham as a man justified by faith, "Who through faith subdued kingdoms, wrought righteousness, obtained promises, stopped the mouth of lions" (11:33). He might serve, therefore, as an emblem of militant religion: in the sixteenth century particularly the icon of Samson fighting the lion carried such a meaning. The composition itself corresponds to an image from the "story" of Hercules, and the two strongman heroes were commonly regarded as analogues.[49] Hercules was also the slayer of other monsters, and the one-man contest with aggressive beasts has many symbolic manifestations, including that of St. George and the dragon, the emblem of the Order of the Garter.[50] The most celebrated early Renaissance image of the subject of Samson and the lion is Dürer's woodcut, made in the 1490s, and widely admired and copied, especially by Lucas Cranach the Elder, artist of the Saxon court at Wittenberg, and friend of Martin Luther. One of Cranach's series of "Tournament" woodcuts, made between 1506 and 1509, shows a tapestry of Samson fighting the lion, based on the Dürer iconography, hanging below a gallery from which an audience watches the chivalric contest in the town square below.[51] A court pastime, the image reminds us, is ultimately connected to religious commitment, and active resistance to evil. Luther's own commentary on Samson underlines his significance as a brave warrior, raised by God from sin and error.[52] Though certainly not exclusively a figure signifying Reformation virtues, then, Samson in Renaissance images might carry a suggestion of the overthrow of contemporary ecclesiastical and political powers. The temple of Dagon that Samson destroys at his death had an evident application in the eyes of the reformers, long before Milton; the destruction of idolatrous shrines and temples was a commonplace of polemical imagery of the Reformation [53]

Further, from Augustine onward Samson had been interpreted as a type of and an analogue to Christ: both men miraculously born, both speakers of paradoxes, both suffering a sacrificial and redemptive death.[54] Such parallelism, a tradition of medieval biblical commentary, was absorbed by the reformers, and survived at least until Milton's time.

The story of Samson as told pictorially could be condensed into one image or extended into a series, in prints, tapestries, or mural paintings. Cranach's panel painting of Samson fighting the lion, from the earlier 1520s, includes the jawbone of the ass, lying on the ground to the left, alluding to another, later episode of heroic slaughter, and connecting the two.[55] The most thoroughly recognizable single-image composition of Samson's story, from Lucas van Leyden to Rubens, is that of Delilah and the cutting of the hair: sometimes by her, sometimes a third figure, with Philistine soldiers lurking in the background. As an emblem of the strong man overthrown it offered an antitype to pictures of the lion-killer, and as an ironically matched pair the two images would tell a good deal of Samson's story. A glass roundel of the early sixteenth century, now in New York, shows the cutting of the hair in the center foreground, Delilah seated, Samson asleep on the ground, with his head on her lap. Helmet and armor lie beside him; with her left hand she wields shears, while his left hand still grasps the jawbone.[56] To the right, midground, a stooping Samson kills the lion, while in a matching position to the left a third representation of Samson carries the gates of Gaza.[57] Simultaneous composition of parts of the story underlines the hero's contrasting strength and weakness.

When Samson's story is shown in narrative sequence the images discussed above remain important visual episodes within the whole. Two prolific and well-known artists from the Low Countries produced Samson sequences as prints in the second half of the sixteenth century: Maarten van Heemskerck in about 1560, and Maarten de Vos in about 1585. The designs of both men were widely copied in other formats, in England and elsewhere.[58] They might therefore serve as models for the story of Samson as it was known visually at about the time of the English Samson play of 1567. The two series differ in number and format. Heemskerck made six designs in circular form, perhaps indicating their market as patterns for glass or pottery decoration, and De Vos seven, in lateral rectangular format, with Latin verses at the foot of each print.[59] The subjects of each differ somewhat, but both begin and end with the same images: first the appearance of the angel to Manoah, Samson's father, followed by the fight with the lion; they close with Delilah cutting Samson's hair, followed by the destruction of the temple. Heemskerck's third picture is Samson's wedding to the Philistine woman; De Vos does not depict this episode. The fourth image in Heemskerck's series is energetic and complex, combining four distinct elements into a simultaneous composition retreating in space. In the foreground a muscular Samson slays the Philistines with the jawbone; in midground he stoops to drink from the spring spouting from the bone. Thus two elements in narrative sequence recess from the viewer. Beyond the drinking Samson a standing Samson watches the foxes ignite the crops (a *narrative* recession, from Judges 15:19 to 15:3–5), and in the far distance, at the top of the circular frame, Samson sets the gates of Gaza on the hilltop (16:3), resuming the correspondence of visual recession and narrative sequence. This lively design brings Samson's triumphs over his enemies together, before moving, in the next vignette, to his fall.

De Vos gives each of his pictures a single episodic focus: his third is Samson setting fire to the crops with the foxes, his fourth the massacre with the jawbone, and his fifth the carrying away of the gates.[60] These two graphic stories largely correspond in subjects, therefore (Heemskerck manages to include one more episode with one less print), and give a sense of the central events of Samson's myth as it was represented in the later sixteenth century, and of what a contemporary audience would have known and might have expected when it assembled in a playhouse or town square to see a dramatic representation of Samson.

Most of these episodes might have been staged in one way or another within the symbolic conventions of the Elizabethan theater. Purely human interactions, naturally, offered no barrier to convincing and engaging representation that might closely reflect the iconography of Samson's story. Thus the seduction and betrayal of Samson by Delilah invites a well-written dialogue and skillful playing. The miraculous and amazing feats relied on stage resources. The annunciation episode, the first picture in both Samson series discussed above, at the end of which "the angel of the LORD ascended in the flame of the altar" (Judges 13.20) might have been represented with the aid of machinery that the Elizabethan stage inherited from the medieval theater.[61] The Red Lion playhouse, at which *The Story of Samson* was mounted in 1567, was equipped with a "turret" having a platform eighteen feet above the stage, from which flying effects might have been managed.[62]

Samson's lion-slaying, a gripping image in graphic format, could easily become ludicrous onstage. Not for nothing is a cowardly lion a target of parody in *A Midsummer Night's Dream*; other lame manifestations of heroic achievements are mocked in *Love's Labour's Lost*. Lions *were*, notwithstanding, represented on the contemporary stage, and perhaps the symbolic shorthand Thomas Heywood employed in *The Silver Age*, in which the killing of the Nemean lion is represented by Hercules entering *"with the Lion's head and skin"* was followed in Samson plays.[63] In 1598 the properties of the Admiral's Men included "j lyone skin," "j lyone," and "ij lyon heades."[64]

In terms of drama one might think that the entire episode of Samson's riddle (Judges 14:7–14), with its parallel to that of Delilah in terms of secret, confidence, and betrayal, is likely to have received more prominence than his revenge in the crop-burning, as represented by the print sequences. Battle and massacre, however, were staple fare in the Elizabethan playhouse, and Samson's smiting of his enemies (there are three distinct fights: Judges 14:19–15:15, culminating in the slaughter of the thousand with the jawbone) was undoubtedly represented with energy and vigor, within the contemporary theatrical principle of synecdoche.[65] The carrying of the gates of Gaza was so thoroughly a sign of Samson's feats that it could hardly have been ignored on the stage; suitably heavy-looking properties could have been provided for the purpose, and a simple "passing over" the stage by the actor bearing them—a dumb show, that is to say—would have served quite adequately as a representation of the episode. The major theatrical challenge came from Samson's demolition of the temple, the culminating act of his story. It was probably also represented in some fashion during the 1602 performance at the Fortune, which was described as "a tragicomedy of Samson and the half tribe of Benjamin."[66] That is to say it included the tragedy of Samson, and went on to dramatise the defeat of Gibeah by the Israelites (Judges 17–21).

If the collapsing masonry and crushed bodies could not be represented on the stage with the same striking and horrific realism as they were in graphic art, some kind of stage effect was not beyond the powers of contemporary technique. A Samson play staged at Aarau in Switzerland in 1557 featured a structure made to fall, suitably lightly built,[67] and there is a native English analogue from the reign of King Edward VI. At Hampton Court in Christmas 1547–48 the Revels Office constructed "a Towre Recembling the Tower of babylon" for a play on the subject.[68] The man who made it, Robert Trunkwell, was a joiner, carver, designer, and expert in stage mechanics.[69] The

Revels title for the scenic structure demonstrates the common Reformation association of the Tower of Babel (Genesis 11:1–9) with the destruction of Babylon announced in Revelation (18:2): contemporary "stories" in pictorial form show "before and after" versions of the tower, and pictures of its collapse are analogous with those of Samson's temple, and might carry the same contemporary application.[70] The property tower made by the Revels, then, must have resembled the "Tower of Babylon" in being constructed so as to collapse, probably directly downward, in concentric sections, once some internal or external supporting mechanism was released at the appropriate cue. Its symbolic significance, under a Protestant monarch, is not difficult to grasp.

We do not know how ambitious the production of the 1567 Samson play may have been, although a good deal of care seems to have been taken on the playhouse that was to present it, and the "turret" referred to above might also have been used to create some kind of mechanism similar to that of the Babylon play of twenty years earlier. As it fell, actors safely positioned in front and upstage of it might simultaneously enact their own crushing and collapse, creating a memorable spectacular moment similar to the pictorial story.

A symbolic alternative, though more appropriate to a parade of worthies like that toward the end of Love's Labour's Lost, is suggested by another representation of Samson, by Pieter Coecke van Aelst, one of the two designers of the Abraham tapestries, of about 1530–40. This is a "Triumph of Fame," one of a series of triumphs based on Petrarch, produced as glass roundels after pen drawings.[71] Samson precedes the chariot with Fame blowing her trumpets: he is a stooped figure, wearing a lion skin, like Hercules, and bearing two classical columns, one over the right shoulder, and the other supported by the left arm, carried at waist level: the two supporting pillars of the temple. The image invokes both the carrying of the gates of Gaza and Christ bearing the cross. As an emblem of Samson's triumph in defeat it is an effective composition; as a show onstage presenting the culmination of Samson's story it would probably have been judged by London playgoers to be rather tame and inadequate.

The context of my discussion so far has made it apparent that Samson plays in the public playhouses are unlikely either to have been chosen by their performers or watched by their audiences entirely without a consideration of Samson's significance within the contemporary moment. Recent study of the earlier Elizabethan theater has made clear the connection between dramatic patronage and politico-religious advocacy.[72] That the Earl of Leicester was both a consistent patron of players and a vigorous supporter of a militant Protestant polity is not coincidental. Samson as a figure nominated by St. Paul as one of the elect gave him a special significance in an England that regarded itself as an Elect Nation, especially favored by God. A strong man constantly surrounded by hostile enemies and misled by deceit, eventually overthrowing false religion, Samson offered a notable mirror for magistrates, his bad judgment in sexual matters not excluded. The 1567 performance of his story, then, would have been received within the context of the early Elizabethan settlement, less than a decade old and still in formation, and of the deteriorating situation in the Netherlands, as reformist initiatives collided with Spanish intransigence. That the play was performed in the summertime at Mile End, a district associated with the musters of the militia, is perhaps not accidental. As a godly warrior, Samson set an example for the survival of England.

What then of the Samson play of 1602? It belongs within something of a revival of Old Testament subjects for plays during the final years of the long reign of Queen Elizabeth, no doubt expressing the hope for a succession that would ensure national security and identity.[73] That most of these plays were staged by the company of the Lord Admiral, Charles Howard, Earl of Nottingham, military hero of 1588 and staunch supporter of the Cecils, and hence of the succession of King James of Scotland, seems suggestive of some kind of program of public opinion formation. The virtues of the Old Testament heroes and patriarchs were to be hoped for in a new monarch who would maintain the political and religious integrity of the nation. While the *History of Abraham* that King James beheld in 1621 was not a play, it was itself an artifact made as a conscious symbol of national destiny and royal power, and James's attention to it part of an unbroken tradition of the application of scriptural history to contemporary circumstances. The monarch took upon himself the best attributes of the ancient leaders, so that Abraham had been King Henry, was in 1621 King James, and would be, some years later, King Charles. Cromwell's choice to keep the tapestries perhaps tells us about more than his mere aesthetic discrimination. The immutable stories of scripture outlived individual kings, but gave each in turn an ideal glass of descent, succession, and divine blessing, of the kind denied to Macbeth but granted, finally, to the spectral Banquo. It was the story told by tapestry, not drama, that held up that glass to the Tudor and Stuart courts.

Notes

1. See Leeds Barroll, *Politics, Plague, and Shakespeare's Theater* (Ithaca: Cornell University Press, 1991), and more recently "Assessing 'Cultural Influence': James I as Patron of the Arts," *Shakespeare Studies* 29 (2001), 132–62.

2. New York: Garland, 1986, 185. *The History of Abraham* is *not* recorded in *Annals of English Drama 975–1700*, 3rd ed., A. Harbage, S. Schoenbaum, and S. S. Wagonheim (London: Routledge, 1989), a work that in other respects is out of date as a guide to theatrical activity in 1621.

3. 7 vols. (Oxford: Clarendon Press, 1941–68).

4. Ibid., vol. 7, 40.

5. On this general topic, see my *English Court Theatre 1558–1642* (Cambridge: Cambridge University Press, 1999).

6. Malone Society *Collections VI* (Oxford: Malone Society, 1962), 119.

7. See Thomas P. Campbell, *Tapestry in the Renaissance* (New York: Metropolitan Museum of Art, 2002), 416–23.

8. Ibid.

9. Platter saw Caesar's death represented in both graphic and dramatic form, the latter at the Globe in September 1599: see Andrew Gurr, *Playgoing in Shakespeare's London*, 2nd ed. (Cambridge: Cambridge University Press, 1996), 222.

10. P. Razzell, ed., *The Journals of Two Travellers in Elizabethan and Early Stuart England* (London: Caliban, 1995), 70.

11. David Starkey, ed., *The Inventory of King Henry VIII* (London: Harvey Miller, 1998), 268. I am grateful to Dr. Tom Campbell for directing me to this source.

12. Campbell, *Tapestry*, 416, 423.

13. See "Assessing 'Cultural Influence'" (note 1).

14. Per Palme, *Triumph of Peace* (London: Thames and Hudson, 1957), 63.

15. See John Nichols, *The Progresses, Processions, and Magnificent Festivities of King James the First*, 4 vols. (London: Nichols, 1828), vol. 4, 664. An impression of a Garter Feast, in a large hall hung with tapestries, may be gained from an etching by Hollar produced for Elias Ashmole's book on the order published in 1672, and quoted below; it is reproduced in my *English Court Theatre*, 72.

16. Quoted in Palme, *Triumph*, 63.

17. See Roy Strong, *Britannia Triumphans* (London: Thames and Hudson), 1980, 39–42. The symbolism of the George was not so exclusively coded, however, as to prevent a leading Catholic nobleman such as the Earl of Arundel from displaying it with evident pride in a portrait by Van Dyck from 1620 to 1621 (J. Paul Getty Museum).

18. Barroll, "Assessing 'Cultural Influence,'" 156.

19. The painting is in the Royal Collection. It is discussed, e.g., by Palme, *Triumph*, 31, and by David Howarth in *Images of Rule* (London: Macmillan, 1997), 125–27.

20. The painting is in the National Portrait Gallery. It is widely reproduced: see, e.g., the cover of Alvin Kernan's *Shakespeare, The King's Playwright* (New Haven: Yale University Press, 1995).

21. *Triumph*, 27. Palme does not note the connection between the Mortlake project and the Order of the Garter, cemented in the person of Sir Francis Crane, the chief animator of the tapestry factory. He held a court post as secretary to the Prince of Wales, and became Secretary of the Order of the Garter under the new king in 1625.

22. Elias Ashmole, *The Institution, Laws, and Ceremonies of the Most Noble Order of the Garter* (London, 1672), 196.

23. See Oliver Millar, *The Age of Charles I* (London: Tate Gallery, 1972), 57–59.

24. Campbell, *Tapestry*, 416, 423.

25. Ibid., 417.

26. John Williams, *Great Britain's Solomon* (London, 1625).

27. See Palme, *Triumph*, Strong, *Britannia*, and Oliver Millar, "The Whitehall Ceiling," *Burlington Magazine* 98 (1956): 258–67.

28. *Tapestry*, 417.

29. Starkey, *Inventory*, 240.

30. Ibid., 191, 209.

31. Ibid., 195.

32. Ibid., 293, 326.

33. Ibid., 209.

34. See Barroll, "Assessing 'Cultural Influence'"; Astington, *English Court Theatre*, 181–82.

35. The hangings were housed at the More. Starkey, *Inventory*, 326.

36. Quotations follow the text of *The Riverside Shakespeare*, ed. G. Blakemore Evans, 2nd. ed. (Boston: Houghton Mifflin, 1997).

37. See Timothy B. Husband, *The Luminous Image: Painted Glass Roundels in the Lowlands, 1480–1560* (New York: Metropolitan Museum, 1995), 51; Ilja M. Veldman, *Profit and Pleasure. Print Books by Crispijn de Passe* (Rotterdam: Sound & Vision, 2001), 308.

38. See Guy Delmarcel, *Flemish Tapestry* (New York: Abrams, 1999), 100.

39. Christiaan Schuckman and D. de Hoop, eds., *Hollstein's Dutch and Flemish Etchings, Engravings and Woodcuts 1450–1700*, vol. 45 (Rotterdam: Sound & Vision, 1995), 19.

40. See Watson Kirkconnell, *That Invincible Samson* (Toronto: University of Toronto Press, 1964); Ilja M. Veldman, trans. M. Hoyle, *Maarten van Heemskerck and Dutch Humanism in the Sixteenth Century* (Maarssen: Schwartz, 1977), 128–32. Veldman also identifies other Dutch visual artists who were members of chambers of rhetoric at various times.

41. E. K. Chambers, *The Elizabethan Stage*, 4 vols. (Oxford: Clarendon Press, 1923), vol. 2, 180, 367.

42. Ibid., vol. 3, p. 120.

43. See John Carey, "A Work in Praise of Terrorism? September 11 and *Samson Agonistes*," "Commentary," *TLS*, 6 September 2002, 15–16, and subsequent letters to the editor.

44. Starkey, *Inventory*, 327.

45. Delmarcel, *Flemish Tapestry*, 18.

46. Starkey, *Inventory*, 196.

47. See Anthony Wells-Cole, *Art and Decoration in Elizabethan and Jacobean England* (New Haven: Yale University Press, 1997), 297.

48. See F. Michael Krouse, *Milton's Samson and the Christian Tradition* (Princeton: Princeton University Press, 1949); Joseph Wittreich, *Interpreting Samson Agonistes* (Princeton: Princeton University Press, 1986).

49. Krouse, *Milton's Samson*, 44–45.

50. Lucas Cranach the Elder created several politically coded woodcuts of St. George, as well as the images of Samson discussed in this essay: see David Landau and Peter Parshall, *The Renaissance Print 1470–1550* (New Haven: Yale University Press, 1994), 184–92.

51. See Tilman Falk, ed., *The Illustrated Bartsch*, vol. 11 (New York: Abaris, 1980), 419. A painting by Cranach of Samson and the lion of 1520–25, based on Dürer's composition, survives at Weimar (Kunstsammlungen zu Weimar, Schloss).

52. See Wittreich, *Samson Agonistes*, 30–31.

53. See, e.g., Margaret Aston, *The King's Bedpost* (Cambridge: Cambridge University Press, 1993), especially 67–81.

54. Krouse, *Milton's Samson*, 40–44, 68–69.

55. The painting is in Weimar: see note 51.

56. The left-handedness probably indicates reversed copying from a drawing or print.

57. Timothy B. Husband, *Stained Glass before 1700 in American Collections: Silver Stained Roundels and Unipartite Panels* (Washington: National Gallery of Art, 1991), 153.

58. See Wells-Cole, *Art and Decoration*.

59. I. M. Veldman and G. Luijten, eds., *The New Hollstein. Maarten van Heemskerck*, 2 vols. (Roosendaal: Koninklijke van Poll, 1993), vol. 1, pp. 84–89; Schuckman and de Hoop, *Hollstein*, 44–47.

60. Only in the Gaza picture does De Vos indulge in simultaneous composition. In the left foreground Samson sets down the gates on the hilltop, before an extensive landscape with a city in the far distance. In the middle distance before it a small second Samson may be seen carrying the gates on his back.

61. See Peter Meredith and John E. Tailby, ed., *The Staging of Religious Drama in Europe in the Later Middle Ages* (Kalamazoo: Medieval Institute, 1983), 94–100, and my "Descent Machinery in the Playhouses," *Medieval & Renaissance Drama in England* 2 (1985), 119–33.

62. Glynne Wickham, Herbert Berry, and William Ingram, eds., *English Professional Theatre 1530–1660* (Cambridge: Cambridge University Press, 2000), 290–94.

63. Alan C. Dessen and Leslie Thomson, *A Dictionary of Stage Directions in English Drama 1580–1642* (Cambridge: Cambridge University Press, 1999), 134–35.

64. R. A. Foakes and R. T. Rickert, eds., *Henslowe's Diary* (Cambridge: Cambridge University Press, 1961), 319–20.

65. "Into a thousand parts divide one man," *Henry V,* Prologue, 24. Presumably this ratio was not followed to the letter in Samson's legendary victory.

66. Chambers, *Elizabethan Stage*, vol. 2, 367.

67. Kirkconnell, *Samson*, 160.

68. Albert Feuillerat, ed., *Documents Relating to the Revels at Court in the Time of King Edward VI and Queen Mary* (Leuven: Uystpruyst, 1914), 26.

69. See W. R. Streitberger, *Court Revels, 1485–1559* (Toronto, University of Toronto Press, 1994), 20, 61, 189, 214, 216, 371.

70. See Aston, *Bedpost*, 73–77.

71. Husband, *Luminous Image*, 160–61.

72. See, notably, Scott McMillin and Sally-Beth MacLean, *The Queen's Men and Their Plays* (Cambridge: Cambridge University Press, 1998).

73. Between 1601 and 1603 the Admiral's Men staged plays on *Jephthah, Joshua*, and *Samson*; other scriptural plays of the same period were *Judas, Pontius Pilate*, and *Tobias*, and older repertory included *Esther and Ahasuerus* (1594) and *Nebuchadnezzar* (1596). See Chambers, *Elizabethan Stage*.

The Theatrical and Other Misdeeds of William Appowell, Priest

HERBERT BERRY

IN November 1584, the Diocese of Bath and Wells accused the vicar of Marston Magna of misdeeds the most serious of which had to do with a puppet show. Marston Magna is a village in Somerset, and the vicar there since 1572 was William Appowell, who was often called simply William Powell. "Powell" is a Welsh name and "Ap" the Welsh equivalent of "Mc" in Scottish and Irish names. The diocese supposed that (to reverse the order of the famous clauses in the Prayer Book) he had done those things which he ought not to have done, and he had left undone those things which he ought to have done.

The diocese brought a case against Appowell in its Consistory Court, which met in the Cathedral at Wells, and the documents of the case provide everything known about Appowell's alleged misconduct. Nearly all these documents are depositions in which deponents answered "articles" drawn up by the diocese. The articles do not survive, but the answers to them suggest much of what they asked.

Early in the proceedings of 20 November 1584, the diocese summoned Appowell to appear. Presumably somebody rode pell mell for Marston Magna, some twenty miles away, and Appowell rode pell mell back, for as the last item of business on that day he was in the cathedral to answer a group of six articles that the Diocese put to him (hereafter group 1).[1]

In answer to the first article, Appowell began by saying that "he was in Come wells." Then he had the clerk line out "Come wells" and write "Glaston" (that is, Glastonbury) instead. He was there, he went on, "at the signe of the Harte in January aboute ij yeares since & confesseth that there was poppett playenge," but (in Latin) he believed the article otherwise to be untrue. His answer to the second prompted the clerk to write "vt supra"—as above, and add that otherwise Appowell believed the assertions in this article also to be untrue. Appowell thought those in the third article untrue as well but did not hint at what they were. Evidently the first two and maybe the third asked whether he had done improper things at a puppet show in an unspecified place and asked when and where the show had taken place. "Come

wells" must mean Combe Wells, a name now unknown by which Appowell
probably meant Walcombe, then and now a hamlet less than a mile north of
the Cathedral. People named Marchaunt were prominent tenants there in
1477 and still in 1645, two of whom in 1580 were William Marchaunt senior
and junior:[2] soon in 1584 a William Marchaunt would tell the Consistory
Court that he knew Appowell well. The sign of the Hart in Glastonbury was
an inn on the south side of the High Street, opposite the Glastonbury Tribu-
nal, that in the 1650s became a coaching inn called the White Hart (or so the
plaque on one of the present buildings there and another on the Crown farther
down the street suggest).

In answering the fourth and fifth articles, Appowell recounted a business
meeting one evening six or seven years before at Ilchester, a small town about
five miles west of Marston Magna. He had heard while in the town that the
wife of one Mocksedge was suing him about a horse he had bought from her
husband and for which he had not paid. He and three or four of his neighbors,
"honest Comepany" who included George Taswell, Nicholas Cutler, and
Silvester Mewe, went to her house to talk to her "thereaboute." While they
were talking, the constable of the town arrived at the house and apparently
for no reason took Appowell and "the woman" to prison and in the morning
set him in the town stocks. Appowell then dismissed the sixth article as untrue without hinting at the question.

If Appowell thought these answers sufficient, he was wrong. The case was
by now in the hands of William Watkins, diocesan procurator, who at a sitting
of the court on 4 December 1584, announced new articles. The court summoned Appowell to appear again on 12 December, then decided that he could
do so on 9 December. There would be twenty new articles divided into two
groups (hereafter groups 2 and 3). Group 2 consisted of seventeen articles to
show that Appowell had done things in his private life improper for a clergyman to do. The events at the puppet show were obviously the most important
part of this case, since the diocese devoted the first four substantive articles
and one other to it (nos. 2–5, 8) and dealt with other accusations in one or
two articles each. Two articles concerned the doings in Mistress Mocksedge's
house (nos. 9–10). Group 3 consisted of three articles to show that Appowell
did not perform his pastoral duties as he should, either.

Watkins found ten deponents including Appowell to provide answers to
these new articles.[3] In a paragraph above each deposition except Appowell's,
the Diocese noted where the deponent lived and for how long, where he was
born, and how long and how well he knew Appowell. Deponents, also called
jurates, were supposed to distinguish direct knowledge from hearsay, and
each wrote his mark or signature after his last answer. All ten men answered
articles in group 2, but none answered more than six from direct knowledge
except Appowell, who answered them all so. Four men who had also answered articles in group 2, including Appowell, answered articles in group 3,

but only Appowell answered all three from direct knowledge. Altogether, the case against Appowell consists of twenty-six articles to which ten men made fifteen depositions comprising fifty-six answers from direct knowledge and thirty-eight from hearsay. Only Appowell answered articles in all three groups of them. (In the appendix below see the list of deponents and the articles to which they gave answers.) One clerk wrote the document having to do with the articles of group 1 and another the documents having to do with the articles of groups 2 and 3. Their rule was to write the headings to depositions in Latin and the answers to articles in English, but even in writing the answers they often strayed into Latin. Neither referred to Marston Magna by those words: the first called it Merston, the other "Brod Merston"—Broad Marston, a common name for the place at the time.

The court need not have concerned itself with whether Appowell could appear on 9 or 12 December. The order summoning him occurs early among the acts of 4 December, and, nothing loath as before, he was in Wells Cathedral to answer the articles of group 2 as the last act on that same day.[4] Other deponents were not so eager, and perhaps the articles of group 3 were not ready. In any event, on 15 December nine others answered the articles of group 2, and Appowell and three others also answered those of group 3[5]— evidently at a special sitting, since 15 December was a Tuesday and the court met regularly on Fridays.

The first article of group 2 asked if something quite general was true, and all ten deponents said that it was—since the clerk wrote for each of them only "deponit [or respondet] eundem esse verum," he deposes, or replies, that the same (article) is true. The last asked whether the deponent had told the truth, since the clerk wrote for each except Appowell, "deponit quod praedeponita per eum sunt [or esse] vera," he deposes that the above depositions by him are true. Appowell made the article a chance for further denial. The clerk wrote for him, "respondet quod Credit Creditio et negat[ivo] negative," meaning, apparently: he replies that he believes not and (the article) not credible. These two articles are not counted in the totals above. What article 16 asked is obscure because nobody answered it at length, though Appowell denied the accusation in it and five others said from hearsay that the accusation was true.[6]

Unlike the articles of group 1, those of group 2 specified where the puppet show had occurred, for the deponents invariably described the place as the "articulated" house. Coincidentally, in doing so they rendered the identity of that place a problem here. The articles also asked particularly when the puppet show had taken place, and they explained what the diocese supposed Appowell had done there and sought confirmation. They suggest, therefore, that the puppet show at the Hart in Glastonbury was not the one the diocese had in mind.

Appowell dismissed the first of these new articles about the puppet show

by admitting "that he was ther" and by saying that otherwise he did not believe the article to be true. For his answer to the second, the clerk wrote only
"similiter"—similarly, and for his answers to the three other articles only
that he did not believe the articles to be true in anything. Two men from
Queen Camel, the village a mile and a half north of Marston Magna, however, were less costive.

They were William Marchaunt and Edward Stone, who had known Appowell for fourteen and ten years and knew from personal knowledge that the
allegations in the articles were true. They were "personally presente" one
night at a puppet show "in the house articulated . . . aboute a xij monethes
since," and each made a point of saying that he did not recall the exact time
and day—or as the clerk wrote, "vt modo recolit et tempus et diem aliter
perfecte non recordatur"[7]—though one (Marchaunt) said that it was "at the
tyme of the sessions." Both "then and ther sawe the articulated Wi^m Appowell put his hande vnder the Coates of one woman" who was "standinge
vppon a forme" according to Marchaunt, "vppon a benche" according to
Stone. "And the Cause of all ther beinge ther was to see pappett players
which was then and ther a handlinge" (Marchaunt), or merely "playinge"
(Stone), together with minstrels, one of whom beat a tabret (a small drum).

Despite the person of the lady standing on the form or bench, Appowell
apparently found the puppets boring, for presently while the show continued
"in the hall" (Stone), Appowell got some minstrels including the one with
the tabret to accompany him to the parlor in the same building. There the
minstrels played and Appowell danced with "diuers women . . . and at the
ende of the daw[n]ces he kissed them." Appowell then sat by the fire with
the wife of one Hawkes of Glastonbury, "a Candle burninge ther & almoste
spent." Finally, when others "were at the Doore [of the parlor] mindinge to
Comme in," Appowell "percevinge it, Conveyed the said woman out at a
backe Doore of the said parlor," and Marchaunt added, "to what ende this
depon^t knoweth not." Three other deponents, John Hurford, Peter Higdon,
and William Wyseman, also thought the assertions in these articles true but
only from hearsay. None of the ladies, however, complained, at least formally. Another article (no. 8) went over the same ground, for both Marchaunt
and Stone said that they had answered it in answering nos. 2–5.

The diocese called on a former constable of Ilchester and his bailiff to answer the new articles about the doings in the Mocksedge house at Ilchester
that led Appowell to the stocks there (nos. 9–10). They were Thomas Jeffery
and Jerome Busshopp both of Ilchester, the first now a tailor, and the second
now a husbandman, neither of whom may have known Appowell before.[8]
Appowell, it seems, was not paying for a horse. Jeffery and Busshopp went
to the "articulated" house of Joan Mocksedge one night six or seven years
ago in response to a hue and cry. It was "suspected to be a very bad house
for harbowringe of evill suspected persons." Inside they found Joan and two

"strange" women, one of whom "was knowen to be a bad woman for that she had a Childe out of wedloke." They also found Appowell, and the "Coates" of the strange women "were at that tyme vnbraced but to what intent this depon[t] [Jeffery] knoweth not." When Jeffery and Busshopp tried to take Appowell away "mindinge to examyne hym concerninge his beinge ther at so vndecent a tyme," he escaped and ran into the nearby house of Robert Bowringes. Jeffery and Busshopp, however, "imediatly tooke hym agayne" in that house "and put hym in to the shiere hall vntill the morninge," when Jeffery put him in the town stocks. After releasing Appowell, presumably later in the day, Jeffery put the two strange women in the stocks. Appowell had been put in the stocks because he had been found in a house of ill repute.

Though small, Ilchester was effectually the county town because the county jail was there. It was also one of the four towns where the quarter sessions of the county took place in turn before the assembled magistrates and justices of the peace of the county. Shire Hall was the public building where the sessions took place. It was also called Sessions Hall and was in the center of the town on the site of the present Town Hall. The stocks were in the market place in front of it, and the jail was some hundred yards north of the market place.[9]

Appowell began his new account of his adventures in Joan Mocksedge's house by saying that he had gone there "for no evill purpose and that was the firste time and the laste." But he now said nothing about paying for a horse, and the three "honest" men who were there with him in his former account became five with diferent names: Thomas Cummocke, Thomas Stone, another man named Stone, Walter Comnocke, and Thomas Morgan. The constable found Appowell and these men in the company of Joan Mocksedge and "thoth[r] suspected woman but wheth[r] they [the women] were vnbraced this respondent remembreth not." He was then committed to Shire Hall "and the same nighte was put in stockes wth one Morgan. And in the Morninge the said women were also togeth[r] wth this respondent Committed to the stockes."

Although a great many people resorted to litigation at the time, seven of the nine deponents who answered articles in group 2 on 15 December 1584, implied that a clergyman should not do so or encourage others to do so. A clergyman should especially not sue his parishioners. Yet, they complained, Appowell had sued many people, including parishioners, in three ecclesiastical courts and urged others to follow his example. The courts were two Diocesan courts, the Consistory Court and Court of Audience, and the Archbishop of Canterbury's Court of Arches in London. Appowell sued his parishioners, presumably, for the fees they owed him. He had sued one deponent in all three courts (and won each time) and another in two of them. These lawsuits were obviously an important reason for the animus against Appowell, and William Hegdon, Hurford, Higdon, and Wyseman agreed that he was "a very

troblous person" because of them.[10] Appowell merely said that the appropriate article (no. 15) was untrue.

"Very neere aboute the tyme" of the puppet show, Appowell urged Marchaunt to sue for money that Marchaunt should have received with his wife
when they married. The money was owing because of an arrangement to
which Appowell had been a witness. She was apparently the widow of Richard Wason, and the man to be sued was Thomas Wason, "her fath^r in Lawe."
Appowell told Marchaunt how to go about it, Marchaunt took the advice, and
Wason was arrested. Then, however, according to Wyseman, who had the
story from Marchaunt, Appowell encouraged Wason "to stand in Law"
against Marchaunt. Marchaunt said that the original conversation between
him and Appowell took place in Edward Stone's hearing in Glastonbury, but
Stone said it took place somewhere in the two miles that lie between that
town and Street (no. 6). Appowell also thought this article untrue.

Two other events that occurred at about the time of the puppet show also
gave offense to the locals. Appowell challenged Marchaunt's accounting of
money owing for merchandise that Marchaunt (who was a merchant) had
supplied, and, having been shown Marchaunt's account book, Appowell then
demanded more time to pay (no. 7). And Robert Clenche of Rimpton (a village about a mile and a half southeast of Marston Magna) saw Appowell so
drunk at the Hart's Head in Wells "that he was not of hym self able to goe to
his bedd" (nos. 11, 12). Appowell thought all these articles untrue. The
Hart's Head, now the White Hart, is in Sadler Street opposite the great gate
to Cathedral Green.

Four deponents, Hegdon, Hurford, Higdon, and Wyseman, did not like Appowell's treatment of a parishioner, Edward Sporle, at Easter, 1584 (no. 13).
Sporle, a smith, went to the church on Easter eve to receive communion and
to pay a fee of 3d. owing to Appowell, but Appowell "repelled" him and
demanded 12d. Sporle said, "shall I not receive else," and Appowell answered "noe." Sporle returned on Easter day with the same result. Appowell
then complained at the next visitation in the parish and managed to have
Sporle excommunicated (no. 14). Appowell admitted that he had refused
Sporle communion because Sporle did not "pay hym suche dutyes as were
accustomably deue to hym." This quarrel became another case in the Consistory Court against Appowell in which a deponent said that in his presence
Appowell "did demaunde all manner of tithes of the said Sporrle."[11]

The first of the three articles comprising group 3 accused Appowell of marrying specified people without having called the banns or procured a license.
One deponent (Hurford) said that Appowell had married the people without
banns but did not know whether he had done so without license. Another
(Wyseman) had heard Marchaunt say that Appowell had married him without
banns or license. Appowell said that he did marry the people without banns
but with the approval of two diocesan judges, Dr. Jones and Mr. Upton.[12]

The second article accused him of corruption. Wyseman happened to be present when Appowell demanded five marks (£3 6s. 8d.) of Thomas Wason to obtain a marriage license for him. Wason offered, as Wyseman thought, £2. Appowell took the money saying that if he could get the license for that much he would, but if not he would perform the ceremony anyway—and keep the £2. Appowell merely admitted that he had received "a Certaine som*me* of mony" from Wason "to obteyne" a marriage license, but how much he "now remembreth not."

The third accused him of not performing routine clerical duties. The three deponents apart from Appowell himself agreed that he did not say the divine service as often as he should, and that, in his absence, parishioners had the clerk say part of it. Two of them (Hurford and Higdon) said that he also did not instruct the youth of the parish as often as he should or read the Queen's injunctions as often or as fully as he should. These two and others then accused him of this last omission at the recent visitation in the parish, for which the visitor required Appowell to pay 12d. to the poor of the parish. Appowell answered that he does say the divine services "orderly" on Sundays, holidays, and weekdays "if he be not at London as" often "vppon occasion he hath ben." He also reads all the queen's injunctions quarterly, "vnlesse it be a ij Leeves of the booke wch ar broken out therof," and, yes, Dr. Cottington has required him to pay 12d. to the poor of the parish for not reading these leaves.[13]

Despite all this, Appowell came to no great harm. Although several further notes about the case survive, the last on 30 April 1585,[14] a judgment does not. The diocese must have let him off with a warning and required him to hire a curate to say services in his absence. For he remained vicar of Marston Magna until he died, and Robert Traske signed the membranes of the parish registers as curate until then. Appowell, "vicar of the p*ari*she," was buried at Marston Magna on 3 April 1597, and John Googe replaced him as vicar "per mortem," on 1 July 1597.[15]

II

The case against Appowell raises two obvious problems. One concerns the puppet show at which witnesses said he amused himself under the "Coates" of a lady standing on a bench. Where and when did the show take place? The other concerns Appowell's surname. What did he call himself, and, since his surname seems to appear in at least five different ways, could the things attributed to him belong to more than one man? The editors of Records of Early English Drama (REED) offer solutions to both problems in their volumes for Somerset,[16] but their solutions do not inspire confidence.

On 20 November 1584, in answer to an article of group 1, Appowell said that he had innocently attended a puppet show at the Hart in Glastonbury (apparently an inn) in January two years before, in January 1583. Three and a half weeks later, however, on 15 December 1584, in answer to articles of group 2, Marchaunt and Stone said that they had seen Appowell misbehave at a puppet show, which, at the particular demand of the diocese, they said occurred "a xij monethes since," in the winter of 1583–84. Three other deponents accepted the thrust of the allegations in these articles, including inferences about the date, though they had not seen Appowell's misbehavior. Did either Appowell or Marchaunt and Stone supported by three other deponents simply lie about the date? The obvious insistence on the date in the articles of group 2 suggests that nobody lied: that diocesan officials had one show in mind and that Appowell at first preferred to assume they had another. There probably were, that is, two shows a year apart, the first at the Hart in Glastonbury, the second at a now obscure place. Appowell was at both, and the one to which the officials referred was the second, "a xij monethes since."

Moreover, Marchaunt and Stone suggested that the puppet show the Diocesan officials had in mind was not at Glastonbury when they described a woman at the show as the wife of one Hawkes of Glastonbury. They would not have identified the man by his residence if he had been a local.

Marchaunt said that the puppet show took place "at the tyme of the sessions," and Stone said that it took place "in the hall," which was near a parlor in the same building. The sessions were the quarter sessions of the county, held before county worthies over several days each quarter in one of the sessions towns. When surviving records begin in 1607, these towns were:

Wells, for the Epiphany sessions, in the second or third week in January,
Ilchester, for the spring sessions, in April,
Taunton, for the summer sessions, in late June or July,
Bridgwater, for the autumn sessions, in mid-September.[17]

Since in 1569 the Ilchester sessions occurred in April,[18] this scheme may also have applied at least to Ilchester in the latter part of the sixteenth century.

Sessions time would have been a useful way of dating an event if the event occurred in one of the sessions towns while the sessions were sitting there. It would also have been a useful way if the event occurred then in Ilchester, because at sessions time the officers of the county jail were busy producing prisoners and their documentation in court and discharging and receiving them as a result of court decisions. Marchaunt's remark, therefore, may suggest that his and Stone's puppet show took place in Wells or Ilchester in the second or third week of January 1584. Stone's saying that the show took place in a "hall" suggests a larger, more stately room than public rooms in inns usually were. The public hall with which two men from Queen Camel would be most familiar was Shire Hall in Ilchester, where for a night five or six years before the town constable and his bailiff had imprisoned Appowell as a found-in.

In April 1266, when Shire Hall was to be repaired, it was called "the king's house at *Ilchester* where the pleas of the county are held," and in a document of about 1530 purporting to copy one of 1476, it was called "Regia*m* Aula*m* voc*atam* le sherhaule." In 1669, the town rented out the "Jury chamber" for 10s. a year and in the 1670s "the Grand Jury Chamber" for 20s. a year. The hall may have been rebuilt ca. 1700, though no good evidence says so. In a drawing by a local man, Charles Lockyer, published in 1724, it is a single-story building with a pitched roof. It was rebuilt in 1812–16 into a two-story building recognizable as the present Town Hall, which has been extensively refurbished in recent years. It is, and Lockyer's drawing shows that it was, a rectanglular building whose long dimension lies east and west and whose front door is roughly in the middle of the north side. East of the front door are single-story rooms, and west of it was until recently a two-story hall.[19] In the 1580s, socializing could have taken place in a parlor on the east side and a puppet show in a hall that rose into the rafters of a pitched roof on the west side.

The editors of REED conclude that there was only one puppet show, which in answering the first article of group 1 Appowell said occurred at the Hart in Glastonbury. In answering articles of group 2, therefore, Marchaunt and Stone meant the same show, and the editors add that "there is no disagreement" with Appowell "about the place." If, however, there is no disagreement, neither is there any agreement. Marchaunt and Stone did not say that the puppet show occurred at the Hart in Glastonbury or anywhere else other than in the "articulated" house. Marchaunt did say that an event occurred in Glastonbury, but the event was not a puppet show. It was his conversation with Appowell about litigation, mentioned in answer to article 6 of group 2, and Stone put the conversation not in Glastonbury but somewhere between that town and Street. The editors date their show in 1584, "possibly" in January. They admit that the remarks of the three men about the date clash but assume that by admitting the clash they resolve it. They think that Marchaunt's remark about the time of the sessions refers to Glastonbury because Wells is "nearby," but Wells is some six miles from Glastonbury across moors notoriously wet in January.

Moreover, the editors read the date of the main body of depositions in answer to the articles of groups 2 and 3 as 10 December rather than 15 December, and they miscount the deponents who answered the articles of group 2 on that day as eight rather than nine. They say that only two deponents responded to articles about the puppet show, but three more also did though only to agree with the accusations from hearsay. They say that Stone was twenty years old, though the heading of his deposition says he was forty (he had lived in Queen Camel twenty years).

According to the Bishop Gilbert Berkeley's register,[20] the name of the man he made vicar of Marston Magna on 8 August 1572, was William Howell. No other of the vicar's contemporaries, however, called him Howell, including many who should have known him better than the bishop or his clerks. He is always William Appowell or William Powell in the depositions reported here. He is William Appowell in the general heading introducing the depositions taken on 15 December 1584. In the headings to individual depositions, he is William Appowell seven times and in the depositions themselves nineteen times. He is William Powell in headings three times and in depositions nine times. In the headings to his own depositions, the vicar of Marston Magna is William Appowell twice and William Powell once. In court acts about the case beginning in November 1584 and continuing until the spring of 1585, he is William Appowell seven times and William Powell nine times. Once he is just Powell, once William Apphowell, and once William Phowell. He was buried as William Powell and replaced as William Powell, the late incumbent. Moreover, there were William Powells and Appowells active in the Diocese who were not vicar of Marston Magna. A William Powell, B.D., was a Diocesan dignitary who had just become archdeacon of Bath (on 1 April 1584) and died in 1614. Another William Powell became rector of Bathwick on 16 January 1586, and the Consistory Court pursued a William Appowell of Bresselton (Brislington?) in 1583.[21]

The vicar of Marston Magna's signatures at the ends of his depositions are much alike and, it seems, the only surviving examples of his handwriting. He began each signature by writing "per me William." He then began his surname with a letter that looks like one of the forms people used for "H," like Hurford here. It could also be a reasonable if curious "P," because it looks like a majuscule version of the character he wrote to signify "per"— "p," that is, with an abbreviation sign. In the signatures at the ends of his first and third depositions, the letter does not have the preliminary curved downward stroke of the character in "per," but in that at the end of the second it does.

He meant to write, therefore, "P" probably with an abbreviation sign, hence "Appowell." He was careful about abbreviation signs in the way he wrote "William." In all three signatures, he correctly used two abbreviation signs (one for "ia" and the other for "mu"), rather than one as many people would have done. Abbreviating "Ap" in this way seems odd, but it is reminiscent of the way the clerks who wrote the depositions regularly wrote, for example, "respondet." The abbreviation sign signifies not only "es," as one might expect, but also "p," and it is over not "r" or even "o" but "n."

The vicar of Marston Magna from 1572 to 1597 must have been one man who was officially called Appowell but was often, even by officials, called Powell. The bishop's clerks in 1572 may have written Howell because he wrote his surname with a letter they mistakenly took for "H." The editors of

The Vicar of Marston Magna's signatures. Photo by Timothy Sofranko.

REED concur that he was one man, but, like the bishop's clerks, they call him Howell. They also seem to think that he was the William Powell who was rector of Bathwick and committed parsonical attrocities in 1606, 1607, and 1610. The misdeeds of the vicar of Marston Magna, however, certainly ended with his demise in 1597, if not with his trial in 1584.

Appendix I

The deponents, together with biographical details mentioned in the headings above their depositions (on 15 December 1584), the articles to which each gave answers, where the answers appear (at the SRO), and how each signed himself. With one noted exception, the places mentioned are in Somerset.

William Appowell. No biographical details given except that he was a priest and the vicar of Marston Magna. Answers articles 1–6 in group 1, 2–17 in group 2 (D/D/Ca 90, 20 Nov. and 9 Dec. 1584), and 1–3 in group 3 (D/D/Cd 20, f. 19v)—all from direct knowledge. Signs with his name (three times).

Jerome Busshopp. Of Ilchester, husbandman, aged fifty-five; has lived in Ilchester forty years; born in Martock; knows Appowell well and has known him six years. Answers articles 9, 10 in group 2 from direct knowledge (D/D/Cd 20, f. 14). Says that six years ago he was the constable's bailiff in Ilchester. Signs with his mark.

Thomas Jeffery. Of Ilchester, tailor, aged seventy years; has lived in Ilchester forty years; born in Langport; knows Appowell well and has known him seven years. Answers articles 9, 10 in group 2 from direct knowledge (D/D/Cd 20, ff. 14v–15). Says that seven years ago he was the constable in Ilchester. Signs with his mark.

William Marchaunt. Of Queen Camel, merchant, aged thirty-four; has lived in Queen Camel twenty-two years; born in Yeovil; knows Appowell well and has known him fourteen years. Answers articles 2–7 in group 2 from direct knowledge, 16 from hearsay (D/D/Cd 20, f. 15). Signs with his name.

Edward Stone. Of Queen Camel, no occupation given, aged forty; has lived in Queen Camel twenty years; born in Somerset, perhaps near Long Burton, Dorset;[22] has known Appowell ten years. Answers articles 2–6 in group 2 from direct knowledge, 7 from hearsay (D/D/Cd 20, f. 16). Signs with his mark.

William Hegdon. Of Marston Magna, no occupation given, aged forty; has lived in Marston Magna all his life; knows Appowell well and has known him ten years. Answers articles 13, 15 in group 2 from direct knowledge (D/D/Cd 20, ff. 16v–17). Signs with his mark.

John Hurford. Of Marston Magna, yeoman, aged thirty-three; born in Marston Magna and has lived there all his life except for seven years; knows Appowell well and has known him seven years. Answers articles 13, 15 in group 2 from direct knowledge, 2–12, 14, 16 from hearsay; and articles 2, 3 in group 3 from direct knowledge (D/D/Cd 20, ff. 17, 20). Signs with his name (twice).

Peter Higdon. Of Marston Magna, husbandman, aged fifty; born in Marston Magna and has lived there all his life except for six years; knows Appowell well and has known him twelve years. Answers articles 13, 15 in group 2 from direct knowledge, 2–11, 16 from hearsay; and article 3 in group 3 (where his surname is spelled "Hegdon") from direct knowledge (D/D/Cd 20, ff. 17v–18, 20). Signs with his mark (twice).

William Wyseman. Of Barwick, sergeant, aged thirty; has lived in Barwick seven years; place of birth not given; knows Appowell well and has known him eighteen years. Answers articles 14, 15 in group 2 from direct knowledge, 2–10, 16 from hearsay; and articles 2–3 in group 3 from direct knowledge, 1 from hearsay (D/D/Cd 20, ff. 18, 20v–21). Signs with his name (twice).

Robert Clenche. Of Rimpton, husbandman, aged fifty; has lived in Rimpton all his life; knows Appowell well and has known him twelve years. Answers articles 11, 12, 15 in group 2 from direct knowledge, 16 from hearsay (D/D/Cd 20, f. 19). Signs with his mark.

Appendix II

The answers to the articles about a puppet show. "CO—" means crossed out and "M—" in the left margin. "I" and "J" are normalized as is the downward stroke at the ends of words signifying "s," "is," or "es." Abbreviations expressed by a superlinear letter appear without comment ("depon[t]"); others are expanded in Italics if a sign appears ("q*uo*d") or in square brackets if not ("q[uo]d").

Appowell's Answers to the Articles of Group 1

Ad primu*m* ar[ticu]^lum [CO—*respo*ndet] et sced*ulam* *respo*ndet that he was in [CO—Come[23] wells] Glaston at the signe of the Harte in January aboute ij yeares since & confesseth that there was poppett playenge et ali*ter* non credit ar[ticu]*lum* et sced[ulam] e*ss*e veru*m* in aliquo

Ad se*cun*dum ar[ticu]*lum* et sced*u*lam annex*am* re*sp*ondet vt supra et ali*ter* non credit ar[ticu]*lum* e*ss*e veru*m*.

Ad 3 ar[ticu]*lum* et sced*u*lam [CO—annex*am*] re*sp*ondet et credit eosdem non e*ss*e veros in aliquo.

Appowell's Answers to the Articles of Group 2

Ad se*cun*du*m* re*sp*ondet [CO—that] that he was ther et ali*ter* re*sp*ondet [CO—negative] q[uo]d no*n* Credit eund*em* e*ss*e veru*m*

Ad tertiu*m* re*sp*ondet simil*iter*.

Ad quartu*m* quintu*m* sextum septimu*m* et octavu*m* re*sp*ondet [CO—negative] q[uo]d no*n* Credit eosdem e*ss*e veros in aliquo

Marchaunt's Answers to the Articles of Group 2

Sup*er* secundo deponit eund*em* e*ss*e veru*m* et reddend*o* ca*us*am sci*e*nti*a*e su[a]e dicit et deponit that he was p*er*sonally p*res*ente in the house articulated togeth[r] w[th] one Edward [CO—Stoninge] Stone [CO—wher and when aboute] at the tyme of the sessions in the night season aboute a xij monethes since vt modo recolit et tempus et diem ali*ter* p*er*fecte no*n* recordat*ur* And then and ther sawe the articulated Wi[m] Appowell put his hande vnder the Coates of one woman beinge then and ther p*res*ente [M—standinge vppon a forme] but her name this depon[t] knoweth not And the Cause of all ther beinge ther was to see pappett players which was then and ther a handlinge et ali*ter* nescit depon*ere*./

Sup*er* tertio deponit eund*em* e*ss*e veru*m* for that he this deponent was in the p*ar*lor and sawe the mi*n*strells playinge and the articulated Wi[m] Appowell then and ther Daw[n]cinge w[th] diu*er*s women whose names this iurate knoweth not and at the ende of the daw[n]ces he kissed them vt dicit et ali*ter* nescit depon*ere*./

Sup*er* quart*o* deponit That the articulated Wi[m] Appowell at that tyme & while some parte of the pappett playinge was, was in the p*ar*lor of the said house w[th] one hawkes wief of Glaston*bury* sittinge by the ffiar ther and havinge a Candle burninge ther [M—& almoste spent] but to what ende they did so sitt ther this depon[t] knoweth not./

Super quinto deponit eundem esse verum for that he [CO—hym selfe] this Deponent hym self Cominge in the parlor Doore saw the articulated Wi[m] Powell putt the said woman out of a backe doore out of the said Doore to what ende [CO—in] this depon[t] knoweth not et aliter nescit . . .

Super octavo Nescit deponere q[ua]m[qua][m] praedeposuit super secundo tertio quarto et quinto ar[ticu][lis] materi[a]e.

Stone's Answers to the Articles of Group 2

Super secundo deponit that aboute a xij monethe agone vt modo recolit et tempus aliter perfecte non recordatur this deponent was personally presente in the house articulated together w[th] Wi[m] Marchant his preconteste[24] beholdinge pappitt players w[ch] was then in the said house wher and when he saw the articulated Wi[m] Appowell beinge then and ther presente puttinge his hand vnder the Coates of [a] Certeine Woman standinge vppon a benche ther and beholdinge also the pappitts then and ther playinge but the name of the woman this depon[t] knoweth not./ et aliter nescit deponere./

Super tertio deponit That at the tyme and place atorsaid he [CO—sawe the articulated Wi[m]] this depon[t] was personally presente when [sic] and when he sawe and hard the said Wi[m] Powell request a minstrell that plaied one a tabrett to Comme in to the parlor of the said house to play ther who at his request did so And then the said Wi[m] Appowell then and ther daunced wth diuers women that were then and ther presente wth hym./ et aliter nescit deponere./

Super quarto et quinto deponit That at the said tyme and in the same place [CO—after the Dawncinge was Donne this deponent] while the poppett playinge was in the hall or while some parte of it was the articulated Wi[m] Powell was in the parlor of the said houss w[th] one hawkes his wief sittinge by the fiar ther et reddendo causam scientiae su[a]e Dicit that as by Chaunce this deponent did looke in to the parlor he saw them sittinge ther by the fier as aforsaid And that when diuers other persons were at the Doore mindinge to Comme in, he the said Wi[m] Powell percevinge it, Conveyed the said woman out at a backe Doore of the said parlor. et aliter nescit . . .

Super octavo Nescit deponere q[ua]m[qua][m] praedeposuit super 2. 3. 4. et 5. ar[ticu][lis] materi[a]e

The Answers of Others to the Articles of Group 2

[Hurford] Super 2. 3. 4. 5. . . . 8. . . . he hard it reported diuers tymes the same articles to be trewe./

[Higdon] Sup*er* secundo et tertio quarto quinto . . . et octavo . . . ex pr*o*pria scientia nescit depon*ere*, sed ex auditu deponit eosdem e*sse* veros./

[Wyseman] Sup*er* 2. 3. 4 et 5. deponit ex auditu eosdem e*sse* veros./

Notes

1. Somerset Record Office, Taunton (hereafter SRO), D/D/Ca 90 (one of the act books of the Consistory Court). The leaves of these books are unnumbered, but they are in chronological order under the date of each day's business. I cite, therefore, the day on which an act occurred, though the acts of a given day often occupy several folios. The Consistory Court met in the chapel under the north tower of the west front.

2. The Combe at Wells is a narrow seven-acre valley that lies beside the old road to Bristol, beginning at the edge of the city and extending north to Walcombe. It is now a park and arboretum open to the public. For the Marchaunts, see SRO, DD/HI 249, 250, 253, 256 (for 1580).

3. Watkins also announced that Robert Bowring and Thomas and Julia Norris would depose (SRO, D/D/Ca 90, 9 Dec. 1584), but if they did their depositions do not survive. Bowring probably had to do with Appowell's appearing in the stocks at Ilchester and the Norrises with his being drunk and incapable in the Hart's Head (of which, according to Robert Clenche, Norris was the innkeeper) at Wells. See below.

4. SRO, D/D/Ca 90.

5. SRO, D/D/Cd 20 (one of the deposition books of the Consistory Court), ff. 14–21.

6. Marchaunt, Hurford, Higdon, Wyseman, and Clenche.

7. For Stone, the clerk inadvertently omitted "et diem." The clerk began Marchaunt's answers to articles 2, 3, 5 by writing "deponit eund*em* e*sse* ver*um*" (he deposes the same [article] to be true), and in that to no. 2 added, "et reddend*o* ca*u*sa*m* scient*ia*e su[a]e dicit et deponit that . . ." (and answering the matter of his [direct] knowledge, he says and deposes that . . .).

8. Jeffery said that the event had occurred seven years before and that he had known Appowell seven years; Busshopp put the event and acquaintanceship at six years.

9. VCH, *Somerset*, III, 180, 186.

10. Appowell had sued Hurford in all three courts and Higdon in two of them.

11. SRO, D/D/Cd 20, ff. 45–49v (the quotation is on f. 49). A case between Appowell and Richard Wason is recorded along with this case.

12. Dr. William Jones and Isaac Upton, M.A., were two of the commissioners who sat as judges on the bench of the Consistory Court: see the headings for many days in the act books of the court, for example SRO, D/D/Ca 65, 14 December 1582.

13. *Iniunctions Geven by the Quenes Maiestie*, of which five editions appeared in 1559 and fifteen more from then until 1583. Injunction 14 required parish clergy to read the *Iniunctions* to their parishioners quarterly. The editions of 1559 consisted of twenty-five quarto pages, which clergy could read out at one service or over two services on the same day. Injunction 44 required parish clergy to instruct the young for

at least half an hour before evensong on the second Sunday of every month and on every holy day. James Cottington, D.D., became precentor of Wells in July 1583: John LeNeve, *Fasti Ecclesiae Anglicanae 1541–1857 . . . Bath and Wells Diocese*, compiled by J. M. Horn and D. S. Bailey (London: University of London, 1979), 8, 43, 55, 107.

14. SRO, D/D/Ca 90, 15, 16 Dec. 1584; 22, 29 Jan., 5 Feb., 30 Apr. 1585 (in addition to the notes on 20, 27 Nov. and 4 Dec. [2] 1584).

15. SRO, D/D/B Reg 18 (Bishop John Still's register), f. 9v; and D/P/mar.m 2/1/1 (the parish registers), burials, pp. 1–8 (notice of Appowell's burial is on p. 8), marriages, pp. 1–3, baptisms, pp. 5–14.

16. Ed. James Stokes (Toronto: University of Toronto Press, 1996), pp. 129–31, 906–07; also 20, 31–32, 876, 1095, and the index.

17. A few scattered records survive for before 1607, but none mentions where or when sessions took place (SRO, Q/SR 1). See *Quarter Sessions Records for the County of Somerset*, ed. E. H. Bates (Somerset Record Society, 1907), xxiv.

18. *Calendar of Patent Rolls, 1566–69*, no. 2091.

19. *Calendar of the Liberate Rolls, 1260–67*, p. 212; VCH, *Somerset*, III, 194; SRO, DD/PH 52, f. 3v; and 223, no. 108, [f. 3–4, also 6v]; D/B/il box 9/2, pp. 48, 57; conversations with Mr. Roy Scutchings, honorary administrator of the Ilchester Museum, about renovations in the 1980s. The drawing, which shows the building from the back, is part of a map of Ilchester in William Stukeley, *Itinerarium Curiosum* (London, 1724), plate 72.

20. SRO, D/D/B Reg 15, f. 35–35v. He had been presented to the benefice by William Stanley, Lord Mounteagle.

21. For the archdeacon of Bath, see LeNeve, 18, 91, 100, 107. He became B.A. in 1564, M.A. in 1569, B.D. in 1577, and D.D. in 1585—all at Oxford: *Alumni Oxoniensis*, ed. Joseph Foster (Oxford, 1891). For the rector of Bathwick and the man of Bresselton, see SRO, D/D/B Reg 16 (Bishop Thomas Godwyn's register), f. 6, and D/D/Ca 65, 11 January and 9 June 1583.

22. The heading gives his birth place as "Long*burt* in Com*itatu* praed[icto]," meaning in Somerset, where there is no such place. Perhaps he was born in an isolated part of Somerset near Long Burton in Dorset, some eight miles south of Marston Magna.

23. The editors of REED transcribe this word as "conu," which at first glance seems reasonable if meaningless. On closer study, however, the word is "Come."

24. I.e., his previous fellow witness.

Henslowe's "Curious" Diary

S. P. CERASANO

THE text that has become known to readers as Henslowe's "diary" retains a central place in the realm of material evidence by which theater historians reconstruct the Elizabethan theater. However, its centrality to this endeavor is concurrently undermined by the very fabric of the book itself. While scholars are keenly interested in the book's variety of play receipts, costume accounts, payments to the Revels Office, and even the other accounts that reveal Henslowe's sideline businesses in pawn-broking and rental property, the book appears to be an eccentric compilation, both in terms of the mixture of evidence it records and in the manner in which the evidence is recorded. For most readers, who are keenly interested in making sense of Henslowe's diary as a whole, the pastiche-like presentation of material is perhaps the most confusing piece of the puzzle. In short, if historians conclude that Henslowe compiled his book unsystematically and even sloppily, then how reliable is the material that Henslowe recorded therein? Thus, although theater scholars are fascinated by Henslowe's book they concurrently waver between certainty and distrust. It is, as some scholars such as Neil Carson have pointed out, completely atypical of account books of the early modern period kept by professional accountants; and it is, as Carson also points out, uneven and inconsistent in both the information that Henslowe chooses to present and in how he represents this information. Therefore, given these considerations, Henslowe's diary might well be an interesting, though enigmatic and unreliable portrait of theatrical practice.

But was Henslowe's book more useful to its maker than it was typical of its type? The answer to this ultimately shapes how the diary and its contents are read. Although Henslowe has undoubtedly left something quite valuable to scholars, further investigation of the manner of presentation by which he recorded his accounts reveals that his work should not be judged by the standards of professionally compiled account books of the early modern period (by which it can so easily be dismissed). In fact—in both its presentation and its content—it is much more typical of memorandum books, an entirely different genre of personal record and one that was created along lines that were materially (and substantively) different from account books of the period. In this way, Henslowe's "diary"—formally thought of by so many readers as aberrant and whimsical, and hence potentially marginal—is actually quite representative of its genre.

In 1790 Edmund Malone published "emendations and additions" to accompany his collection of Shakespeare's plays and poems. Following these emendations, in the same volume, Malone included his well-known history of the English stage. In describing the state of his research at the time of publication he wrote:

> Just as this work was issuing from the press, some curious manuscripts relative to the stage, were found at Dulwich College, and obligingly transmitted to me from thence. One of these is a large folio volume of accounts kept by Mr. Philip Henslowe, who appears to have been the proprietor of the Rose Theatre near to the Bankside in Southwark.[1]

To Malone, the dominant impression was that Henslowe's volume was somehow strange. "The Ms.," he stated, "contains a great number of curious notices"; the register of play performances recorded there he characterized as "still more curious." Moreover, Malone noted that the volume was accompanied by a bundle of loose papers that he could only describe as "very curious materials." Admittedly, Malone did not have ample opportunity to make sense of the Henslowe papers prior to the time when his history of the stage first went to press; but neither did the rhetoric change when Malone's edition was republished in 1821. It remained for him a "large folio volume of accounts" and a "curious" one at that.

Today the "curiosity" of Henslowe's volume continues to fascinate scholars of the Renaissance stage, most of whom make use of its contents selectively. They discuss particular sections of the book—for instance, the register of performances, or the purchases of playbooks and costumes. From these studies our understanding of how playing companies functioned during the 1590s, and perhaps well beyond, has been enlarged and enriched. Yet while it is certainly appropriate for such approaches to be taken, it has been virtually impossible for scholars to make sense of Henslowe's book as a whole, mostly because the diversity of its contents and the complexity of its organization are daunting. In some sense it remains as "curious" to our eyes as it did to Malone's.

In aid of this discussion, however, I would like to suggest that we have much to gain if we depart from previous approaches, taking instead a more "holistic" approach to Henslowe's book, examining it as an artifact made up of all its many parts, that stands within a well-established tradition of memorandum books or, perhaps more properly, manuscript notebooks[2] of its time. In going about this examination I am interested in the physical fabric of Henslowe's book in a very material sense. I hope, by following this path, not only to realign our sense of what Henslowe's manuscript represents, but also to contextualize, in a new and different way, both the manuscript and its owner. As I hope to demonstrate, among other things, Henslowe's book was utterly typical of manuscript notebooks written during the early modern period, including those created by educated authors of rank and station.

The terminology surrounding Henslowe's manuscript has traditionally shaped scholarly interest in its contents, but it has simultaneously stimulated confusion in evaluating the book as a "diary"; and, in addition, it has fueled bias against its creator. Malone referred to Henslowe as the "manager" of the Rose who, he stated, "appears to have been extremely illiterate."[3] By 1845, when John Payne Collier produced his edition of Henslowe's manuscript what Malone had termed a "folio volume" had become a more evocative "diary"; however, Collier's characterization of Henslowe was even more scathing than Malone's, tinged as it was with an obvious note of annoyance. In Collier's words:

> Henslowe was an ignorant man, even for the time in which he lived, and for the station he occupied: he wrote a bad hand, adopted any orthography that suited his notions of the sound of words, especially of proper names (necessarily of most frequent occurrence), and he kept his book, as respects dates in particular, in the most disorderly, negligent, and confused manner. Sometimes, indeed, he observes a sort of system in his entries; but often, when he wished to make a note, he seems to have opened his book at random, and to have written what he wanted in any space he found vacant.[4]

Thankfully, by the time that George F. Warner cataloged the manuscripts at Dulwich College in 1881, the description of Henslowe's volume, and its owner, took on a more objective cast. Bowing to the complex nature of the manuscript, Warner refers to Henslowe's notebook as a "diary and account book." And even more welcome, Warner resisted commenting on Henslowe's character and his scribal habits. Nonetheless, one curious thing did change. Over time the manuscript had apparently shrunk. Malone's "large folio" became Warner's "small folio," and its original 242 folio leaves diminished to 238.[5]

Motivated probably by a combination of custom and convenience scholars in the twentieth century have retained the designation of Henslowe's book as a "diary." W. W. Greg followed this line in 1908, producing a new transcription of the diary and a second volume of commentary to accompany it. More recently, the term "diary" is retained in the title of the preeminent edition published by R. A. Foakes and R. T. Rickert in 1961. However, by 1988 Neil Carson warned that the term "diary" was a misnomer, and consequently he referred to Henslowe's book as a "diary" in quotation marks. Yet even here, after an acknowledgment that "account books were neither so neat nor so homogeneous as today's ledgers" Carson inadvertently drifted toward the negative image of Henslowe that he stated, earlier in his book, should be avoided. To be fair, Carson begins with some level of sympathy. "It is very probable," he writes, "that the book-keeping system that Henslowe learned as a young man was not adequate for the enterprises of his maturity." But by the time that Carson ends he is among those who are shaking their heads in disapproval: "There is no consolidation of entries [in the "diary"] to present a more or less comprehensive financial picture, and indeed, it is difficult to deduce why some of the records were kept at all."[6] Carson points to Henslowe's incomplete records concerning real estate transactions and personal loans in order to support this sense of the manuscript's inadequacy; and finally, in a gesture of reconciliation with his subject, he concludes that what we have so long termed a "diary" might more realistically be termed a "memorandum book." In and among this mixed message, Carson moves both toward and away from the criticism of his predecessors who, in their more generous moments, could only describe Henslowe's volume as a curious puzzle. Yet Carson never leaves his disapproval or his puzzlement completely behind. He comments: "As early as 1592 Henslowe was capable of neat and meticulous book-keeping." However, embedded in this observation is the sense that somewhere along the line confusion and sloppiness set in.

But by what standard is Henslowe's notebook to be evaluated, especially since commentators on the *Diary* have traditionally engaged in this exercise? In forming one opinion Carson notes that the method of Henslowe's volume falls short of other account books when compared with those described in such standard histories of accounting as Basil Yamey's 1940 investigation of double entry bookkeeping.[7] I would suggest that here, and in some ways, Carson's instincts are basically right. Henslowe's manuscript is not necessarily a "diary," certainly in the modern sense of that term; nor does the manuscript conform to professionally written account books of the period. But, alternatively, to compare it with such precisely kept, carefully organized account books and elaborate accounting systems used by the sixteenth-century merchants sets up other, misleading expectations by which to judge Henslowe's method and the content of his volume. Additionally, this approach unwittingly propagates the sense of Henslowe's book as an inadequate curiosity. Still, two general problems remain: by what terminology should Henslowe's manuscript notebook be known (if indeed any single term can be adequate), and by what criteria can it reasonably be evaluated? A careful examination of books that are neither obviously, or primarily merchants' account books provides singular evidence that helps to shape answers to these questions.

An overview of manuscript notebooks written during the sixteenth and seventeenth centuries indicates that Henslowe's contemporaries kept many types of books for many different purposes. Some of these are well known to scholars through printed transcriptions, although it is sometimes difficult to categorize particular books as one type or another. To review some of the better-known examples, the "diary" of Lady Margaret Hoby (kept between 1599 and 1605) is a journal in which the author calendared personal matters, but especially her religious devotions. The "social diary" written by John Manningham of the Middle Temple (1602–3) is a much more public document in which the author entered what its modern editor calls "jottings." The character of Manningham's notebook—marked as it is by witty wordplay and anecdote—brings it tantalizingly close to being a "jestbook"; yet simultaneously its tone ranges from the ironic to the serious, and its content ranges from law and politics to medicine and theology. For Manningham the book clearly provided an opportunity to comment upon a diverse collection of unrelated subjects; and, as many books of its kind, the organization was uniquely, and "curiously" its author's. To take but one example: Manningham included an account of Queen Elizabeth's final hours shortly after a description of the generation of wolves and a synopsis of a sermon delivered by one of the queen's chaplains.[8]

By contrast, the "diary" of Walter Yonge, Esq.—a Justice of the Peace, Sheriff for Devon, and M.P. for Honiton, Devonshire—was used to record events of political interest in London, locally, and abroad (1604–1628).[9] Other books, such as John Milton's commonplace book, were used as a private repository for quotations from classical, western European, or early English authors, including Holinshed. Henry Machin, citizen of London, filled his notebook with elaborate accounts of public funerals, processions, trials, and religious troubles between 1550 and 1563.[10] Thomas Crosfield kept a university diary while a fellow of Queen's College, Oxford (1626).[11] Captain Nathaniel Boteler kept a sea journal (1639–40), whereas Sir Thomas Dawes kept a prison journal while under arrest in 1644 and 1645.[12] Other books from the period under discussion might best be termed astrological diaries, military diaries, puritan diaries, travel diaries, family diaries, parliamentary diaries, medical diaries, country diaries, legal diaries, or ecclesiastical diaries. Yet despite these labels, which offer theoretical possibilities for neat categorization, particular books often resist simple description. And although this list is far from exhaustive it serves to suggest the difficulties embedded in any attempt to define a manuscript notebook by its function or content alone.[13] Even those notebooks that can be loosely termed "diaries" (that is, catalogs of daily activities) lack similarity; and virtually none are defined by the level of personal introspection and exposition that contemporary readers expect when the term *diary* is evoked. Many early "diaries" actually contain little intimate information or psychological revelation. It seems not to have been within the character of their authors to record this.

Aside from the difficulty of assigning specific labels to manuscript notebooks is the fact that those which have been transcribed and printed receive attention primarily because they are of intrinsic interest to some specific area of historical or biographical enquiry. Thus, theater historians have been drawn to Sir Henry Herbert's diary or the notes of Francis Meres; historians of science read the books compiled by Simon Forman and John Dee; and military historians have taken an interest in the war diary of Sir Thomas Coningsby (1591). Similarly, the books compiled by Lady Anne Clifford, the Countess of Pembroke, Lady Grace Mildmay, Edward VI, and Sir Francis Walsingham have all enjoyed the attention of scholars because of continued interest in biographical or historical matters relative to their authors.[14]

There is, nevertheless, a class of manuscript notebook that does not naturally generate such interest, and it is this category that, under examination, perhaps offers the greatest insights for our recontextualization of Henslowe's manuscript. I refer, here, to a class of manuscript that is rarely transcribed or printed, and which is frequently cataloged by archivists under the broad terminology of "memorandum book," "household book," or even "book of account."[15] These are not the books of the great merchants who were operating large trading companies and who—by virtue of the magnitude of their enterprises, and the large amount of money that was changing hands—observed the methods of double entry bookkeeping that had originated among the Venetians. Rather, they are the books created by individuals who are simply interested in keeping track of personal affairs, on a modest scale. Unlike the private ledgers belonging to merchants, or the more public ledgers kept for the great trading companies, these books were not written up for the benefit of hundreds of stockholders who were eager to follow their investments; they were not cataloging the wares of dozens of ships, or the transportation of thousands of crates of goods over land as they moved to their intended market; they were not one among perhaps thousands of books in which every penny, shilling, and pound was entered and in which monetary tabulations were carefully audited. The notebooks in which I am interested were not intended for public use. Such aspects notwithstanding, these single-volume books had their own specific uses, and they do share many common features—in terms of organization and method—enough to suggest that they were created according to customary modes of usage and ways of proceeding, even though these were not codified in the how-to manuals of accounting procedures written during the period.

Although many manuscript notebooks are informative in reexamining Henslowe's manuscript I am limiting this discussion to examples drawn from a collection of books created by Sir William More (executor of Thomas Cawarden, Master of the Revels during the reign of Henry VIII), the Dering family (three members of this, Richard, d. 1612, Anthony, his son, d. 1635, and Sir Edward, a baronet, his grandson, d. 1644), the Key family of Yorkshire, ca. 1561–1642,[16] William, fourth lord Paget (of Beaudesert, Staffordshire,

1572–1628), and Sir William Smyth of Theydon Mount, Essex, ca. 1550–
1626, together with his son, Sir Thomas Smyth, bart., ca. 1602–1668.[17] Together, these books represent a sample ranging chronologically from the mid-
sixteenth century to the mid-seventeenth century. Like Henslowe's manuscript they are all single, self-contained volumes accommodating diverse interests and needs; and like Henslowe's book they are largely meant for
private use. Moreover, all are the work of educated men.

Common features are exhibited by many of the books, though each book
does not look precisely the same as the others. For instance, all appear to
have been bound folios, from their inception. In the number of pages, as in
their actual physical dimensions, there is also some slight variation, although
each numbers over one hundred folio leaves, and several are much heftier
than this.[18] As objects they are of a size and a weight that would have made
them unsuitable for easy transport. As such, they probably remained in the
homes of their owners who—instead of hauling folio volumes up hill and
down dale—more likely carried "size books" or pocket notebooks, or in
some cases, loose sheets of paper from which they later copied information
into larger ledgers. Although such duplication of effort might seem wasteful
to our sensibility this is, in fact, the method by which the entire Royal Exchequer kept its books throughout the early modern period; and, from the appearance of many merchants' ledgers—both English and foreign—it would
appear that this is how they frequently compiled their business ledgers. In
addition, it is probably to this stasis that we owe the preservation of these
notebooks. In private homes or in business establishments folio-sized ledgers
were less likely to be lost or ruined from daily wear and tear, whereas smaller
books extant from the same period, such as almanacs or pocket notebooks
(that moved around with their owners), commonly evidence signs of much
heavier use and subsequent decay.[19]

In terms of overall organization, authors customarily divided their books
into sections in order to segregate types of entries. Sir William More and Sir
William Smyth recorded collections for rent payments separately from building accounts. In Sir William Paget's notebook gambling debts were sectioned
off from expenses for groceries, while notes of his wife's lying in and church-
ing feast kept company with lists of dinner guests for various occasions. In
the midst of the More and Smyth books (L.b. 184 and V.b. 246) each author
turned his book upside down in order to make plain where one section ended
and another began. Probably because one book accommodated many different types of material the authors seem rarely, if ever, to have added foliation
(or, in some cases, pagination) that continued from the beginning of the book
to its end. It would appear as if the notebooks—beginning as uniform, blank
books—were actually conceived of, from their inception, as offering the potential to include many independent sections of unrelated material. Consequently, the owners of these ledgers were unconcerned with projecting any

sense of overall coherence, and therefore they were disinterested in consistent, comprehensive pagination. In most cases, then, whatever foliation (or pagination) now exists was added after the initial creation of the notebook, by subsequent owners or archivists. Here, one final note must be added relating to the "patchwork" appearance of these notebooks. Although some of this physical cast is created by the organization and variety of materials in the books, the number of owners also contributes to its complexion. Not uncommonly, the manuscripts also contain numerous hands, with books being passed from their initial owners to family descendants—as in the case of the More, Dering, Smyth, and Key families—and it is not uncommon to find several seemingly unrelated hands in the same book, whether during the same period of ownership, or in contiguous phases of ownership.

Scribal habits, as they are exemplified throughout these manuscript books, also show a surprising similarity. On occasion leaves were folded inward to create vertical columns, but the more common divisions were those drawn by writers across pages horizontally, freehand, either to divide entries, or to signify that some unit (a year, a week, or a type of entry) was ending. Thus, a category such as "rents" might contain several subsections organized around the locations of properties, with rentals in the same neighborhood grouped together and those in disparate areas separated from others. The continual updating of some sections within a single book, recording information (such as rents or household expenditures) that extended over a period of years, meant that most manuscript notebooks were essentially "works in progress." Entries were made on a regular basis—daily, weekly, or quarterly—as long as space would allow; and blank pages were left for the continuance of a variety of lists. As a result, the ratio of blank space to written space within an individual book varies depending not only upon the actual amount of copy that the author completed, but how much space the writer estimated would be needed in future for the records he or she meant to keep. Into this continuing stream of copy the odd notation was introduced (be it the notation of a loan, a medical recipe, a favorite proverb, or a child's nativity); and notations were added where the available space would accommodate it, even if occasionally this disturbed the flow of other material. In this way the process of the book allowed the marriage of personal content with professional notations, within the same book, and without one type of content finally infringing upon the other; but it is precisely this unusual combination of materials that creates a random appearance, giving such manuscripts a "curious" look.

Not least of all, writers such as More and Paget, together with the Keys, the Derings, and the Smyths all utilized a standard set of abbreviations and notations. They did not always abbreviate a specific word in exactly the same way within a book, or from writer to writer, or even within a single author's work; however, the commonality of abbreviations reflects the fact that they were taking them from the common stock of abbreviations. These and other representational notations are particularly evident in sections of notebooks where accounts or other lists are kept; and it is interesting that such standardization should emerge when the materials under examination here were being recorded over a period of almost a century. Here, at the beginning of accounting entries, one reads such familiar abbreviations as "M^d" ("Memorandum"), "R^{es}" ("Receipts"), and "Itē" or "Itm" ("Item").[20] "Som*m*a" ("sum total") and "tot" (for "totalis," i.e., "total") are common as well, appearing either in margins or at the bottoms of a series of entries, and also at the bottoms of pages. (These are the abbreviations familiar to readers of Henslowe's *Diary* as well. Unfortunately, however, Henslowe's well-known abbreviated "ne" appears nowhere, though generations of scholars would certainly wish it otherwise.)

Symbolic notations, used to draw attention to something of importance (and normally added in after the initial inscriptions) consisted of simple crosses and double crosses with two or more horizontal lines. The well-known finger post sign was used in a similar manner, though much less frequently. It was obviously saved for exceptional circumstances. Moreover, even when a layout of information looks as if it might have been invented uniquely by a writer, further investigation often reveals that it appears in some similar form in another manuscript notebook. For instance, rents for a specific year consistently appear by name, followed by a series of dots or circles divided by vertical lines to indicate payment periods. The series of circles simply grew longer as each payment was collected. Similarly, the terms "lent," "paid," and "received"—followed by the names of the individuals involved in the transactions—constitute the rhetorical formulae that begin entries relating to the exchange of money. Whether one studies the manuscripts of William More, Thomas Paget, the Smyths, or the Keys, amounts of money are recorded to the right side of individual entries in one of two ways: as Henslowe does, sometimes accompanied by the standard abbreviations for "pounds," "shillings," and "pence," and at other times—as is also Henslowe's custom—in a series of numerals separated by horizontal dashes so as to signify pounds, shillings, and pence.

Finally, adding to this sense of a manuscript book as a "work in progress" is a tendency for writers to nullify an old entry, to void a contract when it is completed, or to signify that a loan has been repaid using the same method—by simply striking through script with cross-hatched vertical lines. Interestingly, perhaps, despite the fact that obligations are often rendered null and void in this manner, the physical entries are seldom cut away, or even blotted out with ink so as to make them completely illegible. Consequently, there is a sense that none of the content of the book was ever actually removed or disposed of. One could still read and refer to entries, even after obligations had been fulfilled. Therefore the notebooks were not only working records, but historical records offering access to information both from the present and the past.

These basic, physical elements, shared by the notebooks described here, together with many of the scribal customs of their owners, can be observed in Henslowe's notebook as well. In fact, the similarities that exist, even within the books studied here, are so striking that Sir William More's household book (L.b.550, 1549–1600) and the Smyth family account book (V.b.246, 1601–42) might well have been written by the same scribe. Nor is this to say that these manuscripts share the sorts of well-articulated methodologies that one finds codified in standard manuals of accountancy. In their style of organization and their modes of proceeding it would appear that there were customary habits, generally known and followed by whoever kept notebooks for personal use. In following this line of evidence, I would therefore depart somewhat from Neil Carson's hypothesis that Henslowe's book was "an original book of entry, and that Henslowe (or an associate) maintained another set of books in which accounts might have been laid out in a more systematic manner."[21] There is no indication in any of the other manuscript books that I have cited here that this was the case, or that having other books—if, in fact, other books existed—would necessarily have shaped their organization or content, or the scribal habits of their authors differently.

What is highly significant, however, is that, in its organization, layout, and scribal methods, Henslowe's book is typical of other manuscript notebooks of the period. To summarize its physical aspects, the manuscript is a folio containing 242 leaves, which was rebound sometime after Henslowe owned it. Its contents are divided into sections in order to segregate various types of records. A portion of these are written with the book in reverse. The accounts from Ashdown Forest, which are never transcribed because they lack theatrical interest, would indicate that the book was passed down to Henslowe, in some way, from his older brother John, who was involved in mining and smelting operations in the Forest, located near to the family's Sussex home. Aside from Henslowe's script, other hands—some of them identifiable as belonging to Henslowe's son-in-law, Edward Alleyn, or to dramatists and players associated with the Rose Playhouse—appear throughout the theatrical sections of the manuscript.

Although John Henslowe seems to have supplied the initial foliation, in an irregular eccentric form, this has been superseded by other foliation, in a standard format, added by a later hand. Some specific pages—especially fols. 26r through 27v, with their carefully lined pages—would suggest that Henslowe was familiar with the basic layout of formal accounting; however, the variety of layouts that he used for noting receipts (including those in folios 26r through 27v, which record different sums for the same performance and continue to puzzle scholars) also indicate that he departed from formal protocol, simplifying matters and using procedures that made sense to him.[22] (This is the case in recording most of the theatrical receipts although all entries offer the same information, i.e., the date followed by the title of the play performed and the amount received at each performance. See fols. 7r–25r for examples.)

In terms of scribal habits (with the exception of the well-known "ne," frequently read by historians as an abbreviation for the word "new") Henslowe employed standard abbreviations and symbolic notations found in other manuscript books. He used "Md," "Itm," "pd," and "R^{es}" (which has customarily been transcribed as "Rd," i.e., "Received," but might well be "Receipt*es*"), along with the standard abbreviations for monetary units, all with regularity; occasionally, he used "tt" ("totalis," i.e., "total"), "dd" ("dedit," i.e., "given"), and lower case "p" (with a cross-stroke through its lower stem, as "per," i.e., "by"). Locutions such as "lent unto" and "sold unto" are likewise customary, in Henslowe's book and others, as is the phrase "casting up accounts from the beginning of the world." Similarly, many of these books began a new section with the statement "In the name of God amen" or "In the name of God and good commerce," a phrase that certainly was used typically by merchants in their ledgers.

Even the physical cast of Henslowe's book, and the procedures by which he crossed out dated or irrelevant entries are in keeping with practices in the books of More, Paget, and the others discussed here. Moreover, as I have stated earlier, habits like these underscore the sense that Henslowe's book was a "work in progress," as do other tendencies.[23] For example, some of Henslowe's loans (for instance, one to player William Bird, and another, to Nicholas Bickers)—which are never noted as fully repaid—suggest a "work in progress." So do the rent lists that seem to exist only for selected years (fols. 177r–78r), the blocks of blank space (some of them five inches) and occasional blank folios (fols. 110v–111r, 112v–113r). There is other evidence of a "work in progress" as well. The common occurrence of lists of partial payments scattered throughout the notebook indicate that Henslowe generally noted events over a period of time, but that sometimes he failed to complete his lists (if indeed the loans were ever repaid). Other lists are incomplete as well. Performance receipts, beginning in 1591, fade out in 1597, while loans for playbooks and theatrical costumes emerge in 1596 and continue to 1603. It might have been that, after 1597, performance receipts began to be kept in a separate book, or that Henslowe began a second, all-inclusive notebook (much like the *Diary*) and allowed subsequent performance receipts to spill over into this book. Finally, whatever methods were used to keep track of performance receipts after 1597—assuming that such records continued to be kept—is unknown. But complementing these aspects of Henslowe's record keeping is the fact that, similar to the books of William More, the Smyth family, and William, fourth Lord Paget, Henslowe's book accommodates a variety of interests: theatrical accounts, medical advice from the astrologer Simon Forman, rent collections, loans, and building accounts, along with other things. The diversity and varied organization of these materials is well known. They are, after all, what has made the book such a "curiosity" since its rediscovery by Malone in the late eighteenth century.

Having established that Henslowe's book is typical of other manuscript notebooks of its time requires, then, that scholars set aside questions of competency in forming their portraits of its most famous owner. Moreover, a new understanding of its character perhaps makes it easier to both ask and answer this question: "for what use was Henslowe's book compiled?" I would posit that it was a memorandum book, very much "in process," kept by its owner for personal use, in which Henslowe recorded, in a *typical manner*, a variety of details. It was neither "sloppy" as Collier stated, or "illiterate" as Malone commented, or even necessarily "partial" in the way that Carson hypothesized. Moreover, it was apparently adequate for its owner's purposes, and if it appears extraordinary or confusing to us, then this is due to our misplaced expectations. John Henslowe, the first owner of the manuscript notebook, re ferred to it as "the boke of reconynges ffor this yeare 1576 & 1577." By this term he clearly meant that the book chiefly served as a ledger for accounts. But while his younger brother, Philip, did some "reckoning" of his own, the notebook served other purposes as well.

To summarize, it is certainly true that Henslowe's book has not been transcribed and printed because most readers are interested in Henslowe, but because they are interested in the theater of the 1590s. Nevertheless, even when we are busily ensconced in its details we should remind ourselves of the conventions of the time in which the notebook was created. And we should remind ourselves, as well, that we might evaluate it more productively within the context of similar books produced by authors who stood within the realm of the socially privileged and literate men of their time. Henslowe's diary remains central (not marginal) to the writing of theater history—but as a memorandum book rather than as an account book or a "diary" with the connotations that this term conjures up for modern readers.

Notes

1. Edmund Malone, *William Shakespeare: Plays and Poems* (London, 1790), I, pt. 2, p. 288.

This essay was begun as a conference paper delivered at the University of Reading in June 2001, at a conference entitled "Manuscripts and Their Makers: Philip Henslowe and his Dramatists." I would like to thank Laetitia Yeandle and Peter Beal for advice and assistance offered during the final stages that this paper was in preparation.

2. By the term "manuscript notebook" I am referring to what modern readers would call a "blank book," i.e., a bound book of blank leaves, not a book of leaves that were written separately, gathered together, and subsequently bound.

3. Malone, *Shakespeare*, I, pt. 2, p. 293, n. 6.

4. J. Payne Collier, ed., *The Diary of Philip Henslowe, from 1591 to 1609* (London: Shakespeare Society, 1845), xv.

5. George F. Warner, *Catalogue of the Manuscripts and Muniments of Alleyn's College of God's Gift at Dulwich* (London: Longmans, Green, and Co, 1881), 157–63. This citation is from 163.

6. Neil Carson, *A Companion to Henslowe's Diary* (Cambridge: Cambridge University Press, 1988), 8–13 (quotations from 8).

7. Carson, *Companion*, 6–7. Carson sites Basil. S. Yamey, *The Functional Development of Double-Entry Bookkeeping* (London: Publications of the Accounting Research Association, 1940).

8. Robert Parker Sorlien, ed., *The Diary of John Manningham of the Middle Temple, 1602–3* (Hanover, NH: University Press of New England, 1976), 205–8.

9. George Roberts, ed., *Diary of Walter Yonge, Esq.* (London: J. Nichols, 1848), Camden Society, vol. 41.

10. J. G. Nichols, ed., *The Diary of Henry Machin* (London: J. Nichols, 1848), Camden Society, vol. 42.

11. F. W. Boas, *The Diary of Thomas Crosfield* (Oxford: Oxford University Press, 1935).

12. British Library MS. Sloane 758 and *Surrey Archaeological Collections* 37(1924): 1–36.

13. An excellent handlist of diaries from this period has been compiled by William Matthews, *British Diaries* (Berkeley: University of California Press, 1950).

14. See Matthews, *British Diaries* for specifics relating to the "diaries" mentioned above.

15. The one obvious exception is the Northumberland Household Book (begun in 1512), printed in London in 1770 and 1827, and also reprinted in Grose, *Antiq. Repertory*, IV (London, 1809).

16. The "Key" surname is spelled variously as "Kay(e)" in Dugdale's *Visitation*, as well as in the index volumes to the *Victoria County History of Yorkshire*. The "Smyth" surname attached to Sir Thomas (mentioned below) is spelled variously as "Smyth" and the more common "Smith." The surname is indexed as "Smyth" in the Folger Library's catalog of manuscripts.

17. These manuscripts are part of the collection owned by the Folger Shakespeare Library in Washington, DC. They are identified as Folger MS. V.b.296 (Book of Remembrances, Dering family, ca. 1580–1644), MS. V.b.99 (Household Book, William, fourth Lord Paget), MS. V.b.246 (Account Book, Sir William and Sir Thomas Smyth), MS. X.d.446 (one of the Key (Kay(e)) family manuscripts), MSS. L.b.35, L.b.82, L.b.184, L.b. 331 (a fair copy of L.b. 82, in scroll form), and L.b.550 (Account Books, Sir William More).

Another set of "diaries," those created by Richard Stonley, who served as a teller in the Exchequer, are more typical of modern diaries. They were kept on a daily basis and contain an agenda of the day's events. Additionally, Stonely included personal information regarding his readings (with quotations), prayers and church attendance, visits to friends, synopses of major events such as the spread of plague, and even details of his own illnesses. The manuscripts are identified by the Folger Library as Mss. V.a. 459–61, which cover sporadically the period between 1581 and 1598. It appears that these books were part of a more extensive set, much of which has been lost. The volumes in the Folger collection cover 1581–82, 1593–94, and 1597–98. Stonley's diaries are, however, created along a wholly different model than Henslowe's diary and the other memorandum books discussed in this essay. In this they do not shed very much light on Henslowe's memorandum book.

18. The exception, in terms of page counts, is one of the More manuscripts—L.b. 184—which is incomplete and is now disbound. It has twenty-five leaves.

19. One interesting hybrid example is Folger A1792.8, a small printed almanac (ca.1662–64) in which one owner has made notes of personal expenses.

20. The last example appears in MS. X.d.446, p. 50. It is part of a list that is entitled "parte of the greattist thinges that/ my father dyd in his tyme for ye/ advauncement of this howsse."

21. Carson, *Companion*, p. 17, notes that the word "post" appearing on fol. 12v and in commercial parlance referring to the transcription from a day book to a ledger, is evidence that other books existed. This is, however, slim evidence, and is inconsistent with other evidence on the same folio, as Carson admits.

22. All citations to the transcribed diary are to R. A. Foakes and R. T. Rickert, eds., *Henslowe's Diary* (Cambridge: Cambridge University Press, 1961), cited hereafter as Foakes and Rickert, *HD*. Citations to the manuscript can be seen in the facsimile of the diary edited by Professor Foakes for Scolar Press, 1977, cited as *HDF*. Citations to the actual manuscript (that are not as clearly seen in the facsimile) are simply referred to by folio numbers.

23. A few leaves seem to be missing altogether from the book, although Professor Foakes has hypothesized that these were probably irrelevant to theatrical affairs (*HD*, xii–xiii).

Performance and Text: *King Lear*

R. A. FOAKES

PERFORMANCE criticism of Shakespeare's plays has been haunted by two anxieties in particular. One is theoretical, and, as formulated by W. B. Worthen, concerns "the legislative power of the authorial work."[1] He is troubled by criticism that uses performance as "an interpretive institution for the recuperation of Shakespearean authority" or as a realization of the text so that "performance becomes merely another way of reading."[2] He thinks of performance as not bound by the text, but as "operating in a given social and historical horizon," and as producing meanings "intertextually in ways that deconstruct notions of intention, authority, presence."[3] Every performance transforms "the text into something else, . . . something concrete that is not captive to the designs of the text."[4] The second anxiety relates more to practice, to what Anthony Dawson sees as an impasse between literary and performance criticism.[5] This anxiety informs Harry Berger's attempt to bridge theatrical and textual analysis by the notion of an "imaginary audition," while concerned that "the literary model of stage-centered reading perforce shuttles back and forth between two incompatible modes of interpretation, reading and playgoing."[6] The problem would seem to be that on the one hand performance criticism may collapse back into another mode of critical reading and support of the authority of the text, while on the other hand it may become a description or celebration of ways in which a play by Shakespeare has been adapted or reworked on stage in order to produce new meanings.

I have no solution to offer, but I would like to draw attention to a feature of Shakespeare's dramaturgy that offers authorial guidance without imposing authorial control. In staging a play choices have to be made that limit interpretive possibilities, while at the same time they may produce new meanings, usually by contextualizing the action in relation to contemporary issues. There are various ways in which this can be done. For instance, at the center of *King Lear* is the storm scene in which the old king encounters Edgar, who has transformed himself into the beggar Poor Tom by discarding his clothes:

> My face I'll grime with filth,
> Blanket my loins, elf all my hair in knots,

And with presented nakedness outface
The winds and persecutions of the sky.

(2.2.180)

Identifying with this poor naked wretch, Lear cries, "Off, off you lendings: come, unbutton here" (3.4.106). Playing the king in the 1998 production by Richard Eyre at the Royal National Theatre in London, Ian Holm literally stripped off his clothes and appeared naked, or virtually so. When the televised version of this production was shown in Los Angeles, Holm was interviewed for the *Los Angeles Times*, and remarked how excited he was that Shakespeare's original intention had been restored in this scene. The director and cast were presumably using an edition that retained here a stage direction introduced by Nicholas Rowe in 1709, "Tearing off his clothes." There is no stage direction at this point in the 1608 Quarto or 1623 Folio texts of the play, and it was, in fact, stage practice until the early twentieth century to have Kent and the Fool prevent Lear from disrobing.

Shakespeare's intentions for staging are not often apparent, and at many points, as in this example from *King Lear*, are finally unknowable. So in this scene one actor playing Lear may strip naked onstage, whereas another may remain regally clothed. Some performance critics have claimed that "Shakespeare controls not only what we hear but what we see."[7] but in truth Shakespeare leaves a great deal of freedom to the director, actors, and stage designer who control what we see, and in their cutting, rearrangement, or alterations to the text, they exercise much control over what we hear also. In the end they have to settle for one way of staging each part of the action. The reader is free to imagine at leisure various ways of playing a scene, but the director and the actors have to convert the text into an acting script and decide on a particular way of presenting any incident in the action.

In the case of *King Lear* the choices to be made are affected by the existence of two texts, the Quarto (1608) and the Folio (1623). Many think, as I do, that the later one, the Folio text, includes revisions by Shakespeare, and some of these, like the change in the presentation of Cordelia in 4.4 (see below, p. 91) relate directly to the main argument of this essay. The Folio text has been used to script many productions in recent times, but almost all of them retain the mock trial sequence in 3.6, which is found only in the Quarto. The choices directors make are rarely governed by a strict adherence to either of the texts of the play. Furthermore, however scrupulous a production may aim to be in remaining faithful to the text(s), it will inevitably reflect the times in which it is staged. The aura of royalty and kingly power manifested in *King Lear* has lost its appeal in the twentieth century, while most people are anxious about three problems that immediately affect society, namely, the swelling numbers of homeless people living on the streets; the aging of the population and the burdens this brings; and the decay of the traditional nuclear family evidenced in broken marriages and single-parent arrangements. These matters have influenced recent productions of the play, and help to account for its popularity in recent times.

Stage productions are thus affected by the conditions of the day, not only in such matters as costume and hairstyle (so that photographs of productions tend soon to look old-fashioned), but more importantly in relation to current social and political issues. Rowe's direction to Lear to tear off his clothes suited Ian Holm since his Lear appeared as a widowed middle-class domestic tyrant who was temporarily joining the homeless in order to feel what wretches feel. Directors have to make many decisions that stress some and shut out others of the possible nuances the reader can dwell upon. If Lear does tear off his clothes at 3.4.107, he may be seen as no more than a "poor, bare, forked animal," in a symbolic reduction of the king to "nothing"; if, on the other hand, in accordance with eighteenth- and nineteenth-century stage tradition, Lear remains robed as a king, the visual irony of his reappearance in 4.6 is enhanced when he appears crowned with weeds (as Cordelia reports in 4.4), his robes perhaps in tatters, but still crying "I am the king himself" and "every inch a king." In Eyre's production, the director preferred to disregard the concern of the play with royal prerogatives and rule, by treating Lear as an autocratic old man of some wealth and status who was dealing primarily with a dysfunctional family. In the opening scene Gloucester, Kent, and Lear, all bearded, all dressed in black, looked pretty much alike, and there was hardly any sense of hierarchy or royalty.

In the theatre directors like to achieve an overall style that will give visual coherence to a production and stamp their mark upon it. *King Lear* is not set in a specific historical time, but seems to invoke an ancient pre-Christian world in the opening scene, in which Lear swears by Hecate, Apollo, and Jupiter. A long tradition of giving the play a visual setting that suggested such a world reached its culmination in Michael Elliott's production for Granada Television in 1983, with Laurence Olivier in the title role. Richard Eyre's production, by contrast, began in no particular age in what appeared to be a drawing room in a large, fairly modern house. Other ways of pressing home a contemporary relevance include bringing on Lear in a wheelchair (Brian Cox, National Theatre, 1990), costuming Lear as an eastern European general in a uniform covered with medals (Donald Sinden, Royal Shakespeare Theatre, 1976), and presenting him as a stuffy old country gentleman (Tom Wilkinson, Royal Court Theatre, 1993).

A director also has to make decisions about matters for which the early texts provide little or no guidance. For instance, no exit is marked for Edmund in the opening scene. He can be sent off on the entry of Lear at line 32, but if, as in Eyre's and some other productions, he remains visible onstage, he may at some points exchange "most speaking looks" with Goneril and/or Regan, and so prepare the audience for his later involvement with both sisters. The Fool has no entry before 1.4, but in that scene seems to know all that has happened at the beginning of the play. His presence would be inappropriate in Ian Holm's drawing room, but can be effective if he is seen lurking in a crowded court in 1.1., as in Michael Elliott's television production. Lear talks of being attended by a hundred knights when he sets off for Goneril's house (1.1.133–36), but how many are seen onstage? Four are needed to carry out Lear's orders in 1.4, but there are no more entries for knights after Lear comes on with "a Knight" at 2.2.192. Nor does the text indicate how far Goneril's complaints about Lear's followers as "Men so disordered, so debauched and bold" (1.4.233) are justified. Peter Brooks's 1962 production for the Royal Shakespeare Theatre and later film version (1970) proved sensational and influential in having a crowd of knights wreck Goneril's dining hall, so providing a plausible basis for her hostility to her father.

Directors may also cut and paste or reshape the text by changing the sequence of scenes, or, for example, by moving the Fool's prophecy at the end of 3.2 so that it follows Lear's exit line at 2.2.475, when he rushes out into the storm. This transposition works quite well, since the Fool has not spoken for 150 lines in 2.2, yet Lear's last words are addressed to him, "O fool, I shall go mad." An interval may be inserted here to allow Lear a respite before his rages in the storm scenes. Directors also may feel the need, as it were, to trademark their production by making it different, as in the *King Lear* in Kathakali mode staged at the Lyceum in London in 1990,[8] and the cross-gendered version produced in New York in the same year by Lee Breuer, with a female Lear, Albany, and Cornwall, and Edmund played as a "sulky seductress."[9] Productions also have to be selective in characterization. Lears may range anywhere in the spectrum between a grand tyrant, as in Trevor Nunn's staging with Eric Porter in the title role, which began with "the great sword, the golden map, the hieratic throne. Here was majesty incarnate,"[10] and a "fidgety, unlovable father with delusions of grandeur," weak in body and voice, as played by James Earl Jones.[11] The Fool may be young or old, and has been convincingly played by women actors, as by Emma Thompson in Kenneth Branagh's Renaissance Theatre account of the play (1990). Goneril and Regan may be presented as mature women with a genuine grievance against their father's tyranny, as embodiments of evil, or somewhere in-between these extremes. Cordelia can be played as testy, like her father, in the opening scene, and as a kind of Joan of Arc warrior when she returns in act 4 (at the head of a French army in the Folio), or in a range of more passive and gentler configurations. The text allows similar latitude in characterizing Edgar as something between a wimp and an emerging hero, and Edmund as in the range between a calculating villain and an abused son who is conditioned by and sees through the hypocrisies of his society.

All these changing aspects of the performance of *King Lear* may stimulate viewers by producing "meanings which have to do with the precise specificity of location, history, and audience," and that recognize some potential, some nuance appropriate to the moment. At the same time, they inevitably limit the play to a particular stage embodiment. Yet every production, whatever its style, and however ideologically driven, establishes what reading cannot do, namely visual significances in the action. Critical accounts of the play are likely to dwell on the play's characters and on language, verbal meanings, and cross-connections. Much performance criticism has not moved far beyond an idealized description of how Shakespeare's plays may seek to "control and shape what an audience hears, sees, and experiences moment by moment in the theater."[12] Editors, too, are mostly concerned with possible ways of interpreting the text, and with its intricacies of relationships and values. In the theater, however, an audience goes to *see* a play and engage directly with the living interactions of the characters as people and as bodies. They are caught up in a shifting spectacle in which lines are spoken in rapid succession and resist analysis, while visual impressions have an immediate potency. I am thinking not of factitious visual aspects such as scenery or costume, though these have their importance, but of something more fundamental that has to do with the action played out on the stage.

Understanding of the play in performance I believe is generated through a dynamic relationship between the action witnessed and the words heard spoken, a relationship that can often, especially in key scenes, be very complex.[13] I would like to focus attention on this relationship by considering aspects of the action of *King Lear* involving Cordelia and Edgar. These characters have been interpreted by commentators on the text in various ways. Moralistic critics, for instance, have treated the play as a conflict between good and evil, seeing Cordelia as noble and saintlike, with Edgar as a moral parallel to her. Such a view is not "wrong," but is very limited to a simplifying perspective, and it does not take into account the interaction between verbal meanings and the emotional resonances of the action onstage. In the opening scene Cordelia's behavior gives the audience a range of conflicting signals. She refuses to play her part in an official court ceremony (though this can, as in Richard Eyre's production, be reduced to an informal scene, so ignoring her role as a princess and daughter of a king). She willfully disobeys the monarch, her father. She breaks silence to utter "untender" speeches in a public gathering, admitting love for him only according to her "bond," which makes it sound like a legal requirement, and finally she pours scorn on her sisters. So there are elements of obstinacy and self-will in what she says and does. Yet onstage this is not how the scene plays, for what we see is a young girl oppressed by a largely hostile family and forced on a whim of her father's to defend herself. The action staged in effect works against some of the primary meanings of the dialogue.

Cordelia's responses to Lear's demand that she express her love for him, beginning with the one word, "Nothing," are both harsh and just, offensive in relation to him as her parent and as king, if laudable as a refusal to lie. She is Lear's favorite child, which makes her reaction the more bitter to him, but at the same time he treats her as a chattel, a property to be given in marriage to the highest bidder, and her actions deprive her of a dowry. To the audience she is visibly isolated in court, with only Kent as a lone supporter, so that she appears as an underdog, whose only way of defining herself, of standing out against a patriarchal society that denies her individuality, is to act as she does. So her offense in performance tends to seem much slighter than the offense Lear and her sisters give to her. The scene can, of course, be played with varying emphases, as for example with Lear playing a game that Cordelia refuses to join (Granada TV, 1983), or with Cordelia showing an immediate toughness in opposition (Richard Eyre, 1998). However it is done, there is a tension if not a contradiction between the words spoken on the one hand, and on the other hand, the stage action and group dynamics of the characters. Directors and actors can exploit this tension by choosing some point, as it were, on a sliding scale in the way the interaction between Lear and Cordelia is presented, and I think it is this tension that generates the possibility of a multiple range of meanings that, as they accumulate in the staging of the play, contribute toward a sense of depth and complexity.

When Cordelia returns in act 4 she enters, according to the Folio version, with soldiers, leading an invading army as queen of France. Her tender concern for her father is combined with an urge to claim his "right" and put him back on a throne he no longer wants. In one aspect a sort of healing nurse, in another she is a determined warrior who may appropriately be costumed in armor. Again there is a discordance between the meaning of the words spoken, notably in her echo of the words of Christ at Luke 2.49, "O dear father, / It is thy business that I go about," and what the scene shows. This tension is continued in 4.7, when he wakes from sleep in her presence. He imagines he is in France, which suggests that the Gentleman and attendants in the scene, Cordelia herself also, show French emblems or colors. Cordelia's care for Lear and tenderness toward him ensure a flow of feeling in her favor, yet even as she ministers to her father, the moment he awakes she addresses him as king: "How does my royal lord? How fares your majesty?" He has come to acknowledge that he is feeble in body and mind, a "foolish fond old man" whose only concern now is to "forget and forgive," but this is not what she has in mind as she leads him off saying "Will't please your highness walk?" Her actions are those of a loving daughter caring for her father, but her words and bearing are also those of a princess determined to restore King Lear to his throne. The disjunctions between her actions, as she kneels to him and seeks his benediction, his bewildered anxiety to renounce the past, and her apparent determination to restore him to majesty complicate the scene.

Cordelia's last speaking appearance, as Edmund's prisoner, unites her with her father in a physical embrace. Here, in 5.3, surrounded by enemies, Lear's vision of them as birds singing in a cage and outliving "pacts and sects of great ones" is at once absurd (as we know they must die), self-centered (in his desire to possess her), pathetic (as he stares in love now at a face he swore he would never see again), and renunciatory (as a final distancing of himself from power). In a way he realizes the hope he expressed in the opening scene of coming to rely on his daughter's "kind nursery" (1.1.125). His words now, however, seek to absorb her into his private world, withdrawn, no longer concerned for others; in relinquishing his royalty, Lear has given up, and no longer rails against injustice. The decline in him is registered in the way he makes her an objectification of his desire for love as the daughter who, though married to the king of France, seems virginal, and can serve as surrogate nurse, mother, wife, and daughter all rolled into one. Lear has no more thought of her as a person in her own right than he did when he cast her out.

Here, too, however, the implications of what is said are qualified by what is seen in performance. Edmund, who has signaled that Lear and Cordelia can expect no mercy from him (5.1.66–69), enters in 5.3 "in conquest with drum and colours" (Folio stage direction) with prisoners we know cannot expect to live. Just as audience response in the opening scene is affected by the extent to which Cordelia appears to be oppressed and bullied by the court, so here in act 5 the pathos of an old man, "fourscore and upward," and his daughter, a king and queen both stripped of their dignity and reduced to impotence, and furthermore subjected to the brusque, even brutal, handling of their captors, gives the action its dominant emotional resonance. Feeling muffles interpretation, for the spectacle of Lear and Cordelia clinging bodily to one another as all they have left, and humiliated beyond their due and beyond expectation, demands our compassion. Cordelia is "cast down," distressed for Lear as "oppressed king" (5.3.5), whereas Lear speaks as though prison will provide the pleasures of retirement, gossiping about "court news." Her concern is still for him as monarch, while he has abandoned power and kingship. Lear had said he would never see her again (1.1.265–66), and now in 5.3 there is a sense in which he looks at her but does not see her except as a projection of his own fantasies. If he stands onstage united bodily with her, his words mark a mental distance from her. Instead of playing king, he would imagine them as becoming "God's spies," in effect playing God in understanding "the mystery of things," the mystery perhaps of the existence of wickedness that, according to 2 Thessalonians 2.7, will be destroyed by God. In the theater his words themselves remain mysterious, and the interactions between spectacle and words again complicate the resonances of this scene, which is at once deeply affecting and deeply disturbing.

Maynard Mack asserted, wrongly I believe, that we notice in performance "all that we have learned from reading and discussion." He gave primacy to reading, complaining that "directorial theatre" in productions on the modern stage is "reductive in practice."[14] Well, productions of *King Lear* are bound to emphasize one particular mode of interpretation, and may well cut or re-shape the play to fit, but it makes more sense to turn Mack's assertion round and say, with Harry Berger, Jr., "What we learn from reading and discussion includes what we notice in performance."[15] Mack shifts into high gear, leaving performance out of account, in configuring the play as a universal morality about "man's terrestrial pilgrimage."[16] Berger considers "text against performance" from a different perspective in a concern about "the interaction of the characters and the community of the play," or the "common *ethos* informing the behaviour of all the characters," which he aligns with Stanley Cavell's idea of "the avoidance of love."[17] He is interested, that is to say, in the purposes of the characters and the ways in which we assess them psychologically and morally: "in the struggle of interpretation, we define the character's personhood over against our own."[18] He focuses on the text, on the ironies by which a character, so to speak, "intends to communicate one message, but his language, speaking through him and in spite of his effort to control it, conveys another which he didn't intend." This is an awkward formulation, for if we cannot be sure of Shakespeare's intentions, how is it possible to think of a character as autonomous and having intentions? It may be true that Shakespeare establishes through multiple textual meanings complexity of character and "encourages us to assign responsibility"; more dubiously Berger adds "it does not encourage us to confuse this with assigning guilt."[19] A notable example occurs at the beginning of the play, when Gloucester introduces his bastard son Edmund to Kent with words that say more than he notices: "Though this knave came something saucily into the world before he was sent for, yet was his mother fair, there was good sport at his making, and the whoreson must be acknowledged." Gloucester's relish of the "sport" and his jokiness reveal the absence of any shame or moral awareness of his act of adultery. Edmund does not comment, except through bodily stance and facial expression, and we are left to speculate whether he has suffered public humiliations in this way before; Gloucester's lack of feeling may well help to account for Edmund's callousness to him later. But Gloucester's intentions remain uncertain, a matter of the reader's or actor's interpretation—is he oblivious to the way Edmund may feel, simply unthinking, shameless, or is he merely talking in the customary way of men about the court?

The messages characters communicate are conveyed not merely through language (Berger's main concern), but through their visual and bodily interactions with others onstage, and through feeling or the absence of feeling. In concentrating mainly on the text, Berger has a hard time explaining why he finds the most compelling readings of the character of Edgar to be those that stress "his cruelty, his retaliatory impulse, his shame and guilt."[20] Edgar certainly has some of the most unpleasant lines in the play:

The gods are just, and of our pleasant vices
Make instruments to plague us.
The dark and vicious place where thee he got
Cost him his eyes.

(5.3.168)

Edgar's moralizing here and elsewhere is often taken at face value, as though
he has an unquestionable right to pass judgment on others (Berger goes on to
say "he has assumed the saviour's mantle and feels capable of pronouncing
judgment"). Some productions have even given him a crown of thorns when
he becomes Poor Tom, so linking him with Christ, as though his endurance
of banishment and poverty has earned for him the authority to speak in this
way. If Edgar is perceived as a force for good opposing evil in the play, then
this simple moral assessment may seem adequate, but Berger had reason to
be bothered by him, for when closely examined, his words bite more disturbingly. The "dark and vicious place" is in one sense the vagina or womb of
Edmund's mother. In attributing viciousness to the place rather than to the
person (his father?), Edgar appears to share the misogynistic attitude to
women expressed by Lear in his madness, "there's hell, there's darkness,
there is the sulphurous pit" (4.6.123–24). Also, if Gloucester's blinding can
be attributed to his vice, might we ask what viciousness in Edgar brought
about his exile and misery?

"The place where thee he got" also refers literally to the location, and how
can Edgar know whether it was "dark and vicious"? "There was good sport
at his making" is Gloucester's version, but Edgar takes a stern moral line,
interpreting adultery as the cause of his father's blindness, when we have
seen him as the victim of the cruelty of Goneril, Regan, and Cornwall, who
punished him for what was to them treachery at a time when he was trying
to do good, to help Lear. As self-appointed judge, Edgar speaks as though he
knows the mind of God, and interprets the blinding as a punishment for sin.
His interpretation has been accepted by many, in part because it seems symbolically appropriate in relation to an old tradition of punishing adulterers by
the loss of the sight that first stimulated their lust, and in part because it
makes some sense of Edgar's claim that "the gods are just," a claim contradicted by the death of Cordelia and the play as a whole.

However, in those scenes where Edgar's words are most disturbing when
subjected to close analysis, the visual context and the nature of the action, as
in the case of Cordelia, tend in performance to qualify if not disarm the critic.
The lines cited are spoken over the dying Edmund after the duel between the
brothers, and in context feed into Edmund's recognition that "The wheel is
come full circle." The machinations of Goneril and Regan have been exposed, Regan has just been poisoned, and the "desperate" Goneril has made
her final exit. Fortune's wheel has come full circle for all three, and Edgar's

lines remind us that Gloucester too has met with a kind of poetic justice. The lines thus support the mood of the moment, a certain exhilaration in the physical overthrow of Edmund, a sense that Edgar as Abel has overcome Edmund as Cain, that good has triumphed over evil, a sense shortly to be disrupted by the entrance of Lear with Cordelia in his arms. In witnessing the action we do not have time to pause over Edgar's words as exposing character or motives. In the immediate context they may be heard rather as a plangent cry, both celebratory and anguished, that justice has, for the moment, been done—but at great cost. Even so, there is something unsettling about Edgar's judgmental words to his father.

At Albany's request Edgar goes on to explain how, in his disguise as Poor Tom, he came to know the "miseries" endured by his father,

> Led him, begged for his, saved him from despair,
> Never—O fault!—revealed myself unto him
> Until some half-hour past . . .
>
> (5.3.19)

Here in the Folio text (the Quarto has "father" in place of "fault"), Edgar again gives mixed signals. He acknowledges his fault in not revealing himself, while claiming to have saved Gloucester from despair. The idea of despair invokes Christian values in what is generally a pagan play; Edgar speaks as if he has saved his father from losing faith in the gods and from thoughts of suicide. What then are we to make of his first encounter with the newly blinded Gloucester, who is stumbling along led by another old man? Gloucester speaks words to his guide that may be heard by Edgar, who is onstage when they enter:

> O dear son Edgar
> The food of thy abused father's wrath,
> Might I but live to see thee in my touch
> I'd say I had eyes again.
>
> (4.1.23–26)

These lines are spoken just as the Old Man notices the presence of Poor Tom, and just before Edgar's aside, "Who is't can say I am at the worst?"

Does Edgar pass up an opportunity to reveal himself to his father when he takes charge of him at this point? Apparently, yes. But Gloucester comes onstage led by a stranger, and there is a reason why Edgar, a banished man, his picture "circulated through all the kingdom" (2.1.82), might not make himself known. Furthermore the visual and emotional focus of the scene is on Gloucester's bleeding eyes, and Edgar's words direct attention to this horrible spectacle. A director who wishes to show "cruelty" in Edgar might place him where he clearly hears his father's cry to him, but an audience is likely to attend to the overwhelming pathos of a blind and bleeding old earl.

Yet it is possible that Edgar becomes aware that he may have been responsible for the "despair" he associates with his father. Even when he acts as guide he maintains a certain distance, what Stanley Cavell sees as an avoidance of recognition because he is ashamed and "cannot bear the fact that his father is incapable, impotent, maimed. He wants his father still to be a father, powerful, so that *he* can remain a child."[21] It could also be that in action Edgar enjoys having a power over his father, as when he tricks him into throwing himself off a nonexistent cliff in 4.6. Shakespeare draws attention to Edgar's deception, as he takes on the traditional role of the devil in tempting his father to suicide, pretending to be "some fiend" (4.6.72). There is something disturbing about Edgar's aside, "Why I do trifle thus with his despair / Is done to cure it" (4.6.33); we might well ask whether it would it not have been simpler for him to stop playing Poor Tom and reveal himself as Edgar. Cavell thinks Edgar has a capacity for cruelty that "shows how radically implicated good is in evil."[22] The action onstage, however, does not invite such moral schematization. What is disturbing about Edgar arises from the disjunctions spectators may perceive between his words and his actions, between a concern for principle that makes him judgmental to the extent of playing God, and the feelings of love or compassion that mark his intentions as good.

I think Shakespeare had a superb instinct for opening up a range of the emotional possibilities in his plays, possibilities that in performance are more prominent than issues of judgment, morality, or consistency of characterization. As I suggested earlier, the words spoken in the dialogue often function as a kind of counterpoint to what is shown onstage, and meanings may be generated through choices made in staging the interaction between the verbal and the visual. Still disguised as Poor Tom when he approaches Dover with his father in 4.6, Edgar speaks blank verse again, in "better phrase" than previously, as Gloucester notices; Edgar lies yet speaks truth too in saying "You're much deceived." Edgar continues to deceive his father at the end of the scene, when speaking in his own voice he answers Gloucester's question, "Now good sir, what are you?" by saying

> A most poor man, made tame to fortune's blows,
> Who, by the art of known and feeling sorrows,
> Am pregnant to good pity.

> (4.6.217–19)

Edgar has just applauded Gloucester's rejection of suicide, "Well pray you, father," but still his good pity falls short of revealing himself. However, his words about compassion are spoken just as Oswald enters like a bounty hunter to seize as a "proclaimed prize" the old "traitor," and so immediately precede Edgar's fight with Oswald to protect his father. In the Royal Shakespeare Theater production by Adrian Noble (1993), Edgar savagely blinded Oswald, grinding his staff into his eyes as if to revenge the blinding of his father.[23] This display of cruelty exaggerated the disjunction between Edgar's talk of good pity and his violence in killing Oswald, but did not seem implausible. The effect of emphasizing a gap between his words and the action onstage contributed to a sense of the complexity of Edgar and the way circumstances keep on revealing the inadequacy of his stated principles. At the same time, the emotional focus maintains sympathy for him, since Oswald draws his sword with intent to kill. So on "well pray you, father," does Gloucester fail to recognize his son's voice, or is Edgar still teasingly not revealing himself fully? It is sadly ironic that when Edgar does eventually say what he feels, he has to report the death of his father, brought on by the revelation so long postponed.

It seems obvious enough to say that watching a performance of a play like *King Lear* offers a different experience from reading the text. Much less obvious are the ways in which the significances generated in performance differ from and relate to the meanings that can be teased out from the language in reading the play. The immediate emotional power of the work as staged, or what might be called the affective resonances of the action, may at critical moments run counter to the verbal meanings of what is said by the characters. As the examples of Cordelia and Edgar show, the visual context of what happens onstage enriches our sense of the complexity of these characters as we are made aware of the disjunctions between their words and actions. Directors and actors may use various means to accentuate or diminish the spectator's sense of these disjunctions. Making Edgar brutally grind out the eyes of Oswald is one way of accentuating a sense of cruelty. If Shakespeare was himself responsible for changes in the Folio text, he introduced the military display in 4.4 when Cordelia enters "with drum and soldiers" (F) in contrast to the Quarto, where she comes on with a doctor and attendants. In these and the other instances I have considered there is a spectrum of possible stagings that may permit directors and actors to choose from a range of different emphases, and the stage images and action have an unstable relationship with the dialogue. Directors and actors are always finding new ways of playing scenes, and it seems that we can never exhaust the significance of Shakespeare's great plays, significances that lie not simply in the language or the performance, but in the varying possibilities for interpretation generated by the gaps, discrepancies, and contrasts between the emotional register of what is seen and the verbal meanings of what is said.[24] This may explain why it is that seeing a new performance of a play can be so rewarding in making us aware of new aspects of the shifting relationships between words and action.

Notes

1. W. B. Worthen, *Shakespeare and the Authority of Performance* (Cambridge: Cambridge University Press, 1997), 155.

2. Ibid., 163, 178.

3. Ibid., 180, 190.

4. Ibid., 180.

5. Anthony B. Dawson, "The Impasse over the Stage," *ELR* 21 (1991): 309–27; he argues that performance and reading yield incommensurate values.

6. Harry T. Berger, Jr., *Imaginary Audition* (Berkeley and Los Angeles: University of California Press, 1989), 140.

7. Barbara Hodgdon, "Shakespeare's Directorial Eye," in *Shakespeare's More than Words can Witness: Essays on Visual and Nonverbal Enactment in the Plays* (Lewisburg, PA: Bucknell University Press, 1980), 115–29, citing 115; compare W. B. Worthen, *Shakespeare and the Authority of Performance* (Cambridge: Cambridge University Press, 1997), 6.

8. Described by Worthen, 34–37.

9. See Amy S. Green, *The Revisionist Stage. American Directors Reinvent the Classics* (Cambridge: Cambridge University Press, 1994), 103–14.

10. Robert Speaight, "Shakespeare in Britain," *SQ* 19 (1968): 368–70.

11. Herbert R. Coursen, Jr., "The New York Shakespeare Festival," *SQ* 24 (1973): 424–27.

12. Jean Howard, *Shakespeare's Art of Orchestration* (Urbana: University of Illinois Press, 1984), 2; see also Worthen, 155.

13. David Young proposed something similar in claiming that each play has "some kind of profound and productive tension between dramatic action and expressive language," but in his comments on plays he was concerned with psychological intensity (in *King Lear*), language and themes in a conventional way.

14. Maynard Mack, *King Lear in our Time* (Berkeley and Los Angeles: University of California Press, 1965), 4, 40.

15. Harry Berger, Jr., "Text against Performance: The Gloucester Family Romance," in *Shakespeare's Rough Magic: Renaissance Essays in Honor of C. L. Barber* (Newark, N.J.: University of Delaware Press, 1985), 224.

16. Mack, 117.

17. Stanley Cavell, "Disowning Knowledge" in *Six Plays by Shakespeare* (Place: Cambridge University Press, 1987), 56.

18. Berger, 227.

19. Ibid., 212.

20. Ibid., 223.

21. Cavell, 56.

22. Ibid., 55.

23. Reported by Peter Holland in his review in *Shakespeare Survey* 47 (1994): 202.

24. Shakespeare exploits discrepancies of this kind for comic effect in his consciously hypocritical villains like Richard III and Iago, whose lies are finally penetrated by the foolish Roderigo: "your words and performances are no kin together" (*Othello*, 4.2.184). Such examples illustrate one way in which Shakespeare deliberately uses the kinds of discrepancy I have considered.

Royal Carnality and Illicit Desire in the English History Plays of the 1590s

CHARLES R. FORKER

I

IN a famous passage defending native plays, Thomas Nashe praises dramas "borrowed out of our English Chronicles" such as *The Famous Victories of Henry V* and *1 Henry VI* (glorifying Talbot) that confer "immortalitie" upon the nation's heroes and inspire patriotism, valor, and moral uplift in specta- tors; compared to the theater "beyond sea," he continues, "our Sceane is more statelye furnisht . . . , our representations honourable, and full of gallant resolution, not consisting, like theirs, of a Pantaloun, a Whore, and a Zanie, but of Emperours, Kings, and Princes. . . ."[1] Honor, resolution, and stateli- ness do indeed abound in the stage histories performed during the decade in which Nashe wrote, but a number of these plays also contain a greater ele- ment of lust, adultery, and nonconformist sexuality than Nashe suggests. Nor is it unremarkable that the royal figures who give their names to many of the plays' titles are themselves profoundly implicated in attempted seductions, extramarital affairs, or other illicit expressions of sexual desire as well as sometimes being cuckolded. The intention of this essay is to survey some of the more obvious instances of carnality in the histories of the period, to in- quire what dramatic purposes they serve, and to suggest that the pervasive- ness of these elements may help illuminate the politics and cultural significance of a genre that flowered colorfully in the 1590s and thereafter rapidly declined. It is convenient to begin with the four King Edward plays— Peele's *Edward I* (1590–91), Marlowe's *Edward II* (1591–92), Shake- speare's (?) *Edward III* (1592–93), and the two parts of Heywood's *Edward IV* (1592–99)—not only because these works comprise a range of play- wrights and styles but also because, the difficulties of precise dating aside, they would appear to span the decade chronologically.

II

Peele's play, which probably preceded Marlowe's since the latter seems to have borrowed verbally from it,[2] is episodic, textually garbled as the result of imperfect revision, and inconsistent in its characterization of Queen Elinor: sometimes she appears as a comedic figure, speaking in a tone of unroyal jocosity as King Edward's "sweete Nell" (line 74)[3]—as his earthy, plain-spoken but adored companion in military campaigns (including a crusade) and even as a vulgar boxer of her husband's ear; at other points she emblema-tizes hateful Spanish pride, being portrayed as a witch-like foreign princess (Elinor of Castile) who would have the beards of all her male subjects shaved off and the breasts of all women mutilated, and who is given to haughty, egregiously inflated rhetoric. By the end of the play she has become the "scourge of England" (line 2104), an "accursed monster" (line 2473) guilty of both murder and adultery, although her deathbed repentance is represented as sincere. Apart from the use of chronicle material for the depiction of Ed-ward's conquest of Wales and Scotland and the influence of *Tamburlaine* for the tone of Edward's more vaunting speeches, the play obviously draws upon the traditions of balladry and romantic comedy (several scenes invoke the holiday ambience and greenwood setting of the Robin Hood legend) like that represented by the anonymous *Fair Em* (1589–91?) and Greene's *Friar Bacon and Friar Bungay* (1589–92) and *The Scottish History of James IV* (1590?).[4] A pageant in the middle of the play presents Edward's "beautuous lovely Queene" (line 1452) discovered in her tent, having just been delivered of the Prince of Wales (the future Edward II) whom she ceremoniously pre-sents to the king for christening: "He is thine owne, as true as he is thine" (line 1479). The legitimacy of royal descent is thus celebrated with regal pomp and much lyrical effusion in an episode that echoes the equally cere-monial presentation of the crown to the title character as successor of Henry III in the opening scene.

The final section of *Edward I* then vilifies Elinor almost beyond recogni-tion, concentrating on her barbaric cruelty, her jealousy of the Mayoress of London (whom she poisons by means of an adder applied to her breast), and on her "loose delights" (line 2466) and "lawles lust" (line 2517); in a death-bed confession the queen reveals that she has violated her marriage to King Edward by sleeping with his brother Edmund and by conceiving her daughter Joan of Acon (now married to the Earl of Gloucester) not legitimately as everyone had supposed, but rather by "a leacherous Frier" (line 2579). The "tragic" matter of the drama, which ends with the deaths of both Queen Eli-nor and Joan (after the latter's bastardy has been revealed to her), is drawn from two ballads.[5] One of these, as in the play, recounts the poisoning of the mayoress and the miraculous incident by which the queen is punished for her arrogance by being swallowed up by the earth at Charing Cross and resur-rected at Queenhithe; the other, concerning a different Elinor (the wife of Henry II) but adapted by Peele for the reign he was dramatizing, tells the story of how the dying queen confesses her carnal sins to two French friars who are really the king and a high official in disguise. In Peele the second friar becomes King Edward's offending brother. The play's blackening of Elinor's character seems to reflect popular anti-Spanish feeling, perhaps exacerbated by the recent Armada against England and the memory that "bloody Mary" (Queen Elizabeth's Catholic predecessor on the throne) had been the daughter of Catherine of Aragon as well as the wife of Philip II. Peele's text contains a vague reference to the "Proud incest" (line 1689) of the Spanish royal family into which Elinor had been born. Although Elizabethan audiences would hardly have known the genealogical particulars—the fact, for instance, that the pope had dissolved the marriage of her grandparents on grounds of consanguinity and that her grandfather's earlier marriage had also brought on papal condemnation for the same reason—they would surely be aware that Spanish royalty was notorious for inbreeding and intermarriage.[6]

Edward I is more interested in romance, stage spectacle, and the patriotic celebration of "merrie England" (line 521) than it is seriously concerned with politics. Nevertheless, as Ribner points out, the play makes clear that "kings must treat their subjects as they would be treated themselves" (90), and Queen Elinor, in contrast to her husband, becomes a negative example of good relations with her English subjects. Just as importantly, the play underlines the dangerous threat to stable rule that illicit sexuality within a royal marriage can present. While Edward demonstrates his prowess as a warrior-hero and defender of his country against traitors and military enemies, his foreign wife, although she bears him a legitimate heir, undermines his position by unpopular displays of un-English arrogance and is finally revealed to have been unfaithful to his bed— "a Traitresse to [her] Lord" (line 2477) and the perpetrator of an "incestuous sinne" (line 2552) with the king's closest ally, his brother Edmund.

Peele's drama, like most Elizabethan histories, endorses the doctrine of divine right: the queen herself alludes to Edward's "sacred person" (line 1666) while the Earl of March pursues rebels who "havock . . . Englands sacred roialty" (line 2070). Elinor's extramarital lust thus counts as an insidious form of treason, not only to God but to her liege lord—an assault not only upon the family of which she is theoretically the responsible mother but also upon the state; her infidelities have imperiled both of the king's two bodies, his body natural and his body politic, as united in the sanctity of the anointed Edward and his successors. If, as Thomas Bilson wrote in 1585, the "priuate familie . . . is both a part and a paterne of the common-wealth,"[7] how much more vital is the solidarity of the most prominent of public families—that which embodies national sovereignty and is the breeding place of future monarchs. In the final scene of Peele's play the betrayed king, grieving for his "lovelie Elinor late deceast" (line 2640), decrees that she "Shall have [such] Honor as beseemes [her] state" (line 2629) and orders that an elaborate cross be erected in her memory, thus apparently forgiving her adultery and refusing to moralize upon it. But the play implies nonetheless that the infant Prince of Wales, who embodies the future hope of England and secures the continuity of Edward's line, is legitimate as much in spite of his mother's character as because of it.

In terms of sexual politics as well as in most other respects, *Edward II*, Marlowe's grimly realistic, tightly structured tragedy of royal weakness, is infinitely more sophisticated and complex than Peele's gallimaufry of chronicle epic, romance, and supernatural legend. The dramatic action is based almost exclusively on Holinshed, supplemented by Fabyan, Stow, and probably Grafton,[8] but effectively compressed to dramatize a ruinous sequence of events spanning more than two decades so as to highlight King Edward's regnal ineptitude, the *de casibus* rise and fall of Mortimer (his overreaching chief adversary), the king's rejection of his queen for his male favorites (Gaveston and Spencer, Jr.), the civil chaos resulting from these conflicts, and, most importantly, the degradation, intense personal suffering, and sadistic death of Edward himself as both man and monarch. Showing no interest whatever in the sanctity of kingship despite the savage humiliation of which Edward himself becomes the victim, Marlowe concentrates on the intersection of sexual magnetism with political power at the level of human desire and frustration; and the tragedy is notable for being the only Elizabethan play to portray the homoerotic passions of a major character with honesty, psychological insight, and tragic sympathy.

Illegitimacy as a threat to monarchical succession ceases to be an issue. Edward's sexual liaisons with male lovers obviously present no danger of unwanted progeny, and we learn of Queen Isabella's adultery with Mortimer after she has been driven from her husband's bed (the couple "kiss while they conspire," she continuing hypocritically to bear "a face of love" to the fallen king [4.6.13–14]) only after Edward's son has been clearly established as heir apparent. Mortimer commands a military force in Prince Edward's "right" (4.4.17) well before his father's dethronement and aspires no higher than to be Lord Protector (5.2.12, 5.4.62) after the boy's accession as Edward III. Marlowe is far from demonizing the protagonist's deviant sexuality in a crudely moralistic way as the mortal sin from which the political disasters of the play inevitably flow. Sodomy for Elizabethans was indeed a capital offense, but, as is now widely recognized, remarkably few prosecutions for it occurred,[9] and Mortimer's uncle, a senior baron who opposes Edward for weightier reasons, defends the king's obsession with Gaveston as a passing and relatively harmless proclivity of youth, citing classical precedents— Alexander the Great, Hercules, Achilles, Cicero, and Socrates:

> The mightiest kings have had their minions . . .
> . . . .

And not kings only, but the wisest men. . . .

. . . .

Then let his grace, whose youth is flexible
And promiseth as much as we can wish,
Freely enjoy that vain light-headed earl,
For riper years will wean him from such toys.

(1.4.390–400)

The political conflicts of the play are rooted in a contest of adamant wills—of assertion and defiance involving the clash of egos, class struggle, and the good of the commonwealth in competition with royal prerogative and all-consuming personal desire. Gaveston and Spencer Jr. are hated and hunted to their deaths not because of their sexual propensities but because their amorous relationships with Edward alter the traditional power structure of the realm. From the perspective of the hereditary aristocracy, obsessive love affairs between a reigning sovereign and a "minion," whether he be the "basely born" Gaveston (1.4.402) or the "base upstart" Spencer (3.2.21), invert the time-honored hierarchy of respect and authority, rendering the feudal source of national honor and prestige passive, manipulable, and capable of being exploited for private advantage. Edward outrages his court by turning over the Great Seal of England to Gaveston to "Save or condemn" at will in the king's name (1.1.167–69) and by seating his "base peasant" beside him on the throne where the queen ought to sit in a symbolically disruptive act that makes the favorite politically equal to himself (1.4.7–9).

But Marlowe also ironizes the stereotypical and much satirized relationship between master and minion since Gaveston plays the symbolic role of Edward's submissive "Ganymede" (1.4.180) or adolescent boy (at 1.1.143 Edward likens him to the beautiful lad Hylas and himself to the bereaved Hercules) while nevertheless asserting himself ambitiously as a grown man, thus dominating his protector so as to share royal power and wealth. Holinshed, the principal source, describes the Gascon favorite as "a goodly gentleman and a stout" who "would not once yeeld an inch" to his enemies.[10] Edward is portrayed as the sexually passive partner in the love relationship (he plays Hero to Gaveston's Leander in the latter's opening soliloquy)—a fact that becomes dramatically shocking in the anal ravishment to which the king is subjected in the death scene: Lightborn, Edward's executioner and a political extension of Mortimer's stolen power, overmasters and sodomizes his prostrate sovereign by reaming him with a red-hot spit. And the queen (now Mortimer's concubine) cruelly avenges herself upon the spouse who had estranged her by agreeing to "willingly subscribe" (5.2.20) to any fate for the deposed king that Mortimer shall devise. Her treason as a passive accessory to her husband's destruction thus becomes at once sexual and political, preparing us for the intense pathos of a moment in the murder episode where the bedraggled Edward, half-immersed in sewage and ignorant of his wife's malice, cries out:

> Tell Isabel, the queen, I looked not thus
> When for her sake I ran at tilt in France
> And there unhorsed the Duke of Cleremont.
>
> (5.5.67–69)

Marlowe in fact devises a dramatic structure in which carnal passion and power politics both reinforce and obstruct each other in complex and symbolic ways, involving all the major characters—Edward II, Gaveston, Spencer Jr., Isabella, Mortimer, and even the satanic Lightborn, who caresses his royal victim in a parody of sexual foreplay before the hideous consummation of the murder itself, which takes place on a bed and involves the sufferer's being pressed down under an overturned table in addition to the fiery penetration of his fundament. Kingly failure and sodomitic rape are seen to coincide. The tragedy explores interconnections between monarchical, psychic, and sexual identity in its title figure, as well as raising complicated questions about what is natural and unnatural for a man who is both a head of state and a vulnerable human being—a figure hobbled by stubborn will and strong romantic desire coupled to a dependent personality. Rather than adopting a coarsely didactic stance, the play allows us, as Bruce Smith observes, not only to experience "an eroticization of class difference" (216) but also to "see all sides" of a problem that involves the claims of public duty and private longing, "Gaveston's calculations, Edward's devotion, the lords' distress, [and] England's needs as a kingdom" (217). But the vision thus projected is profoundly pessimistic. Marlowe's embedded dialectic between emotional self-fulfillment and patriotic responsibility, between identity as a lover and identity as a king, erects an impasse that only death can break.

The anonymous *Edward III*, increasingly attributed at least in part to Shakespeare, obviously anticipates *Henry V*, celebrating, as it does, famous English victories over the French at Sluys, Crécy, Poitiers, and Calais as the later play glorifies Henry's conquest at Agincourt. At surface level, the dominant and familiar themes are the grandeur of England's past as incarnated in one of her most heroic warrior-monarchs and the education of a prince—in this case of both Edward III and his eldest son—in the kingly virtues of honor, courage, loyalty, self-discipline, and clemency. While the youthful Prince of Wales successfully passes tests of manhood and chivalry (he earns his knighthood by being forced to defend himself in battle against fearful odds unaided), his father, King Edward, influenced by Queen Philippa, finally masters "his vengeful desire to annihilate his enemy," learning "that mercy and peace are attributes of martial magnanimity"; Edward learns "both publicly and privately that the king's law must subserve moral law."[11] But the sovereign's supposed growth in the acquisition of properly royal and Christian values also involves his confronting a lustful obsession with the Countess of Salisbury; ultimately the king conquers this destructive passion, thereby proving his right, as John Lewis phrases it, to "govern others" by learning to "govern himself." (Warfare "between duty and carnal appetite" within the soul of a monarch, Lewis observes, was a popular motif in the drama of the 1580s and 1590s.)[12]

The play's sources (Holinshed, Froissart, and a highly fictionalized account of Edward's romantic entanglement from Painter's *Palace of Pleasure*) partly account for its double emphasis on King Edward's military exploits and his extramarital infatuation.[13] Melchiori, the editor of the most scholarly edition, suggests that Edward's founding of the Order of the Garter in 1344 may lie behind the play's action, although the almost certainly collaborative text nowhere mentions the incident. According to Holinshed (in a passage translated from Polydore Vergil's Latin *Historia Anglica*), the garter that fell from a lady's leg, occasioning unwanted levity and provoking the king to found "so noble an order" from so "base and meane" a beginning, might have belonged to "some ladie with whom he was in loue"—a lady whom Holinshed in a marginal note identifies with "The countes of Salisburie."[14] Holinshed nowhere gives an account of this supposed relationship, but his tantalizing mention of the countess, as Melchiori points out, could have prompted the deviser (or devisers) of the plot to turn to Froissart and eventually Painter for the story behind the one-sided love affair. If such was the case, we would have a plausible means of explaining the narrative link between Edward's "amours with the Countesse"[15] and his actions as a warrior-king.

As Melchiori has persuasively argued, *Edward III* seems to have undergone substantial and stratified revision—probably involving Shakespeare for the version of the Countess of Salisbury's story that survives in the extant text. Although the play may originally have intended to heroicize its title character as a model prince who had curbed his lust and had risen to a higher level of moral strength, the drama as we have it presents a much more ambiguous and ironic portrait of royal values and behavior. The Victorian critic, Charles Knight, arguing against Shakespeare's hand in the play, believed it to be broken-backed: "In the first two acts we have the Edward of Romance,—a puling lover, a heartless seducer, a despot, then a penitent. In the last three acts we have the Edward of history,—the ambitious hero, the stern conqueror, the affectionate husband, the confiding father. . . ."[16] But even if the perceived asymmetry in Edward's portrayal is partly due to a later reshaping and reconceptualization of the drama, darker and more unflattering aspects of his character seem, on closer inspection, to emerge.

Several of the portrait's more negative details are associated with the pervasive theme of oath-taking and oath-breaking. Edward, for example, violates his original covenant with King John of France (3.3.58–60) when he decides to invade that country, suddenly persuaded by the tergiversating Count of Artois that he now has a valid claim to the French throne (1.1.1–41). Yet he condemns as "Ignoble" (1.1.136) King David of Scotland, who has forgotten "his former oath" (1.1.126) to Edward, invaded English border towns, and is now laying siege to Roxborough Castle where the Countess of Salisbury is immured. Later the countess accuses Edward of "Forgetting [his own] allegiance and [his] oath" to Queen Philippa by seeking to infringe the "sacred law" of marriage (2.1.260–61). Edward saves the countess from King David, who has "besp[oken] her for [him]self" (1.2.44), only to exploit the lady's grateful hospitality as an opportunity to pursue his own "shameful love" (1.2.117) through a strategy of entrapment involving the exaction of misleading oaths.[17] At first he instructs his secretary Lodowick to woo the lady on his behalf by means of poetry, arguing that ingenious rhetoric can make a listener redefine "sin" as "virtue" (2.1.114); then, when conventional praise fails ("I had rather have her chased than chaste" [2.1.154]), he dismisses Lodowick, reveals himself as a doting admirer, and manipulates her into proving her "devout obedience" to her "dread sovereign" (2.1.218–20) by swearing to please him in any way he chooses, by which he privately means the yielding up of her body. Once aware of his nefarious intentions, she ripostes by arguing elaborately that since her body and soul are inseparable, she would be committing "high treason against the king of heaven" (2.1.258) and that she has already sealed an oath of fidelity to her husband (her "sovereign" in marriage [2.1.272] and a loyal subject of the "anointed" Edward [2.2.267]) just as he has similarly pledged himself to the queen.

Still determined to "enjoy her" ("I cannot beat / With reason and reproof fond love away" [2.1.292–93]), Edward springs his second trap by pressing her father, the Earl of Warwick, to swear rashly to do anything in his power to assuage the king's grief, even if the request should mean his death or loss of honor. Thus Edward forces Warwick to perform the "devil's office" (2.1.338)—i.e., to become pander to his own daughter, thereby wronging God, his own child, and his friend (the lady's absent husband) in order to keep the letter of his vow. Reluctantly undertaking his abhorrent duty, a "graceless errand" (2.1.374), Warwick reasons casuistically to the countess that "Honour is often lost and got again" (2.1.389), that life at any price is better than death, and that "The king's great name will temper [her] misdeeds" (2.1.405); she gamely refutes her father by preferring death to becoming "an actor in [the king's] graceless lust" (2.1.430), thus causing him to concede that "An honourable grave is more esteemed / Than the polluted closet of a king" (2.1.433–34) and evoking the proverb (repeated verbatim from Shakespeare's sonnet 94), "Lilies that fester smell far worse than weeds" (2.1.452).

The upshot involves still another entrapping oath, the pledge elicited by the countess from the king that she will grant his wish for her body, provided that he "remove those lets / That stand between your highness' love and mine" (2.2.135–36)—a riddling way of insisting that he first execute both Salisbury and Queen Philippa, their respective spouses and the obvious impediments to a royal marriage. Such is Edward's "lascivious" obsession (2.2.177) that he consents even to this radical condition (2.2.150); whereupon, seizing her wedding knives, the countess gives one to Edward (the better to dispatch his queen) and threatens with the other to kill her "love"—her husband Salisbury "asleep within [her] heart" (2.2.174–75)—by stabbing herself unless Edward "swear[s] . . . never henceforth to solicit" her or ever again to prosecute his "most unholy suit" (2.2.182–83). Caught on the horns of an impossible dilemma, the king finally awakens from his "idle dream" (2.2.198), abandons his carnal purpose, and returns to his role as a military commander and head of state.

The entire sequence of steps during the attempted seduction resembles a chess game, the antagonists checking and counterchecking each other in a manner that exemplifies the resourcefulness of their wit as much as their dedication to sexual passion or lofty principle. Whoever dramatized the historically negligible story of the king and the countess may have wished, following Painter, to valorize the triumph of chastity over the extraordinary pressures of a royal assault. But the resulting effect was to sully the character of King Edward almost irremediably and to create an impression of headstrong selfishness, lust-driven tyranny, willful irresponsibility, and unkingly brutality. Lying behind the story, as Shakespeare or some unknown dramatist met it in the pages of Froissart and Painter, was Jean Le Bel's far more lurid account of how King Edward had "raped [the countess] so savagely that never was a woman so badly treated; and he left her lying there all battered about, bleeding from the nose and the mouth and elsewhere . . . Then he left the next day without saying a word."[18] A tinge of Le Bel's attitude or the tradition of the disgraced Edward that it reflects seems somehow to have leaked through into the play. At a few points, it is true, Edward acknowledges the wrongfulness of his attempt upon the countess, most notably when the sight of his son, the Black Prince, reminds him of his commitment to the queen because of the family resemblance:

> . . . those his eyes are hers,
> Who looking wistly on me make me blush,
> For faults against themselves give evidence.
>
> . . . .
> . . . shall I not
> Master this little mansion of myself?
> Give me an armour of eternal steel,
> I go to conquer kings; and shall I not then
> Subdue myself, and be my enemies' friend?
>
> (2.2.87–98)

But Edward instantly suppresses this qualm of conscience, mentally rejecting his wife as "but black" (= ugly), thus punning on the epithet borne by her son the Black Prince (2.2.107), and resumes his pursuit of the countess, rationalizing his defection from battle with the specious argument that it is more sinful "to hack and hew poor men, / Than to embrace in an unlawful bed" (2.2.112–13).

Additional details of *Edward III* also undermine a positive estimation of the king's character and of the patriotic nationalism he supposedly embodies. If war is a "school of honour" (1.1.165), as the untried Prince of Wales claims, his father abruptly abandons those he has committed to battle both in Scotland and on the continent. In a soliloquy Lodowick bids "farewell" to "Scottish wars," recognizing that a "lingering English siege of peevish love" (2.1.22–23), Edward's affair with the countess, is about to replace martial duty. Conventional Petrarchan imagery of erotic love as warfare is invoked to give point to the effeminizing supersession of the bedchamber over the military camp. The Earl of Derby, who has been sent to solicit the aid of the German emperor for Edward's French campaign, and Lord Audley, who has mustered troops to support the king in Scotland and dutifully brought them to his doorstep, are both ignored by their besotted master. Then Edward promptly undoes Audley's labor by casually dismissing the men so loyally assembled, thereby endangering his own as well as national safety. Totally preoccupied by the countess, the king in a revealing slip of the tongue even substitutes her name for that of the emperor, since she has become "as imperator over [him]" and he her "kneeling vassal" (2.2.40–41). The play also generates skepticism about the supposed glories of English conquest. As Champion (124–25) notes, Edward displays an almost fanatic callousness in refusing "On pain of death" (3.4.47) to send rescuers to his embattled son, whose death at French hands as he "is labouring for a knighthood" (3.4.31) seems otherwise inevitable, even justifying his willingness to sacrifice the heir to his kingdom with the comment, "We have more sons / Than one, to comfort our declining age" (3.4.36–37). Then, when the prince miraculously triumphs over his enemies, his father takes partial credit for the achievement: "Now, John of France, I hope / Thou knowest King Edward for no wantonness, / No love-sick cockney . . ." (3.4.112–14). Horrifying images of death in warfare ("Here flew a head disservered from the trunk, / There mangled arms and legs were tossed aloft . . ." [3.1.165–66]) seem calculated to stimulate more revulsion than patriotic exultation, as does Edward's doom that the burghers of Calais should be dragged alive around the city walls, then quartered (5.1.36–37)—a cruelty forestalled only by the queen's intercession.

The "ideological ambiguity" of *Edward III*, to borrow Melchiori's useful phrasing, turns on the related themes of "divided allegiance" and "the interplay of sexual passion and power" (36–38). King Edward thrusts upon two loyal subjects (the countess and her father) the pitiless necessity of choosing between obedience to their sovereign and obedience to divine law as prompted by conscience.[19] Thus he manifestly abuses his power as a divine-right sovereign—a sovereign who theoretically embodies God's imperatives—by rashly creating a breach in the supposed unity of political and religious authority implied by the doctrine of the king's two bodies. By assaulting the countess sexually, Edward drives a wedge between his body natural (which includes his erotic desires) and his body mystical (the sacramental extension of God's rule, which includes his marriage to Philippa). The motif of divided allegiance arises later in the play when Salisbury releases his French prisoner Villiers for the purpose of securing for him a passport through enemy territory, on condition that Villiers swear an oath to return to captivity, should he fail to obtain the document from the Dauphin Charles. Villiers, placing fidelity to his oath even higher than the authority of his prince, wins Charles to grant the passport by insisting that, should it be denied, he must "in conscience" (4.3.27) recommit himself to his former captor; Villiers is bound to obey the Dauphin, he insists, "In all things that uprightly he commands" but not in a "lawless" order that would cause him to violate "the covenant of [his] word" (4.3.31–34). Salisbury, having obtained the writ of free passage, is nevertheless captured by the French, whereupon King John orders him executed. John only reverses the order for Salisbury's death when his son Charles insists that to hang Salisbury and override his signature on the passport would "disgrace" his royal honor (4.5.73), even though the king attempts to argue that his son's "breach of faith" (4.5.87) would be excusable if it were done in obedience to a royal command.

Thus the play absorbs the element of Edward's sexual rapacity and his ultimate governance of it into a larger context—the potentially subversive issue of limitation on a monarch's power. More complex and multivalent than at first it appears, this particular chronicle play not only presents itself as a panegyric of English heroism and national pride (including an allusion to the defeat of the Spanish Armada);[20] it also casts a critical light upon the problems inherent in absolute monarchy as exemplified by the dangerous conduct of a figure such as Edward III who is at once glamorous and repellent, brave and unfeeling, virtuous and potentially vicious. In some sense, of course, *Edward III* may intend to represent the king's temptations as those of any robust soldier writ large; but, as Warwick says in an eloquent statement evocative of Isabella's appeal to Angelo,

> The greater man, the greater is the thing,
> Be it good or bad, that he shall undertake. . . .
> . . . .
> An evil deed, done by authority,

Is sin and subornation; deck an ape
In tissue, and the beauty of the robe
Adds but the greater scorn unto the beast.

(2.1.435–47)[21]

If the title character of *Edward III* is presented as having been temporarily sidelined by a sudden eruption of sexual desire for the Countess of Salisbury, a passion that seems to evaporate almost as quickly as it descends, his counterpart in Heywood's *Edward IV* comes off as an engaging Lothario who gratifies his fleshly appetites whenever and wherever his roving eye happens to fall. Although Heywood's two-part play concentrates on Jane Shore, Edward's best-remembered mistress (the wife of a city goldsmith), audiences would probably have known that the historical king, a prepossessingly handsome man, was notorious for a multiplicity of concubines and for his easy way with the wives of London citizens whose affections he courted and with whom he remained uncommonly popular.[22] Both Hall (Edward V, fol. xvii) and Holinshed (III, 727), two of Heywood's putative sources, report that before he seduced Mistress Shore, Edward had got with child Lady Elizabeth Lucy; according to the chronicles, it was this relationship that provided Gloucester (the future Richard III) with the opportunity, using the corrupt cleric Dr. Shaw as his mouthpiece, to allege that the two juvenile princes, Edward V and his younger brother, were bastards.[23] Heywood omits mention of Lucy but includes a speech by Shaw declaring his intention to "prove" in a sermon that "King *Edwards* children [are] not legitimate" (II, 1658–59).[24] At least some members of Heywood's audience would also have recalled Shakespeare's popular *3 Henry VI* (1591) in which the widow Grey was depicted as having become Edward's queen only because, in pleading for the restoration of her slain husband's property, she had adroitly refused the royal philanderer's price of sexual favors outside wedlock, holding him off until he finally offered her marriage.

Edward IV evinces a curious fusion of genres. Ostensibly a political drama based on chronicle materials, it devotes a certain amount of space in part 1 to civil unrest (notably the successful defense of London by city merchants and apprentices against the bastard Lord Falconbridge and his Kentish supporters) and in part 2 to foreign affairs (Edward's invasion of France to make good his suzerainty over Louis XI). The coming to power of Edward's brother Gloucester, Lord Protector to Edward V, also includes much machination and court intrigue of the sort already familiar to audiences from Shakespeare's *Richard III*; indeed part 2 with its introduction of Clarence, Brackenbury, the young princes, Buckingham, Catesby, Tyrrel, and Lady Anne covers much of the same ground and reads in part like a competing version of the earlier drama. But Heywood's major interest, as in *A Woman Killed with Kindness* (1603), is domestic tragedy—the wrecking of the happy middle-class marriage of the admirable Matthew Shore and his wife owing to royal coercion. Here the emphasis falls on Matthew's voluntary exile as he copes with the shame of cuckoldry and on his secret return to London in disguise, on Jane's charitable works after she has acquired power as a royal mistress, on her fall from wealth to poverty and her humiliating punishment after the king's death strips her of royal protection, on her pathetic suffering and penitence as a social outcast, and finally on the reconciliation and death from grief and exposure of the married couple in Shoreditch, the London suburb named in their memory.

Comedy, however, is far from absent. The play diverts us with folkloristic episodes derived from a popular ballad—the story of Edward IV's visit in disguise to the house of Hobs, the tanner of Tamworth,[25] where (as in *Henry V* with his soldiers before battle) the monarch exposes himself to uncensored comments from a commoner who thinks he is speaking to "Ned," the king's butler; Hobs then visits the court, intending to persuade Ned to intercede with the king so that his n'er-do-well son may be spared hanging. The plain-spoken tanner treads dangerously close to treason by showing himself hostile to courtiers, by praising his daughter's looks as superior to the queen's, by suggesting that "poore King *Harrie*" (i.e., Henry VI "put . . . down" by Edward and imprisoned in the Tower) is said to be "the honester man of the two" rulers, that the disguised king "lookes like a theefe," and that in comparison to Henry ("a devout man"), Edward is "a merrie companion, and loves a wench well" (I, 1162, 1182–83, 1210–12, 1266–68). At one point the jovial monarch tests Hobs's loyalty by pretending to be a Lancastrian sympathizer: "I say *Harrie* is the lawfull King, *Edward* is but an usurper, and a foole and a coward," to which Hobs gratifyingly responds that Ned may be "speak[ing] treason" (I, 1290–93). Edward's merriment with Hobs seems designed to celebrate the king's common touch and to reify his popularity with ordinary subjects; nevertheless, these scenes contain obvious subversive elements that the incognito monarch can cleverly manipulate into expressions of orthodox affirmation. As new historicists like to argue, established power in the early modern period typically co-opted criticism of idealized royalty by producing deliberate subversions of its own glorification that it then rendered toothless by containment.[26]

The dramatization of Jane's fall also reflects traditions of the morality interlude, the Corpus Christi cycles, and the saint's play. King Edward is presented in part as a powerful tempter who lures Jane into overriding her conscience; and her fellow citizen Mistress Blague functions as an evil counselor who encourages a friend's moral failure and then, like Judas, betrays her while wickedly profiting from the act. Richard III, who not only punishes Jane with disproportionate cruelty but also connives to have the princes murdered in the Tower, emerges as a stock tyrant—a figure like the Herod of the biblical plays, infamous for the massacre of the innocents. Finally Jane, who salves the wounds of her unrecognized husband with "a precious Balme" (II, 2030), recalls the famous subject of the Digby *Mary Magdalene* (ca. 1480–1530). In this influential mystery drama, the penitent harlot of the title, seduced by Curiosity under the aegis of Lady Lechery and richly garbed and bejeweled to manifest her worldliness, anoints the feet of Jesus "With swete bawmys" (line 613) or "*a precius ointtment*" (line 640.3) in token of her spiritual conversion.[27] The dramatist's sentimentalization of Jane as a model of Christian patience and repentance in part 2 raises her almost to the level of secular sainthood.[28]

Heywood in *An Apology for Actors* (1612), encourages us to regard *Edward IV* as homiletic: chronicle plays, he claims, "teach . . . subiects obedience to their King" and "shew the people the vntimely ends of such as haue moued tumults, commotions, and insurrections" (sig. F3v); in dramas that depict illicit sexuality, the "vnchaste are . . . shewed their errors, in the persons of [various foreign courtesans] and amongst vs, *Rosamond*, and *Mistresse Shore*" (sig. Gv).[29] Churchyard's poem on Shore's wife in the second edition of *The Mirror for Magistrates* (1563), another possible source for Heywood's play, takes a similarly didactic attitude, making Jane shoulder the chief onus of blame for her sorry fate:

> Beware, take heede, fall not to follie so,
> A myrrour make of my great overthrowe:
> Defye this world, and all his wanton wayes,
> Beware by me, that spent so yll her dayes.
>
> (lines 389–92)[30]

But Heywood's drama is subtler and more complex than these quotations might suggest.

King Edward exerts such pressure on Jane, a naive and confused young woman who adores her husband (unlike the figure of More's account who has been married off unromantically in her girlhood), that she finds resistance to a man so far above her station, especially one who can command her as a subject, impossible to sustain. As her husband laments when he is forced to give her up, opposition to the will of a king is tantamount to treason: "Oh what have subjects that is not their kings[?] . . . Ile not examine his prerogative" (I, 2521–22). Matthew accepts his cuckoldry with passive resignation: "Where kings are medlers, meaner men must rue" (I, 2333). Jane's response to royal power is essentially that of her spouse's. Like the Countess of Salisbury in *Edward III*, Jane is caught in a conflict of allegiances between fidelity to her husband and obedience to her sovereign; but she is too flattered, too bourgeois, too unsophisticated, and too frightened of evil consequences to defend herself for long with anything like the countess's staunch moral absolutism and aristocratic commitment to family honor. Although she asserts at

first that she "cannot grant" her virtue to Edward (I, 1936), having sworn
hyperbolically that she would sooner die than betray her husband and asking
rhetorically how a king "should so much forget / His royall State" as to
"breake into [her] plighted faith" (I, 2147–49), she is soon swayed by
Blague's argument that "this worlds pompe . . . is a goodly thing," that the
king's "greatnes can dispense with il, / Making the sinne seeme lesser by his
worth" (I, 2167–71), and that her power as a royal favorite will equip her to
"quit the guilt" of "one small transgression" (I, 2186). Then, having yielded,
Jane tries to compensate for her frailty by helping others in need, though all
her charity "Cannot consume the scandall of [her] name" (II, 963). Guiltily,
she confronts Queen Elizabeth, with whom in one sense she has changed
places, but, suppressing an angry impulse to take revenge,[31] the queen offers
forgiveness, killing her rival with kindness in typically Heywoodian fashion.
After Edward's death exposes her to ruin, Jane becomes a weeping penitent
who blames herself rather than her seducer. As one "so readie / To step into
a kings forbidden bed" (II, 2365–66), she even welcomes the severity of her
punishment. The king's disappearance from the play in the midst of part 2
dissolves the moral tension between his and Jane's sexual irresponsibility,
and Matthew's refusal to reclaim Jane as his wife until she is near death
leaves us with the final impression of a martyred whore whose sin has been
expiated by suffering and whom repentance has sanctified.

The portrait of King Edward is perhaps even more mixed. Ever "affable"
(I, 1044), fun-loving, and glamorous, he readily commands the affection and
respect of common subjects—even those, like Matthew Shore, whom he personally wrongs and those from whom he exacts burdensome, though officially
voluntary, "benevolences" (I, 2023, 2039, 2636, 2649) to finance his foreign
war.[32] But he is also woefully careless of his high calling. The opening scene
shows him making frivolous excuses for having betrayed Warwick's embassy
to France for the purpose of negotiating a dynastic marriage, and for having
rashly wedded the politically damaging widow Grey in the interim—a proven
breeder, he argues, who can ensure him of an heir. Rationalized self-indul-
gence has clearly trumped prudent statecraft. His mother, Duchess of York,
refers to him as a "wanton king," blemishing the new queen's previous entanglements with a sarcastic reference to her "Bigamie" (I, 70, 74). When
the Bastard Falconbridge attacks London, Edward absents himself from the
conflict, leaving the defense of his capital to its devoted citizenry, especially
the teenage apprentices—"Without the assistance of their lingring King" (I,
744). Edward arrives to praise their valor only after the rebels have been defeated, excusing his apparent "slacknes" and pleading weakly that he had
"dallied not" (I, 883, 886). This is a departure from Holinshed, who reports
that the Bastard dispersed his men only when he learned of the king's approaching "armie of thirtie thousand men" (III, 690). Edward's dilatory behavior puts his realm at risk, a significant irony of Heywood's treatment

being that a monarch whom his successor accused of having fathered bastards fails strenuously to resist the Bastard who seeks to displace him from his throne and reinstate Henry VI. When Shore with middle-class humility refuses a knighthood for services to the crown, Edward promises some alternative reward "to quittance [his] deserts" (I, 924), only to steal his wife.

Edward's mischievous sport with Hobs may seem innocent enough at the level of festive comedy; but this episode too may be viewed as another example of the monarch's playboy neglect of more serious concerns. While amusing himself with the tanner, Edward fails to attend his mother and the queen at a banquet; the situation causes one of his courtiers to comment knowingly, "the King will have his pleasure" (I, 1364). Edward's erotic compulsions betray themselves even here since one of the attractions of Hobs's hospitality is his daughter Nell, the "prettie wench" with whom "Ned" flirts outrageously and a lass he claims to fancy well enough to take to wife (he jests about becoming Hobs's "sonne in law"; I, 1429–32). The jocular host cannot help noticing that his special guest and his companions are "licorish lads" (I, 1442). Edward's "idle eye, . . . gadding still," first lights upon Jane Shore while she is serving as the Lord Mayor's hostess at a dinner to entertain him in London; his self-admonition addressed to the errant eye, "Keepe home, keepe home, for feare of further ill" (I, 1780–81), makes the point that, at least for the moment, he regards his desire as a form of exile from his better self. Letters containing news that the Duke of Burgundy and the Constable of France will support his claim to the French throne arrive during the meal, and the king suddenly finds it hard to keep his priorities in order: foreign "ayde" may be well enough, but, as he acknowledges privately, Jane's "aid . . . hath more power then *France* / To crowne us, or to kill us with mischance" (I, 1787–90). Thus instantly does Edward's passion for Jane arise—a "fit" that bereaves him "of all reason" (I, 1800–01) and causes him to pursue her lustfully (at first in disguise) until he has possessed her body like the most desirable "jewell" in her goldsmith's shop or the "ring" on her finger (I, 1877, 1888); the "ring," of course, contains a bawdy pun on pudendum (as in *The Merchant of Venice*, 5.1.307) as well as suggesting her wedding ring. Jane tries to parry Edward's addresses by calling him "a merrie man" (I, 1890), finally awakening after much stress to the truth that the insistent wooer is her sovereign, and flying to Mistress Blague for counsel and support. It is Blague who, although affecting neutrality, invokes the pleasures of being "folded in a princes armes" (I, 2179) and who stresses that "a princes hate is death" (I, 2163). As for Edward's dereliction of duty, Matthew's brother-in-law Francis Emersley observes with justice how strange it is that "in this serious busie time" of preparation for war, considering the "day and nightly turmoile of his Lords, / Yea of the whole estate in generall," the king "can be spared from . . . great affaires" of state (I, 2310–15).

It is not Heywood's purpose to vilify or even strongly to denigrate Edward

IV. Such disparaging details as the portrait contains are as nothing compared to the villainy of Richard III; despite his wanton ways, Edward is presented as a much-beloved monarch whose "inauspicious" illness and death (II, 1582) elicit genuine grief and cause great anxiety for the future of England among all but Richard's ambitious subalterns. At the gallows, only minutes before his reprieve, Matthew is able to forgive the ruler who "wrackt [his] state, by winning of [his] wife" (II, 1489) and who has unjustly, though un-wittingly, condemned him. Learning later of Edward's mortal sickness, he seems to speak for the playwright and most of the audience: "God blesse the king, a worse may wear the crown" (II, 1614). By shifting the emotional and moral emphasis onto Jane, especially in part 2, Heywood mutes Edward's sexual misconduct, making the king seem more the occasion of Jane's fall than its efficient cause. Nevertheless, *Edward IV* makes it unmistakable that royal carnality can be tragically damaging both to individual subjects and to the state. And perhaps the most pernicious feature of Edward's character is his selfish unawareness or casual disregard of the harm he has done. But with-out completely alienating our sympathies from Edward, the dramatist con-cludes his play by democratically transferring symbolic royalty from the palace to the city streets—from a dead king to a dying goldsmith:

> A King had all my joy, that her injoyde,
> And by a King againe shee was destroyde:
> All ages of my kingly woes shall tell. . . .

(II, 2932–34)

It is the "kingly woes" of the Shores that Heywood really cares about and that define for him the center of historiographical interest. The affairs of Ed-ward, whether amorous or political, merely furnish the necessary context.[33]

III

Any discussion of the chronicle plays of the 1590s would obviously be meaningless without consideration of Shakespeare—especially of the two tetralogies that made the genre commercially viable and that realized its high-est artistic possibilities. Significantly, the kings of the second sequence are virtually free of the sexual illicitness we have been considering. In *Richard II* Bolingbroke accuses Bushy and Green of having criminally influenced Richard to "Br[eak] the possession of a royal bed," thus making "a divorce betwixt his queen and him" (3.1.12–13), but, as I have argued in my edition of the play, the charge represents political scapegoating on the usurper's part since it contradicts the impression of devoted fidelity between the married pair carefully sustained throughout the rest of the action. The detail, which

has no basis in history, probably reflects the influence of Marlowe's homosexual king, whose passion for Gaveston did indeed divorce Edward II from
his consort.[34] Shakespeare purposefully ignores Holinshed's statement (III,
502) about the "lasciuious living" and the "leacherie and fornication, with
abhominable adulterie," of Richard's court. To have introduced this note
would have robbed the title character of his dignity and pathos and the tragedy of its powerful focus on the king's martyrdom (including Richard's
comparisons of himself to Christ), on his masochistic vulnerability to Bolingbroke, and on his obsession with divine right. *Woodstock* (1591–94?), the
anonymous drama on the same reign, sometimes referred to as *King Richard
the Second, Part One*,[35] illustrates a wholly different approach to the character. The Richard of this play, lacking totally the majesty and poetic charm of
Shakespeare's monarch, is depicted as having enjoyed suspiciously intimate
relationships with two favorites, the Duke of Ireland and Sir Henry Greene,
which contain hints of homoerotic dependency.[36]

Inasmuch as *The Famous Victories of Henry the Fifth* (1583–86) seems to
lie behind the two parts of *Henry IV* and of *Henry V,* we might expect some
Shakespearean dramatization of Prince Hal's amorous sowing of wild oats.
In the anonymous play the wayward prince brags of visiting an Eastcheap
tavern frequented by "a pretie wench / That can talk well": Hal's jest, "I
delight as much in their toongs, / As any part about them" (lines 88–90),[37]
contains an obvious touch of bawdry. But Shakespeare reserves the sexually
illicit aspects of the Henriad for comedy—for the jokes of Falstaff and his
Boar's Head companions (the likes of Mistress Quickly, Doll Tearsheet, and
Pistol) and for Shallow's senile reminiscences of Inns-of-Court "bona robas"
(*2 Henry IV,* 3.2.23). The only Shakespearean reference to Hal's youthful
concupiscence occurs in *Richard II* when his future rival, Harry Percy, reports to Henry IV, that he frequents "the stews" and mocks chivalric tradition
by wearing "a glove" plucked "from the common'st creature" as a favor in
jousts (5.3.16–19). Wooing the princess Katherine after his victory at Agincourt, Hal, now King Henry V, retains a certain lustiness, joking that his bride
"must . . . needs prove a good soldier-breeder" with whom he can "com-
pound a boy, half French, half English" (*Henry V,* 5.2.205–08); but marital
conquest, at least technically, licenses this expression of male sexual aggres-
sion. Apparently the dramatist's increased stress in the second tetralogy on
the isolation of kingship and the tragic burdens of the crown made against
deviations into royal sensuality or sexual attachments apart from marriage.

The case is otherwise with the first tetralogy in which more scattered action
and a wider diversity of narrative elements provided Shakespeare with better
opportunities for introducing royal carnality into the reigns of Henry VI, Edward IV, Edward V, and Richard III. The entire sequence dramatizes a downward spiral of England into chaos and nightmare. The initial play opens with
the funeral of the valorous Henry V, a child king who fails even to appear

until act 3 having acceded to the throne; the final play concludes only after the most unnatural of all monarchs, the "bottled spider" Richard III (*Richard III*, 4.4.81), has brought the nation to its nadir and met his doom at Bosworth, thereby making possible a restoration of order under Henry Tudor. Sexual waywardness not only contributes to the political and dynastic disintegration; it becomes in some sense a sign of the nation's fallenness. In *1 Henry VI*, for instance, Gloucester accuses the Bishop of Winchester, the king's great-uncle, of "lov[ing] the flesh" more than "religion" (1.1.41) and of being a "Lascivious" and "wanton" prelate (3.1.19).

The first and second plays of the group exemplify illicit desire principally in the adulterous relationship of Queen Margaret and her lover, the Duke of Suffolk, whereas the initial play toys satirically with a xenophobic conception of Joan of Arc as a "strumpet" (1.5.12) and "shameless courtezan" (3.2.45) who fraudulently claims to be a virgin of noble birth. In the scene where Joan wins over the Dauphin Charles, he "worship[s]" her (1.2.145) absurdly in the rhetoric of courtly love while she mingles "amorous dalliance, bawdy innuendo, and double-entendres with her claims to heavenly assistance."[38] Though asserting divine authority, she is portrayed as a sorceress who controls him by erotic blandishments more than by holy persuasion. The implied sexual liaison between Charles and Joan caters to English nationalistic prejudice and is obviously intended to provide comedy through ridicule while deflating chivalric notions of warfare; but Suffolk's passion for Margaret of Anjou receives more serious treatment, freighted as it is with baleful and far-reaching consequences.

Pursuing the gratification of his own sexual appetite (he already has a wife), Suffolk manipulates the naive Henry VI into rejecting a diplomatically wise marriage already contracted, and into accepting Margaret instead—the dowerless daughter of the King of Naples and Jerusalem whose titles are politically and monetarily worthless. The price of this disastrous mistake is an unpopular new tax on Henry's subjects to finance his nuptials; the loss of Anjou and Maine as well as other French territories long since won by English soldiers; Margaret's increasing domination over her monkish husband (she reckons him more suited to the papacy than a secular crown); the alienation and eventual murder of Duke Humphrey (Henry's wisest counselor); and the galvanizing of York, who in turn fosters the Cade rebellion, to promote the white rose and seize the crown for himself—in short, civil war. As Suffolk leaves for France to serve as Henry's proxy in the marriage to Margaret, he compares himself to Paris on his way to abduct Helen (*1 Henry VI*, 5.5.104), hoping ironically for a better outcome than the Trojan War. Nor does the unscrupulous Suffolk fail to combine his lust for his "paramour" (5.3.82) with a lust for power: "Margaret shall now be Queen, and rule the King; / But I will rule both her, the King, and realm" (5.5.107–08). This sordid infatuation, developed by Shakespeare from the merest hint in Hall's

chronicle (fol. clviii) that Suffolk was "the Quenes dearlynge," reaches its
crisis when the king is forced to exile the arrogant favorite for the murder of
Duke Humphrey, at which point we are treated to a protracted love duet of
farewells, accompanied by passionate kissing. Then Suffolk, trying to cross
the channel, is beheaded by sailors, one of whom jibes grotesquely, "The lips
that kiss'd the Queen shall sweep the ground . . ." (2 Henry VI, 4.1.75). The
lynching incident serves as a prelude to an even grislier scene in which we
see the queen weeping over the severed head of her beloved, caressing "this
lovely face" that "Rul'd like a wandering planet over me" (4.4.15–16). Ironically, it was Margaret who controlled Suffolk (as she controls the king) rather
than the reverse, and we recognize that the duke's fantasy of power was self-
delusion. Suffolk's errant love affair with the queen assists the effect of King
Henry's weakness and ineffectuality (he accepts his cuckoldom with minimal
protest) just as its violent end contributes to the sense of a whole kingdom
reduced to bloodshed and anarchy.

The third and fourth plays of the sequence further develop the theme of
illicit desire controlling politics. In the scene alluded to above as a probable
influence upon Heywood, the "lustful Edward" (3 Henry VI, 3.2.129), freshly
but precariously seated on his throne, sells out Warwick, the man who made
him king, by undermining his negotiations with Lady Bona (sister-in-law to
Louis XI) and willfully taking Elizabeth Grey as his queen. The impolitic
marriage, opposed by wiser heads, obviously echoes that of Henry VI in part
1; but Shakespeare's point is that Edward's unchecked libido almost fatally
vitiates his statecraft. Shamelessly trying to bargain with the young widow
for her body as she petitions for redress, he offers her marriage only because
she will accept nothing less. But in satisfying his sexual needs at such high
cost, Edward also takes on the baggage of her unpopular upstart family, who
create jealousy, resentment, and dissension at court. Apart from precipitating
Warwick's treason in France, he also breeds disloyalty in his brothers. Clarence defects to the Lancastrian party when Warwick shifts sides and, by marrying the latter's second daughter, "match[es] more for wanton lust than
honor, / Or than for strength and safety of our country" (3.3.210–11). And
the foolish marriage prompts crookback Gloucester to deliver an excited soliloquy of over seventy lines as he revels in ambitious plans to seize the
crown. Scarcely able to wait until his brother's sensually ravaged body is in
its grave, Gloucester tricks Edward in the next play into having Clarence disposed of and maneuvers the council into appointing himself "Protector"
(Richard III, 1.3.14) over the boy princes. Although Mistress Shore does not
appear as a character in either play, she hovers around the margins of Richard
III as a carnal presence, exposing the dynasty of her royal partner to possible
charges of illegitimacy; mentioned no fewer than seven times, she serves as
an evidence of both King Edward's and Lord Hastings's licentiousness, while

as the latter's paramour, she contributes to the endangerment of his political career and even, unwittingly, to his judicial murder.[39]

The theme of sexual energy allied to power politics emerges most histrionically in Richard's seduction of Lady Anne, Warwick's other daughter. The feat is the more astonishing, first, because the seducer, according to his own self-description, is "rudely stamp'd"—not "made to court an amorous looking-glass" or "strut before a wanton ambling nymph" (*Richard III*, 1.1.15–17), and, second, because the subject of his ardor is a mourner whose beloved husband and father-in-law he has just slaughtered. In truth, the encounter with Anne occurs in the very presence of Henry VI's corpse, and Gloucester's bravura accomplishment of the seemingly impossible touches disturbingly upon the dark psychology of the victim entranced by her predator, of beauty sexually mesmerized by deformity. Richard makes Anne's hatred of him the point of entry to her vulnerability, allowing her first to exhaust herself in vituperation and spitting, then baring his chest and challenging her to slay him with his sword, proffered to her for the act of penetration. Jean Howard and Phyllis Rackin analyze this situation compellingly: "Overwhelmed by Richard's aggressive passivity, Anne's resistance quickly collapses, whereupon Richard seals his sexual conquest by enclosing her finger with his ring," a ring that he then compares to her "breast enclos[ing his] poor heart" (1.2.203–04). "Owner of both the sword and the naked breast, both penetrated ring and penetrating heart, Richard has become, as Rebecca Bushnell observes, 'both the man who possesses and the woman who submits.'"[40] Howard and Rackin go on to suggest that Richard's seduction of Anne functions as a metaphor for the demonic hero's actorly seduction of the theater audience—for a way of manipulating them into suspending their disapproval and of converting their revulsion to delight. To quote Bushnell once more, Richard, "like the Vice, . . . fashions power through strategies of seduction, making himself a powerful object of desire and thus reversing the image of tyrannical desire in which passion is expressed through sexual domination" (120).

King John (1595), the Shakespearean chronicle play yet to be discussed, may have intervened between the two tetralogies, although the dating is controversial. Here too illicit sexuality becomes an adjunct of dynastic conflict, not only because the Bastard Faulconbridge, natural son of Richard Coeur de Lion, emerges as the voice of honesty and pragmatism in a politically adulterate and cynical world, but also because the issue of royal legitimacy, John's or Arthur's right to the throne, lies at the heart of the play's subject matter. Elinor and Constance, the warring mothers of the drama, respectively support their sons as claimants, each accusing the other of sexual infidelity and thereby branding their children with the shame of bastardy (2.1.120–33). To an uninitiated audience the genealogy can seem opaque: John's mother, Elinor of Aquitaine (historically married first to Louis VII and subsequently

after a divorce to Henry II), is Arthur's grandmother, the boy's deceased
father Geoffrey (Constance's husband) being also another of Elinor's sons
and John's elder brother. The play nowhere confirms the validity of these
charges (they are indignantly denied on both sides), and, as one editor points
out, they "damn the accuser as much as the accused, for if Geoffrey was not
'true begot' [2.1.130] in Eleanor's marriage to Henry II, Arthur's lineal right
suffers as much as Eleanor's reputation."[41] The passionate crossfire between
the two women settles nothing; yet it advertises dramatically an anxiety about
bastardy, legitimate descent, and inheritance that pervades and infects the
moral climate of the action. As Joseph Candido notices, Constance conceives
of Arthur's political misfortune in terms of adultery when the French withdraw their support and turn hostile to his cause: the boy at his birth was gifted
equally by Nature and Fortune, but Fortune, a "strumpet," "adulterat[ing]
hourly with [Arthur's] uncle John, . . . hath pluck'd on France / To tread
down fair respect of sovereignty, / And made his majesty the bawd to theirs"
(3.1.56–61).[42]

The opening scene explores conflicting claims to a family's property in a
serio-comic contest between two half brothers (Philip and Robert Faulconbridge), one of whom is elder and "well begot" though illegitimate, the other
younger though "true begot" (1.1.75–77); since both boys had the same
mother but different fathers, maternal honor becomes a prominent feature of
the colloquy. When it becomes clear that an English king (Coeur de Lion) is
Philip's biological father rather than the man who reared him (Lady Faulconbridge confesses that she was "seduc'd / To make room for [King Richard]
in my husband's bed" [1.1.254–55]), the Bastard cedes the family land to his
brother Robert and accepts a knighthood from King John, thus acquiring a
royal status (his new title is Sir Richard Plantagenet) symbolically higher
than the one for which he had contended.[43] As he puts it, "new-made honor
doth forget men's names" (1.1.187). Social rank, aristocratic bloodline, and
inherited wealth no longer coincide, and we become conscious of having entered a more ironic, unstable and pragmatic world where traditional conceptions of primogeniture and legitimacy are called into question or no longer
prevail.[44] As his mother points out, John holds his throne by "strong possession" more than by his dubious "right" (1.1.40). As for the Bastard—a divided character who both subverts and subscribes to traditional sovereignty,
who "struggles to mediate between opposed moral and political imperatives"
(Candido 122)—he tries with limited success to reconcile loyalty to a corrupted king of whom he must disapprove with the maintenance of what ethi-
cal standards are possible in a commodified and fallen world. Using the term
nonpejoratively, Candido calls this a "morally defensible 'bastardy'" (122).
In a realm of competing self-interests justified by simplistic definitions of
right and wrong, the Bastard becomes a hero of sorts but necessarily a "hero
by default" (Champion 128).[45]

IV

Royal carnality clearly abounds in the chronicle plays of the 1590s, usually in ways that enrich their characterization, politics, language, and wider significance. Of course erotic behavior, often in its more rebellious forms, has always been a staple of theatrical subject matter; and it might be argued that the comedies and tragedies of the period employ it just as resourcefully as the histories. Yet its remarkable salience in this last group—a body of drama that arose and flourished with particular brilliance during the final decade of the century—prompts us to search for explanations. One obvious way to account for the sexual component of these plays is to invoke the orthodoxy of the divine right of kings. Plays about English monarchs tended not only to pay lip service to the doctrine endorsed by Elizabeth I at her accession in 1558[46] but inevitably to reflect interest in matters of legitimacy and succession logically imbricated with it—especially late in the reign of a queen who remained unmarried and childless and who, although celebrated for virginity, was notorious for young male favorites. Speculation and anxiety about who would succeed became particularly intense toward the end of her reign. Divine right theory postulated two bodies of a sovereign—one mortal and subject to frailties of the flesh, the other immortal and ubiquitous, embodying the grandeur of the state and connected sacramentally through the anointing at coronations to the heavenly source of its authority. Kings were therefore by official definition double-natured—"god[s]" who suffer "mortal griefs" (*Henry V*, 4.1.241–42). It was only natural that dramatists, without denying the exalted nature of kingly supremacy, should wish also to humanize their royal characters by showing that they had "natural" bodies, subject to carnal temptations, as well as "political" ones. Indeed it was often the seeming contradiction or possible conflict between the two that provided the most interesting characterizations and plots. Monarchs might derive their powers from God but this did not prevent their having feet of clay or excitable loins. By the same token, the near deification in art and literary culture of Elizabeth as Astraea-Virgo, linked symbolically to the Blessed Virgin and promulgated to enhance her image as an absolute monarch, was also undermined by subjects who expressed more constitutional views of her power by emphasizing the role of Parliament and by attacking her ministers such as Leicester and Burleigh for their supposedly corrupting influence.[47] Even where no subverting of royal absolutism was intended, the carefully fashioned image of Elizabeth's semidivinity would naturally provoke countervailing opinions and more down-to-earth assessments, often founded perhaps on nothing more substantial than rumor or intuition.

Another way of accounting for the illicit sexuality in so many of the chronicle plays is to regard it as a contrastive element or foil to the heroic emphasis so often taken as the *raison d'être* of such dramas. The stories of past reigns with their battles, conquests, and affairs of state, as in chroniclers like Polydore Vergil and Hall or in poets such as Daniel and Drayton, were seen as composing in their aggregate the epic celebration of England's past, a moral and perhaps even providential embodiment of her greatness. The world so glorified was defined as essentially, indeed almost exclusively, masculine. But negative as well as positive examples proliferated in the source material. Weakness, lust, infatuation, disgrace, and frivolity, most of these qualities involving women in some way, were part of the panorama and indeed were almost necessary to it from the perspective of a practicing dramatist. When the chronicles failed to supply enough of these extraneous features, there were always ballads, novellas, and legends to be drawn upon, since it was traits of personality, tonal variety, moral force, and structural impact that would give life and dramatic viability to a play, and since no writer for the popular theater would feel constrained by mere historicity in the modern sense. At least by intention, if not in fulfillment, Elinor of Castile's incest, Edward III's obsession with the countess, and Edward IV's seduction of Jane Shore may be regarded as belonging to the underside of epic—as antiheroic ingredients of larger, more grandly nationalistic patterns.

Men dominate the history plays because in the Tudor culture of patriarchal England, it was relationships between the fathers and sons of ruling families, between the brothers of noble houses, or between male compeers on battlefields and in council chambers that determined events. For the most part men made policy and had dominion over their wives, children, and servants—or at least should have had dominion over them. Families take their names, titles, and identity from their male progenitors just as nation-states define themselves in relation to their symbolic fathers—the monarchs who govern them. In such a culture women play a subordinate but ambiguous role. Obviously necessary for the engendering of children and the continuation of male bloodlines, they are nevertheless potentially destructive, ironically in some cases because of their function as childbearers. Most of the women in the chronicle plays fall into two broad categories: they are either predatory, lustful, and unnaturally dominant (like Elinor of Castile, Joan of Arc, and Margaret of Anjou) or victims of male power *in esse* or *in posse* (like the Countess of Salisbury, Jane Shore, and Lady Anne). Interestingly, the Isabella of *Edward II* fits both categories, being at first a loving wife whose victimization at the hands of her hostile spouse turns her finally into an adulterous predator, driven as she is from Edward's arms into Mortimer's. Even if they are fundamentally blameless, like Elizabeth Grey in *Edward IV* and *Richard III* for instance, female characters often become the means through whom others are ruined. In the analysis of a feminist scholar such as Coppélia Kahn, "Liaisons with women [in the histories] are invariably disastrous because they subvert or destroy more valued alliances between men."[48] Thus the Countess of Salisbury in *Edward III* and Jane Shore in Heywood's drama divert their royal lovers from kingly duty and responsibility simply by being circumstantially available as sites of attempted seduction. Their sensual desirability is presented as magnetizing and effeminating royal figures who, if not physically tempted, would busy themselves elsewhere with more manly and heroic exploits. There is sometimes a sense in these dramas that the victims of potential violation unjustly bear a measure of blame for the erotic excitement that they involuntarily stimulate. At the same time, however, characters like the Countess of Salisbury who heroically resist their seducers serve as icons of chastity. While the countess exemplifies fidelity to her absent husband, she preserves her sexual virtue intact in a fashion that may glance topically at the strenuously guarded purity of Shakespeare's own virgin queen.

Lastly there is the obsessive fear of bastardy to which irregular sexual relationships may expose the members of royal families, even if only by gossip or vicious innuendo. This issue arises explicitly in the plays by Peele and Heywood as well as in Shakespeare's *Richard III* and *King John*. But all heterosexual liaisons outside wedlock release the menace of illegitimacy for contemplation, even if only latently, and therefore constitute a threat to orderly dynastic succession. Contentions for a throne such as those between the Lancastrians and Yorkists in Shakespeare's first tetralogy, or between Richard II and Bolingbroke in his second, are rooted in anxieties about lawful descent and primogeniture, tensions that sexual illicitness or even the rumor of it can only complicate and exacerbate. Froissart (VI, 377), one of Shakespeare's possible sources for *Richard II*, contains the story, circulated among the partisans of Bolingbroke, that Richard was the illegitimate son of a Bordeaux priest—a circumstance conceivably alluded to in the play at 4.1.155–56.[49] As suggested already, *King John* develops the theme of bastardy with unusual intensity, exploring its various literal and symbolic interconnections. But the concern is fundamental to any play that treats English monarchical regimes and that interests itself in royal authenticity and dynastic security. As Herbert Lindenberger points out, citing the Archbishop of Canterbury's nearly interminable explication of Henry V's right to the French crown (*Henry V*, 1.2.35–95), "The action of historical drama is more precisely a struggle for legitimacy than a struggle for power as such. Dramas that depict a hereditary throne generally present sharply divergent readings of genealogies to justify the rights of various contenders to the throne."[50] In such a context the issue of bastardy becomes unavoidable.

The overarching truth to which all the plays encompassed by this discussion testify is that sexual assault or dalliance becomes a dangerous adjunct of political power. Richard of Gloucester's seduction of Lady Anne dramatizes eros employed not for its own sake but as a Machiavellian strategy—one among many—in his quest for the crown. Edward III and Edward IV pursue their extramarital love affairs less cynically than Richard pursues Anne, but both abuse their power as reigning monarchs by exerting the kind of pressure that female subjects find it nearly impossible to withstand. Edward II's homosexual needs make him a virtual thrall to Gaveston, a social and political inferior who takes advantage of his unique position to dominate his royal partner, although it must be said in extenuation that an element of unselfish romance complicates and to some degree enobles Gaveston's motives. Class conflict and jealousy over the sharing of sovereignty intrude upon and thwart Edward's amours, dramatizing the important point that the love affairs of kings can never be wholly sealed off or protected from the dangerous politics that they create. In royal settings, public and private encroach upon each other in complex ways. The exercise of sexual power in the history plays may take on the dimensions of a microcosm, mirroring in little the dominance and submission or strength and weakness of the social, military and dynastic conflicts that comprise the larger action. Thus Edward's sexual rebellion against the hierarchical norms to which he was born help engender the political rebellion that results in his deposition and death. Carnal relationships involving royal characters can rarely be conducted on a basis of psychological or social equality.

Even queens become engines of dynastic procreation and cannot be wooed for merely emotional reasons. In Heywood's drama, for example, when Edward's mother scolds him for marrying so far beneath him, he tries to pacify her by insisting that his motive is the breeding of "an heire apparant" (*Edward IV*, I, 9). To audiences familiar with the outline of a notorious reign, the king's offhand remark ironically summons up the tragic fate of his son-to-be—the boy king Edward V, murdered by his uncle in the Tower. And the same might be said for Henry V's intention to conceive by Katherine of France "a boy . . . that shall go to Constantinople and take the Turk by the beard" (*Henry V*, 5.2.207–9). As audiences knew only too well, the son thus compounded, far from leading a crusade, "lost France, and made his England bleed" (*Henry V*, Epilogue, 12).

Sexual encounters involving royal persons have a potential for conveying the mysterious power of history in the making, a sense of the future captured in the instant; for, as is widely recognized, chronicle plays usually seek to embed their dramatization of the immediate in the broader context of historical flux, of causes and effects, of past and future—one reason that they typically seem less self-enclosed than comedies or tragedies. Elizabethan history plays occasionally use sexually charged moments or erotic situations to provide an ironic flash of recognition—a kind of epiphany—of what the whirligig of time has in store for its participants and successors. The poet Yeats had something like this in mind when he composed his time-oriented lyric, "Leda and the Swan." In this sonnet Zeus, taking the form of a swan, rapes the mortal girl Leda with the result that she hatches two eggs, one containing Clytaemnestra (the murderer of her own husband Agamemnon), the other containing Helen of Troy—both women who would figure spectacularly in the tragic history of the Trojan War:

> A shudder in the loins engenders there
> The broken wall, the burning roof and tower
> And Agamemnon dead.
> Being so caught up,
> So mastered by the brute blood of the air,
> Did she put on his knowledge with his power
> Before the indifferent beak could let her drop?[51]

Notes

1. *Pierce Penilesse His Supplication to the Divell* (1592) in *The Works of Thomas Nashe*, ed. R. B. McKerrow (Oxford: Basil Blackwell, 1958), I, 212–15.

2. See Marlowe, *Edward II*, ed. Charles R. Forker, Revels Plays (Manchester: University of Manchester Press, 1994), 16.

3. Peele emphasizes the epithet, "sweete Nell," by having Edward repeat it often (cf. lines 175, 728, 739, 1100, 1139, 1462, 1492, 1674, 1951); citations are from *Edward I*, ed. Frank S. Hook, in *The Dramatic Works of George Peele*, 3 vols. (New Haven: Yale University Press, 1952–70), II, 1–212. As Hook suggests (25), the playwright's failure to harmonize the conflicting conceptions of Elinor undoubtedly results from flawed revision.

4. (1) *Fair Em* unhistorically portrays William the Conqueror as endangering the welfare of his realm by deserting it to woo Blanch, daughter of the King of Denmark, disguising himself as "Robert of Windsor," falling in love instead with the more comely Mariana (a Swedish princess captive at the Danish court), and straining his friendship with the Marquis Lubeck to whom Mariana has promised herself. Tempted at first to "yield to lust" (sc. i, 34), King William masters his wanton appetite for Mariana, whom he identifies in the crisis with the masked Blanch, then finally accepts Blanch (who loves him) as his queen when he recognizes that virtue (inward beauty) is more valuable than mere physical allure. William returns to England in time to avert civil war; he passes a trial of honor and maturity in respect of his passion for Mariana ("I count a lover's state to be / The base and vilest slavery in the world" [sc. xvii, 94–95]); chastity is preserved; and he becomes "a reconcilèd foe" (sc. xvii, 226) to the Danish king whose daughter he had unwittingly abducted. Citations are from *Fair Em: A Critical Edition*, ed. Standish Henning (New York: Garland, 1980).

(2) In *Friar Bacon and Friar Bungay*, the Prince of Wales (the future Edward I) amorously pursues a gamekeeper's daughter, "the lovely maid of Fressingfield," to be his "concubine" (sc. viii, 21–23), enlisting the aid of his friend Lacy, Earl of Lincoln, together with the necromantic powers of Friar Bacon, an Oxford scholar. Margaret, the fair maid, falls in love with and is betrothed to Lacy rather than Prince Edward on whose behalf he courts the girl incognito, thus creating a deadly rivalry between the male friends; meanwhile Henry III, the prince's father, entertains Eleanor of Castile, whom he intends for dynastic reasons to marry to his son. Yielding finally to

Margaret's appeals, Prince Edward vanquishes his carnal desires, turning over his friend Lacy to be Margaret's husband in the spirit of rekindled friendship and going willingly to greet the Spanish princess whom the king has chosen for him. After further complications, the comedy ends with a double wedding. Citations are from Greene, *Friar Bacon and Friar Bungay*, ed. Daniel Seltzer (Lincoln: University of Nebraska Press, 1963).

(3) Irving Ribner aptly describes *James IV* as a "quasi-historical will-o'-the-wisp" (*The English History Play in the Age of Shakespeare*, rev. ed. [New York: Barnes and Noble, 1965], 11) despite its reference on the quarto title page to the Scottish monarch of history "slaine at *Flodden*" in 1513 and its possible use of Holinshed for the character of the Machiavellian sycophant (Ateukin in Greene, John Damien in the chronicle). The play takes its plot from a novella in Cinthio's *Hecatommithi*, embedding its main action in a frame story presided over by Oberon, King of the Fairies, and introducing also a clown and a dwarf to provide low comedy. The title figure of the play, an "anointed king" (2.2.67) beset by flatterers like Elizabeth I's brother monarch James VI (whom he is designed partly to reflect), has married the English princess Dorothea; "misled by lust" (Ind., 107), however, James attempts to seduce Ida, daughter of a local countess, with the help of his wicked toady Ateukin. When Ida rejects James's assault upon her honor out of respect for the queen, the king, seeking to remove the impediment to self-gratification, connives with Ateukin to have Dorothea murdered. Being warned in advance, Dorthea escapes in male disguise, is wounded by a pursuer and believed dead by the king, who now promises marriage to Ida. By this time, however Ida has been secretly betrothed to Lord Eustace, her future husband. The play ends happily with King James's repentant reconciliation to a resurrected Queen Dorothea, but not before his lascivious desires and corrupt policies have precipitated open rebellion among his subjects and an invasion led by the English king (Dorothea's father), undertaken to avenge her supposed death. Citations are from Greene, *The Scottish History of James the Fourth*, ed. Norman Sanders, Revels Plays (London: Methuen, 1970); for Greene's possible use of Holinshed, see Sanders, xxxiii.

All three plays, like much of Peele's *Edward I*, are fictional in content and relate to the history play only tangentially on account of the historical names of a few royal characters. Nevertheless, each drama points to a concern that pervades the chronicle play of the 1590s—namely the fear that kings or their spouses may stray from the path of sexual fidelity, thus threatening the good of the state and the stability of "sacred" monarchical authority, as well as raising the specter of illegitimate offspring.

5. *The Lamentable Fall of Queene Elnor* (in the Huntington Library, San Marino, Calif.) and *Queen Eleanor's Confession* (Child, No. 156). Hook discusses both sources, giving full bibliographical details (19–23, 206–12).

6. Elinor of Castile was the daughter of Ferdinand III and Joan of Ponthieu. Ferdinand's parents were second cousins—Alfonso IX of Leon and Berenguela, daughter of Alfonso VIII of Castile. Alfonso IX had earlier married Teresa of Portugal, his first cousin. Although the pope annulled both marriages and placed the kingdom under interdict, the legitimacy of the children was recognized. See "Alphonso," *Encylopaedia Britannica*, 11th ed. (1910). In the play Peele reinforces the negative force of Elinor's incestuous family background by having the speaker quote a familiar tag from

Horace: "*Quo semel est imbuta recens servabit odorem / Testa diu*" (lines 1687–88; *Epistles* 1.2.69)—"The jar will long keep the fragrance of what it was once steeped in when new," i.e., the odor of her inherited reputation lingers and is hard to get rid of.

7. Bilson, *The True Difference between Christian Subjection and Unchristian Rebellion* (Oxford, 1585), Part II, 249.

8. See *Edward II*, ed. Forker, 41–66. Citations are taken from this edition.

9. See Bruce R. Smith, *Homosexual Desire in Shakespeare's England: A Cultural Poetics* (Chicago: University of Chicago Press, 1991), 48–53.

10. Raphael Holinshed, *The Chronicles of England, Scotland, and Ireland*, 2nd ed., 3 vols. in 2 (London, 1587), III, 319. Future citations of Holinshed are from this edition.

11. Larry S. Champion, "'Answere to This Perillous Time': Ideological Ambivalence in *The Raigne of King Edward III* and the English Chronicle Plays," *English Studies* 69 (1988), 118.

12. See "The Rash Oath in *Edward III*," *Allegorica*, 1.1 (1976), 269. Lewis (277) cites Lyly's *Campasbe* (1580–84), Kyd's (?) *Soliman and Perseda* (1589–92), and Greene's *Friar Bacon and Friar Bungay* (1589–92). In Lyly's play Alexander the Great forsakes his attraction to the chaste Campasbe for the military discipline of his calling, his conquest of himself paralleling his conquest of Thebes. Kyd's play portrays Soliman, the Turkish emperor, as besotted with Perseda, the beloved of the Christian knight Erastus, whom he has befriended. At first Soliman resists his desire to force himself upon Perseda, idealistically permitting the lovers to marry; then he relapses, guiltily having Erastus executed on false charges and determining to seize Perseda; she however disguises herself as a man and dies in combat with Soliman, who unwittingly kills the object of his desire, then dies himself by kissing her poisoned lips. For Greene's *Friar Bacon* and other plays that also contain the motif, see note 4 above.

13. See *King Edward III*, ed. Giorgio Melchiori (Cambridge: Cambridge University Press, 1998). Melchiori (25–39) analyzes the play's complex use of sources including Painter's Novella 46 and the (probably collaborative) alteration of its text in three stages of composition, attributing the prominence and content of the Countess of Salisbury section and its problematic integration into the text mainly to revision. Citations are taken from this edition.

14. Holinshed, III, 366; see also Melchiori, 21–22.

15. The phrase is Froissart's; see *The Chronicle of Froissart: Translated out of French by Sir John Bourchier, Lord Berners (Annis 1523–25)*, ed. W. P. Ker, 6 vols. (London: David Nutt, 1901–03), I, 193; also Melchiori, 22–25.

16. Knight, *Studies in Shakespeare* (London: C. Knight, 1849), 279.

17. The countess, contrasting the rude exterior of her castle with the beauty and luxury of its interior (1.2.143–61), invites King Edward to enter it. A trenchant irony of this episode is that her graciousness in offering hospitality becomes the occasion of the king's attempted sexual penetration of his hostess.

18. *Chronique de Jean Le Bel*, ed. J. Viard and E. Déprez, Société de l'Histoire de France, 2 vols. (Paris, 1904), II, 31; trans. in Michael Packe, *King Edward III*, ed. L. C. B. Seaman (London: Routledge and Kegan Paul, 1983), 120; quoted in Melchiori, 23n.7.

19. For a similar conflict between obedience to a king and obedience to conscience, compare Shakespeare's *King John* (4.1), in which Hubert is torn between carrying out John's order to blind Prince Arthur and sparing the innocent boy.

20. Cf. 3.1.64–72 where the "proud armado of King Edward's ships" is described as "Figuring the hornèd circle of the moon." Philip II's Spanish fleet in 1588 was arranged "in half-moon formation" (Melchiori, 108n.)

21. Cf. *Measure for Measure*, 2.2.117–23. Unless otherwise specified, citations from Shakespeare are to *The Riverside Shakespeare*, ed. G. Blakemore Evans et al. (Boston: Houghton Mifflin, 1974).

22. Holinshed, describing Jane Shore, writes that Edward IV "would saie that he had three concubins, which in three diuerse properties diuerslie excelled. One the merriest, another the wiliest, the third the holiest harlot in his realme, as one whome no man could get out of the church lightlie to any place, but it were to his bed"; two of these women "were somewhat greater personages, and nathelesse of their humilitie content to be nameless . . . but the meriest was . . . Shores wife . . ." (III, 725). This passage is incorporated almost verbatim from Hall's *Union of the Two Noble and Illustre Families of Lancaster and York* (1548), Edward V, fol. xvii^v. Hall in turn lifted the words from Sir Thomas More's *History of Richard III, King of England* (ca. 1517), later published in More's *English Works* (1557), 57. Richard Grafton and John Stow in their chronicles (1569 and 1580 respectively) also transcribed More's popular account.

23. Another of Edward's mistresses was Lady Eleanor Butler, daughter of the Earl of Shrewsbury (the Talbot of Shakespeare's *1 Henry VI*); according to some accounts, this lady, too, was said to have been the mother of the "illegitimate" princes later murdered in the Tower. See Paul Murray Kendall, *Richard the Third* (London: George Allen and Unwin, 1955), 215–23; also Eric N. Simons, *The Reign of Edward IV* (New York: Barnes and Noble, 1966), 278.

24. At a later point Shaw, tormented by a ghost who curses him for much wickedness, refers again to his sermon delivered to "prove the lawfull issue of [the] King, / Got out of wedlocke, illegittimate" (II, 2273–74). Citations are from *A Critical Edition of Thomas Heywood's "The First and Second Partes of King Edward the Fourth,"* ed. Whitney A. Peterson (diss., University of Nebraska, 1997).

25. "King Edward the Fourth and a Tanner of Tamworth" (Child, No. 273).

26. See especially Stephen Greenblatt, *Shakespearean Negotiations: The Circulation of Social Energy in Renaissance England* (Berkeley: University of California Press, 1988), 41; also Charles W. Crupi, "Ideological Contradiction in Part I of Heywood's *Edward IV*: 'Our Musicke Runs . . . Much upon Discords,'" *Medieval and Renaissance Drama in England* 7 (1995): 224–56.

27. Citations are from the text edited by David Bevington in *Medieval Drama* (Boston: Houghton Mifflin, 1975), 687–753.

28. The popularity of Saint Mary Magdalene in the later Middle Ages and Renaissance was such that she tended to be accorded a status only a little lower than the Blessed Virgin. See Clifford Davidson, "The Digby Mary Magdalen and the Magdalen cult of the Middle Ages," *Annuale Medievale* 12 (1972): 71–72.

29. Heywood also points out that when the historical Edward IV "would shew himselfe in publicke state to the view of the people, hee repaired to his Palace at S.

Iohnes, where he accustomed to see the Citty Actors" (sig. E^v), thus establishing a precedent for royal patronage of the public theater and the formation of the Revels office for the vetting of plays to be performed at court. Citations from *An Apology for Actors* are to the facsimile reprint of the 1612 edition with a preface by Arthur Freeman (New York: Garland, 1973).

30. *The Mirror for Magistrates*, ed. Lily B. Campbell (Cambridge: Cambridge University Press, 1938; repr. New York: Barnes and Noble, 1960), 386. Churchyard, like Heywood, makes Jane's marriage a love match, although, because she was too young, she "knewe not howe to vse" "meere [= pure] love" (377).

31. Elizabeth contrasts herself with Eleanor of Aquitaine, Henry II's queen, who, upon discovering her husband's adultery with Rosamond, is supposed to have had the mistress poisoned (II, 1176–85).

32. On one occasion the Widow Norton, in "token of her zeale" and "humble dutie," contributes twenty pounds and receives a kiss from the grateful Edward, who calls her "a gallant lustie Girle"; blushing with delight, she extols the king's "honnie kisse, / Able to make an aged woman young," praises the giver as her "sweet and lovely Prince," and then increases her donation by "Fortie olde Angels." Hobs, hinting at the exploitation involved, exclaims skeptically, "Snails [= God's nails], twentie pound a kisse?" (I, 2652–54, 2669–77).

33. Cf. Wendy Wall's comment in "Forgetting and Keeping: Jane Shore and the English Domestication of History," *Renaissance Drama*, New Series 27 (Evanston: Northwestern University Press, 1998), 150n.32: "Although eroding principles of Tudor history, Heywood is not radically skeptical about sovereign power; instead his periodic skepticism is just one element in the play's decentered thematics, countered sporadically by the equally passionate equation of 'king' with 'country.' There are many discourses of power in this two-part play: all are patriotic, some link the king to the national good, others exempt him as insignificant to true English matters, and some show him to be antagonistic to the nation."

34. See *Richard II*, ed. Charles R. Forker, Arden 3 series (London: Thomson Learning, 2002), 310n., 491–92n.; citations come from this edition. That *Richard II* was conceptually and verbally influenced by Marlowe's tragedy has been established; see Forker, *Richard II*, 159–64.

35. Cf. *Thomas of Woodstock, or Richard the Second, Part One*, ed. Peter Corbin and Douglas Sedge, Revels Plays (Manchester: Manchester University Press, 2002); citations are taken from this edition. That *Woodstock* originally formed the first part of a two-part sequence with Shakespeare's play as Part II seems to me mistaken; see my discussion of this point in *Richard II*, ed. Forker, 145–46.

36. The Duchess of Ireland, for instance, alleges that her deceased husband, one of Richard's favorites, "was the cause he left my bed" (2.3.12); and Richard vows vengeance over the slain Greene, kissing the corpse: "Hard-hearted uncles . . . That here have murdered all my earthly joys. / O my dear Greene, wert thou alive to see / How I'll revenge thy timeless tragedy / On all their heads that did but lift a hand / To hurt this body that I held so dear" (5.4.29–34). For the closeness to Greene, see also 2.1.8–10, 2.2.203–04, 2.2.219–20, 3.1.75–80, 4.1.218–20, 5.4.3. These details are fanciful. There is no historical justification for regarding Richard II as homosexually inclined.

37. Anon., *The Famous Victories of Henry the Fifth*, ed. Geoffrey Bullough in *Nar-*

rative and Dramatic Sources of Shakespeare, 8 vols. (London: Routledge and Kegan Paul, 1957–75), IV, 299–343.

38. Donald G. Watson, *Shakespeare's Early History Plays: Politics at Play on the Elizabethan Stage* (London: Macmillan, 1990), 43. Later the Duke of Burgundy describes how he "scar'd the Dolphin and his trull, / When arm in arm they both came swiftly running, / Like to a pair of turtle-doves / That could not live asunder day or night" (*1 Henry VI*, 2.2.28–31). Shakespeare seems to intend a kind of pervasive wordplay on "Pucelle" (= maid, virgin), Joan's sobriquet, and "puzzel" (cf. 1.4.107), a derogatory anglicization of the French word with bawdy overtones (= slut, drab; also perhaps playing on *penis* [from *pizzle*] since Joan adopts male attire).

39. Shakespeare could have known Thomas Legge's academic Latin tragedy, *Richardus Tertius* (1579), in which Shore's wife appears as a mute character doing public penance in procession. He may also have known the anonymous *True Tragedy of Richard the Third* (1591?), the 1594 quarto of which moralistically advertises on its title page the *"lamentable ende of Shores wife, an example for all wicked women."* In the latter play Richard accuses Hastings of bewitching him "with assistance of that famous strumpet" and of having lain with her the night before his condemnation (lines 944–47); later she accuses herself of being a "dishonour to the King, a shame to [her] countrey, and the onely blot of defame to all [her] kindred" (lines 1019–21). At one point she declares that though Edward "was King, yet Shores wife swayd the swoord" (lines 1087–88), her fall serving as a personal analogue to the fall of England under Richard's tyranny. See the Malone Society Reprint edition, ed. W. W. Greg (Oxford: Oxford University Press, 1929), sigs. D4, E, and E2. Conceivably *The True Tragedy*, a contaminated text, reflects Shakespeare's drama as opposed to having influenced it (cf. *King Richard III*, ed. Antony Hammond [London: Methuen, 1981], 83); even so, the similar attitude toward Mistress Shore in both plays shows that the two dramatists regarded her as a corrupting influence in the sexual politics being staged.

40. Jean E. Howard and Phyllis Rackin, *Engendering a Nation: A Feminist Account of Shakespeare's English Histories* (London: Routledge, 1997), 109–10; Rebecca W. Bushnell, *Tragedies of Tyrants: Political Thought and Theater in the English Renaissance* (Ithaca: Cornell University Press, 1990), 124.

41. *King John*, ed. L. A. Beaurline (Cambridge: Cambridge University Press, 1990), 80. Constance implies that both Elinor's sons, Geoffrey and John, are illegitimate; at first she asserts that it "cannot be" that Arthur's father "was . . . true begot" if Elinor was "his mother" (2.1.129–31); then she puns on "her sin" (meaning both Elinor's supposed adultery and its product, John) as unjustly punishing Arthur (2.1.183–90).

42. "Blots, Stains, and Adulteries: The Impurities in *King John*," in *"King John": New Perspectives*, ed. Deborah T. Curren-Aquino (Newark: University of Delaware Press, 1989), 116–17.

43. The Bastard cheerfully excuses his adulterous mother, threatening to send "to hell" anyone who should dare to say that she "did . . . not well / When [he] was got. . . ." How could Lady Faulconbridge be expected to resist Richard's "commanding love"? "He that perforce robs lions of their hearts / May easily win a woman's" (1.1.264–72).

44. John argues paradoxically that the Bastard may be legally judged "legitimate" since he was born to a married woman whose husband had every right to lay claim to him in the same way that a farmer may claim the calf born from his own cow (1.1.116–29).

45. Although Holinshed (III, 160) briefly mentions "Philip bastard sonne to king Richard," the character as developed by Shakespeare is largely fictional. A less sophisticated version of the story Shakespeare dramatizes already existed in the anonymous two-part play, *The Troublesome Raigne of King John* (1591), probably the dramatist's source.

46. See Forker, ed., *Richard II*, 17.

47. Ibid., 5–8, 18–21. The most vocal criticisms tended to come from either Puritans or Papists.

48. *Man's Estate: Masculine Identity in Shakespeare* (Berkeley: University of California Press, 1981), 55.

49. See Forker, ed., *Richard II*, 405n., 499–500n.

50. *Historical Drama: The Relation of Literature and Reality* (Chicago: University of Chicago Press, 1975), 160. For another example of genealogical argumentation, see the opening dialogue in *Edward III* (1.1.1–41).

51. W. B. Yeats, *The Poems*, ed. Daniel Albright (London: J. M. Dent, 1990), 260.

Desdemona, Woman Warrior: "O, these men, these men!" (4.3.59)

JOAN OZARK HOLMER

> Unkindness may do much,
> And his unkindness may defeat my life
> But never taint my love.
>
> (4.2.161–63)

OTHELLO is a tragedy that continually surprises us. Not only did Shakespeare make the blackest man on stage a white man (Iago), I would suggest that he made the bravest warrior onstage a woman (Desdemona). For only one other female character in his works does Shakespeare employ the descriptive term "warrior," predictably for the Amazon Hippolyta, the "warrior love" of Theseus (*A Midsummer Night's Dream* 2.1.71).[1] Because none of the acknowledged literary sources for *Othello* describe the heroine as a warrior, despite the popularity of the Ovidian trope of love as war, Shakespeare catches us off guard when Desdemona is identified as a warrior twice in the play, once by Othello who greets her on the seemingly peaceful battlefront of Cyprus as his "fair warrior" (2.1.180) and once by herself when she calls herself in the subsequent act an "unhandsome warrior" (3.4.152) for uncharitably arraigning Othello.[2] The Duke initially judged her husband "far more fair than black" (1.3.291), but by the end of the play Desdemona proves herself the play's "fair" warrior in both senses of outer beauty and inner virtue.

In his *Artificial Persons: The Formation of Character in the Tragedies of Shakespeare* Leeds Barroll rightly observes, "Desdemona, rather significantly, is Othello's 'fair warrior,'" and "the relationship between Desdemona and Othello's military profession also proceeds through some complexities, for if he sees her as 'warrior,' he also sees her as a possible agency of Cupid's 'toys' in his speech to the senate."[3] As would most critics in responding to this play, Barroll finds that "the motif of Desdemona as 'fair warrior' receives only rudimentary development in the play" (183). It is precisely this important motif that I wish to re-examine in light of some new contexts (Edmund Spenser and Desiderimus Erasmus) and some reconsidered sources

132

(Giraldi Cinthio, Geoffrey Fenton, and Matteo Bandello). Although Othello is a literal warrior in both the Christian and secular senses, Desdemona is literally a warrior in the Christian sense, with faith as her shield (Eph. 6.17), but figuratively a warrior in the secular sense since her tongue is her sword or her only weapon, used defensively against Othello and offensively on behalf of Othello. As moderns we need to recapture an older habit of reading literally and figuratively while we wrestle with Shakespeare's wordplay and the richer meanings then of "common" words we tend to take for granted, such as "honesty" and "honor," both of which have both outer (reputation) and inner (character) nuances.

I

Although Desdemona is no medieval Joan of Arc, Renaissance Britomart, or modern G. I. Jane, her true faith and enduring love in her relationship to Othello and his occupation as a warrior may be surprisingly illuminated by Edmund Spenser's portrayal of Una (truth) and the Redcrosse Knight (holiness) in the first book of *The Faerie Queene*. This contextual relationship of heroines and heroes has been overlooked despite Charles Prouty's earlier argument that Spenser's Archimago helps us to understand better Iago, even though one character inhabits an allegory and the other a drama.[4] Despite the major differences in genres and styles between Spenser's romance epic and Shakespeare's love tragedy, and Spenser's climactic versus Shakespeare's initial presentation of marriage, larger patterns of meaning link the warriors and their lady companions as they venture forth together to engage the enemy, ultimately in the typical one-on-one combat of spiritual warfare. Like Una, Desdemona is no "moth of peace" (1.3.257) to stay at home. Both ladies bravely accompany their beloveds to the field and lovingly "suffereth all things . . . hopeth all things . . . endureth all things" (1 Cor. 13.7) during trials that include temptations to jealousy and suicide. Throughout these trials the women triumph with love that never alters "when it alteration finds" (Sonnet 116) as they attempt to aid, even save, their less steadfast men who afflict them in return with unmerited suffering.[5]

Most significantly, these martial exploits occur within a marital context in which the lovers face challenges to the type of faithful love that constitutes true marriage. The love relationships, therefore, are not supposed to be divorced from the warrior's occupation, as we might typically expect. Hotspur, that warrior of warriors, voices just such an expectation when he prioritizes military over marital duty: "Away, you trifler! . . . / I care not for thee, Kate . . . / And when I am a' horseback, I will swear / I love thee infinitely" (*1 Henry IV* 2.3.90–102). If a warrior were asked what he most fears losing, Hotspur's answer might serve: not the loss of "brittle life" but the loss of "proud titles" (*1 Henry IV* 5.4.79), or his honors. Like Hotspur who divides the duties of war and love into different camps, Othello also reflects the typical awareness of how wives can function as "feathered" Cupid's "light-winged toys" (1.3.269–70) to distract a warrior from his proper business so that "housewives make a skillet of [his] helm" (1.3.273). Once in Cyprus, however, Emilia has to "pray heaven" that "no jealous toy" concerning Desdemona infects Othello (3.4.155–56). The play's shift of locale from Venice to Cyprus ominously suggests potential danger because of its mythological association with Venus. Cyprus is one of the two islands sacred to Venus, Cythera being the other; hence, Venus was frequently called either the Cyprian or Cytherea.[6] In *The Tempest* Shakespeare prevents some "wanton charm" being done by Venus and Cupid on another (unnamed) Mediterranean isle because they are sent "dove-drawn" back to Paphos on Cyprus where Cupid will break his arrows and instead "play with sparrows" (4.1.87–100).

Spenser, however, charts another course in which the love of a good woman is not to be feared for its effeminate potential but is to be integrated into the good man's life as a source of strength, and the betrayal of this love constitutes the knight's *greatest shame*:

> Young knight, what euer that dost armes professe,
> And through long labours huntest after fame,
> Beware of fraud, beware of ficklenesse,
> In choice, and change of thy deare loued Dame,
> Least thou of her beleeue too lightly blame,
> And rash misweening doe thy hart remoue:
> For vnto knight there is no greater shame,
> Then lightnesse and inconstancie in loue;
> That doth this *Redcrosse* knights ensample plainly proue.

(1.4.1)[7]

This stanza appears after the Redcrosse Knight has broken faith with Una because the disguised, and newly met, tempter Archimago used witchcraft, somewhat akin to Iago's "wit-craft," to seduce the Redcrosse Knight to fall for false ocular proof (sprites masquerading as humans) that his beloved "doth her honour staine" (I.2.4.9) in bed with another man whom the Redcrosse Knight does not know. Shakespeare stacks the deck more against Othello by employing insider betrayal. We may overlook that Othello, unlike the Redcrosse Knight, has some legitimate grounds for suspicion. His friend and lieutenant Cassio did indeed betray his trust on the watch; therefore, Othello has a reasonable basis to distrust him in other situations, especially when his ensign Iago, universally reputed for honesty, leads the charge. When Cassio departs from Desdemona "so guilty-like" (3.3.39), he probably does look guilty, not with lust for Desdemona but with shame for having failed Othello. The Redcrosse Knight has known Una for only a short time at the beginning of their journey, but he has already witnessed her brave goodness in action when she helped him defeat the monster Error in "the wandring wood" (1.1.13.6). Othello has had nine months in Venice (1.3.85) to get to know Desdemona, and he too witnesses her courage in action when she wisely testifies on his behalf before her father and the Venetian senate (1.3.180–89) and then eloquently implores the Duke to allow her to stand by Othello's side in war-threatened Cyprus (1.3.244–60).

Othello, for all the criticism accorded his too rapid surrender to jealousy, looks better in comparison to the Redcrosse Knight, the future St. George. Indeed, despite the reputation Moors had for jealousy,[8] our "black Othello" (2.3.29) also looks far fairer than the white Venetian merchant, Corvino, in Jonson's *Volpone*, a comedy written about a year after Shakespeare's tragedy.[9] "With sword in hand" the Redcrosse Knight *immediately* burns with "gealous fire" at the false sight so that "the eye of reason was with rage yblent," and he would have *slain* both his beloved and her squire in his "furious ire" if Archimago had not restrained him (1.2.5.1–9). Archimago, of course, deters the jealous man for no moral purpose but to avoid the exposure of his deception because spirits cannot be slain. Iago similarly suggests to Othello ocular proof too painful to view and too impossible to catch— "Would you, the supervisor, grossly gape on? / Behold her topped?" (3.3.398–99)—knowing that not even a deft director like himself can stage such a scene.

The Redcrosse Knight consequently deserts Una, "flying from his thoughts and gealous feare" so that "will" became his "guide" and "griefe led him astray" (1.2.12.4), and like the Redcrosse Knight, Othello's rational eye becomes blinded by rage once his "clear spirit" is "puddled" (3.4.144) by Iago's temptation to foul jealousy: "O blood, blood, blood!" (3.3.454). Moreover, just as Iago perversely elevates "will" over right reason (1.3.320–22) in self-determination and denigrates "love" as "a lust of the blood and a permission of the will" (1.3.333–35), so also Othello begins unwittingly to incorporate Iago's philosophy as his own rude will, in conjunction with his tormented grief, contribute to leading him astray once he allows his mind to be tainted by "the green-eyed monster" (3.3.168). However, of his own accord Othello intermittently and repeatedly reverts to the right path to love and value Desdemona (e.g., see 4.1.176–85), and left alone, he might have kept to that path, were it not for Iago's persistent plotting. Whose "will" will be done—man's or God's? Both Una ("sore grieued" [1.2.8.8]) and Desdemona ("How have I been behaved that he might stick / The small'st opinion on my greatest misuse?" [4.2.110–17]) are baffled as to what they could have done wrong, knowing in truth their own loyal love. Una even experiences near despair and curses light when she mistakenly thinks the Redcrosse Knight is dead (1.7.20–23), but she spiritually rallies herself to continue the quest (1.7.24–28). Desdemona avoids near despair, but her most "perplexed in the extreme" (5.2.344) moment registers psychosomatically as a "half-asleep" daze in which she claims to have no lord (4.2.99–104). However, she too rouses herself in mid-speech by commanding her wedding sheets to be put on her bed (4.2.107), and then she continues to assert her innocence (4.2.109–66).

Despite the men's betrayals and their failures to resist temptations, neither Una nor Desdemona breaks faith with her beloved. Like their knights, both heroines experience great grief, but both refuse to capitulate to "will" or "wrath." Recognizing his errors in love, the Redcrosse Knight would have taken Despair's proffered "dagger" (1.9.51.2) and committed suicide, but Una saves him by snatching the dagger out of his hand and sharply reprimanding her knight to remember God's mercy: "Ne let vaine words bewitch thy manly hart / Ne diuelish thoughts dismay thy constant spright. / In heauenly mercies hast thou not a part?" (1.9.46.6–9). Othello, likewise tormented by his failure in love, has no lady love living to prevent the hand that threw her away from finding his hidden dagger of suicide.[10] Not only does Spenser seem to be suggestive for various aspects of a love relationship tested by spiritual warfare, but also he may influence some ways in which Shakespeare conceptualizes and images the passion of jealousy.[11]

Spenser's emphasis on spiritual warfare comprises the very emphasis Shakespeare carefully cultivates throughout his play, and it is precisely this emphasis that is lacking in his main literary source of Cinthio's novelle. This same spiritual orientation, with its concern for souls and eternal consequences, also is absent in modern analytical comparisons of O. J. Simpson to Othello and his murdered wife Nicole to Desdemona, such as that of Elaine Showalter.[12] Given the religious history of the Renaissance, we should not be surprised to find such a strongly spiritual emphasis, and perhaps not even too surprised to find in reformed England authors who appreciate the vocation of companionate marriage, rather than the more typical solitary male heroism, for militancy against evil. The martial unit becomes the marital one. But the love relationship of a man and a woman needs to prove true in order to triumph, losing some battles along the way but ultimately winning the war. Pity cushions the falls of the Redcrosse Knight and Othello because, like the original fall of Adam and Eve, they fall tempted primarily by another, not themselves. So Milton's God in *Paradise Lost* will grant grace to humanity but not to fallen angels because the latter fell "self-tempted, self-depraved" while man "falls deceived / By the other first" (3.130–31).[13]

Unlike the Redcrosse Knight who is a warrior in the making, Othello enters his play as a tested and proven hero on the martial (not the marital) front, and he is more than a brave warrior like Hotspur (although both men at death are praised as being "great of heart") because his "patience" (4.2.54) has overcome on numerous occasions "the slings and arrows of outrageous fortune"

(*Hamlet* 3.1.57). His adventures have withstood adversity's assaults, and because of his "solid virtue" (4.1.266), because he is "so good" (5.2.288), he has been a "man / That is not passion's slave" (*Hamlet* 3.2.72) *until* he becomes "much changed" (4.1.268) when he faces the ultimate tempter and succumbs to his temptations to do evil, as does everyone else in the play, except Desdemona. Like the Redcrosse Knight, however, Othello values his soul. One of the deepest ironies, so often overlooked in the criticism on *Othello*, is how much this warrior values *spiritual* qualities, in particular "the worth of [his] eternal soul" (3.3.361). And indeed, one of the reasons Desdemona loves Othello so much is because of the perceived nobility of his "perfect soul" (1.2.31): "I saw Othello's visage in his mind, / And to his honours and his valiant parts / Did I my soul and fortunes consecrate" (1.3.253–55). This virtuous conception of himself is underscored by Othello's recurrent references to his soul, even valuing Desdemona as his "soul's joy" (2.1.182), and the language of "soul" and its variants is used more often by Othello than any other character in the play.[14] Othello should be praised because he values man's soul, but does he rightly "know" or "understand" his own soul? That knowledge of self and discovery of "truth" through "trothplight" is similar to what the Redcrosse Knight has to fight to learn.

Although they undergo no major falls, both Una and Desdemona also learn through adversity. Una learns not to trust too readily (1.7.38), benefits from Arthur's wisdom (1.7.40–42), and in the final canto rightly identifies the hypocrite Archimago, which she failed to do in canto 1, as the "falsest man alive," despite his assumed role now as a "craftie messenger" or a "false footman, clokt with simplenesse" (1.12.34). In the final act Desdemona learns what she denied as possible earlier, namely that "[her] noble Moor" is not so "true of mind" that he cannot fall to "such baseness / As jealous creatures" (3.4.26–28), even though she has in truth given him no cause. Both Spenser's and Shakespeare's paired protagonists try to fight the good fight in which trials test and refine their virtue. The women, forsaken yet faithful and forgiving, persevere. When their heroes fall, their men incorporate the vice to which they are tempted until they attempt to purge their sin through remorseful recognition. While Spenser's *The Faerie Queene* stresses the human inability to do good without divine grace, Shakespeare's *Othello* seems to allow more possibility for human agency to seek divine grace and to do good under adverse circumstances. That amazing agency he stunningly ascribes to a *woman* warrior.

II

I will begin somewhat perversely at the play's end with Desdemona's ending, but before commencing that consideration, the more obvious ways in which Desdemona might be seen as a woman warrior, prior to her death scene, should be indicated, especially in light of the critical trend to see Desdemona as too "passive" or, in Iago's words, "'too gentle'" (Honigmann 56–58). First, in keeping with the natural desire of a lover to partake of the beloved's identity, Desdemona sees herself in warrior terms for wanting to accompany her husband to the battlefield, and so she "may *trumpet* to the world" (1.3.249, my italics) her love to live with him. Because Othello and the Duke expected Desdemona to remain in Venice (1.3.236–41), the play treats her request as unusual and unexpected. The Duke says the matter should be settled "privately . . . / Either for her stay or going" (1.3.276–77), but Othello determines it publicly once the command for departure "tonight" (1.3.279) is given: he assigns Desdemona to Iago's escort in a separate ship (1.3.291). This contrasts with Cinthio's novelle, the main literary source, in which the wife Disdemona, needing no approval from the Venetian authorities, expects to accompany her husband to Cyprus—she "could hardly wait for the hour when . . . she would accompany him to that honourable post"— where the Venetian Signoria has made him the "Commandant of the soldiers whom they sent there," but where there is no threat of imminent war.[15] Cinthio's Moor, on the other hand, is concerned about the peril of the journey for his wife so that either he must cause her "this hardship" and himself "extreme anxiety" on her behalf, or he must leave her behind, which would be "hateful" to him because she represents his "very life" (Bullough 243). Shakespeare's Desdemona wants to brave the dangers of both journey and war, and her extraordinary speech about how and why she physically and spiritually loves Othello persuades him to change his mind and champion the request she directed to the duke's "prosperous ear" (1.3.245). To Othello's credit, he thinks he is being "free and bounteous to her mind" (1.3.266), which contrasts with her disappointed father's refusal to emulate that attitude in rejecting her apparent need for "accommodation" (1.3.239, 241) and in projecting his distrust of Desdemona onto Othello (1.3.293–94). In response, Othello wagers his "life upon her faith" (1.3.295), speaking more prophetically than he knows.

Once on Cyprus Desdemona not only fights on behalf of Cassio, but more importantly she fights for the right reason. Cinthio's Disdemona gives up pleading for the reinstatement of her husband's officer as soon as the Moor becomes angry with her: ". . . but rather than have you angry with me I shall never say another word on the subject" (Bullough 245). Shakespeare's Desdemona, however, retreats in order to reengage repeatedly (3.4, 4.1) despite her husband's temper: "As I have spoken for you [Cassio] all my best / And stood within the *blank* of his displeasure / For my free speech" (3.4.128–30, my italics). Realizing that as a wife who should be obedient to her lord she appears too "free," Desdemona's own generous nature, "framed as fruitful / As the free elements" (2.3.336–37), to do good—abetted by the intercessions of Cassio, Emilia, and Iago—motivates her. She pleads not for her own good but for Othello's own good that he reinstate a man who "truly loves" him (3.3.48), as she rightly interprets Cassio's friendship. Indeed, against the backdrop of racial prejudice that Shakespeare develops in the play, Cassio's true love for his friend and general, like Desdemona's true love for her husband, shines all the brighter. In pleading for Cassio, Desdemona wisely distinguishes between seeking a "boon" for herself, which this is not, and doing "a peculiar profit / To [his] own person" just as she would naturally entreat him to "feed on nourishing dishes, or keep [him] warm" (3.3.76, 78–80). Despite her careful explanation, Othello simply repeats, "I will deny *thee* nothing" (3.3.76, 83, my italics), revealing that "his soul" may be, as Iago believes, "so enfettered to her love," perhaps even enough "to renounce his baptism" (2.3.338–40). Yet he does not seem to understand truly his wife and her good reasoning even before Iago begins his direct assault. In a play permeated with rich structural patterns, Desdemona's "vow" of "friendship" (3.3.21) that opens this crucial scene is offset by Othello's "sacred vow" of "capable and wide revenge" (3.3.462–64) that closes it.

Although some find her "too reticent" in the brothel scene,[16] Desdemona—like Emilia before her—asks the sensible questions regarding "to whom" and "with whom" (4.2.41), adamantly proclaiming Othello does her "wrong" (4.2.81–86), but the general's accusation remains too general because he withholds the specific name of Cassio so that she, unlike Othello when on trial before the senate, cannot summon Cassio as the key witness on her behalf. Only moments before Othello executes her does Desdemona learn from her husband "the cause" of his jealousy. Now she realizes that Othello somehow has become deceived about the missing handkerchief and the true nature of her relationship with Cassio. Complementing her verbal battle to live (5.2.35–83), Desdemona physically fights to live as Othello's textual clue—"Nay, if you strive—" (5.2.80)—indicates. Her will to live is so strong that even the physically superior strength of Othello has to be exerted a second time to silence her: "I that am cruel am yet merciful, / I would not have thee linger in thy pain. / So. so" (5.2.86–88). Nor does Desdemona passively submit after appearing dead; instead, she revives to use, presumably in some pain, the only weapon barely left her—her voice—so that her woman's words "out-tongue" (1.2.19) man's deeds.

Like the final silencing of her voice, critical commentary on her final lines has been relatively muted. How important is it to see and hear Desdemona's revival and not have it cut, as is the case in the 1995 film "Othello," directed by Oliver Parker (starring Irene Jacob, Laurence Fishburne, and Kenneth Branagh) and in the recent adaptation of *Othello* for modern teens, directed by Tim Blake Nelson and titled "O"? Although there may be several ways to read Desdemona's final utterances when she momentarily revives to speak,[17] I would like to offer a reading that, to the best of my knowledge, has not been presented and that illuminates how the play and early modern audiences might have perceived Desdemona as a fair warrior far more readily than we moderns may. Scholarly editions of the play are curiously silent about the blatant contradiction between the revived Desdemona's first two utterances and her last two lines. When Desdemona recovers enough breath from Othello's suffocation of her, her first concern is not to pray but to clear her name, that is, to reaffirm her innocence of adultery to her lord while she properly defines his attempted ritual sacrifice as actual murder: "O falsely, falsely murdered!" (5.2.115). But during the time Desdemona has seemed dead or been unconscious, the situation in her bedroom has changed unbeknownst to her, changed from a private scene with only her husband present to a public one with Emilia's entrance. As Desdemona regains consciousness, her cry that she has been falsely murdered is probably intended for Othello's ears.

But Emilia is the one who responds to Desdemona's cry and opens the bedcurtains that Othello had drawn (5.2.103), begging her "sweet mistress" to "speak again" (5.2.119–20). Now, directly to Emilia, Desdemona asserts, "A guiltless death I die" (5.2.121). Emilia specifically inquires, "O, who hath done / This deed?" (5.2.122). Naming "who" would affix blame for the deed of being "falsely murdered." After her double admissions of honesty, Desdemona's answer does, and should, stun us: "Nobody. I myself. Farewell. / Commend me to my kind lord—O, farewell!" (5.2.122–23). How might this reply, which appears to be a lie and so Othello interprets it— "she's like a liar gone to burning hell" (5.2.127), cue us as to how an early modern audience might have seen her despite her gender, more readily than we do, as not only Othello's but indeed the play's "fair warrior"? Honigmann interprets Desdemona's final line as a "lie" in order to "protect" Othello (56), a lie that almost "sanctifies" her (58), and I concur. So does Othello *after* he becomes enlightened about the truth, changing his view of Desdemona from damned to saved as he simultaneously changes his view of himself from saved to damned: "When we shall meet at compt / This look of thine will hurl my soul from heaven / . . . Whip me, ye devils, / From the possession of this heavenly sight!" (5.2.270–76).

But how and why has Shakespeare scripted for his heroine such a remarkable ending when deathbed speeches are traditionally noted for their veracity? A brief review of possible sources helps to sharpen our awareness of Shakespeare's originality in crafting Desdemona's ending.[18] In Cinthio, there is no revival of the lady who is bludgeoned to death, although she does manage to pray for herself during her death throes: "The wretched Lady, hearing this and feeling herself near to death (for the Ensign had given her another blow), called on Divine Justice to witness to her fidelity, since earthly justice failed, and as she called on God to help her, a third blow struck her, and she lay still, slain by the impious Ensign" (Bullough 251). But two other possible sources—Bandello's Italian tale and Fenton's English translation of it—

present an innocent wife who appears dead but briefly revives to speak after her jealous husband, an Albanian captain, has stabbed her and then himself to death.[19] I suspect the differences between these two versions may suggest that Shakespeare was familiar with both. In Fenton's English translation of Belleforest's French translation of Bandello's original Italian story, the good wife "with great ado to speake" salvages some time to pray for herself and to request that her body be laid in the tomb of her first, good husband: " . . . the want of breath abridged her secret shryft and confession to God, with lesse leasure to yield her innocent soule (wyth humble praier) into the handes of her Redemer and *commende* the forgevenes of her synnes to the benefit of his mercie."[20] Several critics have argued that Shakespeare most likely used Fenton, especially at the end of his drama.[21] If Shakespeare knew Fenton, he might recall the verb "commend" for Desdemona's final line; although "commend" is a common enough word in Shakespeare, in this play he uses it only in this one instance. His Desdemona, however, had begged for time to pray, unlike Fenton's lady who did not know she was about to be slain. Despite Othello's initial good intention, he denies her time for even one prayer (5.2.82), although he knows she had already prayed before going to sleep (5.2.25).

Desdemona's, "O Lord! Lord! Lord!" (5.2.83) as Othello smothers her, a line that appears in the Quarto and not the Folio, sounds like a cry that is a prayer, unlike Emilia's repetition of calling "my lord" in the subsequent line in order to be admitted by Othello to the bedroom.[22] This prayerful repetition of "Lord" might recall for the audience the Lord's Prayer, which concludes with an emphasis on the human need for forgiveness—"And forgiue vs our dettes, as we also forgiue our detters" (Matt. 6:12). This call for mercy Desdemona has explicitly invoked moments earlier: "The Lord have mercy on me . . . / And have you mercy too" (5.2.57–58). But when Shakespeare's Desdemona revives, she does not pray for herself, as does Fenton's lady, but rather she asserts her innocence twice (once privately to Othello, once publicly to Emilia) before she literally lies about *who* "falsely murdered" her. Nor does she then commend herself to God but rather to Othello, her "kind lord." Does Desdemona's own awareness of her essential innocence, despite her former white lie about the handkerchief not being "lost" (3.4.85–90) and her present lie about the identity of her murderer, indicate that she knows she does not need to pray again at the hour of her death? Does her faith justify her belief in her own salvation because she honestly knows that she has fulfilled the primary commandment to love charitably?

Unlike Nathaniel Hawthorne's Hester who concludes in *The Scarlet Letter*, "But a lie is never good, even though death threaten on the other side,"[23] the less puritanical Shakespeare often allows for deception as a means to greater good, especially to do good lovingly for the welfare of another.[24] This is not surprising given his medium of drama because the make-believe art of theater uses lies or fictions to convey truths, whereas the real world's use of lies usually promotes falsehoods. Indeed, the etymology of "hypocrisy" tends to capture this tension in its meaning of "actor."[25] Likewise, Emilia's "theft" of Desdemona's handkerchief to please her husband Iago (5.2.227–29), as well as her deliberate silence about this impropriety despite her intuitions of Othello's jealousy (3.4.29, 100) and her firsthand witnessing of Othello's anger and Desdemona's distress about the missing handkerchief (3.4.51–107), do not deter Emilia's hope for salvation as she transfers her allegiance from her "pernicious" (5.2.151) husband to her "heavenly true" (5.2.133) mistress and tells the truth, and nothing but the truth: "So come my soul to bliss as I speak true!" (5.2.248). Genre, however, generally governs consequences, and while well-intentioned deceptions in comedy produce prosperous outcomes, similarly motivated deceptions in tragedy litter the stage with multiple deaths.

Bandello's original Italian version presents more to the matter, and I am inclined to agree more with Shaheen who suggests Shakespeare read Bandello in Italian than Honigmann who remains unconvinced.[26] Suggesting that if Bandello is not a source then at least an "interesting analogue" (205), Bullough provides the pertinent translation, noting that in Bandello the wife gets to make a confession to a priest, insists her husband is not to blame for her death, blames her death on her own misfortune, and asks to be buried in her first husband's tomb: "The wife, returning somewhat to consciousness, sent for one of the priests of Saint George, and made confession, pardoning her husband with all her heart, not willing to let anyone speak ill of him, and accusing *nobody* but her own misfortune" (261–62, my italics). I think the overlooked word "nobody" ("*nessuno*") seems deliberately echoed by Shakespeare in Desdemona's few and significantly chosen words, as she painfully draws her last breath.[27] Moreover, Bandello's wife disallows ill speaking of her husband, which is recalled in Desdemona's "Let nobody blame him, his scorn I approve" (4.3.51). This line, which develops Desdemona's attitude of forbearance a few lines earlier (4.3.17–18), gains significance as an addition to the willow song, and Desdemona self-consciously catches her own improvisation—"Nay, that's not next" (4.3.52).[28] Although Fenton's version omits the priest, the pardoning, and the wife's blaming her own misfortune, keeping only her personal prayer and burial request, in both Fenton's and Bandello's versions an emphasis is placed on how "unfortunat" (Fenton 188) is the unnamed lady in her "misfortune" (Bullough 262), which may recall for Shakespeare the meaning of Desdemona's name as "unfortunate," provided by Cinthio (Honigmann 386).

However, Shakespeare creates two strikingly original additions for Desdemona's last two lines: (1) the "lie"—Desdemona's assumption of blame for her own death in what amounts to an admission of suicide and no general scapegoating of fortune—"Nobody. I myself"; and (2) the nature of her fare-

well—"Commend me to my kind lord—O, farewell!" Given the tradition of
deathbed veracity, the magnitude of Shakespeare's innovative assignment of
tragic blame as a bold lie has not been critically considered. Desdemona's
"I myself" amounts to self-slander of self-slaughter, rendering her a suspect
suicide. By explicitly pinning the blame for her death on herself, Desdemona
is "undone" (5.2.75). She courageously sacrifices the loss of her good
name—"the immediate jewel" of her soul (3.3.159)—and gains the infamous
reputation of a suicide, who like Ophelia in *Hamlet* could expect maimed
burial rites or even burial at a crossroads with a stake in her heart.[29] Although
Desdemona lies about her death and never about her chastity, she dies knowing that she has tried but failed to convince Othello that she is no strumpet
so that not only does her lord think her a whore, but now the world will brand
her a suicide. Insult is added to injury.[30]

In this play so vitally concerned with "reputation" (a word repeated nine
times, excluding synonyms like "good name," "opinion," or "estimation"),
what man would so bravely and generously sacrifice the honor of his reputation? Othello, like Hamlet, expends some of his final breath in attempting to
clear the air about his wounded name and establish the truth as he sees it. As
Honigmann observes, Shakespeare probes many stereotypes in this play (56,
60–61), and here a woman sets an example of moral courage to which the
men can only aspire. If men, especially warriors, were supposed to die for
the honor of their reputations, how exceptional is Desdemona to lay down
the honor of her reputation to try to save Othello? Shakespeare crafts a fitting
exit for Desdemona. She deceived her father in order to marry Othello, and
now she deceives the world in order to love Othello ideally, especially from
an Erasmian perspective as I will explain later. She enters the play with an
act of deception (her adventuresome elopement out of honorable love for
Othello), and she exits the play with a verbal deception—the saving grace of
her lie out of "humble love" (3.3.461) for Othello that risks her own self-
abasement in the eyes of the world. Unlike Fenton's heroine who immediately earns "due fame . . . after her deathe, beinge worthelye invested wythe
the wreathes of honoure amonge all the ladies of that contreye" (191–92),
Desdemona risks that very fame, risks having "her name, that was as fresh /
As Dian's visage" now become "begrimed and black" (3.3.389–90).

Why lie? As mentioned earlier, Desdemona is probably trying to shield
Othello. From what? Several possibilities. She probably hopes to defend
Othello's physical life from the rigor of the law. Although some critics have
suggested that Venice would tolerate, even approve in some cases, a jealous
husband's taking of the law into his own hands and executing his wife suspected of adultery, this does not seem to be the expectation for Othello's case
in this play.[31] In the first place, Desdemona is innocent so Othello would not
be excused for taking an innocent life. Secondly, the Venetian authorities
who have arrived in Cyprus, along with the Cyprian governor Montano, voice

their disapproval. Ludovico is appalled that Othello slapped his wife in public (4.1.241–43, 272); Gratiano and Montano are stunned that Othello has murdered his wife (5.2.182–86, 204–07); and Gratiano cries shame upon Iago (who moments later brands his wife a "villainous whore") for drawing his sword upon his wife (5.2.222–27), even though Emilia rebels against Iago's commands to be silent and go home; and Montano pursues Iago as a "notorious villain" (5.2.237–41) for killing his wife and tempting Othello to kill his wife, not yet knowing Iago's role in the murder of Roderigo and the maiming of Cassio. Most importantly, Montano puts Gratiano in charge of guarding Othello, commanding that Othello be *killed* rather than allowed to escape (5.2.239–40), and once the full extent (although not the motive) of Iago's villainy is discovered, Ludovico continues to keep Othello a "close prisoner" for the Venetian state (5.2.333–35).

What might Othello's penalty be? More historical work needs to be done regarding the possible legal consequences, but given English law, an English audience would probably expect Othello to be judged guilty of the felony of murder, and he could receive the death penalty.[32] Under Venetian law, neither jealous rage nor injured honor would suffice to excuse Othello who would not have gone unpunished, and although the council would decide the precise penalty, the conviction of murder usually resulted in "either the serious mutilation of the criminal or his execution."[33] Because Desdemona now realizes that Othello has somehow been deceived about the true nature of her relationship to Cassio, she probably expects that if Othello's life is spared, he has more time to discover the truth and repent. Given Desdemona's faith in her husband's essentially noble nature, she would expect him to repent his "fall," which he does indeed once his error in judgment has been exposed to him. Therefore, her lie may also anticipate Othello's concern about damnation (5.2.65, 135–37) and attempt to preserve him for spiritual salvation.

The character most militant against slander ironically lies stifled on her deathbed after slandering herself with a lie that not only illuminates her magnanimity but also triggers ultimately the stifling of Iago's slanders through Othello's immediate truth-telling that in turn enables Emilia's unraveling of Iago's web of lies. With positively shocking irony, it is precisely Desdemona's lie that provokes Othello's self-confession of truth: " 'Twas I that killed her" (5.2.128). Othello's voluntary correction of Desdemona's lie with his admission of guilt deserves much credit, but is often overlooked to find "Othello's death speech serves as his confession" (Honingmann 74). Shakespeare seems obsessed with having the truth come to light, in contrast to Cinthio whose Moor never confesses. Not only do Roderigo's letters supply new evidence in the play's closing minutes, but like Desdemona, Roderigo revives after appearing dead and vocally tells the truth that exonerates Cassio. But *how* the truth begins to emerge is crucial. Had Othello's own love of honesty never exposed Desdemona's lie, Emilia would have been constrained to report Desdemona's lie as truth—"She said so; I must needs report the truth" (5.2.126). When Othello takes this first step of self-conviction, the pieces of the puzzle can begin to fall into place as Emilia rises to take down the culprits. Emilia's "iterance" of "my husband" (5.2.137, 142, 145) ironically parallels Iago's "iterance" of "honest" and "think" (3.3.104, 108) as Shakespeare uses this same speech strategy for *peripetia,* reversing now Iago's deception with Emilia's clarification. Her moral and physical heroism is inspired by that of her mistress, whose song she dies singing as she requests to be laid on the same bed by her side. Her request perhaps allies the two women in a positive parody of marriage that visually reverses and replaces the negative parody of marriage in the alliance of Othello and Iago who kneel together, Othello vowing revenge and Iago vowing obedience: "I am your own forever" (3.3.482).

It is easy to fault Desdemona for not being less naive like the more worldly wise Emilia. However, all of Emilia's sophisticated assets—her incisive intuitions about jealousy (3.4.29, 100), her awareness of her husband's waywardness (3.3.296) and accusation of adultery with Othello (4.2.149), her observations of Othello's changed behavior over the missing handkerchief (3.4.100), her knowledge that he now regards Desdemona as unchaste (4.2.12–19), and her instinct for smelling out villainy (4.2.132–35; 5.2.188–89)—do not suffice to enable Emilia to connect the dots and detect Iago as *the* villain: "I know thou didst not, thou'rt not such a villain" (5.2.170). Despite suspicions, no one sees through "honest" Iago until too late, and appropriately it is Iago's first victim, Roderigo, who first sees through the Ensign's false signs. Unlike the more "divine" (2.1.73) Desdemona, the more earthly Emilia approves the payback of revenge (4.3.91–01) and does not forgive (5.2.156–57) the "cruel Moor" (5.2.247), even though she witnesses, as Desdemona could only imagine, his agony of remorse upon realizing the truth. Desdemona can even pray for the villain abusing her husband's conception of her, "If any [villain] such there be, heaven pardon him" (4.2.137), whereas Emilia speaks for most of us mortals, "A halter pardon him, and hell gnaw his bones!" (4.2.138). Bemoaning "why should honour outlive honesty" (5.2.243), Othello decides to "let it go all" (5.2.244), but he ends up trying to salvage some of his honor (reputation) through his honesty (character) and how he interprets the truth about what he has done and why. Desdemona's paradoxical "dishonesty," on the other hand, is truly honorable in attempting to be honest ("kind") to Othello.

Let us now consider Desdemona's final line. When Desdemona seeks to save Othello with her dying breath, she purposefully ends with a goodwill wish that speaks volumes: "Commend me to my kind lord." Why "commend"? Why "kind"? As noted earlier, Shakespeare may be simply echoing Fenton's verb choice in his selection of "commend." But the fact that Desdemona's line is a death utterance might also recall for Shakespeare's audience the most biblically famous of all death utterances, namely Christ's "Father, into thy hands I *commend* my spirit" (Luke 23:46, my italics).[34] The gloss in the Geneva Bible refers the reader to Psalm 30.8 (misprinted as 6): "Then cryed I unto thee, o Lord, and prayed to my Lord." This psalm could remind one of Desdemona's prayerful cry—"Lord, Lord, Lord"—when Othello stifles her. The reiterated emphasis on Othello's intended "sacrifice" would linguistically signal a parallel between the sacrifice of innocent victims who die as scapegoats assuming others' guilt for salvific purposes.[35]

Why "my kind lord"? Other monosyllabic adjectives would have worked poetically, e.g., "good" or "dear." This is significantly the only time in the play when Desdemona explicitly addresses Othello as her "kind lord, " even though elsewhere the play's rhetoric of "kindness" (2.3.315) and "unkindness" (3.4.153, 4.1.225, 4.2.161–62) does get associated with Desdemona. The adverb "unkindly" in the play's very first line keynotes the opening mood as Roderigo complains against Iago: "Tush, never tell me, I take it much unkindly / That thou, Iago, who hast had my purse / As if the strings were thine, shouldst know of this" (1.1.1–3). Who knows what and when in this tragedy of epistemology and theology—of knowing and believing—a tragedy long valued for its powerful psychology? Othello's "dear heart strings" (3.3.265), like Roderigo's purse strings, will be untied maliciously by Iago. Yet Iago cannot unmoor "true hearts" (4.2.119) like Desdemona's because, among its many virtuous attributes, love truly defined is kind (1 Cor. 13:4–7). The language of kindness is crucial in the play (and as we will discover in Erasmus); "kindness" as a word was richer then than now, having the meanings of "naturalness" as well as "benevolence." In fact, Othello has been unkind in both senses. Othello could have condemned her supposed adultery but forgiven the adulterer. Othello has at least one nonlethal option, and he knows it. He initially thinks of divorce: "If I do prove her haggard, / . . . I'd whistle her off and let her down the wind / To prey at fortune" (3.3.264–67). Likewise, when she discovers he intends to kill her, Desdemona begs, "O, banish me, my lord, but kill me not!" (5.2.77). Earlier even Iago anticipated this possibility: "[Brabantio] will divorce you" (1.2.14). However, Othello spirals downward to murder with Iago's pestilent persistence as Iago follows his own advice to "plague him with flies" (1.3.70). Unlike Desdemona, why does Othello fail to consider the option of forgiveness for either her or himself? No longer suborning the witness as the "unhandsome warrior" she had envisioned herself as in act 3, Desdemona now admits Othello's life-threatening "unkindness" (4.2.161–62) as she recognizes that his "soul" may not be as "perfect" (1.2.31) as either of them had thought.

Although both spouses need to grow in wisdom, they do recognize the existence of evil. Desdemona distinguishes between those who err in "ignorance" as opposed to those who err in "cunning" (3.3.48–51), and Othello knows "the tricks of custom" adopted by "a false disloyal knave" (3.3.121–27). But they, like everyone else in the play, cannot be expected to detect Iago's hypocrisy, "the only evil that walks Invisible, except to God,"[36] until the hypocrite slips up and tips his hand. They also deserve credit for how genuinely they value the human soul. Despite Othello's change for the worse, or as Emilia puts it, "Here's a change indeed!" (4.2.108), Desdemona maintains her undying love so that she appears to love him more knowingly now than she did earlier. When Othello makes his intent of killing known to her, Desdemona correctly instructs him about the unkindness of such mistaken behavior that punishes "loves" as "sins" (5.2.40): "That death's unnatural that kills for loving" (5.2.42). However, in publicly identifying him to Emilia as her "kind" lord, she shows she has forgiven his unnaturalness and hurtfulness, and she does so not naively, but *knowingly*. Bandello's heroine closes with an explicit articulation of forgiveness. Shakespeare grants his heroine less breath and less time, preferring to indicate directions by indirections, characteristically leaving more open to his audience's fertile imagination. Like Prospero, whose rejection of magic demonstrates self-mastery in recognizing the superiority of the power of virtue over the virtue of power, Desdemona, whose rejection of revenge demonstrates knowledgeable forgiveness, understands that "the rarer action is / In virtue than vengeance" (*The Tempest* 5.1.27–28). Desdemona sets the example of Christian kindness for Othello regarding how to avoid hate, whether of self or other, in love that is both giving and forgiving. In so doing, she upholds Erasmus's conception of the woman warrior.

III

An especially fruitful, yet neglected, context for understanding Shakespeare's construction of Desdemona as a woman warrior, who is both "fair" and "unhandsome" in the play's two references to her as a "warrior," is Erasmus's *Enchiridion Militis Christiani*, that is, *The Handbook of the Christian Soldier* (first published in February 1503 by Martens). Erasmus told Thomas More that this book became "'universally welcome'"; he described it to John Colet as "'a method of morals'" (for matters of religion "'that have to do with true goodness'") and to Maarten van Dorp as "'the pattern of a Christian life.'"[37] Although the metaphor of the "Christian soldier" is as old as the New Testament, receiving its first expression from Paul,[38] Erasmus pointedly gives it fuller meaning in his own treatment of the spiritual warfare against the allurements of vice that should be the life of the Christian. Earlier, medieval drama presented such warfare in the *psychomachias* of the morality plays that staged the conflict necessary to drama either between humans and supernatural powers or within human nature as strife between body and soul.

Erasmus, however, self-consciously affirms that his *Enchiridion* presents the reader with "the method and rules of a new kind of warfare" (126).

In his version of our spiritual combat, Erasmus specifically redeems Eve, allegorically our "carnal passions" (48), through the marriage trope and the figure of the obedient wife as a heroic female warrior:

> Paul wishes the woman to be subject to her husband. . . . The carnal passions are our Eve [Sir 42:14], whose glance the clever serpent attracts daily. . . . But what do you read about the new woman, the one who is obedient to her husband? "I shall create enmity between you" (obviously the serpent) "and the woman, and between your seed and her seed. She will crush your head, and you will strike insidiously at her heel." [Gen.3.15] . . . The serpent has been thrown down on his belly . . . All he can do is lie in wait to strike blows at her heel from ambush. But by the power of faith the woman has been turned into a female warrior and with great heroism crushes his poisonous head. Grace has been increased; the tyranny of the flesh has been diminished. (48)[39]

If Shakespeare had Erasmus's description of the Fall in mind, he would find here both the old nature of woman as corrupted temptress and the new nature of woman as heroic warrior. Shakespeare captures this contrast by combining two characters in Cinthio to create the single character of Bianca (Bullough 249) so that she embodies onstage the idea of woman as "whore" (carnal passions). While Bianca is no spouse, despite her desire for Cassio as a husband (4.1.128–30), she can be seen as a type of "enfleshed" Eve. Nonetheless, Bianca joins Desdemona and Emilia in demonstrating female bravery when she immediately withstands, far better than the male Roderigo has done, Iago's best attempt to intimidate her: "[Cassio] supped at my house, but I therefore shake not" (5.1.119). Moreover, Shakespeare would also find two notable elements that suit his play but that do not do not appear in Genesis 3.15, the biblical text to which Erasmus refers.[40] Erasmus's serpent needs "ambush" in order to strike "insidiously," and likewise Iago, called a "viper" (5.2.282) though but a man, uses the mask of honesty as his ambush for insidious attacks. The "poisonous head" of the serpent complements Iago's deliberate use of verbal "poison" (3.3.325) to strike at the Achilles' heel of the newlyweds so that the play ends with a scene that "poisons sight" (5.2.364).[41] Desdemona is the only one of Iago's intended victims that he cannot corrupt but can only make to *appear* corrupt. She may lose the earthly battle for physical life, but more importantly she wins the eternal war for spiritual salvation. Emilia who rebelliously but justifiably transfers her allegiance from Iago to Desdemona in act 5 becomes the disobedient wife whose heroic championing of the obedient wife ironically contributes to Iago's downfall.[42] But what I wish to emphasize here is not so much detailed as *general* applicability of Erasmus's version of the Fall and his significant and surprising depiction of the *woman* of faith as the heroic *warrior* over evil.

The *Enchiridion* might also shed light on Desdemona's surprising self-description as "unhandsome warrior" (3.4.152). Shakespeare uses the adjective "unhandsome" only 3 other times in his canon, twice in the usual sense of "unattractive" (*Much Ado about Nothing*, 1.1.175; 1H4, 1.3.44) and once in the sense of "unfitting" (*As You Like It*, Epilogue 2P). In his careful note on "unhandsome" (250), Honigmann presents the possible meanings of "unhandsome," primarily as "unskilful" (noting that this is the first and only such instance cited in the *OED*), and secondarily as "unseemly, discourteous" and "unsoldierly" (noting that the first citation for "handsome" as "soldierly" is 1665). Because the etymological meaning of Desdemona's name is "unfortunate," as noted earlier, I would suggest that perhaps Shakespeare is also playing on the meaning of "unhandsome" as "unfortunate, unhappy" (*OED* 5), although the first instance cited is 1633. But I think it is the soldierly sense that a literal translation of Erasmus's Latin title conveys best. As Fantazzi observes, the first English translation, published by Wynkyn de Worde in 1533, was followed by a thoroughly revised edition in 1534, which translated the Latin original more literally and rendered the title: "'The hansome [ie ready to hand] weapon of a christen knyght'" (6). One meaning of "unhandsome" is "unhandy, inconvenient, ill-adapted" (*OED* 2) which complements the meaning of "inexpert, unskilful" thought to be the primary sense of Desdemona's term. As Fantazzi explains, the Greek word *enchiridion* has both the meanings of "'dagger'" and "'handbook'" that Erasmus earlier used in a letter to Jacob de Voecht to play on Menander's saying that "'virtue is mortal man's mightiest weapon'" and that a few years later he used again to entitle this treatise "to exploit its double-edged connotation, although in the context of the military metaphor the more concrete sense must have been uppermost in his mind" (2).

Erasmus cleverly took pains to create a handy handbook or weapon to be used for virtue and against vice by all Christian warriors. Desdemona, therefore, recalls Othello's description of her as his "fair warrior" when she finds herself unfair or unhandsome, not in the sense of physical but rather spiritual beauty, because she lets down her guard against imperfect charity and unskillfully wounds herself when she sought to wound Othello: "Beshrew me much, Emilia, / I was, unhandsome warrior as I am, / Arraigning his unkindness with my soul, / But now I find I had suborned the witness / And he's indicted falsely" (3.4.151–55). Throughout his treatise Erasmus emphasizes the heart of Christian *pietas* as the new law of love, as "kindness" (11, 97), as pure or perfect "charity" (94, 97), as "forgiveness" (123–25) so that when we err, we should try to err on the side of love (13–15, 19, 123–24).

Given Erasmus's rich wordplay on handiness, skill, dagger, and handbook for his *Enchiridion*, it should not catch us so much by surprise, as it might otherwise, to find Iago sneers at Othello for his lack of bookish knowledge as an appropriate self-defense regarding the vice of jealousy: "As [Cassio] shall smile, Othello shall go mad. / And his unbookish jealousy must construe / Poor Cassio's smiles, gestures and light behaviour / Quite in the wrong" (4.1.101–04).[43] Had Othello been fully armed with Erasmus's handbook as his dagger, as it can be argued his wife as the Erasmian fair warrior truly is, he might not have found his own dagger so ready to hand. Othello has already been doubly disarmed, once by Montano (5.2.238) and once by himself (5.2.268–69), but both times the weapons are significantly swords: (1) swords as stage props help to signify Othello's identity as a Christian Moor, unlike the scimitars that Honigmann notes are assigned to Moors in other plays (323); and (2) these two swords have personal meaning for Othello: the one Montano takes appears to be the sword he wears daily (its confiscation makes Othello see himself as no longer valiant), and the other seems to be a trophy sword that represents his glorious past victories, one that he initially flaunts but then permanently retires. Regarding the removal of his first sword Othello bemoans how "every puny whipster gets my sword" (5.2.242), and Ross glosses "puny" as "skilless," thinking "*puny* has the force of 'puisny' in *As You Like It* III.iv.39—'having but the skill of a novice'" (Ross 238). No one suspects Othello has another weapon (5.2.358), but the ever resourceful soldier produces a hidden dagger when he (self-divided in fighting simultaneously for and against himself) decides to kill himself as paradoxically both the Turk and the Christian Moor.[44]

Erasmus's *Enchiridion* also presents both a literal and figurative use of the Turkish threat that is not found at all in Shakespeare's main literary source, Cinthio, although one literal allusion to a past fifteenth-century Turkish siege appears in Fenton (165). Likewise, Shakespeare's use of contemporary historical sources regarding the Turkish-Venetian wars in the sixteenth-century and his awareness of James I's poem on the Battle of Lepanto (Bullough 212–14) reflect a literal or factual representation of the Turks, but these sources tend not to emphasize a symbolic reading of the Turks.[45] In his preface Erasmus lays the groundwork for how he will use the Turk in his text, beginning with the historically literal to emphasize later the spiritually figurative significance, an organizational structure that Shakespeare reflects in his play because he begins with a strongly literal use of the Turks but shifts increasingly toward a figurative emphasis on "the Turk" as a symbol of evil that threatens not just Christendom but every Christian as the danger within us all, according to Erasmus: "this is . . . a war with oneself, and the enemy battle line springs unbidden from our own entrails . . ." (40–41; cf. 83).[46] Both Cinthio's and Fenton's (Bandello's) stories of a jealous soldier's murder of his innocent wife occur in times of peace. Shakespeare adds the emphasis on literal war between the Turks and the Venetians over the island of Cyprus. If "what's past is prologue" (*The Tempest* 2.1.253), Erasmus, in language that hauntingly recalls somewhat the 2003 international crisis over the war in Iraq, agonizes over the current (1518) Christian preparation for war against the Turks, worrying about the image and message Christians represent if they don't live up to their *true* ideals, should they physically triumph in literal battle but spiritually fail to convert their enemies to those ideals by living a good example of "a pure and simple life" (10).[47] Erasmus even contemplates staging first a paper war of "pamphlets" to win the minds and hearts of the Turks.[48]

Shakespeare, however, has his Turks take the offensive and, like Iago, use "a pageant / To keep us in false gaze" (1.3.19–20), but he avoids actual bloodshed by creating a tempest that destroys the external threat of the Turks while he allows the internal threat of the Turk—both in the person of Iago and the potential for darkness within each person—to breed on Cyprus. Hence, the curiously brief scene (3.2) of Othello's inspection of his outer fortifications ironically precedes Iago's attack on Othello's inner fortifications that he has not inspected sufficiently. So also in *Hamlet* Shakespeare shifted the threat from outside (Fortinbras) to inside (Claudius) the realm. Once Iago's engineered chaos begins on Cyprus, Othello remonstrates: "Are we turned Turks? and to ourselves do that / Which heaven hath forbid the Ottomites? / For Christian shame, put by this barbarous brawl" (2.3.166–68). Othello's metaphor of Christians shamefully "turning Turk" reflects the same idea of erroneous conversion that Erasmus articulates when he explains that "we shall degenerate into Turks long before we convert the Turks to our way of thinking" if Christian militants do not promote the flowering of "religion and charity and peace and innocence" (11).

The jewel of Erasmus's metaphorical uses of the Turk, who is the enemy of the Christian soldier, is a passage that relates most poignantly to both Desdemona's and Othello's final speeches, and the following context for that passage is very important. In his articulation of the "beliefs worthy of a Christian," Erasmus begins by emphasizing that we live not for ourselves, but for God, and charity is the rule: "Christian charity knows no exclusivity. Let him love the pious in Christ and the impious for the sake of Christ, who so loved us first when we were still his enemies that he expended himself wholly for our ransom [Rom. 5.10]. Let the Christian, therefore, embrace the former because they are good, and the latter as well so that he may render them good" (93–94). In his concrete example that Christian charity embraces all humans, regardless of race or nation, Erasmus explains: "It is not fitting for a Christian to entertain thoughts like this: 'What have I to do with this fellow? I don't know whether he is black or white [Catullus 3.2]. He is unknown to me, a total stranger. . . . he offended me once . . .' None of this! Recall only for what merit of yours Christ bestowed all his gifts. It was his wish that the *kindness* he conferred upon you would be reciprocated not to himself, but to your neighbor" (94, my italics). These beliefs, then, frame the following passage on the Turk that pertains to *Othello* because Desdemona embodies them—she who has loved faithfully a black man, a stranger to her native city, a misled murderer, she whose romantic love manifests pure charity in returning kindness for "unkindness" (4.2.161–62) that defeats her life but never taints her love:

> [The Christian] should not hate any man at all in so far as he is a man, any more than a devoted doctor hates a sick man. Let him be the enemy only of vice. The graver the illness, the greater the care pure charity will administer. He is an adulterer, a sacrilegious person, a Turk; one should abhor the adultery, not the man; show one's aversion for the sacrilege, not the man, kill the Turk, not the man. He should make every effort that the impious man that the other has made of himself should perish, but that the man that God made should be saved. (94)

Over two decades ago I tried to study the importance of this passage for Othello's final speech in arguing for the Folio's "the base Judean" reading over the Quarto's "the base Indian," but I overlooked its significance then for Desdemona.[49] I would like to revisit briefly this difficult textual crux as well as suggest another possible reading in light of Desdemona as woman warrior. As I demonstrated in the earlier article, there is no philological evidence to show that "base" could mean "ignorant," either in Shakespeare's era or ours.[50] However, the interpretation of "base" as "ignorant" continues to prevail in criticism devoted to this textual crux. For example, Richard Levin glosses "base" as meaning "ignorant" if it modifies Indian, which is the reading he prefers.[51] M. R. Ridley emphasizes the aptness of the "Indian" reading on grounds of the Indian's "ignorance" because "'they know not the value of their own commodity.'"[52] Reading "the base Indian" in light of the contemporary stories about Indians who threw away jewels because they did not know the gems had any value whatsoever tends to predispose scholarly editors to interpret "base" as meaning "ignorant" even when that is not the specific gloss supplied by them. For example, Norman Sanders glosses "base" as meaning "'low in natural rank or in the scale of creation'" or as meaning "'deep-coloured, dark,'" but he concludes by finding that among other flaws "Othello is lamenting his ignorance."[53] Honingmann glosses "base" as "lowly" if it modifies "Indian" but "depraved, despicable" if it modifies "Judean" (330), but he too concludes that "the ignorance of Indians, unaware of the value of their gold and precious stones" defines Othello's action as similarly resulting from "ignorance" (342). Summarizing the arguments for and against "Judean" and the arguments for "Indian," Honingmann adopts the "Indian" reading and supports Levin's argument as the "best analysis" of this crux because it ends with a telling point: "It is appropriate for Othello to compare himself with the Indian, whose action results from ignorance, and 'very inappropriate for him to compare himself to Judas, whose action was regarded as a conscious choice of evil'" (342–43). While Othello may be "ignorant" in the sense of "stupid" or "foolish"—"O gull, O dolt, / As ignorant as dirt" (5.2.161)—he is not totally ignorant of the value of what he threw away, which is the sense of absolute "unknowing" that the "Indian" reading necessitates, but rather he believes Desdemona has betrayed or cheapened her original value so that he "will kill [her] / And love [her] after" (5.2.18–19).[54] Shakespeare's texts (Quarto and Folio), however, present the word "base," not "ignorant."

In addition to the inaccuracy of interpreting "base" as "ignorant," there is another problem that confronts us here. Whose Judas do we have in mind? We may think of Judas's choice as a deliberate or conscious choice of evil, but this overlooks the biblical presentation of Judas, especially in the gospels of Luke and John, as having been tempted, as having been corrupted from outside influence, like Othello: "the devil had now *put in the heart* of Judas Iscariot . . . to betray him [Jesus]" (John 13:2, my italics). But unlike Othello, Judas encounters the devil himself and not a "demi-devil" (5.2.298) human: "Then entred Satan into Judas" (Luke 22:3); "And after the soppe, Satan entred into him" (John 13:27). Once deceived by the tempter and fallen to temptation, both Othello and Judas can be seen as having "changed" ("change" being a major theme in Shakespeare's play) because evil does "gnaw [their] inwards" (2.1.295) as they ingest the temptation fed them and respond to its poison. Thus Othello incorporates Iago's view that women are hypocrites (2.1.109–13) so that now he can "see" Desdemona as only seeming pure when she is really foul. Desdemona verbally refutes Iago as a "slanderer," but Iago parries, "Nay, it is true, or else I am a Turk" (2.1.113–14), which figuratively he is. Desdemona's life and death, however, offer the best rebuttal to Iago's slandering of good women.

But to return to "base." "Base" modifying "Indian" can mean "deep-coloured" or "lowly," and it might be argued, as it has not been, that both meanings could also possibly modify "Judean" if "Judean" refers to "Judas" because from an English or Venetian perspective Judeans would be considered darker in skin color and Judas has humble origins. If "Judean" refers to Herod, who jealously killed his good wife Mariamne, then "base" as "lowly" could not be applied since Herod was a king. But do the senses of "lowly" or "deep-coloured" really suit the context of Shakespeare's simile that is meant to describe Othello as he now sees himself? Othello does not see himself as "lowly," but of "royal siege" (1.2.22). Moreover, Ludovico recognizes Othello as a wealthy figure or he would not be concerned enough to order Gratiano to "seize upon the fortunes of the Moor / For they succeed to [him]" (5.2.364–65). Sanders's "deep-coloured" seems to have more merit because darker skin color is characteristic of Othello, Indians, and Judeans.[55] If this is the literal meaning Shakespeare intended for "base," then I would suggest perhaps there is wordplay to suggest the "darkness" of the deed done by the dark-skinned man, as Shakespeare does, for example, in Emilia's "racist" condemnations of Othello as Desemona's "most filthy bargain" (5.2.153) or "as ignorant as dirt" (5.2.160). However, this reading seems to invert priorities because the primary emphasis in Othello's simile is not on what is "external" to the man and over which he has little choice (skin color or natural/social birthright), but rather what is more "internal" and over which he has more choice: what he has done and why. What is at stake here is the nature of the deed done and how that deed reflects the doer's perceived identity of self and how he wants others to see him for the record.

Rhetoric might shed some light on these tough issues. Shakespeare's rhetorical strategy of *anaphora* (repetition) should be carefully considered regarding how it works and stylistically contextualizes meaning.[56] Othello insists, "Speak of me as I am," and if so, "then must you speak" (5.2.340) of one whom he describes in four successive, and I would suggest, *related* phrases that comprise one grammatical sentence in verse, each beginning with the phrase "of one" and each conjoined by colons in the Folio's punctuation as part of one sentence that arrives at a final period when the comparisons end in line 349. Shakespeare's figure of speech presents four different expressions that are connected by an introductory repetitive phrase and one governing idea, namely the description of one who *erred* and who now *realizes* that error. Therefore, Othello can describe himself *now* as one "that loved not wisely, but too well"; as one "not easily jealous" but once provoked capable of extreme distraction; as one whose hand "threw a pearl away / Richer than all his tribe" (the gem specifically recognized as a pearl and not just any pearl, but one of inestimable value); and finally, as one who does not easily weep, any more than he was one to be easily jealous, but who now weeps profusely in grief-stricken awareness of what he has done. Given the paralleled rhetorical structuring of Othello's self-conscious descriptions, the idea of "ignorance" as "destitute of knowledge" (*OED* 1) does not seem to suit this context any more than "ignorant" can be used to define "base," according to the *Oxford English Dictionary*. Unlike a Judas, a Herod, or an Othello, an "ignorant" Indian cannot judge and bewail his own action if he accords no significance or value to what he has done. Nor do we tend to feel tragic pity for a person who is indifferent to what he has done, who does not suffer *anagnorisis* as a result of his *hamartia* because ignorance is bliss: "He that is robbed, not wanting what is stolen, / Let him not know't, and he's not robbed at all" (345–46). The "Judean" reading, whether taken to refer to Judas or Herod, disturbs sensibilities because such a reading seems to preclude the response of "pity," or as Levin indicates, the Judean (Judas) reading treats Othello's killing of Desdemona "allegorically" as "meriting eternal damnation" whereas the Indian reading allows us to view Othello's murder "in literal terms as a tragic error committed by a particular man worked upon by a particular set of circumstances who merits some pity" (36). Need it be so starkly "either/or"?

Enter Desdemona, woman warrior. As I have tried to indicate throughout this essay, I do think Othello elicits pity, and in fact, I think Shakespeare deliberately cultivates our pity for Othello. Shakespeare assaults our senses with Othello's agony; our ears hear his moans and his anguished eloquence, and our eyes watch Othello's "subdued eyes" (5.2.346) rain tears, a sight rare to see for a military general of Othello's stature, whether onstage or in public life. Not to pity Othello would be not to pity ourselves, that is, not to pity anyone who falls to temptation. As mere mortals we are all sinners and err to varying degrees and for various reasons. Ross makes this idea even more explicit by not allowing us to demonize even Judas as dismissively "the other": ". . . every mortal sinner could be regarded analogically 'as' a Judas and Judean ('they crucify unto themselves the son of God afresh' Hebrews 6:6)" (246). Desdemona responds with charitable wisdom to Emilia's understandable argument in favor of "revenge" (4.3.92): "God me such usage send / Not to pick bad from bad, but by bad mend!" (4.3.103–4). That response foreshadows her ultimate act of what Erasmus defines as "perfect charity" for a Christian warrior when one imitates Christ by overcoming evil with good (cf. Rom. 12:21): "Perfection is reached when, having indignation only against vice, you replace insult with an act of charity. . . . Not to be angry at all is to be most like God and therefore most beautiful" (126). Desdemona, therefore, proves herself to be the play's "fair warrior" in the "new kind of warfare" (126) Erasmus describes so that one might arm oneself against "the vices of detraction, obscenity, jealousy," vices being "the sole enemies of the Christian soldier" (126).[57]

Therefore, I suggest that Shakespeare may cultivate our pity for Othello *especially* through Desdemona's final response as an Erasmian woman warrior. Othello sees himself now as damned. But he earlier saw Desdemona as unchaste and was proven wrong. Othello mistakenly envisions Desdemona's "look" as that which "will hurl his soul from heaven" (5.2.272), but her "look" has already been contradicted by her voice because her dying words spoke for him in forgiveness, not against him. Desdemona wisely cautions that "we must think men are not gods" (3.4.149). Nor are women. No matter how greatly good Desdemona is, Shakespeare remarkably succeeds in making her human with recognizable fears, desires, and deceptions, or as Marvin Rosenberg states: "It seems to me as dangerous to rob Desdemona of her human frailty as it is to steal her essential goodness from her. . . . But we care intensely for this young, passionate woman who ran away secretly from her father's house to the arms of her lover, who has a healthy desire to be with her husband on her wedding night, who cries when she is struck, and who fears death terribly."[58] However, if she in her mortality can forgive Othello, does Shakespeare also invite us to ponder what God can do whose greater love far surpasses the pale reflections that even the best of humankind can mirror? The inebriated Cassio claims, "Well, God's above all, and there be souls must be saved, and there be souls must not be saved" (2.3.98–100). Fortunately for us fallible folk, that ultimate judgment rests not with us but with an infallible God whose perfection of both justice and mercy challenge human comprehension. Athough Ludovico voices dismay for the ending of Othello's peroration, "O bloody period!" and Gratiano objects, "All that's spoke is marred" (5.2.355), Shakespeare's play leaves us with thought-provoking possibilities and avoids the kind of definitive judgment found at the end of Marlowe's *Dr. Faustus* with the despairing protagonist dismembered and dragged down to hell.

Given the insistence on jealousy as a "base" passion (3.4.27–28) and given Erasmus's association of this weakness especially with women,[59] Shakespeare's use of jealousy in connection with Desdemona should also surprise us. In a play more than any other in Shakespeare's canon that explores negative jealousy, Desdemona refreshingly exemplifies positive jealousy in the biblical sense of "godly gealous," that is, jealousy in the sense of being "zealous . . . for the well-being of something possessed or esteemed" (*OED* 3). Whether Desdemona tries to be kind to her father by not provoking impatient thoughts (1.3.242–43), speaks up publicly on behalf of Emilia (2.1.102, 162–63), befriends Cassio (3.3.21), or prays for villains (4.2.137), she evinces a positive jealousy that Iago ironically apes in presenting the quality of his "love" for Othello—"oft of my jealousy / Shape faults that are not" (3.3.150–55). Given the tragic trajectory of evil coming out of good, Desdemona's good jealousy on behalf of Othello ironically provides the "ocular proof" (3.3.363) he demands. After being exposed to Iago's germ of jealousy, Othello struggles to "not believe't" (3.3.283), and Desdemona, noting Othello's uncharacteristically faint speech, inquires about his health. He complains of a headache, and Desdemona immediately seeks to heal him by binding his head with the handkerchief that he then brushes aside as insufficient or "too little" (3.3.291) so that Desdemona drops it. Both are so preoccupied—he with negatively jealous thoughts, she with positively jealous concern—that neither observes what happens to the "fallen" handkerchief that Emilia picks up to please Iago's "fantasy" (3.3.303).

In the next scene Othello asks for her handkerchief because he feigns a specific illness that indicates to Shakespeare's audience, as it does not to us, the psychological change Othello is undergoing in his fall to false jealousy. James Winny explains that Othello's complaint, "I have a salt and sullen rheum offends me" (3.4.52), warns that "Othello's habitually phlegmatic nature" that is "temperamentally cold despite his torrid background" and makes him "a man most unlikely to commit crimes of passion" is about to undergo a dangerously passionate change to choler because in humoral theory, as explained in Timothy Bright's treatise on melancholy that Shakespeare used for *Hamlet*, "a salt phlegm" changes a phlegmatic temperament: "'*then approacheth it to the nature of choler, and in like sort thereof riseth anger and frowardness.*'"[60] Winny also observes that in addition to seeing the storm (2.1) "as a symbol of disorder" in general, Bright clarifies how this storm imagery, common to "sixteenth-century treatises of the passions," has "pointed relevance" for Othello's later tempestuous rage given the Elizabethan belief in the "sympathetic link" between human nature and Nature: "'*those domestic storms that arise more troublesome and boisterous to our nature than all the blustering winds in the ocean sea*'" (15). Desdemona could tame Nature's storm: "Tempests themselves, high seas, and howling winds / . . . As having sense of beauty, do omit / Their mortal natures, letting go safely by / The divine Desdemona" (2.1.63–73). But her husband's jealous tempest did not let her body go safely by, although he could not drown her godly jealous love.

Shakespeare's praise for the nobility of an honorable woman, like the Christian soldier Desdemona, would not be lost on Shakespeare's audience, especially the female patrons who comprised a significant portion,[61] Honigmann observes that Desdemona may "seem passive" once her "self-confidence is checked" by Othello's rejection of her "handkerchief" in the third scene of act 3, and I agree with him that "it would be kinder to describe her as bewildered, out of her depth, not as defeated" (43). However, I would disagree that she "suppresses [her impulsiveness] and thus denies her own nature, almost becoming another person in the last two acts" (48), because that view of her "impulsiveness" does not do justice to Desdemona's charitable courage in sacrificing her reputation or "honor" as a self-proclaimed suicide in order to save Othello. Honigmann, however, astutely appreciates the "moral strength" of Desdemona's "'sweet soul'" (56–57), and my exploration of her heroism as a woman warrior hopefully supplements his awareness of the Christian view of heroism articulated by Milton when he finds "'the better fortitude / Of patience'" to be "'not less but more heroic than the wrath / Of stern Achilles'" (56). From the perspective of some in Shakespeare's audiences, Desdemona, as Emilia's human "angel" (5.2.128) but no modern "kickass" Charlie's angel, may well deserve a medal of honor for courage under fire on the moral battlefield.

Notes

1. All citations from Shakespeare's works, except *Othello*, are to *The Riverside Shakespeare*, ed. G. Blakemore Evans, 2nd ed. (Boston and New York: Houghton Mifflin, 1997).

2. All citations from *Othello* are to *Othello*, ed. E. A. J. Honigmann, 3rd Arden (Walton-on-Thames, Surrey: Thomas Nelson & Sons Ltd., 1997).

3. See J. Leeds Barroll, *Artificial Persons: The Formation of Character in the Tragedies of Shakespeare* (Columbia: University of South Carolina Press, 1974), 183.

4. See Charles Tyler Prouty, "Some Observations on Shakespeare's Sources," *Shakespeare Jahrbuch* 96 (1960), 64–77.

5. Unless specified otherwise, all biblical citations are to *The Geneva Bible (a facsimile of the 1560 edition)*, intro. Lloyd E. Berry (Madison: University of Wisconsin Press, 1969).

6. See Edith Hamilton, *Mythology* (Boston: Little, Brown and Co., 1949), 45. In Ovid's story Pygmalion was a sculptor on Cyprus, and once Venus transformed his statue into a woman, Pygmalion and Galatea had a son named Paphos who "gave his name to Venus' favorite city" (145–50).

7. All citations from Spenser are to *The Faerie Queene*, ed. Thomas P. Roche, Jr. (Harmondsworth: Penguin, 1978).

8. See, e.g., Geoffrey Bullough, ed., *The Narrative and Dramatic Sources of Shakespeare* (London: Routledge and Kegan Paul; New York: Columbia University Press, 1973), 7:209–10.

9. The white King of Sicilia, Leontes, in Shakespeare's *The Winter's Tale* also falls to false jealousy much more rapidly than Othello does, and unlike Othello, Leontes also falls tempted by himself and not by another like Iago.

10. For the symbolic significance of Othello's suicide weapon, see Lawrence J. Ross, ed., *The Tragedy of Othello the Moor of Venice* (Indianapolis and New York: Bobbs-Merrill, 1974), 248 n. 352. In his book 1 Spenser presents Wrath with a dagger (1.4.33.8).

11. In a forthcoming essay I will examine this matter of influence.

12. In her newspaper feature article, Showalter quotes Lance Morrow as referring to O. J. Simpson as a "'Santa Monica Othello,'" and she suggests that "for many women, the case was another drama of female powerlessness, with Nicole the innocent Desdemona." See Elaine Showalter, "Othello of Santa Monica," *The Guardian*, 4 October 1995, T4. Cf. also, Anthony Hecht's interesting comparison of "uncanny" parallels between Simpson's letter (read by his friend Robert Kardashian) and Othello's final speech in Hecht's letter to the editor, *The Washington Post*, 4 July 1994, A18. Cf. also, Faith Nostbakken, *Understanding Othello: A Student Casebook to Issues, Sources, and Historical Documents* (Westport, CT and London: Greenwood Press, 2000), "Contemporary Applications," 171–85.

13. See John Milton, *Paradise Lost*, ed. Scott Elledge, 2nd ed. (New York and London: Norton, 1993), 3.130–31.

14. Of the play's forty instances of "soul" used either in the singular, the plural, or the possessive, Othello's speech accounts for fifteen references, Iago's for ten, Desdemona's and Emilia's for 5 each, and other characters are limited to a single usage (Roderigo, the Duke, and Brabantio) or two (Cassio). "Soul" interestingly appears in Emilia's discourse (3.4.159) only after Othello has begun to mistreat Desdemona due to jealousy.

15. See Giovanni Battista Giraldi Cinthio, *Gli Hecatommithi* (1566 edn.), The Third Decade, Story 7, in *Narrative and Dramatic Sources of Shakespeare*, ed. Geoffrey Bullough (London: Routledge and Kegan Paul, and New York: Columbia University Press, 1973), 7:242. All citations from Cinthio's novelle will be to this translation by Bullough (pp. 239–52).

16. See, e.g., Kenneth Gross, *Shakespeare's Noise* (Chicago: University of Chicago Press, 2001), 123.

17. For example, Desdemona's "lie" that she is to blame for her death might be interpreted as figuratively "true" from the perspective of the marriage mystery that two individuals become one flesh so that she could identify herself with Othello, but such an interpretation conflicts with Desdemona's preceding assertions of her own innocence.

18. Honigmann notes that in English domestic tragedy predating *Othello*, there occur two revival scenes in the anonymous *A Warning for Fair Women* (1599), a play that was performed by Shakespeare's own company, but he also observes that in one of those scenes the identification of the murderer by a servant *contrasts* with Desdemona's attempt "to shield her murderer instead of accusing him" (74).

19. See Bullough, 202–05.

20. Geffraie Fenton, trans., *Certain Tragical Discourses of Bandello* (1567; repr. New York: AMS Press, 1967): 1:189, my italics. All citations from Fenton will be to this edition.

21. See, e.g., Paul N. Siegel, "A New Source for *Othello*," *PMLA* 75 (1960): 480; Lawrence J. Ross, ed., *The Tragedy of Othello the Moor of Venice* (Indianapolis and New York: Bobbs-Merrill, 1974), 274–75; Naseeb Shaheen, "Like the Base Judean," *Shakespeare Quarterly* 31 (1980): 93–95, and *Biblical References in Shakespeare's Plays* (Newark: University of Delaware Press; London: Associated University Presses, 1999), 600–01.

22. Ross refers Desdemona's "prayerful iteration of the divine name" to Isaiah 42:8: " 'I am the Lord, this is my Name'" (225). Honigmann cites Granville-Barker's defense of Q's line: " 'Imagine it: Desdemona's agonised cry to God, and as the sharp sound of it is slowly stifled, Emilia's voice at the door rising through it, using the same words in another sense. A macabre duet'" (312).

23. See Hawthorne, *The Scarlet Letter*, ed. Seymour Gross, Sculley Bradley, Richmond Croom Beatty, and E. Hudson Long, 3rd ed. (New York and London: Norton, 1988), 132.

24. Hal, e.g., magnanimously "gilds" Falstaff's lie about the credit for killing Hotspur in order to befriend Falstaff or to do him "grace," thereby sacrificing the embellishment of his own reputation for killing the most reputed warrior in the realm: "For my part, if a lie may do thee grace, / I'll gild it with the happiest terms I have" (*1H4* 5.4.157–58).

25. See the etymology from the Latin and Greek of "hypocrisy" in the *OED*: "the acting of a part on the stage, feigning, pretence."

26. See Honigmann, 387. See Naseeb Shaheen, "Shakespeare's Knowledge of Italian," *Shakespeare Survey* 47 (1994): 161–69.

27. For Bandello's Italian, see Matteo Bandello, *Le Novelle*, ed. Gioachino Brognolio, 5 vols. (1910–12) (Bari: Gius Laterza & Figli, 1910), vol. 2, 230: "*Ella alquanto in sé ritornata, fece chiamar uno dei sacerdoti di San Giorgio e confessosi, di core perdonando al marito, non potendo sofferire che nessuno di lui dicesse male, non incolpando altro che la sua disgrazia.*" Bandello's story is numbered fifty-one.

28. For the full text of the willow song, see Honingmann, 392–93.

29. For practices regarding suicide burials, see Rowland Wymer, *Suicide and Despair in the Jacobean Drama* (Brighton, Sussex: Harvester Press Limited, 1986), 15.

30. Fenton's heroine cautions her husband against the loss of reputation—"a crowne of infamie" (184)—as a result of suicide due to unbridled passion; if he uses "unnaturall force" against himself and sacrifices his body, he will certainly "leave to the remeinder of [his] house, a crowne of infamie in the judgement of the worlde to come, and put [his] soule in hazarde of grace afore the troane of justice above" (184).

31. See, e.g., Rodney Poisson, "Death for Adultery: A Note on *Othello*, III.iii.394–96," *Shakespeare Quarterly* 28 (1977): 89–92: "For a man of honor like Othello, who is presented as living in the Venetian world of the sixteenth century, the thought of executing his wife . . . would have been considered proper, even inevitable" (90); Sarup Singh, *The Double Standard in Shakespeare and Related Essays: Changing Status of Women in Sixteenth and Seventeenth Century England* (Delhi: Konark Publishers, 1988), 43: "Perhaps most husbands in that period—whether Venetian or not—did act as Othello did, if their sense of honour was as highly developed as his and they possessed his courage."

32. For evidence from English law that Othello would probably be judged guilty of the felony of murder, see Michael Dalton, *The Countrey Iustice* (1618; rpt. Amsterdam: Theatrum Orbis Terrarum; Norwood, NJ: Walter J. Johnson, 1975), 211. In his section on "Murder" in his chapter, "Of Felonies by the Common Law," Dalton (a gentleman of Lincoln's Inn) cites the case of a husband who was in a quarrel with his wife and who suddenly struck her, and she died. Even though the act was "done vpon the sudden, and vpon prouocation" with "no precedent malice" appearing, "it was adiudged Murder at the Assises at Stafford before Walmesley. 43 *Eliz.*" (211). The title page of Dalton's book indicates its focus and purpose: *"The Covntrey Ivstice, Conteyning the Practice of the Ivstices of the Peace out of their Sessions.* Gathered for the better helpe of such Iustices of Peace as haue not beene much conversant in the studie of the Lawes of this Realme." My suggestion here contradicts the view presented by Sarup Singh that "for an Elizabethan audience . . . what Othello did was justified" (42). Cf. also J. H. Baker, *An Introduction to English Legal History*, 3rd ed. (London: Butterworths, 1990), "Homicide" (600–603); I am grateful to my colleague Lindsay Kaplan for this reference.

33. See Guido Ruggiero, *Violence in Early Renaissance Venice* (New Brunswick, NJ: Rutgers University Press, 1980), 171. Because of the political significance of Othello's case, the Avogadori and the Forty would probably handle it (171). For Venetian legal punishments of adultery during the Renaissance period, see Guido Ruggiero, *The Boundaries of Eros: Sex Crime and Sexuality in Renaissance Venice* (New York and Oxford: Oxford University Press, 1985), 66–69. Ruggiero notes that "lost honor was not in itself an excuse for murder in adultery cases" (67), and punishment was required for "passionate murders and rationally committed ones" (68) so that "neither offended honor nor jealous rage" (68) excused a crime. Ruggiero cites a case from 1441 in which a nobleman, Domenico Grimaldi, killed another young noble, Francesco Bembo, after Grimaldi caught Bembo with his wife in "a compromising moment" (68). Grimaldi fled the city, escaping Venetian justice, but he was "banned perpetually," and if he was caught, "he was to be taken to the scene of the crime, where his hand was to be cut off and hung around his neck," and then "he was to be taken between the columns of justice and decapitated" (68). Ruggiero finds that "only a slight inequality in penalties for women is a surprising indicator of female status in

patriarchal Venice" (68) where "a certain independence for women in sexual matters, especially at the higher social levels" (69) obtained. Penalties for adultery for both men and women were "typically restrained and ameliorative" (68) and "seemed to be concerned not with eradicating a moral vice but with reconstituting the family unit and protecting property" (69).

34. The verb form "commend" is used surprisingly less than ten times in the Bible, and the only time "commend" appears in a death utterance is this instance in Luke's account of the crucifixtion.

35. For William Tyndale's coinage of the word "scapegoat" and its biblical applicability to Christ as the innocent sacrifice for others' sins, see the present writer's *The Merchant of Venice: Choice, Hazard and Consequence* (Basingstoke and London: Macmillan; New York: St. Martin's Press, 1995), 239. For a study of religious imagery, the theme of sacrificed innocents, and parallels in scenic form between the mystery plays and the last scene of *Othello*, see Cherrell Guilfoyle, "Mactacio Desdemonae: Medieval Scenic Form in the Last Scene of *Othello*," *Comparative Drama* 19 (1985–86): 305–20. Although I agree with her emphasis on Desdemona as "innocent," I disagree with the emphasis on her "passivity" (306–07).

36. Milton, *Paradise Lost*, 3.684.

37. All citations, hereafter documented parenthetically, are to Erasmus, *The Handbook of the Christian Soldier* (*Enchiridion militis christiani*), trans. Charles Fantazzi, in *Collected Works of Erasmus*, ed. John W. O'Malley (Toronto: University of Toronto Press, 1988), 66: 1–127; quotations are from Fantazzi, p. 3. Fantazzi suggests the composition of the *Enchiridion* dates from "between the early months of 1499 and the publication of the *Lucubratiunculae* in February 1503 (2); he has based his translation on the 1519 Schürer edition (7). By 1561 Erasmus's text had gone through eleven editions in England. John W. O'Malley cites Margo Todd's *Christian Humanism and the Puritan Social Order* for demonstrating the influence of Erasmus's text on Puritan social thought in England (xxxi). In his edition, John P. Dolan maintains that this text had "a lasting influence in the Church of England" (58). See Erasmus, *Handbook of the Militant Christian* (Notre Dame, IN: Fides Publishers, 1962).

38. See 1 Tim 1:18; 2 Tim 2:3–5, 4:7–8. See O'Malley's introduction, *Collected Works of Erasmus*, vol. 66, xliii and n. 78.

39. In a letter of 1523 to Johann von Botzheim, Erasmus interestingly explains that his *Enchiridion* originated from the request of a good wife, "a lady of a deeply religious turn of mind," who "was fearfully concerned for her husband's salvation" because he was "plunged in fornication and adultery," and she hoped that Erasmus "might get a little religion into the man . . . on condition that he must not know that this was his wife's initiative, for he was cruel even to her, to the extent of beating her, as soldiers will." See *The Correspondence of Erasmus: Letters 1252 to 1355 (1522 to 1523)*, trans. R. A. B. Mynors, in *Collected Works of Erasmus* (Toronto: University of Toronto Press, 1989), vol. 9, 321–322. For early English translations (1533 and 1534) of the passage cited from *Enchiridion* in the text, see Erasmus, *Enchiridion Militis Christiani: An English Version*, ed. Anne M. O'Donnell, S.N.D. (Oxford: Oxford University Press, 1981), 74. This translation does not use the word "warrior" in this passage; instead, ". . . the woman thrugh grace of fayth, *changed as it were in to a man*, boldly tredeth down his venymous heed" (74, my italics).

40. For Genesis 3.15, Erasmus appears to be rather unique in gendering the victor as female and not specifically identifying that female as Mary but rather more generally as a faith-filled "woman" who is "a female warrior." The Geneva Bible (1560) genders the victor as male: "He shal breake thine head, & thou shalt bruise his heele." Biblical scholar and editor, Father James Walsh, S.J., informs me that the Hebrew is clearly masculine, but Jerome writes "*ipsa conteret*," following the Old Latin, and the feminine "she" has always been taken in a Marian sense.

41. Shakespeare may be adapting his earlier motif of literal poison in the ear in *Hamlet* for Iago's figurative poison in the ears of others. For example, just as Iago seeks to "poison [Brabantio's] delight" (1.1.68) with obscene accusations, so also he plots, "I'll pour this pestilence into [Othello's] ear" (2.3.356), rejoicing three scenes later that "the Moor already changes with my poison" (3.3.325). Although sin figured as disease is commonplace imagery, to the best of my knowledge, however, it has not been noted that Shakespeare's use of the disease nuance of "pestilence" may owe something to Fenton's translation of Bandello's story of the Albanese captain who murders his wife because Fenton consistently uses disease imagery for the passion of jealousy, as Shakespeare's main source, Cinthio, does not. See Fenton, e.g., "sickness" and "disease" (185–86), "traunce" and "fyttes of straunge and diverse disposition" (186), and "violence of sicknes" (187).

42. See Erasmus who objects to obeying "ungodly" commands by citing Acts 5:29: "'We ought to obey God rather than men'" (Fantazzi 23).

43. As Honingmann notes, "unbookish" is Shakespeare's coinage (261).

44. The hidden weapon is brilliantly concealed in Janet Suzman's film of *Othello* (1987) based on her direction of the play for the Market Theatre in Johannesburg. Jon Kani, who plays Othello, wears an African style metallic necklace that unclasps to reveal a hidden dagger so that the necklace literally "converts" to a dagger. The only drawback is that Kani's death gesture is a "slicing" of the jugular vein rather than the "smoting" that the play's language indicates.

45. For the figurative sense of "the Turk" as representing "all that was barbaric and demonic, in contrast to the Christian's civil and moral rightness" (13), see Virginia Mason Vaughan, *Othello: A Contextual History* (Cambridge: Cambridge University Press, 1994), 13, 23, 31.

46. Cf. Milton, *Paradise Lost*, 9.348–49: ". . . within himself / The danger lies, yet lies within his power."

47. Erasmus cautions: "At this moment war is preparing against the Turks, and whatever the intentions of those who started it, we must pray that it may turn out well, not for a chosen few but for all in common. . . . We shall have found the most effective way to defeat the Turks, once they have seen shining forth in us Christ's teaching and example, once they realize that we are not greedy for their empire, we have no thirst for their gold and no desire for their possessions . . . Nor does it make sense to prove ourselves truly Christians by killing as many as we can, but by their salvation . . ." (10). The date of 1518 for war preparations against the Turks is derived from Erasmus's letter to his friend Thomas More, dated 5 March 1518. See *The Correspondence of Erasmus: Letters 594 to 841 (1517 to 1518)*, trans. R. A. B. Mynors and D. F. S. Thomson, annot. Peter G. Bietenholz, in *Collected Works of Erasmus* (Toronto: University of Toronto Press, 1979), vol. 5, 325–29. With this letter Erasmus

also sent to Thomas More, Pope Leo X's "Proposals for a Crusade against the Turks" (issued 12 November 1517) as well as Luther's Ninety-five Theses ("the Conclusions on Papal pardons"), and a book by the Englishman Richard Pace (5: 327).

48. Although understandably writing with the religious bias of his era, Erasmus furnishes a pacifist opinion that it would be a good plan "long before we make attempt by force of arms, to seek to win [the Turks] by letters and pamphlets," of course, not political but spiritual documents that avoid scholarly, theological jargon for clear, pithy expression: "They are human beings, as we are; there is neither steel nor adamant in their hearts. It is possible they may be civilized, possible they may be won over by kindness which tames even the wild beasts. And the most effective thing of all is Christian truth" (11).

49. See the present writer's "Othello's Threnos: 'Arabian Trees' and 'Indian' Versus 'Judean,'" *Shakespeare Studies* 13 (1980): 145–67.

50. I argued if "base" modifies "Judean," it means "low in the moral scale" (*OED, a.*, 9), that is "ignoble" or "vile," which is the sense most frequent in Shakespeare (152–55). Cf. "base" as a synonym for "ignoble" in sixteenth- and seventeenth-century dictionaries. For example, John Florio, *A Worlde of Wordes* (London, 1598): "Ignobile, *ignoble, infamous, unrespected, base, dishonored*"; John Bullokar, *An English Expositor* (London, 1616): "*Ignoble*. Base, that is not noble"; and John Minsheu, *Ductor in Linguas* (London, 1617): "*Base, vile, abject*" with synonyms being *"unnoble, vile."*

51. Richard Levin, "*Othello's* American Indian and the Nu Principle," *The Shakespeare Newsletter* 50:2, no. 245 (Summer 2000): 36.

52. M. R. Ridley, ed., *Othello*, 2nd Arden (London: Methuen, 1958), 196.

53. Norman Sanders, ed., *Othello*, New Cambridge Shakespeare (Cambridge: Cambridge University Press, 1984), 192.

54. See Holmer, 153.

55. The evidence cited in the *OED*, however, leaves much to be desired. Both sixteenth-century examples of "base" as "deep-coloured" refer medically to the color of urine, not to skin color. The *OED* questions whether this sense defines Shakespeare's use of "base" in *Titus Andronicus*, "IV.ii.72: Is black so base a hue?" See *OED* 5. Given Aaron's response to the Nurse's view of his black baby as "loathsome as a toad / Among the fair-fac'd breeders of our clime" (4.2.67–68), I think that the "depth" of color is not so much the issue (black is the darkest color) but rather the sense of "base" as "befitting an inferior person or thing; degraded or degrading, unworthy" (*OED* 10) better suits the context. Although the *OED* questions the meaning of "base" in this line from *Titus Andronicus*, none of the seven recent editions of the play I checked (including the 1995 Arden) gloss "base."

56. For *anaphora*, see George Puttenham, *The Arte of English Poesie*, ed. Gladys Doidge Willcock and Alice Walker (Cambridge: Cambridge Univrsity Press, 1936). Regarding "*anaphora*" or "the Figure of Report" as one of the seven different figures of repetition, Puttenham writes that *anaphora* is "repetition in the first degree . . . when we make one word begin and . . . lead the daunce to many verses in sute" (198). The three English examples of *anaphora* furnished by Puttenham illustrate the idea that many verses perform "*one daunce*" (198, my italics). Moreover, this figure is singled out for eloquence and therefore contributes to the power of Othello's final

self-report: "your figure that worketh by iteration or repetition of one word or clause doth much alter and affect the eare and also the mynde of the hearer, and therefore is counted a very braue figure both with the Poets and rhetoricians . . ." (198).

57. In emphasizing that the pious Christian soldier must "be gentle at heart" (15), Erasmus also illuminates the degree of Desdemona's generous mercy for even the "unworthy" (97–98), who might be "worthy of compassion, not punishment" (125), when he cites Augustine's evidence that "in the old days, even when criminals were justly condemned, bishops used their authority to appeal for them, and sometimes rescued a criminal from the hands of his judges . . ." (14).

58. Marvin Rosenberg, *The Masks of Othello* (1961; repr. Newark: University of Delaware Press; London: Associated University Presses, 1994), 209.

59. In the *Enchiridion* Erasmus discusses Paul's use of the terms "flesh" and "spirit," and he indicts the Christian who practices ceremonial observances (e.g., vigils, fasts) but who still indulges in "the works of the flesh," e.g., "jealousy worse than you find in a woman" (77). Regarding the baseness of false jealousy in love, Othello unwittingly prophesies what happens when he assures the senate that if he neglects his military duty for Desdemona, then "all indign and *base adversities* / Make head against [his] estimation" (1.3.274–75, my italics).

60. See James Winny, ed., *The Frame of Order* (London: George Allen & Unwin Ltd., 1957), 15. For the view that Bright's *A Treatise of Melancholy* (1586) is a "subsidiary source" for *Hamlet*, see Harold Jenkins, *Hamlet*, Arden Shakespeare (London and New York: Methuen, 1982), 108.

61. See Andrew Gurr, *Playgoing in Shakespeare's London*, 2nd ed. (Cambridge: Cambridge University Press, 1996), 58: "women from every section of society went to plays, from Queen Henrietta Maria to the most harlotry of vagrants." See S. P. Cerasano and Marion Wynne-Davies, eds., *Renaissance Drama by Women: Texts and Documents* (London and New York: Routledge, 1996). Although the debate over the influence of the English theatre was "a controversy that was to coexist with the playhouses throughout this period up to 1642 when overwhelming puritanical sentiment forced their closure" (Cerasano and Wynne-Davies 157) and women were the subjects of much of this controversy, women did not vacate the playhouses until they closed for men too.

"A Jointure more or less": Re-measuring *The True Chronicle History of King Leir and his three daughters*

GRACE IOPPOLO

SINCE 1608, *The True Chronicle History of King Leir and his three daughters* has drawn attention from scholars and critics only as a slightly defective touchstone by which to measure the true value of Shakespeare's *King Lear*, which appears to have used *Leir* as one of its main sources. While critics have complained for almost four centuries of the exceptional cruelty and lack of redemption in Shakespeare's grim play, it has fared significantly better as a piece of theater and a literary work than the anonymous *Leir*. Faulted for its supposedly creaky verse, one-dimensional characters, and simplistic conclusion, *Leir* was called "execrable" in the eighteenth century, "mechanical" in the nineteenth (Goethe and Tolstoy voiced minority views in preferring it to *Lear*), "flawed" in the twentieth, and "pleasant" in the twenty-first, always in comparison with Shakespeare's play.[1]

It almost goes without saying that *Leir* has not been properly evaluated on its own merit. The reasons for this are many, but seem particularly to rest on critics' lack of understanding of the numerous sources from which both *Leir* and *Lear* were adapted. Thus, for example, critics have attributed to the *Leir* author the creation of plot and character devices, including "antifeminist" stereotypes, an unlikely love test, and a subsequent feud between a king and his three daughters, which the author in fact inherited from his sources.[2] Critics have especially derided the use of the mixed genre of chronicle history and romance in *Leir*, finding it decidedly inferior to the tragic grandeur of *Lear*, even though such grandeur perturbed A. C. Bradley, among others.[3] If the *Leir* author can be faulted for anything, it is for relying *too* heavily on his sources for the genre and plot, which preserve the fairy-tale like conclusion of a rescued and triumphant Lear, whose daughter Cordella will live to inherit his kingdom.

The truth is that *Leir* is so bound up in the cult of Shakespeare, and in modern hermeneutics of the Shakespearean text, that critics' failure to understand the text and context of *Leir* seems to be the least of the problems in

appreciating the play. As Leeds Barroll has persuasively argued, "many critics urging a twenty-first century sense of Shakespeare's texts as interrelated
with his culture continue to privilege a nineteenth-century daguerreotype of
Shakespeare the dramatist and even build on its colorless angles and lines."[4]
So, the further forward that modern criticism moves, the further back plays,
even those, like *Leir*, that exist only in the shadows of those by Shakespeare,
will be fixed with such colorless angles and lines. In this essay I want to strip
The True Chronicle History of King Leir and his three daughters of its colorless shadows, dispel some of the misconceptions about it, and reexamine it
strictly on its own terms without comparison to Shakespeare's play. In doing
so, I will try to enlarge what is known about the play's composition, performance, and printing history. I especially want to consider the appeal and power
of *Leir* on the Elizabethan and Jacobean stages as well as its strength as a
literary text. As a relative object or touchstone, *Leir* has no real existence. As
an individual play, it stands out as cleverly structured and well-plotted drama
that provides theatrical and reading audiences with a cathartic exploration of
early modern family, monarchy, and culture.

The text eventually printed in 1605 as *The True Chronicle History of King
Leir and his three daughters, Gonorill, Ragan, and Cordella* was almost certainly the "kinge leare" play for which Henslowe noted receipts for performances on 6 and 8 April 1594. With spring 1594 as the latest date for its
composition, critics have suggested the earliest possible date of sometime in
1588.[5] The first performance of the play earned Henslowe thirty-eight shillings and the second twenty-six shillings. As receipts ranged from three to
forty-three shillings for a variety of plays, including *The Jew of Malta*, performed "by the Quenes men & my lord Susexe to geather" during this Easter
period in 1594,[6] the takings for the "leare" play were better than average. No
other records appear to exist that provide any further performance history for
Leir other than the Stationers' Registry entry for the 1605 Quarto as well as
its title page that boasts that the play "hath beene diuers and sundry times
lately acted," a generically ambiguous form of advertisement that is impossible either to verify or dismiss.

On 14 May, just five weeks after these performances, Edward White paid
to enter *The moste famous Chronicle historye of LEIRE kinge of England and
his Three Daughters* in the Stationers' Register.[7] White's claim to the play
may have been assigned to him by Adam Islip, whose name has been can-
celed in the entry, or Islip, who entered a number of other plays in this period,
may have been named in error. Such a quick attempt at publication suggests
that whichever company owned the play regarded it as popular enough to sell
it off to a printer, or they had decided that *Leir* would not remain active in
the repertory, or both. The timing of the publication would link the play's
ownership solely to the Queen's Men, which broke up and sold off a number
of playbooks in 1594.[8] However no printed text of the play from this date

survives, so most likely it was not printed at this time, possibly for a number of reasons. White may have lacked title or been challenged by another publisher, or he may simply have been registering his claim without any plan to publish in the immediate future. It is also possible that the Queen's Men, which re-formed after 1594, thought better of relinquishing *Leir* to print, which would have provided an available text from which other companies could act the play. It certainly drew respectable audience numbers on the two dates recorded by Henslowe.

The play was entered again, perhaps retroactively,[9] in the Stationers' Register on 8 May 1605, and this entry also shows some confusion about the play's title and the ownership of that title. The entry reads:

> **Simon Stafford** Entred for his copye vnder th[e h]andes of the Wardens A booke called *"the Tragecall* [altered from *Tragedie*] *historie* [interlined] *of kinge LEIR and his Three Daughters &c." As it was latelie Acted.*
>
> **John Wright** / Entred for his Copie by assignement from **Simon Stafford** and by consent of Master **Leake**, *The Tragicall history of kinge LEIRE and his Three Daughters* / Provided that **Simon Stafford** shall haue the printinge of this booke.

This entry raises two immediate questions: why was the title altered from "tragedie" to "Tragecall historie,"[10] and how did John Wright, who acted as publisher, and Simon Stafford, who assigned his title to Wright in exchange for printing it in his shop, acquire ownership of the play?

The alteration in title may seem to imply that Shakespeare's tragedy was already in performance at that time and that Wright and Stafford put *Leir* into print, and an acting company staged revivals of the play, in order to capitalize on favorable response to Shakespeare's play.[11] However, the alteration of the title may simply signify an error in the entry (errors are not uncommon in the Stationers' Register and genres remarkably fluid in this age), rather than a conspiracy to defraud Shakespeare's fans. After all, Shakespeare appears to have stolen the fans of the *Leir* author in using that play as a main source. Nor can the entry be definitively used to date the composition of *Lear* by early 1605, whose earliest performance could have been no later than 26 December 1606, according to the 1608 Quarto 1 title page. Not uncommonly, both the 1594 and 1605 Stationers' Register entries fail to list the play's author or authors, and no satisfactory evidence has emerged since its printing by which to attribute its authorship.

The acquisition of the play by Wright and Stafford is more complicated to unravel. Wright was apprenticed to John White, who had registered his claim to the play in 1594, and some have argued that Wright purchased or stole the text of the play from his employer.[12] However, Donald M. Michie explains that White retained ownership of the play until his death in 1613, when it passed to his son, whose heirs sold it in 1624 to Edward Allde, and afterward it passed to Allde's heirs at least through 1640.[13] Michie also argues that, due to a lack of stage annotations in the text, the printer either used authorial fair papers or foul papers that a scribe had "tidied up," removing "the marks of stage adaptation from the prompt-book before the manuscript went to the printer."[14] Richard Knowles concludes that by 1605 only two manuscripts of the play were available, the company "book" carrying the censor's license and another manuscript that was not theatrical in origin, and that Wright and Stafford borrowed this latter manuscript from White to print their edition.[15] However, Michie's and Knowles's arguments are both faulty here. It is true that there is no extant record that White lodged any written complaint with the Stationers' Company about Wright and Stafford. So either White granted them formal or informal permission to print *Leir* (as perhaps Adam Islip had granted White in 1594), perhaps for payment, or White took no interest in this event, possibly because he did not actually acquire the rights to the play in 1594. That is, as with some other entries in the Register, White's entry staked a claim to ownership that was still forthcoming, or even temporarily borrowed from Islip. It is also possible that the *Leir* owned and registered by White, which makes no mention in the Stationers' Register that it had been "acted," was not the play but another text, such as a poem or prose version of the story, in which interest had been revived due to the play or the vogue in printing English chronicle histories.

As for printer's copy, there is no need to suppose that Wright and Stafford borrowed White's manuscript or that only two manuscripts of the play existed by 1605. The claim that the 1605 Quarto of *Leir* "shows no signs of theatrical provenance"[16] is difficult to support. Although the printed text lacks act-scene notations, other than "Actus 1" at the opening, the thirty-two scenes can easily be delineated by the fact that every new scene follows a cleared stage that is consistently marked by "*Exit*" or "*Exeunt.*" In my experience in examining both autograph and scribal dramatic manuscripts, one common characteristic of autograph manuscripts is missing exit directions, so the presence of absolutely regular exit directions points to someone other than the author. Nor does the fact that the stage directions in the play are sometimes brief point *only* to authorial copy, as Michie assumes. Not all the directions are brief, and those that are are consistently offered are very precise, rather than vague, as in "*Enter the King of Cambria booted and spurd, and his man with a wand and a letter*" in scene 5. Such precision, which calls attention to stage properties needed, certainly does not rule out theatrical origin. The lack of formal act-scene notations is also not unusual, even in scribal copy made from company books. In two such manuscripts of Middleton's *Hengist, King of Kent*, the scribes are similarly inconsistent in making scene notations.[17] In addition, the *Leir* text often contains stage directions printed in the right margin that are split over several lines. This characteristic also appears in the

Hengist manuscripts copied from the company's book, and is, in fact, typical of scribes copying dramatic manuscripts, who cannot always fit their text onto one line but carry it over to subsequent lines. In my experience, such split directions appear to point to scribal copyists, not composing authors.

Knowles's contention that the company "book" from which the Queen's and Sussex's Men acted the play in 1594 had to contain the license is also flawed. As no extant manuscript still carrying a censor's license shows signs of having been used in the theater as the company book, it is more likely that licensed copies were too valuable to be used in this way and another copy was made to serve as the book. Thus, any number of manuscript copies of *Leir* could have been extant, including the author's foul papers and/or fair copies; a scribal copy of either (perhaps used as the copy sent to the censor to license) or both; and the Queen's Men's book and a transcript of it made especially as printer's copy in 1594 or 1605. The consistency of the play's style would suggest that it had a single author but this may also be due to a bookkeeper or playhouse scribe regularizing the text, and it would not be unusual for one author to have written the main plot with another adding the numerous comic scenes. In summary then, the lack of act-scene notations and the presence of some brief stage directions cannot be used to support arguments that the printer's copy for *Leir* could not have been "theatrical" in origin. In fact, the text looks as if it has been subjected to very careful correction and regularization that enhanced its use in the theater. Although Greg argued that printer's copy was a "play-house manuscript,"[18] I think it is reasonable to conclude that the copy was a transcript of the 1594 or later company "book," possibly made especially for use as printer's copy.

What is much more intriguing about the 1605 edition of *Leir* is the claim in its Stationers' Register entry that it had been "*latelie Acted*," which is expanded in the Quarto's title page to "hath beene diuers and sundry times lately acted." If these claims do indeed refer to *Leir*, rather than *Lear*, *Leir* lived on the stage and in some company's repertory, probably the re-formed Queen's Men (which performed until 1603), for up to ten years after its early performances. W. W. Greg and Roslyn Lander Knutson, among others, have argued that the "book" or another transcript of *Leir* had not remained with the Queen's Men but had been sold to the Lord Chamberlain's Men after 1594. Such arguments rest on the notion that Shakespeare had access through the King's Men to a manuscript of *Leir* when writing his play before May 1605.[19] Shakespeare had some connection to Sussex's Men around 1594, as the 1594 Quarto 1 of *Titus Andronicus* lists it as acted by Darby, Pembroke, and Sussex's Men. If his knowledge of *Leir* preceded its 1605 publication it may have been due to his exposure to the play as actor or dramatist with Sussex's Men in 1594 rather than the Chamberlain's/King's Men between 1594 and 1605. However, it is far easier to conclude that Shakespeare used the printed text to write his play at some point after May 1605.

If *Leir* continued to be acted in the age of James I it had moved beyond the purpose assigned to it recently by Scott McMillin and Sally-Beth MacLean. They claim that the play typified the repertory of the Queen's Men, which was "formed to spread Protestant and royalist propaganda through a divided realm and to close a breach within radical Protestantism." For this reason, "the English history play came to prominence" in a company that had the personnel to do "big" English plays, especially as narrative sources for those plays were being published. *Leir*, they calculate, would require at least fourteen actors, with five roles for boys. McMillin and MacLean further contend that *Leir* and other chronicle history plays reached the stage because they could be "presented as 'true' rather than 'poetic,' the sort of entertainment English people could be drawn to see in crowds without abjuring the combination of God, queen, Protestant church and nation which the government depended on." They conclude that the "signs of reduction in the printed texts" of plays like *Leir* signifies that they were kept in the repertory "even when they had to be reduced for smaller versions of the Queen's Men."[20]

As persuasive as this general contention is, it becomes problematic for *Leir*. The play does draw on a number of sixteenth-century chronicle histories of England, all of which derive in some way from earlier histories, beginning with Geoffrey of Monmouth's *Historia Regum Britanniae* (ca. 1135), apparently available only as a Latin manuscript until an English translation was printed in 1718.[21] Geoffrey presented the story of Leir's test of his three daughters' love, his division of the kingdom, and the resulting foreign and civil wars, ended only by his reunion with his youngest daughter and her husband, the Gallian king, and their victory over his older daughters and their husbands. After her father's death, Cordella peacefully rules England for five years, until her two evil nephews overthrow her and send her to prison, where she commits suicide. Geoffrey may have invented this story of the Leir family, borrowing it from traditional folk-tales of ungrateful children and their fathers, or even from the parable of the prodigal son who finally redeems his father's love and allegiance. Or Geoffrey may have been relating what he thought was the historical truth, albeit in parable form. The Leir story appeared in the works of succeeding historians, including an English translation of a fourteenth century French prose history of *Brut* about the line of early Celtic kings (of which Leir is the tenth after King Brut); Robert Fabyan's *New Chronicles* (1516); Polydore Vergil's *Anglicae Historiae* (1534); John Stow's *Summarie of Englyshe Chronicles* (1563) and *Annales* (1592); Raphael Holinshed's *Chronicles* (1577 and 1587); William Harrison's *Description of England* (printed in Holinshed); and William Warner's *Albion's England* (1586).

But Leir's story appeared not only in the chronicle histories on which McMillin and MacLean focus, but in poems, notably John Higgins's *The Mirror for Magistrates* (1574, 1587) and in book 2, canto 10 of Spenser's *The Fairie*

Queene (1590), both of which the *Leir* author appears to have used.[22] In these poems, the history of Leir is displaced by the tragedy of Cordella, who eventually slays herself in prison. In fact, she narrates her own story in *The Mirror for Magistrates,* under the heading "Cordila shewes how by despaire when she was in prison she slue herselfe. the yeare before Christe. 800." This later suicide may be what the theatrical audience focused on, even in watching the happy conclusion to *Leir.* Thus, the audience saw in 1594 or afteward not solely "Protestant and royalist propaganda" but a historical romance that served as prequel to genuine tragedy. Perhaps this tragic connotation to Cordella's suicide, which takes place several years after *Leir* but is prominent in the poems and chronicle histories, is what caused the confusion about the play's genre, both for the clerk making the 1605 Stationers' Register entry and the play's later critics.

Although the *Leir* author has been separately credited with following the vogue at Court for romances from 1570 to 1595,[23] and, as noted above, for acceding to the demands of the Queen's Men for chronicle plays to celebrate the reign of Elizabeth I,[24] he seemed unconcerned that the play seamlessly blended elements of comedy, tragedy, history, and romance. Such a fluid genre would help it move from the age of Elizabeth I to James I, when its fantastical elements, such as the masque-like pastoral celebration and reunion of Leir and Cordella in scene 24, would suit a more sophisticated audience in the early 1600s. More importantly, Leir's feuds with his children and his division of the kingdom would also resonate with James I, who had warned in *The True Law of Free Monarchies* (1598, 1603) and *Basilikon Doron* (1599, 1603) against provoking "monstrous and unnaturall" sons to rise up against a king, as well as the folly of "devliding your kingdomes."[25] In fact, *King Leir* was an especially topical play and more than suitable for revival in 1603 and afterward, possibly with alterations or revisions to update it, an issue no previous critic of the play has considered. Furthermore, the notoriety of the 1603 case of Cordell Annesley, daughter of the aristocrat Bryan Annesley, who petitioned the government to protect her "poor aged and daily dying father" from the cruelty of Grace, the elder of her two sisters, could also have contributed to a revival of *Leir.* After her father's death in 1604 Cordell erected a monument to testify to her "dutifull love unto her father and mother."[26] So, the 1605 claim that *Leir* had been "lately" acted may in fact be legitimate rather than a publisher's exaggeration. If the play remained with the Queen's Men, they probably continued to act from their 1594 book, which may have been updated or altered. From this copy the 1605 printer's copy could have been made, by which time the play had ceased being performed and could be sold off for publication.

In order to understand why the play could remain fluid in genre, staging, and presentation, I want to trace its major aims and accomplishments from beginning to end (offering plot summary when necessary). I particularly

want to defend it against the standard attacks made against it, typified by
Michie's contention that the author is "not very skillful in creating consistent
and sustained dramatic effect," and that "for the most part," his "characterizations are as unskilled and mechanical as his plot."[27] I also want to challenge McMillin and MacLean's contention that this "stilted and self-
conscious" play could be presented as "true" rather than "poetic," and that
"when *Leir* grows moral, which is most of the time, the tendency toward
iambic regularity and rhyme pushes the speakers into their virtual stanzas,
and the action grows heavy with prefabrication."[28]

The play opens with an ill and weary King Leir mourning the death of his
"(too late) deceast and dearest Queen" (line 2)[29] and lamenting his lack of a
male heir. He confesses that he will divide his kingdom into equal parts as
dowries for his three daughters for whom he has already chosen husbands.
Although the courtier Skallier tries to persuade him to "make them eche a
Joynter more or less, /As is their worth, to them that love professe" (lines
37–38), Leir refuses, preferring "to try which of my daughters loves me
best: / Which till I know, I cannot be in rest" (lines 79–80). In doing so, he
assumes that once his recalcitrant daughter Cordella admits that she loves
him "best" she will no longer be able to refuse the Hibernian king as Leir's
choice for her husband. Although McMillin and MacLean claim that Leir's
opening monologue offers "gnomic and sententious familiarity,"[30] it presents
instead a finely detailed, compassionate, and rational monarch, father, and
man. Leir's beloved wife is not really absent here but will infuse the scene,
especially as he acknowledges that "fathers best do know to governe
sonnes; / But daughters steps the mothers counsell turnes" (lines 19–20).
Leir's unusually sensitive concern for gender difference and the construction
of family life sets the tone for the rest of the play and marks *Leir* as extraordinary for its time.

Although Michie, among others, claims that the play is "very crudely constructed,"[31] the author of *Leir* structures the play dialectically, juxtaposing
scenes of compassion and openness with those of jealousy and deception.
Words, images, and actions are mirrored in every set of two scenes for the
first part of the play, creating dramatically effective binary opposition. For
example, following this first scene, Gonorill and Ragan enter together to
present their reading of family life, focused on their rage at Cordella for attempting to use her perfect nature and behavior to "exceed" them at court
(line 104). Once again, Skalliger acts as tempter, warning them of Leir's intention to test their love and counseling them to rehearse their answers. Also
revealed here is that Leir's choice of the Prince of Cambria to marry Ragan
and the King of Cornwall to marry Gonorill reflects the two women's own
desires. Thus in the second as well as the first scene we see through the father
a mirrored family unity and structure, expressed both seriously and ironically.

Scenes 3 and 4 continue this duality, as, in the first, Leir confronts his three daughters at court and asks them to measure their love, not in order to assign the sizes of their dowries but to hear the words of love that a grieving and suddenly bereft husband needs to hear. In doing so, Leir hopes to fix a stationary and stable point for himself and to end the desolation and desertion brought by his wife's death. Gonorill and Ragan give him this stability while Cordella's refusal to pledge more than "what love the child owe the father" (line 279) repositions him as the lover who has been deserted. In her test as Leir's surrogate wife, or that of the Hibernian king for whom Leir has tried to woo her by proxy, Cordella has failed completely. The following scene offers the Gallian king, his clownish courtier Mumford and other nobles at his court. Like Leir, he wishes to be suitor to Gonorill, Ragan, and Cordella and to test their love in order to make a match. But he will woo them in disguise, with Mumford acting as his surrogate.

> Such courtship by proxy is mocked by Mumford:
> Do not tye my toung from speaking,
> My lips from kissing when occasion serves,
> My hands from congees, and my knees to bow
> To gallant Gyrles; which were a taske more hard,
> Then flesh and bloud is able to indure.
>
> (lines 369–73)

In a sense then, Mumford will play the fraudulent wooer, as Leir had done in the previous scene.

In the next two paired scenes, 5 and 6, two more sets of suitors practice their speaking and kissing. In scene 5, Cornwall and Cambria, each "booted and spurd," reveal their pleasure at being chosen as husbands to Gonorill and Ragan, and, in scene 6, they formally present themselves at Leir's court where they draw lots to fix which half of Leir's kingdom they will receive as dowries. Both scenes ironically echo the type of courtship established by Leir and then adopted by the Gallian King. Scenes 7 and 8 seemingly continue to deconstruct the world of Leir, as in the first of these scenes, when the Gallian king, appropriately disguised as a pilgrim, meets the banished Cordella and courts her just long enough to win her love and her hand. The language is highly sentimental, as in Cordella's pledge,

> What e're you be, of high or low descent,
> All's one to me, I do request but this:
> That as I am, you will accept of me,
> And I will have you whatsoe're you be:
> Yet well I know, you come of royall race,
> I see such sparks of honour in your face.
>
> (lines 717–22)

McMillin and MacLean argue that in the play there is "little stylistic technique besides the rhyming pace," with the result that the dialogue is "poised and formal, virtually an exchange of stanzas."[32] However, the author does not allow this particular rhyming pace to stand but immediately undercuts it with Mumford's sarcastic comment, "Have Palmers weeds such power to win fayre Ladies?" (line 723). This rhyming pace is a not a fault but a device to remind the audience that the author satirizes such sentiment on its own, seeing it only as existing, as in scenes 1 and 2, relative to its opposite.

As the play continues, the plot and characters develop not in colorless angles and lines but in blended and subtle hues. In scenes 8–10, Leir's most loyal courtier, Perillus discusses in a soliloquy Leir's "mild patience" in the face of Gonorill's lack of hospitality (line 755), and immediately after, Gonorill and Skalliger plot to humiliate her father. Finally Leir expresses his pain at Gonorill's treachery and cruelty. In scenes 11, 12, 14, 15, 17, and 18, we witness Ragan and Gonorill mistreating and conniving against their father, finally employing their Messenger to murder him. In juxtaposition, we see Cordella, alone in scene 13 and with her husband in scene 16, attempting to redeem his love, either in having her ambassador bring him back to France or to join him herself in Britain. The scenes are tightly written and theatrically effective, especially scene 17 in which Ragan masterfully contracts the Messenger's services, and scene 18, when another type of messenger, the French ambassador, hears from Gonorill and Cornwall that his services are not required.

But the center and climax to the play comes in scene 19 with Leir and Perillus's confrontation with the murderous Messenger. In a play of confrontations, courtships, love tests, and seductions through words, this scene stands alone as the masterpiece. Whatever practice, success, and failure that Leir had in attempting to persuade his daughters in scene 3 to frame themselves within his realm of experience and desire he puts to stunning use here. McMillin and MacLean decide that the only "stroke of brilliance in *King Leir* lies in playing the murderer as a comic character in the first place, one who is allowed to break the metrical norms before getting to the regular couplet at the end."[33] Yet, the scene's mix of blank verse and prose shows off a well-paced and smoothly structured scene that builds in several steps, each with its own emotional climax. The scene begins with intellect stripped away by action, as the Messenger symbolically removes books from the sleeping Leir and Perillus. The two men awake as Leir starts from a nightmare of "dread" (line 1479). But the messenger takes on a more sophisticated role by offering to "expound" Leir's dream (line 1487), and in this way he becomes not just Leir's interpreter but a projection of his subconscious. In fact, the Messenger appears to have been conjured up by the fears of the exhausted and depressed men, rather than simply hired by Gonorill and Ragan. In the second movement of this powerful scene, the Messenger, armed with two daggers, takes on the role of highwayman, asking the two men to "stand" and "deliver," explaining,

> You should have prayed before, while it was time,
> And then perhaps, you might have scapt my hands:
> But you, like faithfull watch-men, fell asleep.
>
> (lines 1508–10)

This last image plays nicely on the actual and metaphorical watchmen, almost all of whom fail to offer any form of protection, who populate the play.

The Messenger's adoption of roles, first as subconscious guide and then as thief, continues. Once he has acquired their purses he reveals himself as a murderer contracted by Leir's "children." Leir immediately assumes that Cordella and her husband have hired him, but whatever fear or despair the scene has raised collapses at this point with this exchange:

> *Leir.* Camst thou from France, of purpose to do this?
> *Mess.* From France? zoones, do I looke like a Frenchman? Sure I have not mine own face on; some body hath chang'd faces with me, and I know now of it: But I am sure, my apparell is all English. Sirra, what meanest thou to aske that question? I could spoyle the fashion of this face for anger. A French face!
>
> (lines 1571–86)

Such comic indignation, and a joke for the English audience at French expense, in a seemingly tragic scene may undercut it, but the play centers on comic indignation at the absurd, both from the characters and the audience. The author particularly deconstructs anything taken too seriously or tragically in the play. The frustrated murderer changes tack and adopts yet another role, a hellish ambassador, whose resolve is soon weakened by the heavens' thunder and lightning and by the "strong Magician" Leir's debating and rhetorical skills (lines 1634–40). Just as Leir gains psychological and verbal control of the scene, the Messenger provides Leir with Gonorill's letters contracting his murder. Leir attempts, without success, to convince the Messenger to spare Perillus's life by arguing that his murder was not included in the contract. Even as supplicant on his knees, Leir fails to sway the Messenger, until his arguments become more rationally structured and self-assured. Leir cautions the Messenger that Gonorill and Ragan will have to kill him to ensure his silence about the murders, and his soul will be eternally damned. Once again the heavens thunder and the quaking Messenger drops his daggers and flees. His hasty exit from the stage leaves the audience wondering if he was real or a projection of Leir's psychological need to reestablish his own identity.

The repeated movement in this climactic scene from inflation to deflation may imply that the scene is absurd and simplistic or merely an example of "extreme Christianity."[34] But, in a sense, the author is mirroring the effects within one scene of the force of the climax on the entire play. At this point the audience is prepared to release any sense of tragedy, and as the play continues, Cordella, her husband, and Mumford emerge in scenes 21 and 24 as central and stable points upon which the plot will rest. Leir and Perillus escape to France in disguise by exchanging clothes with two sailors, so, although metaphorically or psychologically killed by the Messenger, the two men will be reborn a few scenes later. Finally in scene 24 we have a slowly structured scene of reunion of Cordella and Leir that begins as a pastoral celebration with Cordella, her husband, and Mumford "disguised like Countrey folke" and celebrating life and the rebirth provided by nature. Leir and Perillus will stumble in "very fayntly," and although they do not immediately recognize Cordella, she recognises them and nourishes them with food and drink. When Leir was last on his knees he was begging the Messenger for his life, and in this scene he and Cordella, after an excruciatingly long wait, kneel to each other in recognition and pledge their lives to each other. The scene may seem trite and sentimental, but the fact that the audience becomes impatient for Cordella finally to reveal herself ensures that the scene is emotionally complex rather than simplistic.

In scenes 25–30, the joint armies of Leir and Cordella and of Gonorill and Ragan and their husbands prepare for battle and finally engage. Mumford, still the clown, manages to subdue two drunken watchmen and assorted "halfe naked" men and women (line 2476). Such comedy seems to promise that death and despair will not be the result of this armed conflict. In scene 31, Leir confronts Ragan and Gonorill but does not punish them, and in the final scene, 32, Leir, Perillus, Cordella, her husband, and Mumford celebrate their triumph over the forces of Gonorill and Ragan. Leir's final speech neatly ties up all the loose ends, with appropriate thanks to Cordella, Perillus, and Mumford, and with Gonorill, Ragan, and their husbands declared "fugitives." No hint of the tragic fate of Cordella appears, but the play actually lacks closure in Leir's last two lines: "Come, sonne and daughter, who did me advaunce, / Repose with me awhile, and then for Fraunce" (lines 2662–63). Life will continue after the play's conclusion, but the future of the main characters is not assured, and the future suicide of Cordella looms large, as the play's historical and poetic sources remind us.

Although much of the *Leir* story is adapted from the sources, Skalliger, Perillus, Mumford, the Messenger, and the two bumbling watchmen who fail to capture Mumford are not found in any source material. Nor does the wooing scene of Cordella and Gallia, the attempted murder of Leir by the Messenger or the reunion scene on the coast of France appear in any of the sources.[35] It is these three scenes that center and fix the play and its characters and themes, and that move and engage theatrical and literary audiences. Simply put, this play *makes sense*, as the author has provided enough psychological motivation for Leir's folly in conducting a love test, for Gonorill and Ragan's jealousy of their sister and eventual betrayal of their father, for Leir's abdication, and other key points to allow the audience to remain engaged. The author also offers consistency in the continuing and comforting presence of Cordella throughout the play and the growth of her ability to love.

It seems exaggerated to claim, as numerous critics have, that *King Leir* influenced nearly half of Shakespeare's plays, most notably *Richard III, The Merchant of Venice, As You Like It,* and *Hamlet,*[36] as well as *King Lear.* Nevertheless, the play's power and appeal are such that it is easy to understand how *King Leir* could have remained "a remarkably pervasive presence in Shakespeare's career for well over a decade and exercised considerable power in shaping the formal and thematic structure of several quite different plays."[37] It seems to me that this play wields considerable influence, both on authors and audience, and offers a perfectly constructed, self-contained, and powerful deconstruction and reconstruction of family life and love. *The True Chronicle History of King Leir and his three daughters* needs to be regarded on its own terms, not just as a "colorless" series of lines and angles in the shadow of Shakespeare, but as a multicolored and multidimensional representation of the power of a single drama, both in the early modern age and our own.

Notes

1. For a discussion of critical reactions to the play, see *A Critical Edition of "A True Chronicle History of King Leir and His Three Daughters, Gonorill, Ragan and Cordella,"* ed. Donald M. Michie (New York: Garland Publishing, 1991), 38–43; Stephen J. Lynch, "Sin, Suffering, and Redemption in *Leir* and *Lear,*" *Shakespeare Studies* 18 (1986), 161–74; Mark J. Blechner, "King Lear, King Leir, and Incest Wishes," *American Imago* 45 (1988), 309–25; and Richard Knowles, "How Shakespeare Knew *King Leir,*" *Shakespeare Survey* 55 (2002): 13.

2. Many critics make this error of failing to read or acknowledge the sources for *Leir* or even *Lear.* See for example, Claudette Hoover, "Goneril and Regan: 'So Horrible as in Woman,'" *San Jose Studies* 10 (1984): 49–65, who blames the *Leir* author for his antifeminist representations of Gonorill and Ragan, without explaining that such stereotypes go back as far as Geoffrey of Monmouth. Also see Blechner, "King Lear, King Leir, and Incest Wishes."

3. See Bradley, *Shakespearean Tragedy: Hamlet, Othello, King Lear and Macbeth* (1904; repr. New York: Meridian Books, 1960), 200–201.

4. Barroll, *Politics, Plague and Shakespeare's Theater: The Stuart Years* (Ithaca: Cornell University Press, 1991), 4.

5. For discussion of the play's composition history, see Michie's, 18–19.

6. *Henlsowe's Diary,* 2nd ed., ed. R. A. Foakes (Cambridge: Cambridge University Press, 2002), 21.

7. *A Transcript of the Registers of the Company of Stationers of London; 1554–1640 AD*, ed. Edward Arber (London, 1876), 2:307.

8. See W. W. Greg, "The Date of *King Lear* and Shakespeare's Use of Earlier Versions of the Story," *The Library*, 4th series, 20 (1940): 378; and Scott McMillin and Sally-Beth MacLean, *The Queen's Men and their Plays* (Cambridge: Cambridge University Press, 1998), 88.

9. See the editor's annotation on this entry in *A Transcript of the Registers of the Company of Stationers of London; 1554–1640 AD*, 3:123.

10. Greg, 138, notes this alteration; Arber does not.

11. Greg, 383–84.

12. Ibid., 379.

13. Michie, 75n.11.

14. Ibid., 18.

15. Knowles, 29–30, 33–34.

16. Ibid., 33.

17. See *Hengist, King of Kent, or, The Mayor of Queenborough by Thomas Middleton*, ed. Grace Ioppolo (Oxford: Oxford University Press, 2004).

18. Greg, 380.

19. See Greg, 378, 385, and Knutson, *The Repertory of Shakespeare's Company 1594–1613* (Fayetteville: University of Arkansas Press, 1991), 59, 170.

20. McMillin and MacLean, 166–67, 100, 107.

21. See Aaron Thompson's translation, *The British History . . . of Jeffrey of Monmouth* (London, 1718).

22. For extracts from *Leir* source material as well as a full text of the play, see *Narrative and Dramatic Sources of Shakespeare*, ed. Geoffrey Bullough (London: Routledge and Kegan Paul, 1973), 7:269–308. See also Wilfrid Perrett, *The Story of King Lear from Geoffrey of Monmouth to Shakespeare* (Berlin: Mayer and Muller, 1904).

23. Michie, 36.

24. See McMillin and MacLean, 136–37.

25. James I, *The True Law of Free Monarchies: or the Reciprok[al] dutie betwixt a free King and his naturall subjects* (Edinburgh: Robert Waldegrave, 1598), signatures B4v–B5r, D4r, and *Basilikon Doron: or His Maiesties Instructions to his dearest sonne, Henry the Prince* (Edinburgh: Robert Waldegrave, 1603), books 2–3, signatures H1v–H2r, H8r, I4v.

26. See Bullough's discussion of this story, 309–11.

27. Michie, 45–46.

28. McMillin and MacLean, 146–47.

29. Scene and through-line numbers are keyed to Bullough's text as printed in *Narrative and Dramatic Sources of Shakespeare*, 7:337–402. The play, edited by Jay L. Halio, also appears in *The Cambridge "King Lear" CD-Rom: Text and Performance Archive*, ed. Christie Carson and Jacky Bratton (Cambridge: Cambridge University Press, 2000).

30. McMillin and MacLean, 146.

31. Michie, 44.

32. McMillin and MacLean, 146.

33. Ibid., 147.

34. William R. Elton, *King Lear and the Gods* (San Marino, Calif.: Huntington Library, 1966), 63.

35. On this point, see Michie, 21.

36. See Martin Mueller, "From Leir to Lear," *Philogical Quarterly* 73 (1994): 195; also see Knowles, 19, who discounts apparent borrowings in a number of other Shakespearian plays.

37. Mueller, 212.

Dulwich MS. XX, *The Telltale:*
Clues to Provenance

WILLIAM B. LONG

THE papers of Edward Alleyn at his College of God's Gift at Dulwich have long provided valued information for researchers into the workings of Elizabethan theatrical companies and their stagings. Chief among them is Philip Henslowe's "Diary," much quoted, used, and misused. Without these documents, our knowledge and understanding of Elizabethan theater would be immeasurably poorer. Yet the "Diary" and many of its satellite documents bring their own problems, or at least limitations on researchers' expectations. As (mis)chance would have it, of all Philip Henslowe's theatrical and public entertainment activities, only some of the theatrical records pertaining to The Rose in the 1590s have been preserved. Records of early theatrical activities before the building of The Rose as well as those from the operation of The Fortune are missing.

Thus we know chiefly things connected with The Rose, almost nothing about pre-Rose activity, and frustratingly little about The Fortune in both its original and rebuilt versions which Henslowe used far longer than the two versions of The Rose and which no doubt were far more important to the family finances and to theater history in general. The documents remaining in the Alleyn papers indeed comprise a great treasure, but they can be only a fraction of what once must have been contained in Alleyn's and Henslowe's "papers" relating to their theaters.

I should like to look at one document in the Alleyn papers, the anonymous manuscript play, *The Telltale*, to which no certain links can be made to any particular playhouse. It reposes in the Alleyn papers and surely has been there for over two hundred years and most likely long before, but that is hard to prove. We do not know when this manuscript or the playbook from which it was copied entered the Alleyn archives.

There is, of course, another source for dramatic materials entering the Alleyn Papers which is not dependent upon previous ownership by or even contact with either Alleyn or Henslowe. It is possible and even probable, given the late date (in terms of the lives of Alleyn and Henslowe) of *The Telltale* manuscript, that it was one of those owned by the player-turned-bookseller William Cartwright, the younger (ca. 1606–86). In the inventory of Cartwright's estate, is (among many printed books, some titled, most not) the intriguing item "about 100 *Manu Scripts* of plaies".[1]

Gerald Eades Bentley recorded that "Tell Tale: a Comedy" appeared in a list of "Books in the Presse, and ready for printing" advertised by publisher Nathaniel Phillips in *The New World of Words* (1658).[2] Unfortunately, publication seems not to have occurred. Thus it would seem likely that the unpublished manuscript of *The Telltale* passed from Cartwright's estate to Dulwich College.

Not being able to document provenance exactly is frustrating, but in its own way this lack of knowledge offers a valuable opportunity for the study of Elizabethan-Jacobean-Caroline play manuscripts in general. For the very paucity of information about this manuscript makes it available for a kind of "blind" study which is difficult to apply to a play about which playwright, company, and even sometimes the writer of the manuscript itself is known. *The Telltale*'s very anonymity forces the researcher to be more objective than would be likely (and probably possible) in a case where more facts are known. Instead of being guided by subjective assumptions, the researcher would be better advised to consider the evidence here as being analogous to the shards of pottery that regularly confront archeologists whose task it is to assemble them into an intelligible form and to set that object in its historical context.

The Telltale manuscript presents a nearly barebones case where the researcher almost literally must dig to understand what kind of artifact is to hand. Even to approach deciphering the riddles of *The Telltale*, one must attempt to place its features in the contexts of those of other manuscript plays of the period. Thus I should like to examine the features of this manuscript, particularly the stage-directions, in comparison with what we know about stage-directions appearing in playbooks that bear irrefutable markings proving their theatrical provenance.[3] In so doing, and in coming to at least partial determination about facets of *The Telltale*, I suggest that procedures and comparative evaluations made here might be used for the study and classification of other Elizabethan-Jacobean-Caroline play manuscripts as well.

To return to the play at hand, *The Telltale* is an attractive manuscript, carefully written and, for the most part, easy to read. For the theater historian, however, the manuscript of *The Telltale* poses many questions but reveals only some answers. It is, of course, the Alleyn/Henslowe connection that has provided such interest as has been shown in this manuscript play. In the introduction to their 1960 Malone Society edition, R. A. Foakes and J. C. Gibson agree with W. W. Greg in dating this manuscript ca. 1630–40 and marshall convincing evidence to establish this manuscript as a scribal copy rather than a playwright's holograph.[4] But were it merely another early seventeenth-century copy of a current play, it would lack the cachet and concomitant interest that clings to *The Telltale* merely because of its preservation as part of the Dulwich treasure trove and to its distinction of being the only play remaining there (after being returned to the collection) among various other kinds of documents.

But it is present there with little documentable history. Too many people had access to the Alleyn papers for too many years to give solid authority to the mere proximity of storage. We know only that the manuscript was seen in the Alleyn papers by George Stevens before 1780.

If the ca. 1630–40 date of the present manuscript is correct (and there seems to be little reason for supposing that it is not), then the question of how this particular copy made it to the safety of the Dulwich collection is fraught with questions and with at least one borrowing/sequestration. The Rose was not used for playing after 1603; The Fortune burned down in 1621; Henslowe died in 1616; Alleyn himself in 1626—all events worrisomely before the 1630–40 date, thus giving considerably more credence to the Cartwright connection.

There does exist one important thread of connection well worth following, particularly for *The Telltale*'s possible early connection with Alleyn. The extant folded sheets of this copy of *The Telltale* once were wrapped in the "plot" of *2 Seven Deadlie Sins*, a sheet of paper still in the Alleyn papers (returned at the same time as *The Telltale*) and now far better known, reproduced, and commented upon than the play for which it once was deemed a fitting wrapper—a small irony of theatrical history. The "plot" is titled in the hand that wrote the rest of it: "The Booke and platt of the Second part of the 7 deadly sinns" although the playbook itself long ago disappeared. Apparently this wrapper was pressed into service as the cover for *The Telltale* after the removal of the book of *2 Seven Deadly Sins*.

W. W. Greg assigns the *2 Seven Deadly Sins* plot to the Lord Strange's Men playing at The Curtain about 1590. How this sheet of paper migrated to Dulwich by the 1630s possibly may be traced by the very hand that wrote it. That person has been identified by Greg as "Hand C," the bookkeeper of the manuscript playbook of Anthony Munday's *Sir Thomas More* (1592/3) and the person who also endorsed the wrapper of Munday's holograph playbook of *John a Kent and John a Cumber* (1590).[5]

"Hand C" thus is the first identifiable (but unfortunately nameless) bookkeeper in the entire Elizabethan-Jacobean-Caroline period. He would appear to have been a longtime employee of Henslowe/Alleyn, accompanying them from playhouse to playhouse over the years. His handwriting is one of the ways, however small, of chronicling that peregrination. At whatever point *The Telltale* was acquired, prepared for production, and entered the repertory (and whatever its success), it obviously was deemed worth retaining and supplying with a wrapper to aid its preservation. Whether or not Hand C was the bookkeeper who prepared *The Telltale* for the playhouse of course is unknowable since the extant manuscript is a copy of the original playbook. Additionally, it is well to note that although Hand C's autograph wrapper was used for *The Telltale*, there is no proof whatsoever that Hand C was the one who placed it there. By the time of *The Telltale*, Hand C may have moved on or have died.

In his important examination of the plot of *The Second Part of the Seven Deadly Sins*, David Kathman persuasively argues that the date and provenance of this plot and play is the late 1590s and with the Lord Chamberlain's Men. These changes from Greg's conjectures are important for a number of facets of theater history, but do not change the generally agreed dates for the manuscript of *The Telltale* and add support to the suggestion that the manuscript came to Dulwich in the Cartwright bequest rather than remaining from the Henslowe-Alleyne years.[6]

Like other papers in the Dulwich archives, *The Telltale* did have its own late eighteenth- early nineteenth-century peregrinations; but unlike many other documents, it eventually returned home. With many other theatrical papers, *The Telltale* was lent or traded to Edmond Malone during his researches and eventually surfaced as Item 3140 in the 30 May 1825 Sotheby sale catalogue of the Library of James Boswell, Jr., Malone's literary inheritor, from whence it was claimed by officials of the College and returned, hopefully never more to roam. The *2 Seven Deadlie Sins* plot/wrapper was Item 3136 in the catalogue and also was duly returned (Greg, ibid., I: 6–7n., 8–9).

Whatever may have happened to the playbook itself, this particular manuscript of *The Telltale* is highly unlikely to have been planned for anything but a reading copy, and its use even for that is limited because of its large lacuna and other scribal failures to read the hand of the manuscript he was transcribing, presumably the playwright's. Greg assigned this manuscript to his "Class B": "manuscripts with definite relation to the theatre but which show no definite evidence of having been used in the playhouse and if written there were probably prepared for some private purpose" (ibid., I: 191).

It would seem that the extant manuscript of *The Telltale* is a scribal copy of the playwright's holograph that was used as a theatrical playbook which now was being prepared as a reading copy for a private person, or for some other nontheatrical use. Let us then proceed in an orderly fashion to examine the features of this manuscript to support this rather cursory observation.

"The play occupies twelve sheets of paper, folded once to give a page measuring up to twelve and one quarter by nearly eight inches" (Foakes and Gibson, v). This produces a book, allowing for slight variations in sheet size and wear, of the same proportions as the eighteen manuscript playbooks that survive from 1590 to 1635, but these measurements are also approximately the size of most surviving copies of contemporary manuscript plays not related to theatrical production.

Furthermore, nearly all of the surviving playbooks bear signs, some faint,

some quite distinct, of two additional vertical folds which produce a page
divided into four equal longitudinal columns, done seemingly both for ease
of copying and, more importantly, for producing useable blank marginal
space for theatrical notation as well as for easily separating dialogue from
directional material. *The Telltale* manuscript bears no such signs, and the
margins are consequently, for play manuscripts, atypically small. Such an
absence signals a scribe, writing "in the hand of a literary type" concludes
Greg, (ibid., I: 340), who was not familiar with theatrical copying.

Foakes and Gibson continue: "The number of lines to a page varies between forty-eight and sixty. The play is divided into acts, but there is no
heading for ACT I; scenes are not indicated in the original" (vi). Unfortunately, these features are so general and so common that they point nowhere.
In most manuscripts meant for the stage as well as many meant only for reading, stage-directions and speech-headings often are inscribed in Italian style
for easy differentiation from the secretary hand of the dialogue itself. Such
switching from hand to hand is done so frequently that it seems almost a
second nature for those composing or transcribing plays. Not so with this
scribe, however.

> A few stage directions are written in an Italian style, but as a rule this is not very
> distinctive, and it quickly shades off into the scribe's usual English hand. Some
> speech-headings . . . are commonly written in what seems meant to be an Italian
> style; and once or twice . . . where there is a change of ink or a change or mending
> of pen, a positive attempt was made for a time to distinguish directions and speech-
> headings in this way. But always the scribe lapses into his English hand, and is
> reasonably consistent in his use of Italian forms only in the writing of *exit* and
> *exeunt*. As Greg noted, it may well be a sign of his awareness of this failure to
> distinguish his italian hand that the scribe consistently underlined speech-headings,
> and enclosed most stage-directions in rules.
>
> (ix)

These rulings are, indeed, a distinguishing feature of this manuscript; here
is an illustrative group, Figure 1: folio 5a, middle portion, lines 464–68.

Greg noted that the scribe "was apparently conscious that his Italian script
habitually lacked distinction" (ibid., I, 340). Two manuscript playbooks have
roughly analogous emphasizings of stage-directions, done in both cases, it

would seem, for ease in noticing them; there the scribes had no difficulty in consistently using their Italian hands. But with theatrical playbooks, the Italian hand is for the benefit of the bookkeeper and not for that of a reader in the study. In the manuscript playbook of the anonymous *Thomas of Woodstock* (company unknown, ca. 1604), most stage-directions in the hand of the scribe whether centered, or in the left or right margins are over- and underscored, and many of these scorings are connected by parentheses (Figure 2: folio 179a, upper portion, lines 2147–53).

In looking at this manuscript playbook, it would seem that such unusual emphasis was needed to make the stage-directions easily visible to the bookkeeper glancing ahead to what was to happen on (or back) stage. In generally similar fashion, in the playbook of the anonymous *The Two Noble Ladies* (Revels Company, 1619–23), most directions in all positions are boxed. In addition, the scribe adds a row of dots across the page at the end of each act (Figure 3: folio 5a, lower portion, lines 366–70).

Again, such markings appear to have been added to aid the bookkeeper to keep tabs on what was approaching in the action. Looking at this manuscript itself (in contrast to looking at the ample spacing provided in the Malone Society edition) shows how helpful such added markings could be.

In *The Telltale,* the scribe begins by centering the title "The Telltale" at the top of the first page, underlines it, and then adds two decorative squiggles at either side (Figure 4: folio 1a, upper portion, lines 1–7).

It would seem that he then wrote the text of the play, setting off directions at the right and emphasizing them by over- and underscoring and by adding similar squiggles left and right as he had with the title. Again, such markings appear to have been done originally to aid a bookkeeper who was giving a quick glance at what was coming up in the text, and they are reproduced here by a scribe who tries to remain faithful to his text even though the original reason for some markings no longer pertains to the reading copy the scribe is creating. This scribe observes the convention of using speech-rules; his are about three-quarters of an inch elongated ticks. After completing the copying of the dialogue lines on a page (at least, if not for a longer portion of text), he then goes back and enters the speech-headings (which he atypically underlines for emphasis) and left-marginal stage-directions. It is interesting then, even though he did not use the traditional folded columns, that nonetheless he first copied the dialogue before he went back for the left margin markings—the practice of professional playwrights and theatrical scribes.

Because of this copying process, the speech-headings are quite clearly out of line, most often inscribed slightly above the baseline of the speech they identify (Figure 5: folio 2a, middle portion, lines 132–43).

No scribe copying every word in a line from one side of a page to the other would be so regularly and consistently off. The placement of the opening stage-direction also is curious (see Figure 4). It occurs in the left margin in the very upper left-hand corner of the page: "A florish. / enter Duke / of florence / solus" with a single line under it. Most playwrights (and most scribes) would center a play-opening stage-direction. Why not here? Was this placement an idiosyncrasy or a mistake of the playwright that the scribe was copying faithfully? If this latter is so, then the original manuscript was very curious indeed. If not, then what? If the scribe was changing what he found, what was the purpose? Why would he go to the extra trouble of rethinking and rearranging what he found before him?

A clue may lay in his choice of phrasing: "A florish" is a curious phrasing for playwright, theater scribe, or bookkeeper; usually the noun appears without the article. At line 36, another "A Florish" is boxed in the left margin before the entrance of eleven characters. Playwrights rarely bother with the indefinite article in such instances; bookkeepers also focus attention on that vital noun which demands that something be done offstage at a particular time. I believe that the scribe's use of the article here and elsewhere has to do not so much with what he is copying but rather with the nature of what he is creating. And I think that his persistent use of the article is one of a number of indications that he is consciously making a reading text.

Racing ahead to the very end of the play, we find "A florish" in the left margin opposite a nearly centered "ffinis"—a formal musical closing bracketing a formal musical opening (Figure 6: folio 23a, lower portion, lines 2300–03).

| that they so long haue wishd for, all the right | 2300 |
| that Ioy Can giue vs weele enioy this night | |

| A florish. | | |
| | ffinis | Exeunt |

I include the Malone Society diplomatic transcription to underscore the inadequacy of even good print redactions as an aid to understanding space relationships which cannot be duplicated when moving from manuscript to print. (The monogram of "NICHOLAS" may be that of the scribe; if so, further identification stops there.) That the method and the wording of inscription for the direction is the same indicates to me that it was done by the scribe. I would guess that some sort of rewriting had shuffled elements at the beginning of the play, leaving space for the opening entrance only in the left margin, a highly atypical placement but for various reasons now not recoverable, probably the only available space.

Slim evidence that this use of the indefinite article is, it would seem to be part of the scribe's reasoning that led him to box the stage-directions. If one looks at pages of text without reading them, boxed stage-directions stand out—not so much in the manuscript as they do in The Malone Society redaction to print, but they are easily distinguishable from dialogue nonetheless. Indeed, they are far more easily seen than they would need to be for theatrical personnel. However, they do help to make what is going on clear for a reader. Similarly, the difference between "A florish" and the far more usual "Florish" is what I will call, for want of a better term, "literary"—or at least, intended for reading and not for theatrical use, whether that be a playwright's letting the players know what he wanted or a bookkeeper's notation for an offstage noise needed at a particular point.

Inscriptions in the manuscript playbooks would seem to bear out this difference of origin. *Thomas of Woodstock* has two instances of *"a florish"* (folio 168b, line 914) and *"A Florish"* (folio 170a, line 1120) both in the hand of the scribe; however, when the bookkeeper highlights such calls, he uses merely "florish" five times ("fflorish." folio 166a, line 628; "fflorish" folio 167b, line 794; "florish" and "ff[ ]she/" folio 168a, lines 820, 823; "Flourish" folio 169b, line 109). (Figure 7: folio 167b, middle portion, lines 787–96; folio 169b, upper portion, lines 1008–15).

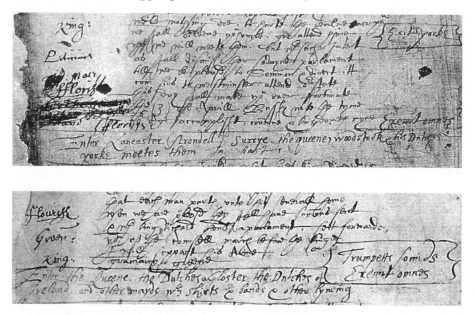

Opposite the ending of Philip Massinger's holograph manuscript playbook of *Believe as You List* (King's Men, 1631), Edward Knight, the King's Men's bookkeeper, has over- and underscored a bold "fflorish" (Figure 8: folio 27b, lower portion, lines 2892–95).

Farther down on the first page of *The Telltale*, the scribe boxes an *"exit"* on the right and then two lines later boxes a centered entrance for eleven players, completing this entry by boxing this example of *"A florish"* in the left margin opposite the entry. On folio 3a, he boxes *"Exeunt"* and *"Exit."* Players usually do not have to be told when to get off the stage—witness all

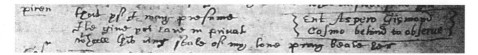

those "missing" exits in the plays of Shakespeare and others; and certainly neither the players nor a bookkeeper need to have exits boxed for noticeability. For a reader, however, it is quite handy in his/her constructing a mental picture of what is happening onstage to keep clearly in mind who is present and who is not.

At the top of folio 4b, "*Enter Captain, Lieftenant Antient*" is underscored and boxed on the left and right sides. The second scene ends with a boxed "Exeunt" (folio 5a, line 344) immediately followed by "*Enter victoria &* *picinto*" scored top, bottom, and sides and with an empty extension to the box on either side, presumably to more easily indicate stage clearance and the entrance of new characters. Farther down on the same page occurs what in earlier studies I have labeled a "playwright's advisory direction." In such inscriptions, playwrights instruct the players not just what to do, but also how or why to do it: "*Ent Aspero, Gismond / Cosmo behind to observe*" (Figure 9: folio 4a, lower portion, lines 368–70).

It is toward the right and, of course, boxed. Since the reader cannot see what is happening onstage, the scribe ensures that this stage-direction will be seen. This direction surely seems to be one originating with the playwright, and it apparently has not been altered or supplemented by a playhouse bookkeeper (again the expected practice, or nonpractice); it then has been transcribed by our scribe who carefully boxes it so that his reader[s] will be aware of the playwright's intentions. This is the observable pattern for most of the stage-directions surviving in *The Telltale*.

It is, at this point, well to note something else which I think is important about the playwright's advisory directions in *The Telltale*; there are an atypically large number of them—thirty to be exact. A number of plays have very few. A manuscript playbook of similar length, Anthony Munday's *John a Kent and John a Cumber* has only seven.[7] It is certainly possible that some plays had none at all. Most often, there are a relatively small handful. Playwrights' advisory directions are added by a playwright who is in some way or other, for some reason or other, distant (or at least absent) from the company of players. Either the playwright is an amateur and does not know how capable professional playwrights are in adapting a playwright's words to stage action or the playwright is not in frequent contact with the playing company to offer explication of his text and/or advice on how to bring it to life. Which of these options is operative in *The Telltale*, I do not know, but I very much believe that one of them is.

Folio 5a continues with *"Enter Iulio as a slaue"* boxed after the dialogue and partially into the right margin, plus two *"Exeunt"*s and *"Enter Iulio."*, all boxed and similarly located. Act 1 ends at the bottom of the page with *"Exeunt"* boxed at the right, "Actus Secundus" centered and boxed to contain an empty space extending through the left margin, the top line enclosing "Actus Secundus" extends across the page to become the bottom line boxing "Exeunt" (Figure 10: lower portion, lines 493–96).

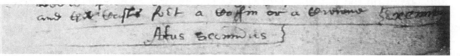

The change of act is thus well highlighted on the page, a situation of use to readers, but unless there is interact music, a situation of no use to the theatrical personnel—or to the theater audience, for that matter.

After its well-announced arrival, Act 2 actually begins under the box with "Enter Elinor, fernese Garulo" which is only underlined (folio 5a, line 497). At line 522, after a short line, but before the right margin, appears the boxed "Ent Clowne" and at line 541, the boxed "ent benti: wth two wepons" also after a short line and ending at the completion of the dialogue. The vagueness as to exactly what weapons are to be brought onstage is a not unusual playwright's vagueness relying on the players to decide upon the particulars—a practice rarely modified by theatrical bookkeepers. It would seem that this scribe's clarification process extended only to emphasizing stage-directions, not to providing additional information.

On folio 6a, the boxed and unusually phrased "Exiturus" appears near the right end of the dialogue line. Shortly thereafter, halfway through a twenty-one-line speech by Bentivoli, "ent Gismond / whisp elinor" appears boxed in the left margin similar to the arrangement at the opening of the play shown in Figure 11: middle portion, lines 578–80.

Elinor and Gismond begin to speak just after Bentivoli's boxed exit at the right after his last words (line 589). This, of course, is not only an entry, but also a playwright's advisory direction; it is, however, the left-marginal placement that is atypical. A more usual placing can be seen with a "whisper" direction from the anonymous manuscript playbook *Charlemagne* (company unknown, ca. 1604) where the scribe, presumably following the playwright, has entered the direction in the right margin (Figure 12: folio 131b, upper portion, lines 2130–34.)

The phrasing of the direction is that of the playwright, and its expected placement would be either centered or in the right margin. The right margin here in *The Telltale*, however, is taken up with long prose lines. It is, of course, possible that the playwright placed it there originally and for the same reason. Such a situation would be highly unusual although not excludable from possibility. There is another possible explanation: because of his failure to fold the pages into equal columns, this nontheatrical scribe has left himself no room in such tight situations created by long prose lines, thus leaving him no choice but to use the left margin. The shortened "whisp elinor" rather than what would be expected from a playwright, "whispers to elinor", adds strength to this explanation.

Folio 7a brings the boxed "*exeunt*" (line 670) and "*exit*" (line 671) at the right after the completion of the characters' speeches. Here too is the continuation, which becomes a continual pattern, of boxing the exeunt ending a scene with the entrance which begins the new scene (Figure 13: middle portion, lines 679–81).

Not only is this something not expected from a playwright, but also neither is placing both exit and entrance in the same line. A playwright nearly always would have placed the exeunt after the last line of the closing scene and positioned the entrance of new characters in the center on its own line. There are instances of a playwright's opening his manuscript with "Actus I Scena i" and adding no further indication of Latinate breaks anywhere else thereafter; but most often playwrights add no indication of scene change which is simply assumed by the clearing of the stage and the entrance of different characters.

Thus the picture here of a box beginning with the dialogue at the left margin followed by a space, then "Enter Isabella & lesbia" set off by squiggles, then another blank space, then "exeunt" set off by squiggles looks very much like a scribal arrangement for the convenience of and explanation to a reader (Figure 14: folio 10a, middle portion, lines 995–1001).

And it is an effective device. It highlights the changes noticed, and the scribe adds a similar device with the close of each succeeding scene. This scribe was no fool; he knew what he was doing in constructing a reading text. His problems arise from his not being familiar with stage practices.

On folio 7b, the boxed *"Exeunt"* appears alone on line 719 because the boxed squiggle [space] / "Enter Aspero Cosmo Gismund Bentis / Elinor Isabell: Lesbia Ambassed /" takes up too much space to include the "Exeunt," but the format is identical. Further down the page, however, there is something quite different and provides a very important piece of provenancial evidence.

At the end of the dialogue and extending into the right margin occurs the boxed *"A cry wthin* / ent Count lik a foole" (lines 738–39). In the left margin opposite line 738 occurs unboxed "Wthin". The two-line, right-hand direction is an almost archetypical playwright's advisory direction: a call for an off-stage noise and an entrance that includes a playwright's advisory direction. And similarly, the left-marginal "Wthin" is an extremely typical example of the kind (and placing) of an alteration to a playwright's stage-direction made by a playhouse bookkeeper (Figure 15: folio 7b, middle portion, lines 734–40).

He does not alter the playwright's words; he merely adds a near-duplicating, and thus emphasizing, word in his own hand and ink in the left margin so that the notation for the offstage noise will not be missed. His addition is an attention-getting rather than a changing. Because the "Wthin" is so cramped

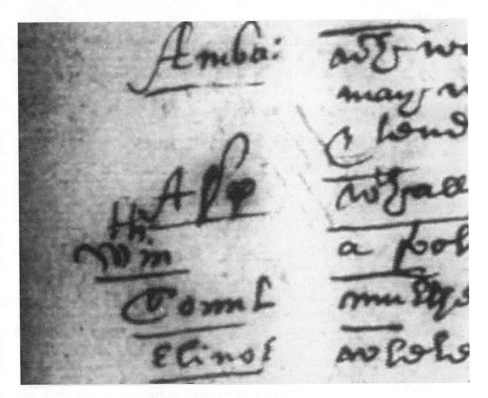

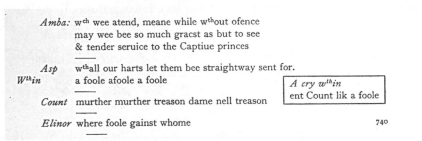

Amba: wch wee atend, meane while wthout ofence
        may wee bee so much gracst as but to see
        & tender seruice to the Captiue princes
        _____

        Asp   wthall our harts let them bee straightway sent for.
Wthin   a foole afoole a foole
        _____

    Count   murther murther treason dame nell treason

    Elinor where foole gainst whome

> *A cry wthin*
> ent Count lik a foole

                                                            740

and so important, I include an enlargement as well as an actual-size copy of
the manuscript. As a contrast to emphasize how misleadingly obvious it all
looks in a type redaction (and thus how unnecessary a marking for the bookkeeper), I also include the Malone Society rendition.

   This set of directions alone demonstrates that the manuscript from which
the extant *Telltale* manuscript was copied had been prepared in anticipation
of theatrical production. It is additionally curious that the scribe copied, but
did not box, the bookkeeper's "Wthin". Perhaps he felt that fidelity to the
text meant copying everything he could decipher even though he did not un-

derstand the purpose of the duplication and thus chose not to highlight it. In
the context of reading, of course, the bookkeeper's addition is redundant. Had
the scribe, in the interest of clarity for the readers, deleted the bookkeeper's
addition, he would have eliminated the single strongest piece of evidence for
establishing the provenance of this manuscript. Of such chances is theater
history made.

Folio 8a contains three entrances: "Ent Borgias" (line 768), "ent ii doc-
tors" (line 796), and "Enter hortenza." (line. 804)—all boxed and near or
into the right margin at the end of a line of dialogue which reflect playwrights' usual practices found in surviving manuscript playbooks. *The Telltale* scribe's persistent placing of such short entrances in the right suggests,
given the scribe's reluctance to interfere with what he is copying, that the
playwright placed such short entries there originally, an unusual but not impossible choice.

Folio 9a contains more of the now to be expected right-hand boxed exits:
"*Exit Hort*" (line 871), "*exit* doctor" (line 778), "*exit*" (line 880), and "*exit*"
(line 888), and a playwright's advisory direction "*enter* Duke like a / hermit"
(lines 889–90). Folio 9b bears the boxed "*Enter* Iulio. / like a slaue" (lines
924–25), and "*Exit*" (line 938) at the right edge of the dialogue. Folio 10b
begins with "*exit Duke / ent a messinger / wth a letter*" (lines 978–79) and
"opens the letter" (line 983) both boxed at the right, the second two being
playwright's advisory directions, and closes with two of the scribe's signature boxed scene closings/entrances: "*exeunt*" / [space] "Enter duke & fide-
lio" (lines 999–1000) and "*Exeunt* / [space] Ent victoria in a poore habitt
Iulio like [space] / A slaue" (Figure 16: folio 10b, lower portion, lines 1029–
31).

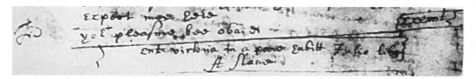

More playwright's advisory directions are boxed on the right on folio 10b:
"*offers to cut her face*" (line 1051) and "*vmbers her face*" (line 1053). Act
3 begins with the by now expected boxed formula: "*Actus tertius*" [space]
"*exeunt*" / [space] *Enter Duke Cap: Leiftenant Antient*" (lines 1066–67).
Only two further boxed directions occur before the scene changes: "ent 2
sold: vict: & Iulio" (line 139) and "Enter a boy dressed like Elinor / & a
doctor [space] *Exeunt*" (lines 1190–91). The last entrance, a playwright's
advisory direction, has an additional boxed space before the words, thus extending the entire boxed stage-direction into the left margin and heightening
its noticeability. These lines have been scored through for deletion and now
are difficult to read.

The next scene begins on folio 12a with the centered, boxed "Enter a boy drest like Elinor & doctor" followed by a squiggle to separate off "*Exit*" at the end of the boxed material, but set half a line higher than the entrance (l. 1209). The scene expands at line 1215 with the boxed "Ent Borgias & Hortenza" at the right, after the end of a line of dialogue. The group leaves with Hortenza's "are they gone? then hence" followed by a boxed "*exeunt*" (line 1272). At line 1276, the group expands with "*ent Amb: asper: Cosmo Gismond*" boxed at the right of a short line. Line 1300 brings more with "Ent Elinor & Count a foole", similarly boxed and placed. Folio 13a, brings a rash of activity including two playwright's advisory directions, all duly boxed and added at the right, after dialogue lines: "*exit*" (line 1327), "*exit*" (line 1335), "*ent a gent: whispers asp*" at the end of a line by Aspero (line 1336), "*exeunt*" (line 1340), "*exeunt*" (line 1344), and "*enter Duke in hast*" (line 1345).

Folio 13b adds "*exit*" (line 1375) and "*exeunt*" (line 1380) boxed and at the ends of dialogue lines to end the scene. Immediately following the "*exeunt*" is the centered and boxed "*Ent: Aspero Cosmo Gis: Fernisi Isabella sick / Picentio* as a doctor wth her water" (Figure 17: folio 13b, middle portion, lines 1379–82).

Once again, the playwright's advisory directions clarify much for the readers, but perhaps not enough. Isabella must be identified quickly as "sick." How does she look "sick"? A doctor at her side holding her "water" might well suffice, but there is another stock device (which conveniently happens to be used later in the play [folio 22b, lines 2231–32]). Andrew Gurr and Mariko Ichikawa discuss the use of the "sick chair"[8] which is conspicuously absent here, but which materializes near the end of the play with "Garullo brought / in a Chaire wth / a doctor" (folio 27b, lines 2231–33).

Those researchers interested in torturing themselves by looking for consistency in staging practice will want to add this instance to their journals. These two entrances can well be used as a cautionary example: even though we know that certain staging devices or methods were known, and available, to certain players in certain theaters on certain occasions, one can by no means be sure that they always were used. They well may have been, but we do not *know* so. Editors and theater researchers must be more cautious than has been the rule in the past about making *ex cathedra* pronouncements about what was or was not done.

Later (line 1403), Aspero leaves with a boxed "*exeunt*", and still later Picentio leaves the stage with his boxed "*Exit*" at the end of his last speech line (line 1480). Folio 14b begins with the somewhat curiously placed "Enter picentio in / his owne shape" boxed and in the right margin at lines 1493–94; but Picentio does not enter until 1496. Why this is so placed is unknown. It is at the right side because the scribe (and possibly/probably the playwright) eschew centered directions. The possible crowding of long prose lines does not apply here because this stage-direction is in a verse passage, and the last line of this passage is the shortest in the speech. A marginal placing to save a line rather than use a lineal space with a centered direction does not apply here because the length of this page is fifty-seven lines, the same as the preceding one and only four more than the next folio's fifty-three. Playwright's habit seems the most likely explanation for this placing of stage-directions in or toward the right margin after the dialogue.

Farther down on folio 14b (at lines 1528–29) occurs "*She offers to / embrace him*", a boxed playwright's advisory direction in the right following dialogue. Folio 15a brings the boxed "Exit" at line 1550 and "Ent Picentio as Doctor" (1555) before the closing of act 3 with the elaborately boxed "*Actus quartus . . . Exeunt* / Enter Cosmo Gismond fernesi bentivoli" at 1590 and 1591. Each unit in each line is marked off with vertical squiggles within horizontal lines. Line 1591 also bears boxed empty space on both sides of the entrance (Figure 18: folio 15a, lower portion, lines 1589–92).

Folio 16a begins (line 1652) atypically with the merely underlined and thus seemingly almost nakedly presented "*Enter aspero, Ambassador doctor*". Elinor joins the group at line 1680 "Ent Elinor." and Bentivoli at 1680, "Enter Benti wth a letter" both boxed and following dialogue lines at the right. The same boxed-end of the dialogue-in-the-right formula is employed to bring on "*Enter Hortenzo*" (1725), take off "*Exit Hortenzo.*" (1738), and bring on Hortenzo again, "Ent Hortenzo" (1750). This last is made further noticeable by the addition of a small boxed empty space at each end of the direction. Folio 17a begins with "*Exeunt* manet nobles" (l. 1767) boxed at the right as a preparation for the boxed scene change at 1772–73: "Enter Captaine, Leiftenant, Iulio / antient, duke, Barber as hauing trimd him"—yet another playwright's advisory direction. "*Exeunt*" is separately boxed at the right of the first line of the entrance. At line 1799 "ent victoria as before" is boxed at the right, after dialogue.

Picentio's changes are carefully recorded on folio 19a: "*Exit* Picentio" (line 1836), "enter picentio as adoctor" [*sic*] (line 1842), both boxed, to the right, and after a line of dialogue. A few lines farther down the page Aspintor leaves the stage with *"Exit"*, boxed with long side bars dropping down to be closed on the bottom with the top line of the box for "Enter Cosmo Gismond fernese" (lines 1851–52). The page ends with Picentio's boxed (advisory) direction to "discouer himself" (line 1872), followed immediately overleaf with "embrace him", underlined only (line 1873). At the end of line 1878, the boxed "Ent Benti" is the last before the beginning of the final act, the centered, boxed "Actus qintus [*sic*] / Enter fernese & porter."; at the right of the first line appears the expected "Exeunt". The scene continues at line 1923 with the boxed "enter Count Lesbia Clow" at the right of the dialogue.

Folio 20a, line 1971 carries the unexpected and surprisingly located and presented "wine", boxed at the right. Wine is used several lines later; what is of interest here is this word and its placement (Figure 19: lower portion, lines 1970–72).

In a text where the playwright had been so careful to provide even seemingly unneeded advisory directions, one wonders why he did not inscribe something like: "Enter servant with wine"? If he did so in his manuscript, it is missing in this copy. What we have here is but a single word—the sort of thing that one would expect to see inscribed in the left margin by a book-keeper to ensure that wine would be onstage when needed.[9] Were this word in the left margin, I unhesitatingly would assume it similar in inspiration and origin to the "Wthin" on folio 7b.

However, it is near the right margin, not in the left. Surviving playbooks offer possible explanations other than the obvious, but highly unusual in this text, answer that the playwright simply wrote "wine" and that the scribe correctly copied it. On a few occasions where a bookkeeper is greatly concerned that a noise be made at the proper time or that a particular property be ready to be carried onstage at the right moment, he would enter an appropriate word like "swords" or even "wine" in both the left and the right margins as a kind of double-check, ensuring that the property would not be late or missed altogether in the rush of performance. For example, here is a bookkeeper's call for "Blanks" [i.e., blank charters] from *Thomas of Woodstock* (Figure 20a): folio 170b, upper portion, lines 1132–38. Another bookkeeper adds a very insistent call for "Barre" in the left margin and a "Table" in the direction itself in addition to playhouse scrivener Ralph Crane's "A Bar brought in" in the right (Figure 20b) from John Fletcher's *Sir John van Olden Barnavelt* (King's Men, 1625, folio 23b, upper portion, lines 2154–60).

Bookkeepers most often mark primarily in the left margin because it is easier to notice something there, and they made it their habitual territory. It would seem that, for whatever reasons, the main (left-hand) notation was missing or had been deleted and that what remained (and which was faithfully copied by the scribe) was the secondary right-margin "insurance" inscription by the bookkeeper.

On folio 20b, the foolish count leaves with a simple right-margin boxed "*Exit*" on its own line rather than at the end of a dialogue line as would be expected in this manuscript. At line 2015, everyone else leaves with an "*Exeunt*" which is boxed in the line after the last speech and which is connected to the new entrance by sharing the top line of its box. The direction begins with "*A Sennit.*" in the left margin and continues: "*Enter Cosmo Gismond bare: 2 bearing / the Crowne and scepter: then aspero. / 2 Churchmen betwixt them Isabella. / Hortensio Elinor Borgias Bentivoli / Picentio as a doctor.*" The entire direction is boxed, with "*Exeunt*" separately set off at the end of the first line of the direction. The direction *cum* advisory directions and its placement is standard for this manuscript.

What is unusual is "*A Sennit.*" carefully inscribed in the left margin in the same line of the beginning of the entrances but outside the box (Figure 21: middle portion, lines 2025–30).

The question is: was this the creation of the playwright or was it added by the playhouse bookkeeper? As these words stand now, it is impossible to be certain. Had the playwright included in the body of the direction the words "florish", "tucket", or "sennet", by themselves or as part of a description, then one might well take this lefthand margin "A Sennit." to be an addition by the bookkeeper to be sure that this offstage sound would happen at the proper time. And perhaps this is the case.

On the other hand, one could argue that this sennet is needed at such a large entrance which involves so many players that the person in charge of producing this sound could not possibly miss the proper timing, and thus that this inscription is the playwright's in spite of its left marginal placing—much like the curious left-margin placing of the opening entrance of the play itself. *Thomas of Woodstock* contains "sound A Sennett" as the opening of a large centered entrance direction; it is in the hand of the scribe presumably copying the playwright's direction, not that of the bookkeeper, who does not add a

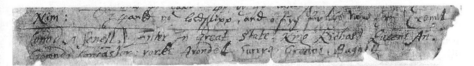

highlight of his own (Figure 22: folio 163b, lower portion, lines 349–51). Sometimes in reconstructing an object, pieces can fit into similar slots in differing objects, and one hesitates to say which is correct. It is rather like trying to fit together pieces of a jigsaw puzzle without knowing what is represented by the picture one is attempting to assemble. A good fit—i.e., a viable explanation—is not necessarily the correct answer. One could end up with a picture of a tiger with rosebuds for ears.

Still later in the scene appears a conventional entry *cum* playwright's advisory direction, boxed in the right after the end of a dialogue line (lines 2101–02): "ent duke, dutches Iulio Captain / lieftenant antient lik ghosts". The most elaborate directions in the play do not involve an entrance at all, but the climactic and symbolic dance: "The duke taks the Crowne the dutches / the scepter, Captaine fetches of hortenzo. / leiftenant elinor & the antient Borgias." This is lined top and bottom (Figure 23: folio 21b, middle portion, lines 2144–50).

At the end of the first line, there is a line after the last word (dutches), then another line parallel into the right margin with the initial boxing line. These three lines, two long and one short, thus form a box open only on the narrow right side into which "*A Daunce*" has been written. (In point of composition, of course, the words were most likely written first, then the lines added.)

After all this, the direction continues: "in wch they reioyse & embrace the duke / dutches & the rest take a new state in order". The last line of text is underscored. Opposite the first of these two lines, the words *"Another strained"* have been added in the right margin (three lines under *"A Daunce"*), the new call for more music underlined and a three-line bar was placed after the dialogue to complete a three-sided box for this direction. Another squiggle then was added to connect the underscoring of the last line of directional text with the underscoring of the second musical direction (Figure 24). On the page everything is all quite obvious: this simply is a five-line advisory direction with two music directions to complement it; each element is separately boxed within the larger box encompassing the entire direction. A person glancing at it *in toto* thus easily could separate who is doing what from the music calls.

Folio 22b provides an instance of the classic stage presentation detailed by Gurr and Ichikawa of a person who is ill: "garullo / brought / in a Chaire wth / a doctor", boxed in the right margin after dialogue (Figure 24: middle portion, lines 2231–33).

And the play ends (lines 2302–03) with an almost centered "ffinis" boxed top and bottom (not on the left) followed by an *"Exeunt"* several inches to the right, barely into the margin. The top and bottom lines boxing *"ffinis"* also enclose "Exeunt" which is additionally undivided, thus providing left and right vertical lines to complete the box (see above, Figure 6). The first question to present itself here is why is there a second line under *"Exeunt"* when it is already boxed? It hardly would be needed to emphasize the players' final leaving of the stage. They surely could have figured this out without an underlined direction (and so could readers). If I am correct in my supposition that the boxing of stage directions is the addition of the scribe to make an easier-to-read manuscript, the first long and flowing line under *"Exeunt"* might have been simply an emphasizing flourish by the playwright upon completion of the play: "Exeunt" / [stroke] / ("I'm finished with it!"). Being a careful copyist, the scribe then picked this line up, later "duplicating" it when he boxed the entire direction.

But he did not box quite everything. He left open the left-margin side of his box, beginning his lines with the beginning of the dialogue. In the left-margin, a line or so higher than *"ffinis"* stands *"A florish."* totally unboxed, unseparated from *"ffinis"* except by vertical and horizontal space. The second question obviously is: "Who was responsible for the initial inscription of *"A florish."*—the playwright or the bookkeeper? And also obviously, either could have been. Here I would opt for the bookkeeper not only because the direction is in the left margin, but also because the scribe handles it similarly to the way he handled the "Wthin" back on folio 10b. He does not know quite what to do with this word because he does not quite fathom its function. He includes it because it is there, and he records it in the position in which he found it because he is a careful copyist. But it is odd—and it does not fit the pattern he has observed and continued and emphasized. And, of course, he is right; neither of these markings (and a few others) "fit" the suppositions this nontheatrical scribe is or should be following. They are inscriptions for the theater, not for the study. They indeed do belong to a different world—one that is often idiosyncratic, sometimes messy, many times difficult to fit neatly into a pattern, and occasionally just plain contradictory.

Having moved from shards to larger joined pieces, these fragments must be fitted into some sort of more or less coherent configuration. The material presented here demonstrates that this manuscript of *The Telltale* is a copy made by a scribe who was not familiar with the vagaries of theatrical playbooks. The manuscript he was copying would seem most likely to have been the playwright's holograph which then was supplemented by at least two theatrical bookkeeper's calls for offstage sounds. That there are so few may indicate that some were deleted or not copied; but it very well also might mean that they were not made in the first place. Proportionate to the numbers of playwrights' directions, playhouse bookkeepers add very few additional markings. Their markings reveal no desire for completeness or for overriding supervision, but rather they are meant only to mark spots in which the bookkeepers see trouble or its possibility. Offstage sounds, whether from the human voice or from musical instruments are what most drew additional inscriptions from bookkeepers' pens.

I have dwelt at some length, actually considering every entrance and exit, in the (perhaps obsessive) interests of completeness and realizing that in doing so, I run the risk of some measure of tediousness. But in sifting through such evidence as comes down to us, I believe that no details can be ignored, no matter how obvious they are in function nor how insignificant any single one may be. For a short perspective comparison, let us look at sheer totals.

The manuscript as it stands, or rather, slightly more accurately, as presented in the Malone Society diplomatic rendition allowing one line count for any line with writing on it, totals 2303 lines (shorter than most plays (although, of course, with a lacuna), but almost exactly the size of *John a Kent and John a Cumber*. Of these lines, 51 are taken up with stage-directions alone, reducing the number of lines bearing dialogue to 2262. There are 117 stage-directions; of these, 87 are only simple entrances or exits bearing no additional descriptions. Thus there is a stage-direction for every 26 lines of dialogue. When one adds the number of playwright's advisory directions, 30, to the mere entry/exit ones, the percentages change significantly to one direction for every 19+ lines.

For playwrights connected closely to a group of players, Shakespeare and Heywood for example, playwright's advisory directions are fewer: compare for instance, in F1 *Hamlet*'s 3906 lines, there are 104 lines containing only directions. There are 111 entrances and exits for 3802 lines of dialogue, giving a percentage of one direction for every 34+ lines; adding in the eighteen playwright's advisory directions without separate lineation brings the percentage to one for every 29.3 lines. In F1 *Richard III*'s 3887 lines, 171 contain only stage-directions, leaving 3716 lines of dialogue. There are 145 entrances and exits yielding one direction for every 25.6 lines; adding in the sixteen not separately lined advisory directions, this brings the percentage to one direction for every twenty-three lines of dialogue.

The playwright of *The Telltale* uses approximately 20 percent more advisory directions than does Shakespeare in this sample. This percentage indicates that the *Telltale* playwright is a playwright considerably more concerned with directing the players than is usual for a playwright who was in close, regular contact with the players.

Thus in determining what kind of manuscript *The Telltale* is, it is vital to remember the two most important shards which direct this identification. The first is the added, unboxed, left-marginal "Wthin" signaling the boxed "*A cry wthin*" in the right margin of folio 7b; the other is the boxed, right-marginal "wine" on folio 20a. As I noted earlier, these seem very much to be theatrical in origin and thus to being very important considerations for attempting to discover provenance for this manuscript. They would be very strange items, indeed, to be added by a playwright. That they would have been volunteered by any scribe, let alone this one, would seem to be more than highly unlikely.

Other questions such as why missing text was not filled in and the exact purpose for which this copy was undertaken remain as unknown as the name of this scribe and the playwright.

It thus seems relatively certain that Dulwich MS. XX was made as a reading copy for further purposes or for persons unknown by a nonplayhouse scribe sometime between 1630 and 1640 copying a theatrical playbook of unknown date which (most likely) was written in the playwright's holograph;

this playbook additionally bore some notations by the playhouse bookkeeper. Such a supposition explains the existence of a scribal copy suffering lacunae presumably because the scribe could not read portions of an unavailable playwright's manuscript, and yet bearing many stage-directions which are authorial and at least two additional directions which are of the sort that would be added by a playhouse bookkeeper to guide productions.

But, like all too many other aspects of late sixteenth- and early seventeenth-century drama, there is much more about *The Telltale* that cries out to be discovered.

Acknowledgments

Reproductions from *The Telltale*, Dulwich College MS. XX, are made By Kind Permission of the Governors of Dulwich College. I should like especially to thank Dr. Jan R. Piggott, Keeper of Archives, for his assistance and hospitality.

Reproductions from *Charlemagne*, British Library MS. Egerton 1994, Item 6; *Thomas of Woodstock*, British Library MS. Egerton 1994, Item 8; *The Two Noble Ladies*, British Library MS. Egerton 1994, Item 11; *Sir John van Olden Barnavelt*, British Library MS. Additional 18653; and *Believe as You List*, British Library MS. Egerton 2828 are made with the kind permission of The British Library.

Notes

1. E. A. J. Honigmann and Susan Brock, *Playhouse Wills 1558–1642. An Edition of Wills by Shakespeare and His Contemporaries in the London Theatre*, The Revels Companion Library (Manchester and New York: Manchester University Press, 1993), 242.

2. Gerald Eades Bentley, *The Jacobean and Caroline Stage*, 7 vols. (Oxford: Clarendon Press, 1941–68); V (1956), 1418–19.

3. For a general description of the surviving manuscript playbooks, see William B. Long, "'Precious Few': English Manuscript Playbooks," in David Scott Kastan, ed., *A Companion to Shakespeare* (Oxford: Blackwell Publishers Ltd., 1999), 414–33.

4. Anon., *The Telltale*, Dulwich College MS. XX, prepared by R. A. Foakes and J. C. Gibson, checked by Arthur Brown (Oxford: The Malone Society, 1960 [for 1959]).

5. W. W. Greg, *Dramatic Documents from the Elizabethan Playhouses: Stage Plots: Actors' Parts: Prompt Books*, 2 vols. (Oxford: Clarendon Press, 1931; repr. 1961); I: 19, 225.

6. David Kathman kindly and generously supplied me a copy of his, at this date, unpublished study "Reconsidering *The Seven Deadly Sins*."

7. See William B. Long, "*John a Kent and John a Cumber*: An Elizabethan Playbook and Its Implications," in *Shakespeare and Dramatic Tradition*, ed. W. R. Elton and William B. Long (Newark: University of Delaware Press, 1989), 125–43.

8. Andrew Gurr and Mariko Ichikawa, *Staging in Shakespeare's Theatres*, Oxford Shakespeare Topics (Oxford: Oxford University Press, 2000), 59, 64–65.

9. See William B. Long, "'A bed for woodstock': A Warning for the Unwary," *Medieval & Renaissance Drama in England* 2 (1985): 91–118.

Shakespeare and the Chamberlain's Men in 1598

SCOTT McMILLIN

LEEDS Barroll has shown the benefits that can flow from thinking, exactly and in detail, about the individual years of Shakespeare's career. The early chapters of *Politics, Plague, and Shakespeare's Theater* are a close reading of Shakespeare and the King's Men in the first year of the Jacobean regime, from the royal patent that was issued to the company in May 1603 through their performances at court in the winters of 1603–04 and 1604–05. That period consists of over eighteen months, so I use "individual year" in a broad sense, but if we could find in every year and a half of Shakespeare's career as much as Barroll has seen the months between May 1603 and January 1605, we would know just about everything involving the writer and his acting company, or would at least have a theory about everything.[1]

What opened the way to Barroll's study of 1603–05 was the extraordinary evidence in the accounts of the Revels Office, where the titles of the plays performed before the king and queen in the winter season of 1604–05 are included, giving us a picture of the repertory of the King's Men at a particular moment. The actual scheduling of plays by title—which Henslowe's Diary makes available for the Admiral's Men and the other companies that played at the Rose—is the kind of detail normally lacking for the Chamberlain's/King's Men (although the Revels accounts offer similar title-writing for 1611–13). I have no such windfall of evidence for my "year" in the affairs of Shakespeare and company, some eighteen months between 1597 and 1599 that I am calling "1598," but there is nevertheless ample space for detailed thinking about this spot of time in the affairs of the playwright and his fellow actors. I would like to zero in on the English history plays that were being written and performed in "1598," with particular attention to the question of whether these were recognized as a "series" in their own time. We permit ourselves to talk of the First Tetralology and the Second, a far cry from anything the Elizabethans would have called the histories. But a "series" of plays would have been taking shape in the playhouse by the later 1590s, and it may also have been taking shape at the sign of the Angel in St. Paul's Churchyard, where the stationer Andrew Wise had his shop.

In February of 1598 Wise entered the play we know as Shakespeare's *1 Henry IV* in the Stationers' Register, as a preliminary step to the publication of the play later that year. The Stationers' Register and the published quarto both use the title *The History of Henry the Fourth* (modernized spelling), giving no sign that this was the first part of a two-part *Henry IV.* But a broader sequence of history plays was being fashioned. Andrew Wise had published two other plays about English kings, *The Tragedy of Richard the Second* and *The Tragedy of Richard the Third*, just a few months earlier, the first appearing sometime after a Stationers' Register entry of 29 August 1597, the second after an entry of 20 October 1597. When the *History of Henry the Fourth* came out, if the other two had not already sold out, there were three plays on the reigns of English monarchs available for purchase at the sign of the Angel in Paul's Churchyard.

Did Wise conceive of these as a group? Would he have been aware that more English history plays would be coming along from the Chamberlain's Men, to form a series of connected plays? We do not know. What we do know is that Wise published second editions of the plays about Richard II and Richard III in the same year as he brought out the new play on Henry IV, 1598, and that the second editions added something that was left off the title pages of the first editions, the name of the author. The second editions of the Richard II and Richard III plays named Shakespeare and the Chamberlain's Men, whereas the first editions named only the Chamberlain's Men. When in 1599 Wise published a second edition of *The History of Henry IV* he named Shakespeare again, this time rather improperly: "newly corrected by W. Shakespeare." The Chamberlain's Men were not named on either edition of the Henry IV play. So a group of three English history plays was available at the sign of the Angel in 1598, two of them naming the Chamberlain's Men as the originating agents, and second editions of the group were available there the following year with the author's name added on all three second editions. That is worth thinking about.

Wise certainly knew he had a coherent group of plays to sell—a group he could identify by spelling out the name of the acting company on two of the three first editions, and the name of the author on all the second editions. When Wise published respectable books, such as sermons or essays on poetics, he customarily listed the authors' names. His edition of a sermon by Thomas Playfere, *The Pathway to Perfection*, 1597, named the minister; his *Book of the seven planets . . . of W. Alabaster,* 1598, named the author, John Racster; his *Observations on the Art of English Poetry*, 1602, named the author, Thomas Campion. (This last item was printed by Shakespeare's Stratford acquaintance Richard Field.) One can virtually see the drama rising in the literary scale as Wise decided to add "Shakespeare" to his second editions of the history plays. Commercial success and respectability have their affinities. Wise was keeping these plays on English monarchs in circulation as "Shakespeare" plays.[2]

If these three plays by Shakespeare and the Chamberlain's Men were available as a group at the sign of the Angel in 1598, there was a noticeable gap. The plays on Richard II and Henry IV connected to one another by the flow of events represented and especially by the character of Henry Bullingbroke, returning to depose the king in the first play and suffering from the guilty aftermath of that deposition in the second. But the play on Richard III left a stretch of eighty years untreated in the "series," covering the reigns of Henry V, Henry VI, and Edward IV, not to mention the remainder of the reign of Henry IV (for the 1598 *History of Henry IV* went only as far as the Battle of Shrewsbury).

This gap would be filled on one bookstall or another between 1598 and 1600. Although it is hard to believe that other booksellers were keen to fill the available spots in Andrew Wise's inventory, or that there was much money to be made by publishing stage versions of English history, it can be reported that between 1598 and 1600 eight plays on the reigns in question were published, potential gap-fillers of different sorts. Four of these came from other acting companies. An older play on *The Famous Victories of Henry V* from the Queen's men, going back at least as far as 1588, was published by Thomas Creede in 1598, and in 1599 a two-part play on *Edward IV* was published by John Oxenbridge from the company known as Derby's Men. A new play from the Admiral's Men, concerning the reign of Henry IV and called the *First Part of the true and honorable history of Sir John Oldcastle*, was published by Thomas Pavier in 1600. The old *Famous Victories* had a part for a supposed rogue-knight, "Jockey Oldcastle," one comic follower among several for the rapscallion youth of Prince Hal. The new *Henry IV* play by Shakespeare turned this into a tour-de-force for one of the comic actors in the Chamberlain's Men. The role was such an outrageous success on the stage that it was deemed prudent among the acting company, probably under pressure from descendants of the Oldcastle line, to change the name from "Oldcastle" to "Falstaff" before the text was published.[3] The *1 Sir John Oldcastle* published by Pavier from the Admiral's Men in 1600 was reacting to the comic version of Oldcastle/Falstaff, presenting Oldcastle as the Protestant martyr he was in history. Thus the issues surrounding Falstaff were an important reason for the popularity and publication of the plays (Wise spelled out his name too, on the title pages of the plays on Henry IV).

The remaining history plays, all belonging to the Chamberlain's Men and published in 1600, were closer to being true gap-fillers in a series. Wise himself brought out *The Second Part of Henry the Fourth* in 1600, keeping the series identity clear by naming Shakespeare and the Chamberlain's Men. (He also used both names for his *Much Ado about Nothing*, 1600.) There is no clearer sign of the rise of authorship as an important category in English drama than the addition of Shakespeare's name to the group of English history plays Wise was selling in St. Paul's Churchyard by 1600: *Richard II, 1 Henry IV, 2 Henry IV,* and *Richard III.*

The other three plays, on the reigns of Henry V and Henry VI, were published by Thomas Millington in 1600. Two were republications of older plays. Years before anyone thought there was a gap to fill, Millington had published two plays on the reign of Henry VI, one called *The First Part of the Contention of the Houses of York and Lancaster*, the other *The True Tragedy of Richard Duke of York.* These reached back to before the formation of the Chamberlain's Men in 1594. Their title pages mentioned no authors, and only *The True Tragedy* gave an acting company—Pembroke's Men, a predecessor company to the Chamberlain's Men. Apparently Millington did not care who wrote or performed his editions of the history plays. But the second editions of two Henry VI plays in 1600, after Wise had published his group of *Richard II, 1 and 2 Henry IV,* and *Richard III*, suggest that Millington was alert to the market, and somehow he obtained the one gap-filler remaining, the latest one being staged by the Chamberlain's Men, their *Henry V,* and published that too in 1600 (with another stationer, John Busby). Millington may have stolen a march on someone with *Henry V,* for a "staying order" for a Henry V play and for three other titles from the Chamberlain's Men appears in the Stationers' Register for 4 August 1600. Nevertheless, *The Chronicle History of Henry the Fifth* appeared in 1600, naming the Chamberlain's Men. It did not imitate Wise's notion of naming the author. Moreover, Millington's second editions of the two Henry VI plays left the title pages unchanged from the earlier editions, with the outdated advertisement that Pembroke's men were the agents for *The True Tragedy* and saying nothing about the provenance of the other play. Compared to Wise's endeavor, it was a backward piece of publishing, but it did help to make seven of the Chamberlain's sequence of English history plays available to readers in 1600.

Millington's three plays of 1600 differ strikingly from the Wise group. They run only about half as long as the Wise plays and their dialogue is often garbled. Three hundred years later they would be defined by an influential scholar as among the "bad" quartos, whereas Wise's plays would be among the "good." This moralistic distinction has faded from more recent scholarship, and it is now being recognized that short and imperfect texts of the kind Millington brought out may represent the plays as they were staged, perhaps under straitened conditions of some sort, perhaps even under normal circumstances in the London playhouses. The issue is not yet settled, and the question of what sorts of manuscript Millington's short and imperfect texts represent is an enduring mystery in Shakespeare studies. A study of his group of three histories set against Wise's contrasting group of four, all seven published in first or second editions between 1598 and 1600, might well help to advance a solution.

For our purposes, the point is that the Chamberlain's Men were broadly readable in the group of English history plays by 1600, with "Shakespeare" becoming commercially visible as the author of the more respectable texts.

The question of whether the history plays were apparent as a "series" in our year of 1598 has a sharper feel when it comes to the acting company performing the plays, the Lord Chamberlain's Men, Shakespeare among them. A year or so earlier, let us call it 1597, the Chamberlain's Men not only knew they were engaged in a sequence of English history plays, they also thought they were nearly finished with it. They had played *Richard II*, in about 1595 or 1596. They had *Richard III* in repertory, with their star actor Richard Burbage making a strong impression in the title role. These two scripts were being sold to Andrew Wise, for printing, and this does not look like happenstance, not at a time when Shakespeare would have been writing a Henry IV play, which Wise would also publish. The Chamberlain's Men were putting these history plays into circulation at the extremes of the series, the first and last, then the second. They also had older scripts on Henry VI available for staging—*The First Part of the Contention* and *The True Tragedy of York*—along with another Henry VI play, not yet published (it wouldn't be until 1623), which began with the king as an infant.

If there was a sense of the series in the playhouse, not many of the plays could be staged in succession. The repertory depended on changing the bill every day, a comedy followed by a chronicle play followed by another comedy or a tragedy. That was the standard way of luring spectators to return—the now-for-something-entirely-different principle of audience development. But a sequel method was also being tried in the commercial theaters, as a different way of drawing spectators. The Admiral's Men at the Rose were doing a number of two-part plays in the later 1590s, and in 1598 they were even planning three parts of a venture called *The Civil Wars of France*. Sometimes the two-part plays were performed on successive days, but not always. The sequel to a successful play would draw spectators back to the playhouse whether or not the performance days were successive.[4] The series on English history taking shape at the Globe by 1598 was almost certainly not being staged on successive days in anything like its entirety, but it would have been understood as a series to anyone engaged in making the costumes, copying the scripts, learning the roles, writing the next play, or seeing the plays in the theater over a period of months.[5]

Let us think for a moment about how the series would have appeared to an acting company that had staged *Richard II* in the mid-1590s, had several scripts on Henry VI at their disposal from days gone by, and had a crowd-pleaser in *Richard III* in repertory from time to time. *Richard II* ended with 1400. Henry VI was born in 1422. The gap apparent in the acting company's plays, visible by the time *Richard II* was being staged, amounted to only twenty-two years. One more play would certainly finish the series—anyone could see that, except perhaps for the playwright. One play would cover the twenty-two years of Henry IV and Henry V (as the Queen's Men piece on *The Famous Victories* had done), and then the histories would reach all the way to the Battle of Bosworth Field and the origin of the Tudor line from which Queen Elizabeth herself descended. There would be six plays in the series—no one had ever tried anything this vast in the commercial theater. This was something more than audience development. The Chamberlain's Men must have felt that something else was being developed too. *They* were being developed, as an acting company, a troupe with the staying power to take on this venture—especially as the six plays became seven. When the first script of the Henry IV play was ready, it turned out to cover only to the Battle of Shrewsbury. The actors playing Hal, Falstaff, and the King would have another play to go, learning continuations of their parts, while the actors playing Hotspur and other roles would go on to new parts in the sequel. These players were learning how to enact the most serious events of the nation's past and make them comic too, turning the theater toward a new combination of popular entertainment and national self-awareness, but their writer was also building in long episodes of common life, as though scenes in an Eastcheap tavern or in the orchard of a Gloucestershire justice belonged to the range of dynastic chronicle. As the seven-play group became *eight* (for the second play on Henry IV did not get past the coronation of Henry V), the actors, the costume sewers, the scribes, and those who came back to see these plays, must have sensed that "playing" was being advanced into outlandish territory. Eight plays? Burbage's role as Prince Hal and then Henry V now amounted to the longest part ever played in the theaters, and he was being seen as Richard III too.[6] The sheer realistic *detail* these actors and their playwright were learning to supply in chronicle plays made history seem to linger over lives actually lived, as though London playhouses could transform entertainment into high culture.

At least that would have been part of the story. There are always other concerns breaking in, even when a historical moment is happening. The pressing issues for the Chamberlain's Men in our long year of 1598 would have been about finances and theaters. One reason for selling history plays to Andrew Wise was that the company was strapped for funds.[7] They had lost their lease on their famous playhouse, the Theatre, in 1597. In 1598 they were probably acting at the nearby Curtain, but as they produced one installment after another of what we regard as a landmark series of English history plays, they literally did not know which theater they would be playing in next year. A plan to open a roofed-over playhouse in the Blackfriars district of the city had come to grief in 1596, as had a substantial financial investment on the part of the Burbages in that venture. Newer playhouses, one of them housing the chief rival company, the Admiral's men at the Rose, stood south of the city, on the Bankside. That is the direction the company eventually took, when by the end of 1598 they were resorting to the extreme solution of taking down the Theatre in the landlord's absence (he owned the land, not the building, but he had some rights in the question of what stood on the land), carting the heavy structural timbers across the Thames, and contracting to have a new theater built on the Bankside, the Globe. This plan was being hatched by our year of 1598, but in its doubtful legality it cannot have seemed a simple solution to the financial problem. The costumes for one history play could be used in another—that's a reason for eight history plays. The most important thing to know about 1598, if we are trying to grasp the moment itself and not the long-term outcome, is that major financial and logistical problems saddled the company—just when their fellow Shakespeare was turning the twenty-two-year-gap into *three* new history plays.

There were other things for an ambitious playwright and company to be doing, of course. *Romeo and Juliet* and *Midsummer Night's Dream* were probably two of the plays being performed while the gap was becoming apparent in the history plays. This in itself increases one's impression of the astonishing fecundity of company and playwright in the mid-1590s, and as the *Henry IV* plays took the stage, the vein of romantic comedy was being deepened with *Merchant of Venice* and *As You Like It*. The hindsight by which we operate makes all this look magnificent, when the air was probably filled with uncertainty and argument in the day-to-day affairs of the company.

Theater historians are only now discovering that another set of plays on Henry VI was being played by the Chamberlain's Men around 1598. These were the two parts of *The Seven Deadly Sins*, an experimental blending of history play and allegory that has come down to us only in the form of the backstage outline of entrances for the second part. The "plot" of part 2 of *The Seven Deadly Sins*, which has long been assigned to an earlier date and an earlier acting company, has now been re-dated to the Chamberlain's Men of 1597–98.[8] This play was not just about the Seven Deadly Sins. It was also about Henry VI when he was imprisoned, and then released, after being forced to cede the crown to Edward IV. The poet Lydgate, who actually was court poet to Henry VI, is shown staging a number of moral playlets on the Seven Deadly Sins as edification for his imprisoned monarch. In the plot of part 2, Envy is represented by the story of *Ferrex and Porrex* (i.e., *Gorboduc*), Sloth by the story of Sardanapalus, and Lechery by Tereus and Philomela. This was a huge play, with the plot calling for more than twenty actors. Part 1 must have concerned the other four Deadly Sins—indeed, the plot shows the second part beginning with Envy, Sloth, and Lechery driving away the other four. In the final scene the Earl of Warwick releases the king from prison, an event represented in realistic terms toward the end of the *True Tragedy of York* soon to be available once again at Millington's bookshop (*3 Henry VI*, 4, 6). That the company should be experimenting with other ways of staging English history suggests that the Shakespearean way was not the only way.

Indeed, the Shakespearean way was itself undergoing important changes in about 1598. Battle scenes were becoming a thing of the past in Shakespeare's history scripts. The battles in the first *Henry IV* play are fundamental, but the sequel lets the Falstaff attitude toward swordsmanship and combat prevail (Falstaff wins a parodic one-on-one combat because of the fame of his swollen belly). *Henry V* does away with battle scenes entirely—it is *about* battles, but it does not stage them. The company was practicing a different kind of stagecraft in the later 1590s (they have no group battle scenes in new plays from 1599 on), and joining *Henry V* to their early plays on Henry VI might have seemed retrograde. The old plays specialized in large-scale combat and had themselves been experiments in building dialogue into battle scenes. Would an *allegorical dream vision* have seemed a more up-to-date drama for the reign of Henry VI? Were the *Sins* plays considered an alternative to the older pieces? Or were the *Sins* plays being staged *along with The True Tragedy of York* as an allegorical elaboration on the king's experience in prison, extending the cycle to upward of ten plays? The questions cannot be answered here—they are only now becoming apparent. They show the complications that arise when one thinks of the entire repertory of the Chamberlain's Men and not just the plays that have gone on to long-term cultural status.

One of the company's plays of 1598 went so far as to drive History and Comedy from the stage in an opening dumb show. This was *A Warning for Fair Women*, which sends History and Comedy away so that Tragedy can present a London murder-thriller. This is the first play centered on contemporary London in the extant repertory of the Chamberlain's Men.[9] It was an attempt to change the direction of the company's repertory, and like the *Sins* plays it fuses the virtual choreography of the allegorical dumb show with a type of plot normally treated realistically.[10] History is allegorized in one play, History is driven from the stage in the other (although the final remarks of Tragedy say that History and Comedy will be back soon, a reminder that changing the bill was still the paramount concern). An adulterous seduction is shown in one dumb show of *A Warning for Fair Women*, and the murder itself is represented in another when a large tree suddenly rises from under the stage, representing the cuckolded husband, and is cut down by the adulterers. Sex and violence in contemporary London are being treated to allegorical representation. The experiment of elaborating a moment of Henry VI's reign with allegories on the Deadly Sins may look old-fashioned to us today, but it has an understandable place in what I take to be the artistic and commercial questioning of the Chamberlain's Men in about 1598. The great Shakespearean achievements of the 1590s—romantic comedy in addition to the history plays—may have seemed outdated in the rivalry of the commercial theaters, or perhaps in need of allegorical shock treatment.

Shakespeare was listening to these plays, and acting in them too. One reason his new plays on Henry IV and Henry V seem different from the old pieces on Henry VI is that the new ones take an ironic tone toward the staging of history itself. The *Henry VI* plays are unconditional in their assertion that history can be staged. Their mode is "anything goes." The choruses at the end of *2 Henry IV,* where dancing takes the place of speech, and throughout *Henry V,* where the "wooden O" of the playhouse comes in for some teasing remarks about the staging of these events, not only add ironic points of view about history in the theaters, they also *sound* like Tragedy in *A Warning for Fair Women.* Tragedy in *Fair Women,* like the *Henry V* chorus, speaks to the auditors about the theater they are in ("All this faire circuit here is left to me. . . . My Sceane is London, native and your own") and tells them how to imagine the locations of the plot ("Suppose him on the water now for Woolwich," lines 1249ff.)[11] The *Henry V* chorus did not come out of nowhere. I would say that he came out of *A Warning for Fair Women,* except that both may have come out of another play that has left no trace behind.

We will never know the full story of Shakespeare and his actors in 1598, but the snapshots available in the extant plays and records let us glimpse a company caught in cross-currents of dramaturgy at the same time as they faced an uncertain financial future *and* built lasting monuments of Elizabethan drama in the history plays and romantic comedies. That the financial crisis would be solved through building the Globe could not have been apparent in 1598. The allegorical experiments of *The Seven Deadly Sins* and *A Warning for Fair Women* would turn into a dead end, but this was not apparent either—nor was the long-term success of the history series that Shakespeare was building up as he supplied one script after another on the brief reigns of Henry IV and Henry V. Their decision to sell the earliest and latest plays to Andrew Wise in 1597, then the two new plays on Henry IV to the same publisher, suggests that the company had designs on making their history plays into a recognizable sequence for Londoners, both in the theaters and on the bookstalls. Wise's second editions of *Richard II* and *Richard III* were printed before the end of 1598, and now the publisher was identifying the group by the name of the playwright. At the same time, the acting company was trying other kinds of play, setting the reign of Henry VI into an allegorical mode with their two-part drama on the Deadly Sins, and venturing on a genre Shakespeare never wrote, the contemporary London play, with an allegorical mode there too. If these were resistances to Shakespeare's design, they also caught his ear. There was some vigorous give-and-take in the acting company, with the new style of humors comedy by Ben Jonson also making its presence felt in the repertory of the late 1590s.

We will leave the story at that point, for a glance ahead shows that other major issues lie just after the turn of the century. There are no romantic comedies by Shakespeare there, and no English history plays, not for a decade. If we were to take up a broad eighteen-month year called "1601," *Hamlet* would come into view, and further discussion would require vast detail. That the Chamberlain's Men were staging *Thomas Lord Cromwell* as a new play and reviving *A Larum for London* at the same time as *Hamlet* was being rehearsed gives a hint of what lies ahead!

Notes

1. *Politics, Plague, and Shakespeare's Theater* (Ithaca: Cornell University Press, 1991), chaps. 1–4

2. See Lucas Erne, *Shakespeare as Literary Dramatist* (Cambridge, Cambridge University Press, 2003), 56–69 for the role Meres's *Palladis Tamia* may have played in Wise's title-page attributions.

3. The pressure would have come from Lord Cobham, whose wife's ancestors included Oldcastle. Cobham was briefly Lord Chamberlain in 1596–97, a period when Shakespeare's company was known as Hunsdon's men.

4. See Roslyn Lander Knutson, *The Repertory of Shakespeare's Company, 1594–1613* (Fayetteville: University of Arkansas Press, 1991), 50–52.

5. Millington's decision to republish *The Contention* and *The True Tragedy* in 1600 suggests the plays had been staged recently. The final chorus to*Henry V* states that "our stage hath shown" plays about the reign of Henry VI, although this speech did not appear in print before 1623 and we are not sure when it was written or first spoken in the theater. Andrew Gurr has argued that Millington's 1600 quarto, which lacks the chorus, represents the play as it was first staged in the London theaters. See *The First Quarto of Henry V* (Cambridge: Cambridge University Press, 2000). Alternatively, the speech could have been written by then and cut for performance. Below I suggest that the chorus and the presenter of *A Warning for Fair Women* of about 1598 were written at the same point in the company's career.

6. There is no evidence as to which actor played the Hal/Henry V combination, but Burbage was already famous for his Richard III and he was playing Hamlet soon after *Henry V* was staged. The development of inward self-awareness in the long role is important in all these undertakings, and it seems a sound guess that the company's star actor was the vehicle.

7. See Andrew Gurr, *the Shakespearian Playing Companies* (Oxford: Clarendon Press, 1996), 282–84 for the company's financial plight.

8. The key evidence concerns two boy-actors named for female roles on the plot, "T. Belt" and "Saunder." David Kathman has learned that boys named Thomas Belte and Alexander Cooke were apprenticed to John Heminges, a leading actor of the Chamberlain's Men, in 1595 and 1597 respectively. See Kathman, "Reconsidering *The Seven Deadly Sins*," forthcoming in *Early Theatre*. I am indebted to the author for letting me read this article before publication. It now appears that the plot of *Seven Deadly Sins* must date from about 1597–98, with the names of the actors giving

a virtual roster of the Chamberlain's Men of that time (three main roles are unassigned, and Shakespeare and Heminges are not listed).

9. A point I owe to Andrew Gurr, who kindly let me see his forthcoming book on The Chamberlain's/King's Men before publication.

10. Dumb shows were cutting edge techniques in the academic theater, and Legge's *Richardus Tertius* had used them for an English history play.

11. I use the edition by C. D. Cannon (The Hague: Mouton, 1975).

Samuel Daniel's Gifts of Books to Lord Chancellor Egerton

JOHN PITCHER

THIS is an article about twelve rare books. Eleven of these books are in the Huntington Library in California and one of them is in the Beinecke Library at Yale.[1] The books, containing poems, plays, and histories written by the poet Samuel Daniel (1562–1619), arrived in the United States late in 1917. Daniel's books were a small part of the famous Bridgewater Library purchased from the Earl of Ellesmere for a million dollars by Henry E. Huntington who made it the cornerstone of his new library in San Marino in Southern California.[2] Some of the treasures of the Bridgewater collection—the Ellesmere manuscript of *The Canterbury Tales* for instance—far exceed this small set of books in importance, but there are nevertheless good reasons why we should examine the books closely. For one thing, they point to a sustained connection between Daniel and Sir Thomas Egerton—the founder of what became the Bridgewater Library—over a period of fifteen to twenty years; for another, they show how carefully Daniel chose to present his poems and histories to Egerton, at the appropriate moment and in the proper format.

Scholars have known for two centuries and more that Sir Thomas Egerton (1540–1617) was one of Daniel's patrons.[3] The important verse epistle that Daniel addressed to Egerton in print in 1603 implies as much. The starting point of this austere and impressive poem is the confused condition of civil law at the end of Elizabeth's reign. Egerton is the officer of state entrusted by the monarch with the job of protecting people from the delays, wrangling, and over severity of the law courts. He has been chosen, Daniel tells him, to preserve the "sanctuarie" to which (lines 122–24)

> Th'opprest might flie, this seate of Equitie
> Whereon thy virtues sit with faire renowne,
> The greatest grace and glory of the Gowne.[4]

One measure of Daniel's high standing with Egerton is that he is able to write to him so openly in these terms, and to express his own opinions. Daniel's views on equity, perhaps informed by passages from Aristotle's *Ethics*, were not out of line with Egerton's,[5] but the poem has some straight-talking passages in it about harsh law and corrupt lawyers. It is inconceivable that Daniel could have written like this unless he was already, in some sense, a client of Egerton's. The poem was published early in May 1603, at the head of a folio collection of six verse epistles Daniel had written to other members of the Jacobean court elite (Lord Henry Howard, Lucy, Countess of Bedford and so forth).[6] In this folio, the epistle to Egerton is placed immediately after the *Panegyric Congratulatory* that Daniel wrote to King James at his accession (he presented the poem to the king in an autograph manuscript on 23 April). The title Daniel uses to address Egerton at the outset of the epistle, "Lord Keeper of the Great Seale of England," is another indication of a degree of familiarity between them. Egerton, who been had Lord Keeper since May 1596, gave over this office in June 1603 when he was appointed Lord Chancellor,[7] but in the epistle, at least a month earlier, Daniel is already addressing him as the "Great Minister of Justice" who sits in the court of equity (the reference to the "seate" in the lines above is probably an allusion to the woolsack, the symbol of the Lord Chancellor's position). Daniel was only a minor player on the fringe of the court set that was bringing in the new king, but he was close enough to the Egerton circle to know, weeks or months before it was made public, that the Lord Keeper was due to be made Lord Chancellor.

The image Daniel used to describe Egerton's new office confirms that the connection between them was not a distant one. The poem opens with King James's "powreful hand of Majestie" setting Egerton in "th'aidfulst roome of dignitie" (that is, giving him the office in which he could be of most help):

> As th'*Isthmus*, these two Oceans to divide
> Of *Rigor* and confus'd *Uncertaintie*,
> To keepe out th'entercourse of wrong and pride,
> That they ingulph not up unsuccoured right
> By th'extreame current of licentious might.[8]

Daniel made this striking comparison out of well-known lines early in the first book of Lucan's *De Bello Civili*. For a brief time, Lucan writes, the triumvir Crassus kept Pompey and Julius Caesar at peace, despite them wanting to make war on each other. He was like a strip of land between two raging seas (I.99–103):

> Nam sola futuri
> Crassus erat bella medius mora. Qualiter undas
> Qui secat et geminum gracilis mare separate Isthmos
> Nec patitur conferre fretum, si terra recedat,
> Ionium Aegaeo frangat mare.[9]

This wasn't the first time Daniel had drawn on this passage in Lucan, and his return to it for the Egerton epistle was, most likely, deliberate. In Book 4 of the 1595 *Civil Wars*, his epic poem on the wars of the barons, Daniel had described how the murder of Humphrey, Duke of Gloucester, had removed the only man (like Crassus in Lucan) who was preventing a civil war. With Gloucester's death, the flow towards war in medieval England became an unstoppable torrent, and the full force of mischief began (IV.91.6–8):

> T'a vniuersall ruine to extend,
> That Isthmus failing which the land did kepe
> From the intire possession of the deepe.[10]

This time the isthmus is Gloucester, the great Lord Protector whom Daniel praises in earlier stanzas for—in this respect he is like Egerton—observing strictly "due forme of Iustice towards euery wight" (IV.78.1–2).

The evidence that in 1603 Daniel was consciously recalling lines in a poem he had published in 1595 comes in a private letter he wrote to Egerton in or around 1602. In this, Daniel thanks the Lord Keeper (his title at the head of the letter) for, in some unspecified way, assisting his brother. "Amongst all the great workes of your worthynes," Daniel tells Egerton at the start of the letter,

> it will not be the least that yow have donne for me, in the preferment of my brother, with whome yet now sometimes, I may eat whilst I write, and so go on with the worke I have in hand, which, god knowes, had long since bene ended, and your Honour had had that which in my harte I have prepared for yow, could I have but sustayned myself and made truce within, and peace with the world.[11]

Daniel sent this letter to Egerton attached to a presentation copy of his 1601 *Works* folio, one of the Huntington rare books to be examined in a moment. When he refers to the "workes" of "worthynes" that Egerton has done for him (presumably small gifts of money or speaking on his behalf to others or perhaps loaning or buying him foreign books),[12] Daniel obviously intends a parallel with his own *Works*: the moral is, good works by patrons draw good works from poets. The particular help Egerton has given Daniel in this case is the "preferment" of his younger brother, John, who at this date was an undergraduate studying music at Christ Church in Oxford, where he graduated in 1603. John went on to write some of the best lute music of the age—in achievement not far behind Dowland so the musicologists tell us—and it is no surprise that Egerton, who was fond of music, was prepared to help a talented Oxford student whose brother was a leading poet.[13] What this preferment of John amounted to is not clear. Daniel almost certainly wrote the letter in London (see below) where, because of Egerton's kindness, he and John were now able to dine together occasionally. Perhaps Egerton found John a temporary (or vacation) job with someone at court who needed a music tutor for their children, or who simply wanted musical entertainment from an accomplished player. Whatever the explanation, John doesn't seem to have received any further help from Egerton, at least (as we shall see) as a composer or music teacher.

The letter, which begins as a thank you note, quickly becomes an apology. It appears that Daniel is working on two distinct pieces—poems we must assume—the first an unfinished work, which should have been completed long before, and the second something he has planned (or perhaps promised) to write for Egerton but which he hasn't started yet. A little later in the letter we learn that the unfinished work is the *Civil Wars*, six books of which Daniel had completed in the 1601 *Works* folio, but which left him no more than half way through the projected history. We cannot know for sure what the second piece was—at this stage perhaps no more than an idea or rough notes—but there is a good chance that it emerged, a year or so later, as the 1603 verse epistle to Egerton.[14]

If we accept this, it becomes possible to offer a plausible scenario for the exchanges between Daniel and Egerton in this period of 1602–3. At the end of the 1590s Daniel had been acknowledged in public, on the strength of the *Civil Wars*, as the "English Lucan," as well as Spenser's successor.[15] He was already familiar with several of the top people at court—Lord Mountjoy was his chief patron, and through him there were connections with the Earl of Essex—but he had doubts about whether he should carry on writing, and whether he could afford to (in the letter he speaks of needing to sustain himself and to make "truce within, and peace with the world").[16] Egerton had done him some favours, but evidently these didn't include giving him a regular income, since he had been forced to become a tutor, "constrained to live with Children" is how he puts it. One of his pupils was Lady Anne Clifford, a demanding and self-willed young aristocrat (she was twelve in 1602) who must have taxed his patience and taken up a large amount of time.[17] Daniel had few if any other options, however, since by 1600 Mountjoy was out of the country, serving as Lord Deputy in Ireland, and Essex was in too confused and perilous a state to be of any help to him. How Daniel made contact with Egerton, and exactly when, is discussed below, but certainly by the date of the letter Daniel already had it in mind (in his "harte" is what he says) to write a poem for Egerton. It would be perfectly natural for him, since he was well known as the English Lucan, to want to make some link between the *Civil Wars*, his unfinished long epic poem modeled in part on *De Bello Civili*, and the smaller piece he intended for Egerton. This link, which Daniel could be sure Egerton would recognize, was made, in all likelihood, through his reuse of the image of the warring factions and isthmus in Lucan.

There is a good deal of evidence to show that Daniel, like other poets then and now, wrote his poems around a single image or a cluster of metaphors or even an emblem or *impresa*.[18] Perhaps the accession in March 1603, and the acceleration of everything around it—courtiers scrambling to be noticed by the king, poets writing against the clock to congratulate him—released something in Daniel so that he was able to write the verse epistle to Egerton quickly and with none of the delay he refers to in the 1602 letter.[19] The image of the isthmus may indeed have been what finally ignited his writing. In several of the 1603 verse epistles, as a unifying motif perhaps, there are fluvial images—tempests, oceans and storms, flowing rivers—set against settled earth and shorelines, and even gardens.[20] We probably ought to view the isthmus image chosen from Lucan, which is the opening to the collection of the epistles as a whole, as Daniel's way of identifying himself, his poetic signature as it were.

Another possibility exists, that there is a more private allusion folded inside the public one. All Daniel is doing, it appears, is focusing on one aspect of the Lucan image. Crassus stood between warring factions, and so did Humphrey, Duke of Gloucester; Egerton stands between, on the one side, inflexibility in applying the law and on the other, the vagaries and injustice of pleadings and lawyers' cant. But is there any sense in which Daniel meant that Egerton too had prevented a civil war? In his 1602 letter, he told Egerton that, in writing the *Civil Wars*, whatever his limitations as an epic poet, he hoped to "give the best hand" he could to the perpetual 'closing up of those woundes' and the

> ever keeping them so, that our land may lothe to looke over those blessed bounds (which the providence of god hath set us) into the horror & confusion of farther and former claymes.

When Daniel wrote this it was probably about a year after the Essex rebellion and a year before Elizabeth died. At that date, the prospect of civil war in England, if James didn't come the throne, was not remote. The most likely cause, if war broke out at the queen's death, would be a power struggle at court between factions, probably with Cecil and his allies set against the survivors of the Essex coup. The hidden alliances and interconnectedness of aristocrats and court bureaucrats make it difficult for us to know, in retrospect, what the groupings might have been, had it come to a fight. Egerton's conduct as a mediator in this crucial period—doing what he could to save Essex from destroying himself, working behind the scenes with Cecil to bring in the king—may have convinced Daniel that the Lord Keeper, with others, had played a decisive role in avoiding war. In his verse epistle to Egerton, completed when the succession was a settled thing, it wouldn't be politic for Daniel to dwell too much on past fears, but a subtle private compliment, drawing on Lucan, might be appropriate. Daniel put similar compliments and personal allusions in other poems (to Lady Cumberland, for instance, and later to Prince Henry).[21] This allusion would have something extra in it too, by way of contrast: where Crassus had failed to keep the antagonists apart, Egerton had succeeded.

At the close of the letter, Daniel thanks Egerton again. The poet plans "to retyre" to his "pore home"—to leave London for the West Country in other words[22]—and not to see Egerton again until he has paid him his "vowes," which presumably means until he has completed the poem he has promised him. This he did, if the conclusions above are correct, with the publication a year later of the 1603 verse epistle. At this point, documentary evidence of Daniel's contacts with Egerton dries up: no more letters, no more poems, no more signs of preferment. The silence may mean nothing—perhaps we simply haven't found later letters, or they were destroyed—or it may mean a lot. When Daniel was called before the Privy Council early in 1605 to explain why he had written *The Tragedy of Philotas*, which looked like a political comment on the Essex affair, one of the Privy Councillors, Lord Mountjoy, wasn't present. We don't know whether Egerton, also a Privy Councillor, was there, but if he was he said nothing on Daniel's behalf, at least not while the poet was in the room.[23] For the period after 1605, up to 1617 when Egerton died, there are other questions we might wish to pose, if only because answers to them would help us to assess Daniel's standing among the Jacobean elite. Did Egerton and Daniel fall out over *Philotas*, or did they lose interest in one another, or did they maintain a close contact, patron and client, throughout these years?

Gaps in the documentary record are not uncommon at this date, and to fill them we often have to make do with guesswork. In this case, though, we have those twelve rare books, formerly in the Bridgewater Library, to add to the story. It will become clear in a moment that ten of these books were among Egerton's personal collection from the very beginning, while the other two were probably given to his heir, John 1st Earl of Bridgewater (1579–1649), or perhaps to his widow, Alice Spencer, Dowager Countess of Derby (who is discussed further at the end of this essay). The Daniel books are in fact an unusual run of presentation copies, from which we can learn several things. Just how unusual this run of copies is needs a proper context. Around seven hundred copies of Daniel's editions have survived, a little under half of which are now in eight major libraries: the British Library (70), the Bodleian Library in Oxford (70), the Folger Shakespeare Library in Washington, DC (62), the Harry Ransom Humanities Research Center in Austin, Texas (38), the Beinecke Library at Yale (27), the Houghton Library at Harvard (28), the Firestone Library at Princeton (14), and the Huntington Library (39). Something like two-thirds of the surviving copies are the prose histories that Daniel published in 1612–1613 (quartos) and 1618 (a folio which was reprinted four times up to1634).

Among these, only the Huntington collection has a gathered group of gift copies, with a single identifiable recipient. The major prize, for students of Daniel's life and work, would have been the recovery of the copies he must certainly have presented to his chief patron, Mountjoy, but so far none of these has been located.[24] Daniel's custom of not signing or inscribing gift copies in any way makes the job of identifying books he presented very difficult. In most cases, it is only because a recipient wrote something on the title page that we know that Daniel gave him the book, and what their relationship was. On his copy of the 1618 history, John Holles, later 1st Earl of Newcastle (d.1600), writes "The author Sam. Daniel gave me this book. 1618," while the antiquarian Sir Peter Manwood (d. 1625) has written on his copy of the 1612 history, "The first day of July. 1612. sent mee by Mr Danyel my good ffriende."[25] Most times we have to rely on the present location of a Daniel book to guess who received it. The copies of the 1612 history in Westminster Abbey and in Lambeth Palace, for instance, although they are not signed, were almost certainly Daniel's personal gifts to, respectively, William Camden (d. 1625) and George Abbot, Archbishop of Canterbury (d. 1618). By contrast, the copy of the 1612 history at Holkham Hall, although it is listed as part of Sir Edward Coke's library, may have been acquired by Coke (d. 1600) rather than presented by Daniel, or it may have been given to Coke's second wife, Lady Elizabeth Hatton (d. 1600), with whom Daniel had a known connection.[26]

When we turn to the Daniel copies in the Huntington Library, we find that the Bridgewater (formerly Egerton) group comprises about a third of the total holding. The revised Short Title Catalogue lists thirty-five of Daniel's editions published between 1585 and 1634 (including separate issues and variant imprints, but excluding the 1591 and 1597 editions of *Astrophel and Stella* which contained sonnets from Daniel's *Delia*). The Huntington has all but a couple of these titles, and in a few instances more than one copy per title (STC2 6238, for instance, and 6243.2, 6244, and 6261). There would have been more titles with duplicate copies had it not been Henry Huntington's policy, like other nineteenth-century collectors, to sell off duplicates as soon as he acquired new books. For example, one Daniel book sold by Huntington as a duplicate, a folio copy of the *Panegyric and Epistles*, STC 6259, is now in the Folger Shakespeare Library, call number STC 6259 Copy 1 1603. Only one of the Bridgewater (Egerton) copies was sold, however, *The Tragedy of Cleopatra*, a bibliographically independent part, with separate title page and signatures, of the 1599 collected edition of Daniel's *Poetical Essays*. This copy was subsequently purchased, probably from the Clawson library in 1924, for the Beinecke at Yale.[27]

The twelve Bridgewater (Egerton) copies of Daniel were published between 1595 and 1623. Their STC2 numbers, dates of publication, and present locations are these (all but one are in the Huntington):

STC2	Date	Format	Title	Call Number
6244.3	1595	Quarto	Civil Wars	RB 60932
6261 (part)	1599	Quarto	Cleopatra	Beinecke, Ig.D226.599
6236	1601	Folio	Works	RB 60958
6258	1603	Folio	Panegyric and Epistles	RB 60957
6259	1603	Folio	Panegyric and Epistles	RB 60950
6260	1603	Octavo	Panegyric and Epistles	RB 60948 (with 60949)
6239	1605	Octavo	Certain Small Poems	RB 60949 (with 60948)
6262	1606	Octavo	Queen's Arcadia	RB 60936
6245	1609	Quarto	Civil Wars	RB 60930
6246	1612	Quarto	History	RB 60923
6248	1618	Folio	History	RB 60952
6238 (part)	1623	Quarto	Whole Works in Poetry	RB 59013

The provenance of these copies as a group is straightforward. None of the books has an inscription by Daniel or Egerton on the title page, but the copies all have one or more of the indicators used to identify books that were once in the Bridgewater Library: (1) a limp vellum binding with distinctive gold tooling, or (2) the distinctive Bridgewater bookplate, or (3) a dull brown calf binding, stamped with the Bridgewater crest (a lion on its hind legs holding a spear pointing down), or (4) a handwritten number on the title page, enclosed in a three-sided frame, probably in the hand of John, 2nd Earl of Bridgewater (1623–1686).[28]

The descriptions of the Daniel copies given below in the Schedule of Copies (bindings and handwritten markings in the books) show that they were indeed all once in the Bridgewater Library. Further confirmation comes from catalogs of the Library and from occasional references to particular books. In 1908, almost a decade before they were sold to Huntington, all the printed books at Bridgewater House were listed by Strachan Holme, in twenty-seven handwritten volumes arranged alphabetically.[29] All twelve copies of Daniel are recorded, each with its library shelf mark, and a brief note of its contents and condition (from which we can be sure that the copies described match the ones now in the Huntington). Holme lists no other Daniel books, which is something we must be careful about since the Bridgewater catalog that preceded his, published in 1837, was compiled by John Payne Collier.[30] The tangled story of Collier's Shakespearean forgeries, and his connection with the Francis, Earl of Ellesmere and the Bridgewater Library, is too well known to need repeating here.[31] Collier evidently had a special interest in Daniel—he liked his poetry and he knew a a great deal about his life—but we need to be circumspect about his description of the copies of Daniel at Bridgewater House in the 1830s. In his *New Facts Regarding the Life of Shakespeare*, which appeared a couple of years before his catalog of the Bridgewater books, Collier tried to pass off a letter he claimed Daniel had

written to Egerton early in 1603, in which Daniel is supposed to speak dispar-
agingly about Shakespeare. Collier said he had found the letter among the
Bridgewater House papers, but in truth he forged the letter, in a pseudo-Eliza-
bethan hand, borrowing phrases from the genuine 1602 Daniel letter discussed above.[32]

Once our suspicions are aroused over this forgery, we are bound to doubt
everything else Collier said about Daniel, including the 1837 list of the
Bridgewater copies. Of the twelve Daniel books in Holme's list, Collier mentions only eight. Some of these omissions are understandable—in the 1837
Catalogue Collier was avowedly selective, often concentrating on fine paper
and association copies, unknown imprints and so forth, about which he could
write impressive notes—but at least one of the unmentioned ccpies ought to
have been listed. Perhaps the 1599 *Cleopatra*, even though it had a Bridgewater crest on its calf covers, didn't seem important to him or he had nothing
new to say about it, and he may simply have been uninterested in the gift
copy of the 1606 *Queen's Arcadia*. This explanation won't do for the 1603
folio first issue *Panegyric and Epistles* in vellum, STC2 6258 (Huntington
RB 60957), however, because it is clear that Collier was particularly interested in the unusual way Daniel had published these poems. In the *Catalogue*
Collier lists and discusses the Bridgewater copy of the second issue, STC2
6259 (RB 60950, which has additional contents and title pages and a calf
binding with the Bridgewater crest), but he ignores the first issue copy entirely. It may be no accident that this copy, RB 60957—an extremely rare
one—has had its title page removed. Collier certainly acquired a title page
detached from another of Daniel's large folios, which he kept in a scrapbook,[33] and we know too that he forged the signature of Mary, Countess of
Pembroke, on the vellum cover and title page of a copy of the folio second
issue *Panegyric and Epistles* he himself owned and which he planned to publish a print facsimile of (or to put on sale in a catalog).[34] It is difficult to resist
the conclusion that Collier not only forged a Daniel letter, but also stole the
title page from the special first issue Bridgewater *Panegyric and Epistles* and
tampered with two or more other folios of Daniel's.

The reason for prosecuting Collier like this so long after the event is that
his pilfering and fabrications may have extended to stealing other (now un-
identified) Daniel copies that he found at Bridgewater House.[35] One thing we
can be sure of is that the twelve Bridgewater presentation copies are a good
indication of what Daniel believed Egerton would wish to receive, and also
what he himself regarded as his most gift-worthy and important collections
of poems and prose. It is an unnerving thought, therefore, that a Daniel book
may be missing from the list not because the poet didn't give it to Egerton but
because Collier stole it two centuries later. There is another instance, wholly
unconnected to Collier, of a Bridgewater Daniel that may have gone missing
or been sold at the beginning of the eighteenth century. Henry John Todd, by

this date already a leading editor of Milton, was engaged by the Duke of Bridgewater in the later 1790s to sort out the library, and he was permitted to sell books pretty much as he thought fit.[36] In the catalog of books for sale by Thomas King at the "Francis Egerton 3rd Duke of Bridgewater" Part 1 Sale, Tuesday 27 April 1802, there is listed, at the foot of the first page, "*17 The Queenes Arcadia, *extremely rare* 1606." The sale catalogue places the book among anonymous plays, but it is certainly Daniel's (*The Queen's Arcadia* was the only book published without his name or initials on the title page). From this it seems either that the Bridgewater collection had two copies of *The Queen's Arcadia*, or that this one for sale in 1802 wasn't bought and remained at Bridgewater House (and is now RB 60936 in the Huntington).

It will be helpful at this point to summarize what we know about the Holme and Collier catalogues, and to draw together some details of the bindings, sizes of paper, and marks on the title pages (these are described below in the Schedule of Copies).

Title	Binding	Size (mm)	Title-page mark	Collier	Holme
Civil Wars	vellum	201x147	21/180	yes	25/A76
Cleopatra	calf (crest)	184x132	"5" within frame	no	21/B35
Works	vellum	277x185	N 6./4	yes	26/a11
Panegyric and Epistles	vellum	277x190		no	15/E14
Panegyric and Epistles	calf (crest)	288x168		yes	15/E15
Panegyric and Epistles	calf	158x115		yes	20/B22
Certain Small Poems	calf	158x115	A: 12/17	yes	20/B22
Queen's Arcadia	calf (crest)	163x131	21/38	no	21/B33
Civil Wars	vellum	212x161		yes	20/B18
History	vellum	204x172	D: 2./4	yes	20/B19
History	vellum	340x222	G: 4./7	yes	26/a10
Whole Works in Poetry	calf (crest)	175x130	21/38	no	21/B37

The next question—how many of these books were presentation copies—can be answered with some confidence. It is impossible for one of the copies to have been a gift from Daniel, since he died in 1619, four years before the publication of the 1623 *Whole Works in Poetry*, and another of the copies can't been received by Egerton (he died in March 1617, a full year before the 1618 *History* was published). Among the remaining copies, it is the four in vellum with gilt tooling on the covers that we can group together at once as Daniel's gifts to the Lord Chancellor, that is, the 1595 *Civil Wars*, the 1601 *Works*, the folio *Panegyric and Epistles* (first issue), and 1609 *Civil Wars*. Since we know for sure that one of these, the 1601 *Works* folio, was a presentation copy (it was the gift Daniel sent with the 1602 letter attached to it), it is reasonable to suppose that the three others that resemble it closely—with similar frames of gold fillets and fleurons, with acorns at the center—were also given by Daniel. The two copies in vellum that don't have tooling and ornaments must also be gifts. The first is the copy of the 1612 quarto *History*, an edition which Daniel says specifically was for private circulation to friends and patrons (pp.239–40), while the second, a 1618 folio *History*, is a very large fine-paper copy—the largest surviving copy of any of Daniel's works—in which, most unusually, the poet has corrected the text in places in his neat italic hand. Daniel must surely have given this book to Egerton's heir, John, 1st Earl of Bridgewater, or perhaps to Egerton's widow, Alice Spencer, the Dowager Countess of Derby (*d.* 1637).

Four of the remaining copies are bound in calf, stamped with the Bridgewater crest. These bindings can't have been put on the books until after Egerton had died (at his death he was still only Baron Ellesmere, and it was his son John who was made the 1st Earl of Bridgewater in 1617). It is possible, perhaps probable, that these four copies were originally bound in vellum too. The latest of the copies, the 1623 *Whole Works in Poetry*, does not have a complete set of contents—poems, drama, and prose—merely the section with the plays in it. Perhaps John Danyel, whose preface introduces the whole edition, gave this part copy to the 1st Earl as it is, as a remembrance of his brother, or perhaps it wasn't a gift at all, but simply a secondhand dismembered copy that someone in the Egerton family picked up in a bookshop decades after the edition was first published.[37] It is conceivable, though not likely, that this was the case with the final two copies, the 1603 octavo *Panegyric and Epistles* which is bound, in an inferior later seventeenth- or eighteenth-century binding, with the 1605 *Certain Small Poems*. Copies of these books are now sometimes found in separate bindings, but most often they have survived bound together, and it is certain that Daniel's publisher, Simon Waterson, coupled and sold many of the original copies as a complete item, two editions in one, from 1605 onward.

This is the point at which, having considered the evidence piecemeal, we can begin to fill out our account of the connections between Daniel and Lord Chancellor Egerton. Caveats are necessary, as we have seen (were all the books gifts? did Collier remove any others?), but in outline the story looks clear enough, at least from around 1602 when Daniel sent Egerton the *Works* folio with the letter of thanks. After that, in the following four years, Daniel presented the Lord Chancellor with nearly everything else he wrote (most notably, all three editions of the *Panegyric and Epistles* which contain the verse epistle addressed to Egerton).[38] Then, in 1606, there start to be more significant omissions, first the small pamphlet *A Funeral Poem* on the Earl of Devonshire (formerly Baron Mountjoy), which was probably issued as a private publication for circulation at the funeral in April 1606,[39] then the *Certain Small Works* octavo collected edition published in 1607. Negative evidence of this kind must always be handled carefully, but the gaps here really are telling. When Mountjoy died, he was deeply out of favor at court over his marriage to Penelope Rich, and it is entirely possible that Egerton stayed away from the funeral to avoid any taint of the disgrace;[40] perhaps the last thing he would want in his library was a poem in which Daniel tried to defend Mountjoy and to celebrate his achievements as a general and a scholar. The reason that the 1607 *Certain Small Works* is missing is probably simpler. This edition contains major changes that Daniel made to several poems, particularly *Musophilus*, but it is also by far the most poorly produced of his books, with printing errors and other mistakes throughout. Daniel was very ill—close to death in fact—when the book was being manufactured, and the printing house itself was in disarray, with the compositors and workmen stricken with plague.[41] The edition is a complete mess and it is no wonder that Daniel, when he recovered, chose not to present a copy to Egerton.

From 1608 onwards Daniel turned to writing history almost exclusively, publishing first (in 1609) another instalment of the verse *Civil Wars*, followed by the two editions of the prose *History* (1612 and 1618) both of which were planned for private circulation to friends and patrons, Egerton among them evidently. In this period, though, there are once again books that Daniel didn't give to Egerton, the 1610 investiture masque *Tethys' Festival*, the 1615 court tragicomedy *Hymen's Triumph*, and the two small reprint editions of 1607 and 1611.[42] It is obvious that Daniel was making a choice here, in not presenting Egerton with smaller format books, reprints and ephemera (that is, books of plays and entertainments). If we turn back to the period *before* 1602, we find here too that Daniel chose not to give Egerton his smaller books or reprints. The Bridgewater collection has none of the editions that Daniel published before 1595, that is, the half dozen little books of poetry (quartos, octavos, and tiny duodecimos) that made him famous in the early 1590s, *Delia, Rosamond and Cleopatra*.[43] The earliest edition he gave to Egerton was the four-book version of the *Civil Wars*, published in 1595. The subject of this poem—a sober and sophisticated analysis of medieval power, law, and rebellion—would probably have appealed to Egerton straightaway, but we don't know whether he already knew Daniel personally by this date. He may have contacted the poet because he admired the 1595 *Civil Wars* (and possibly because he knew Mountjoy had taken him up), at which point Daniel would naturally present him, as a new patron, with a copy of the book. Another possibility is that the first meeting between them didn't take place until two or three years later, 1598 say, when the only appropriate book Daniel had to hand for presentation (one that would suit Egerton's serious and severe Protestant tastes) was the *Civil Wars*.

Another of the Bridgewater books suggests a date of ca.1598 for the first contact between Daniel and Egerton, that is, the 1599 *Cleopatra*, the copy now in the Beinecke. As was explained earlier, this was a bibliographically separate piece in a composite volume, the 1599 *Poetical Essays* (which comprised five books of the *Civil Wars*, published 1595 and added to ca.1597, with two new pieces, *Musophilus* and *Octavia*, and revised versions of the existing works, *Rosamond* and *Cleopatra*). The *Poetical Essays* was Daniel's first collected edition and its presence among the Bridgewater collection, albeit only the *Cleopatra* portion, probably indicates that Daniel presented the book soon after it was first published, by which time Egerton may have declared himself his patron. (It is difficult to know why only *Cleopatra* has survived, but the number 5 on the title page, in the hand of the 2nd Earl of Bridgewater, makes it very likely that the book was indeed at one time the fifth item in an untraced complete *Poetical Essays*, perhaps a rebound one since when it was first published *Cleopatra* was the *fourth* piece in the edition.)[44] The implication in Daniel's 1602 letter of thanks to Egerton—that he had had to delay for a while writing something personal for his patron—may be relevant here. An apology for the delay of a couple of years (from ca.1599 to 1602) is perhaps more likely than an apology for the nondelivery of a poem that had been promised for six or seven years (that is, ca.1595–1602).

Some of these dates are guesses, of course, but surely we won't be that far out if we conclude that Egerton wasn't a patron of Daniel's before 1595, and probably not until ca.1598, but that then, in the following two decades, there was a sustained, although possibly intermittent connection between them. The years immediately before and after the accession of King James appear to have been the time when they were in closest contact. Perhaps the loosening of their connection in later years, if that's what happened, was due in part to Daniel's writing of *The Tragedy of Philotas* and the criticism the play attracted, and to his closeness and loyalty to Mountjoy, a courtier tainted with scandal at his death in 1606. From a survey of what's missing and what's present among the Bridgewater books, it looks likely that Daniel, as we might expect, took particular care in later years to present poems and historical writing he knew the Lord Chancellor would approve of, and that he didn't bother him with reprints and pieces of slighter value, such as the printed texts of court masques (the exception being *The Queen's Arcadia*, a pastoral tragicomedy acted before the Queen and Prince Henry in Christ Church in Oxford in August 1605).[45]

Again, it will help to summarize here in a chronological list the most likely dates that the Daniel books were given or acquired for the Egerton library (see table on page 227).

This is about as much as we can deduce from the Bridgewater copies of Daniel, but there are a couple of related points that need to be made too. First, it is intriguing that the Bridgewater collection has no copy of John Danyel's *Songs for the Lute*, a large, attractive book with musical settings and lyrics that was published in London in 1606. Given the "preferment" Egerton arranged for John, which Daniel thanked him for in 1602 (see the quotation above), it comes as a small surprise that Egerton isn't even mentioned in *Songs for the Lute* (we might have expected "The Lord Keeper's Pavan" or

Title	Likely date of presentation
Civil Wars	1595–ca.1598
Cleopatra	1599
Works	1602
Panegyric and Epistles (first issue)	May 1603
Panegyric and Epistles (second issue)	late 1605[46]
Panegyric and Epistles (octavo)	1603
Certain Small Poems	late 1605
Queen's Arcadia	1606
Civil Wars	1609
History	mid-1612
History	after March 1618
Whole Works in Poetry	1623 or later (not presented by Daniel)

something of the sort). The book is dedicated to Mistress Anne Green, a relatively modest member of the elite (she was the daughter of a knight), not at all at the same elevated social level as the Lord Chancellor.[47] John Danyel could hardly have refused the opportunity to have Egerton as a dedicatee if it had been offered to him, so it's reasonable to think it wasn't. Moreover, although Egerton was fond of music, and his daughters in particular were given a good musical education, there is no evidence that John Danyel had any place in the Lord Chancellor's entourage, either as a tutor or a performer.[48] Perhaps John was simply taken up by other patrons soon after 1602 (by Edward Seymour, Earl of Hertford, for instance),[49] and he simply couldn't give the time or commitment Egerton would require. This is plausible, but still one can't escape the nagging feeling that part of this story, of patronage bestowed on one brother but not the other, is hidden from us.

The most interesting side issue in relation to the Bridgewater books is something we have considered in part already, the question of how and when Egerton and Daniel met each other. We need to return to this even though the simpler explanation proposed above is perfectly sound (that is, that by the end of the 1590s, at the latest, Egerton would have wanted to meet England's new historical writer, championed by Mountjoy, the poet whom everyone said was a rival of Lucan, and who was likely to be Spenser's successor). The reason for giving this matter a second thought, even at the risk of overturning some of the dates suggested above, is that in 1600 Lord Keeper Egerton married, as his third wife, Alice Spencer, Dowager Countess of Derby (1559–1637), a lady with impeccable credentials as a patron and promoter of literature. In the 1590s the Countess had had several connections with Spenser and, through her first husband, Ferdinando, Earl of Derby (d. 1594), links too with Nashe, Robert Greene, and the public theater.[50] It isn't impossible that in 1600—not all that long after Spenser's death in 1599—the Countess urged her new husband to meet Daniel and to offer him patronage.

A good while before 1600, however, Egerton was already well known as a patron of letters, so there is no compelling reason why his interest in Daniel should need to be prompted by his wife, however keen she was on literature and drama. Nevertheless, it is worth noting, as a final instance of what early ownership of a book may tell us, that Daniel and the Dowager Countess had at least one association, albeit at one remove, through her family and through another poet, a minor one, Sir William Skipwith (ca.1594–1610). In 1607, when the Countess visited her daughter and son-in-law, Lord and Lady Hastings, the Earl and Countess of Huntingdon, at their home in Ashby-de-la-Zouche in Leicestershire, an entertainment was written for the occasion, containing poems and eclogues by the dramatist John Marston. As part of the entertainment, there was a gift-giving, for which further verses (speaking parts for the noblewomen and ladies present) were written by Skipwith.[51] It may be of particular importance, in our search to situate Daniel in relation to Egerton, that Skipwith owned one of the few special copies of Daniel's 1601 *Works* (all of which the poet himself may have presented in person),[52] and that Henry, Earl of Huntingdon (the Dowager Countess's son-in-law), owned a copy of Daniel's 1613 *History*—a copy he had to buy, it's true, but one that he bothered to trick up in his family arms.[53] Perhaps, in time, archival or other evidence will show us in more detail just how intimately Daniel was connected with Egerton, and with his family and circle.

Schedule of Egerton Copies

The standard descriptions of the contents of Daniel's editions are in Sellers and in Greg.[54] The brief notes below—chiefly concerned with bindings, handwritten markings, and some of the contents—supplement the evidence already presented that these copies belonged to Egerton and his immediate heirs. STC2 numbers for the copies are listed above, p. 223.

1595 *Civil Wars*
This copy is in the original limp vellum binding. The covers, which formerly had pink ties, are tooled in gilt with a single frame of fillets with fleurons at the corners, and with a single acorn gold ornament in the center.

1599 *Cleopatra*
This is bound in calf with the Bridgewater crest, a lion on its hind legs holding a spear pointing down, on upper and lower covers. There are telltale signs that this copy was once bound up with other items, most probably with

other parts of the 1599 *Poetical Essays* collection from which, for some reason, it has become separated.

1601 *Works*

This is in the original limp vellum binding with four sewing bands. The covers, which formerly had green ties, arc tooled in gilt with two frames of fillets, the second with fleurons at the outer corners, with acorns and oak leaves as the center ornament. There are six small gilt ornaments on the spine. This copy is not bound, as other *Works* folios are, with a folio *Panegyric and Epistles*, which indicates that Daniel gave it to Egerton before spring 1603, the date the *Panegyric and Epistles* were published. The remnant of a seal is visible on the inside front cover, which matches the broken seal on the letter Daniel sent to Egerton presenting this copy to him. There are a few small manuscript corrections, one or two in Daniel's hand, most probably made soon after the book was printed.[55]

1603 *Panegyric and Epistles* (first issue)

This is in the original limp vellum binding with eight sewing bands. The covers, with pink ties still in place, are tooled in gilt with two frames of fillets, the second with fleurons at the outer corners, with acorns and oak leaves as the center ornament; this is very similar to (perhaps intended to complement) the binding on the 1601 *Works* folio. There are seven small fleurons on the spine. The original title page is missing, its place supplied with a photostat from the British Library copy of the first issue, BM 837. K9(1). E and F signatures have been transposed, presumably when the book was first bound, since there is no indication of later rebinding.

1603 *Panegyric and Epistles* (second issue)

This is bound in calf with the upper and lower covers tooled with a frame of fillets in gilt and the Bridgewater crest in blind as a center ornament. This copy has the extra, deliberately misdated leaves that Daniel added late in1605 (see below, p. 238, n. 46), but these have been misplaced when the book was first bound, or in a subsequent rebinding.

1603 *Panegyric and Epistles* (octavo)

This is bound with the 1605 *Certain Small Poems* in three-quarters calf, with a red label and blue marbled edges.

1605 *Certain Small Poems*

This is bound with the 1603 *Panegyric and Epistles*. Copies of the *Certain Small Poems* survive by themselves, but most were put together and sold, as the first item, with the *Panegyric and Epistles*. In this volume, the *Certain*

Small Poems has been misplaced as the second item, perhaps when the volume was rebound.

1606 *Queen's Arcadia*
This is bound in calf, with tan morocco labels and marble endpapers pasted down. The upper and lower covers are tooled in blind with a frame of fillets with the Bridgewater crest as center ornament.

1609 *Civil Wars*
This is in the original limp vellum binding with five sewing bands and a red label on the spine. The upper and lower covers, which formerly had pink ties, are tooled in gilt with two frames of fillets, the second with fleurons at the outer corners, with acorns and oak leaves as the center ornament; this is very similar to (perhaps intended to complement) the bindings on the 1601 *Works* folio and 1603 *Panegyric and Epistles* folio (first issue). There is a small manuscript correction on Q3v, where the misprinted phrase 'recorder equity' has been corrected, properly, to "re order equity" by a single penstroke made through the letter "c." This may indicate that Egerton, with his profound and professional interest in equity, read the passage very carefully.

1612 *History*
This is in the original limp vellum binding, with four sewing bands: the label on the spine was added much later, probably in the eighteenth century. There is no tooling or ornament on the covers, and there are no ties.

1618 *History*
This is the largest surviving copy of any of Daniel's books. There is no tooling or ornament on the original limp vellum binding, although a title has been added in gilt on the spine, well after the book was first printed, perhaps in the early eighteenth century. The dedication leaf to Queen Anne is missing, which may have a bearing on the circumstances in which the book was published.[56] Daniel, most unusually, has made small corrections by hand, in his usual neat italic script, in a few places in the printed text: on p.160, for instance, opposite the date "1289" the phrase "the hatred to the people of men" is corrected to 'the hatred of the people to men', by penstrokes made through "to" and "of," with "of" and "to" written respectively above the corrections, with carets. Some but not all of these corrections were incorporated into the reprinted texts, 1621, 1626, 1634 (the misprints on p.160 were corrected).

1623 *Whole Works in Poetry* (only 2A–2T⁸, masque and plays)
This is bound in calf with tan morocco labels, with the Bridgewater crest in blind on the upper and lower covers, with red edges. John, 2nd Earl of

Bridgewater, has written on the title page "Sam: Daniel's Poeticall Workes in ye Title Page at ye End of this Booke": the 1623 title leaf and dedicatory preface by John Danyel have been misplaced between 2T4 and 2T5 in re-binding.

Notes

1. Much of the work for this article was done in the Huntington Library in April 2003. I am indebted to the Trustees of the Huntington Library and Art Gallery for the award of a William Ringler Fellowship, which gave me the opportunity to examine Egerton's books and papers in detail.

2. The Bridgewater copies joined the Huntington collection throughout the latter part of 1917 and early 1918 (the dates are noted in pencil on the endpapers). The history of the Bridgewater collection, and its acquisition by Henry Huntington, is told concisely and authoritatively by Stephen Tabor, in his article "The Bridgewater Library" in *Pre-Nineteenth-Century British Book Collectors and Bibliographers*, Dictionary of Literary Biography, vol. 213, ed. William Baker and Kenneth Womack (Gale Group, Detroit, San Francisco, and London, 1999), 40–50

3. The connection between Egerton and Daniel was noted first in print by Francis Henry Egerton, 8th Earl of Bridgewater, in *A Compilation of Various Authentic Evidences tending to illustrate the Life and Character of Thomas Egerton* (privately printed, 1798), 57.

4. Quoted from *Poems and A Defence of Ryme*, ed. Arthur Colby Sprague (Chicago and London, 1965 Phoenix edition), 104 (hereafter cited as Sprague).

5. There are recent studies of Egerton's views on equity in Mark Fortier, 'Equity and Ideas: Coke, Ellesmere, and James I', *Renaissance Quarterly* 51 (1988): 1255–79, and Simon Markham, "Samuel Daniel's idea of Law and Equity," *Studies in Law and Literature 1580–1652*, unpublished Oxford D.Phil thesis, 1996, 127–181. For the sources in Aristotle, see *Samuel Daniel's Occasional and Dedicatory Verse: A Critical Edition*, ed. John Pitcher, 2 vols., unpublished Oxford D.Phil thesis, 1978, 2: 271 (hereafter cited as Pitcher)

6. The verse epistles are printed in Sprague, pp.101–21. The background to the poems and their sources are set out in Pitcher, 2: 266–97.

7. Before he was made Lord Keeper, Egerton was Solicitor General (1581), Attorney General (1592) and Master of the Rolls (1592). His life, and his legal and political careers are considered by W. J. Jones, "Ellesmere and Politics, 1603–1617," *Early Stuart Studies*, ed. Howard S. Reinmuth (Minneapolis, University of Minnesota Press, 1970), 11–63; Louis A. Knafla, *Law and Politics in Jacobean England* (Cambridge University Press, Cambridge, 1977) passim; the entry by Jones and Hasler in *The House of Commons, 1558–1603*, ed. P. W. Hasler, 3 vols. (HMSO, London, 1981), 2:80–83; and Louis A. Knafla, "The 'Country' Chancellor: the Patronage of Sir Thomas Egerton, Baron Ellesmere" in French R. Fogle and Louis A. Knafla, *Patronage in Late Renaissance England* (William Andrews Clark Memorial Library, University of California, Los Angeles, 1983), 33–115.

8. Sprague, 101

9. Quoted from the Loeb edition, *Lucan*, edited with a translation by J. D. Duff (Loeb, Cambridge, Mass., 1928), 10–11: "Crassus, who stood between, was the only check on imminent war. So the Isthmus of Corinth divides the main and parts two seas with its slender line, forbidding them to mingle their waters; but if its soil were withdrawn, it would dash the Ionian sea against the Aegean."

10. Book 4 of the *Civil Wars* was first published in 1595 (for the gift copy of this edition that Daniel presented to Egerton, see the Schedule of Copies, p. 230 above). The *Civil Wars* was much revised for the next edition (the first part of the 1601 *Works* folio), and the 120+ stanzas in Book 4, with some stanzas added and others deleted, appeared as Book 5: in 1601 the lines referring to Gloucester as "that Isthmus" became, without any substantive alterations, 5.89.6–8 (see *The Civil Wars by Samuel Daniel*, ed. Laurence Michel (New Haven: Yale University Press, 1958), 58–60 and 199–200)

11. This letter was believed to be a John Payne Collier forgery for a long time, but it was shown to be authentic by John Pitcher, "Samuel Daniel's Letter to Sir Thomas Egerton," *Huntington Library Quarterly* 47 (1984): 55–61. The text of the letter is printed on p. 56; see pp. 59–60 for the suggestion that it was written in 1602.

12. Daniel would also have had access to English and foreign books through a close friend, the London stationer Simon Waterson, who published nearly all of his works.

13. Biographies and estimates of John Danyel (the way his surname is now spelt), are included in the entry on him by David Scott in *The New Grove Dictionary of Music and Musicians*, 20 vols., ed. Stanley Sadie (Macmillan, London, 1980), 5:233–34; and in *Lyrics from English Airs*, ed. with an introduction by Edward Doughtie (Cambridge: Harvard University Press, 1970), 259–69 and 549–53.

14. Another possibility should be noted—if only to dismiss it—that when Daniel says "[I shall] go on with the worke I have in hand, which, god knowes, had long since bene ended, and your Honour had had that which in my harte I have prepared for yow," the gift he intends for Egerton is not a separate poem (the verse epistle), but the long-delayed completion of the *Civil Wars*. We can rule this out on several grounds, however, the most important that Egerton is never mentioned at all in the prefaces or text of the *Civil Wars*, let alone as a dedicatee or a special patron of the poem.

15. Descriptions of Daniel as a "Lucanist"—the satirist Everard Guilpin's term for him in 1598—are noted by Michel, *Civil Wars*, 341. In his 1602 *A Poetical Rapsody*, E9v, Francis Davidson went so far as to claim that Daniel had even surpassed Spenser because of his range (drama as well as lyric and heroic verse).

16. Mountjoy's patronage is discussed by John Pitcher in the entry on Daniel in the *Oxford Dictionary of National Biography* (Oxford: Oxford University Press, forthcoming 2004). Earlier accounts of Mountjoy and Daniel are available in Joan Rees, *Samuel Daniel: A Critical and Biographical Study* (Liverpool University Press, Liverpool, 1964), pp.67–70 and 126–29, and Cecil Seronsy, *Samuel Daniel* (New York, Twayne Publishers, 1967), 60–61 and 123–29. Daniel's doubts about what to do with his life, and whether to give up writing, are most visible in *Musophilus*, the long colloquy poem he published in 1599 that shows the influence, not always benign, of Fulke Greville.

17. Modern historical literature on Lady Anne Clifford is extensive. A useful starting point, which notes Daniel's connections with her, is Richard T. Spence, *Lady Anne Clifford, Countess of Pembroke, Dorset and Mongomery (1590–1676)* (Stroud, Sutton Publishing, 1997), see especially 12–17.

18. The argument that Daniel used *imprese* (devices with mottos) as dominant images in his verse epistles is considered in John Pitcher, *Samuel Daniel: the Brotherton Manuscript* (Leeds, University of Leeds Texts and Monographs, 1981), pp.32–35.

19. Daniel wrote the first (472 lines) version of the *Panegyric Congratulatory*, addressed to the King, in less than a month: see Pitcher 2:232 ff (especially 238–40).

20. Among Daniel's fluvial keywords are "course" and "passage" (movements of water as well as abstractions for the ways to conduct ourselves) Examples of seas and land in the verse epistles are in Sprague, p.111, lines 12ff, p.118, lines 93ff, p.123, lines 45ff.

21. Personal allusions are identified in Pitcher 2:277–84 (epistles to Lady Cumberland and Lady Hatton), 2:305–6 (elegy on Mountjoy), and Pitcher, *Samuel Daniel: The Brotherton Manuscript*, 31–34 (epistle to Prince Henry).

22. In 1605, in the letter of apology he wrote to Robert Cecil over the *Philotas* scandal, Daniel offered to withdraw the "booke"—the manuscript of the play—and himself to his "poore home," the same phrase with the same meaning as in the letter to Egerton, that is, his home in Somerset, perhaps in Beckington (the 1605 letter is quoted in *The Tragedy of Philotas by Samuel Daniel*, ed. Laurence Michel (New Haven, Yale University Press, 1949), pp.37–38; for Beckington, see Rees, 167).

23. The record of the Privy Council meeting has not survived, but Daniel is reported to have said that at that point he had no "friend in power to help him" other than Mountjoy (Michel, *Philotas*, 37).

24. I have personally examined 400 copies of Daniel's editions, but I have found no sign that Mountjoy owned any of these. I have also drawn a complete blank with sale catalogues and descriptions in library catalogs.

25. The Holles copy is in the Bodleian, shelfmark D.2.16.Art; the Manwood copy is owned by Dr Bent Juel-Jensen (Pitcher, 1984, p.60, article cited in n. 11)

26. Camden's copy is in Westminster Abbey, Abbott's in Lambeth Palace. For the copy that may have belonged to Coke, see *A Catalogue of the Library of Sir Edward Coke*, ed. W. O. Hassall (New Haven, Yale University Press, 1950), p.49, item 586. Daniel's links with Lady Hatton are set out by Arthur Freeman in "An Epistle for Two," *The Library* 5.25 (1970): 226–36.

27. Tabor, pp.49–50, explains Henry Huntington's policy of selling duplicates, even ones as important as the presentation copy of *Comus*. The 1599 *Cleopatra* was lot 173 in *Catalogue of Early and Modern Literature: Part VII*, Sale 1333, 4 February 1918. It was sold again as item 175 in the Clawson sale (Seymour de Ricci, *A Catalogue of Early English Books in the Library of John L. Clawson*, Philadelphia and New York, 1924, 60–61). The book has the Bridgewater bookplate, Clawson's bookplate, and the notice that it was bought for the Beinecke by the "Albert H. Childs Memorial Collection." I take this opportunity to thank the Beinecke Library for the award of an A. Bartlett Giamatti Fellowship that I held in April and May 1994, when I was able to examine the Daniel books in Yale and Harvard, as well as papers relating to Lady Anne Clifford.

28. Tabor, 50.

29. Strachan Holme, *Catalogue of the Books of the Right Honourable Francis Charles Granville Egerton Earl of Ellesmere at Bridgewater House St James' London*, undated, bound manuscript volumes "reproduced by an autograph process" (what is probably the unique copy is now in the British Library).

30. *A Catalogue, Bibliographical and Critical of Early English Literature, forming a Portion of the Library at Bridgewater House* (London, 1837). Entries are arranged alphabetically, with the Daniel books listed on 78–84.

31. Most of the materials relevant to Daniel are discussed by C. M. Ingelby, *A Complete View of the Shakespeare Controversy* (London, 1861), 247–49 and 307–9.

32. *New Facts Regarding the Life of Shakespeare* (London, 1835), 47–53: the forgery is on pp.48–49, the genuine letter on pp.52–53. Two versions of the forgery have survived in the Huntington collection: EL 137, in Collier's "Elizabethan" hand, and 11751 in an even less "Elizabethan" hand (illustrated in Ingelby, Sheet No. IX facing p.248). One explanation for the two versions is in Collier's account of how, when he found various manuscripts, he copied them, as the Earl of Ellesmere asked him to (Ingelby, 242–43). Perhaps EL 137 was supposed to be the original and 11751 Collier's honest copy of it. Both letters are spurious, as the Ingelby expert witnesses indicate, 249, and as Collier's fake Elizabethan language confirms (phrases in the forgeries, such as "Most bounden," certainly aren't ones Daniel ever used).

In *New Facts*, footnote on 51–52, Collier also said he owned one of Daniel's manuscripts—a holograph copy of book 5 of the *Civil Wars*—but since he didn't repeat the claim, and the manuscript hasn't surfaced, the presumption must be that this was another of his inventions.

33. Collier's scrapbook, containing fragments from several STC editions, is in the Folger, shelfmark 26145 No.1a. There is a signature, "John J<. . .>ng," now barely legible, in the right-hand corner of the detached 1602 *Works* title page; the same hand has practised scroll marks on the verso.

34. Only two copies of the first issue *Panegyric and Epistles*, STC2 6258, are known, this one in the Huntington, the other in the British Library, which has its title page intact. More than a dozen copies of the second issue, STC2 6259, have survived (this issue has an additional item, the prose *Defence of Rhyme*, and in some copies, including the one Daniel gave Egerton, it also has additional leaves: see the Schedule of Copies, p. 230). Collier's own copy of the second issue is now in the Pierpont Morgan Library, PML 16312. On the flyleaf facing the title page he has written in pencil "This copy (see the autograph above the imprint) belonged to the Countess of Pembroke, the patroness of Daniel &. Her name has also been inscribed on the vellum cover but nearly effaced." The name on the cover is indeed all but lost—Collier may have contrived this, to make it look authentic—but the "autograph" on the title page doesn't resemble any known signature of Lady Pembroke's.

Collier referred to this "Pembroke" copy in a letter to *The Times*, dated 5 July 1859, in the course of defending himself against accusations about the pencil additions in the 1632 "Perkins" Shakespeare Second Folio (which were then being exposed as his forgeries). In the fifth paragraph of the letter, he claims that the binding of the Shakespeare folio "is considerably older than the reign of George II," and that the date of fly-leaves provide "no criterion as to the date when the leather covering was put on" because "fly-leaves are often added at a subsequent period for the protection of the title-page" when "the original ones have been torn or destroyed." He then says that he has "several distinct proofs of this," but will only mention one, a copy of Samuel Daniel's *Panegyricke Congratulatory* folio (1603), which "the poet presented to the Countess of Pembroke; Daniel wrote her name on the gilt vellum cover, and she put her signature on the title page. It is likely that Daniel also placed an inscription on the fly leaf, which has disappeared, perhaps to gratify the cupidity of some autograph collector. A comparatively modern substitute has been inserted; it has no watermark, but a moment's inspection is enough to show that it was much posterior to the time when the book was printed." The mention of "the cupidity" of someone who might tear the title page out of a rare book is another (possibly unconscious) pointer to what Collier himself may have done with the title leaf in the first issue *Panegyric and Epistles* at Bridgewater House.

Evidence that Collier intended to publish a facsimile of this "Pembroke" copy, or perhaps to describe it for auction or a private sale, is to be found in a short note, in his normal handwriting, preserved in the Folger manuscript, Y.d.7(27). In this, he claims once more that this is Lady Pembroke's copy, but he adds this time that in its contents it "agrees precisely" with the Ellesmere (now Huntington) copy, which he had previously thought was unique. I have not been able to establish whether Collier's short description of the book—which supplements the one in the "Bridgewater Catalogue"—was ever printed, either as a preface to a facsimile or as an entry in a sale catalog.

35. Arthur and Janet Freeman, who know more about Collier than anyone else, tell me, privately, that this charge is probably unfair. They are not persuaded that Collier would have mutilated a book in the Ellesmere library or stolen one. Indeed, in their researches they have found no evidence that Collier was light fingered at all with old books, as opposed to manuscripts. In their view the absence of the vellum first issue *Panegryic* from the 1837 catalogue may have the simple explanation, that at that date Collier didn't know that there were separate issues of the poem, and that he didn't describe the book because it looked to him like an imperfect copy.

36. See Tabor, 47

37. It is interesting, and possibly significant, that in 1635 some copies of this drama portion of the *Whole Works* were reissued, with a new title page, as a set of "Drammaticke poems": see STC2 6238 and 6243.8.

38. He didn't give Egerton the 1604 court masque *The Vision of the Twelve Goddesses*, STC2 6265.

39. See Pitcher, 2:303–6.

40. Pitcher, 2:308–9.

41. See Mark Bland, "John Windet" in *The British Literary Book Trade, 1475–1700*, Dictionary of Literary Biography, vol. 170, ed. James K. Bracken and Joel Silver (Detroit, Washington DC and London: Gale Research, 1996), 319–25 (324–25).

42. STC2 13161, 6257, 6242, and 6263.

43. STC2 6243.2–6 (1592–8)

44. Tabor, 50, describes the 2nd Earl's way of marking the binding order for separate sections in books. The contents of the 1599 *Poetical Essays* are listed by Sellers, pp. 34–35, and Greg, (full citations in n.54 below).

45. This book may have been acceptable to Egerton, among other things, because of the close links he had with Oxford University throughout his life.

46. The second issue of the *Panegyric and Epistles* differs from the first in its title page, but both issues were published in late spring 1603. Two years after, probably in November 1605 around the time the *Certain Small Poems* collection was published, Daniel had a couple of extra leaves added to a number of copies of the second issue (Pitcher 2:242–50). The Egerton second issue has these additional leaves.

47. Doughtie, *Lyrics from English Airs*, 549.

48. There is no sign of John Danyel or his brother among the Egerton papers I have examined (for instance, the lists of retinue and servants in the Egerton households in 1603 and 1615, Huntington EL 290, 291, 137, 288, 296, and the lists of payments in 1604, 1606, 1607, and 1608, EL 148, 151, 159, 161, 169, 171, 172, and 174). Danyel certainly wasn't a lute tutor for the Egerton family at this date or a dozen years later (in 1615–16 it was a Mr Newport who taught the lute to Egerton's granddaughter, Frances, as the payments in EL 320, 324, and 331 show).

49. John Danyel's connections with the Earl Hertford were through his brother: see John Pitcher, "Samuel Daniel, the Hertfords, and a Question of Love," *Review of English Studies* 35 (1984): 449–62.

50. French R. Fogle, "'Such a Rural Queen': the Countess of Derby as Patron" in Fogle and Knafla, *Patronage in Late Renaissance England*, 1–29 (14–18)

51. James Knowles, "Marston, Skipwith and *The Entertainment at Ashby*," *English Manuscript Studies* 3 (1992): 137–92 (171–77).

52. This copy is now in the Houghton Library at Harvard, shelfmark 14453.48*. The name "William Skipwith" is written in neat letters on the title page, immediately below the printed motto. The book didn't come from the Bridgewater collection, although it did pass through Huntington's hands (*Catalogue of English Literature*, Anderson Galleries, Sale Number 1351, lot number 109).

53. This copy is now in the Folger, STC 6246 Copy 2. Huntingdon's signature is on the recto of the page preceding the title page, and the calf binding has the Hastings crest stamped on the upper and lower calf covers.

54. Harry Sellers, "A Bibliography of the Works of Samuel Daniel," *Oxford Bibliographical Society Proceedings and Papers*, vol. 2, 1927–30 (Oxford, Oxford University Press, 1930), 29–54, 341–42; and W. W. Greg, *A Bibliography of the English Printed Drama to the Restoration*, 4 vols. (Bibliographical Society, London, 1939–59), 1:216–19, 331–32, 349–50, 354–5428–9, 466.

55. Some of the printing-house corrections are listed in Pitcher 2:359–60.

56. See I. A. Shapiro, "The Dedication of Daniel's *Collection*, 1618," *The Library* 3 (1981): 62–4.

Propeller's Staging of *Rose Rage*

PATRICIA TATSPAUGH

UNLIKE other English companies that have presented adaptations of the three parts of *Henry VI*, Propeller, founded in 1997 at the Watermill Theatre, Newbury, might best be described as a co-operative. Its twelve male actors, director Edward Hall, designer Michael Pavelka, lighting designer Ben Ormerod, and text adviser Roger Warren worked together at every stage of the production of *Rose Rage*.[1] This close communication between artistic team and actors distinguishes their work from the more well-known, large-scale adaptations by the Royal Shakespeare Company—*The Wars of the Roses* (1963–64) and *The Plantagenets* (1988–89)—and by the English Shakespeare Company, *The Wars of the Roses* (1986).[2] So, too, their approach to staging the adaptation, as well as unadapted Shakespearean plays,[3] sets them apart. Influenced by both Elizabethan and Brechtian practices, the company seeks to break down the barrier between audience and actor and to reveal in the course of the production how the performance is created. Strategies include (1) incorporating a "set piece" designed to draw the audience into an argument, played with house lights up; (2) doubling of roles; (3) casting all roles with male actors; (4) placing actors not directly involved in a scene as observers on the periphery of the acting space; (5) using actors to create lighting and sound effects, to sing and play musical instruments, so that they perform tasks more generally undertaken by stage management and professional musicians; (6) introducing contemporary cultural references.[4]

Another factor distinguishing Propeller's *Rose Rage* is that the adaptation of the *Henry VI* trilogy does not take its place in a cycle of Shakespeare's histories or, as did *The Plantagenets*, with *Richard III*. From Shakespeare's trilogy, Hall, Warren, and the company have shaped two plays; each play has two acts, with a running time of one hour for each act.[5] *Rose Rage* concentrates on the dynastic struggles in England between two well-defined historical moments—the deaths of Henry V, in 1422, and Henry VI, in 1471.

To achieve its sharp focus on England's royal family and the nobility, *Rose Rage* retains only those French scenes in act 4 and 5.3 of *1 Henry VI* and 3.3 in *3 Henry VI*; it eliminates characters, including the Duchess of Gloucester, Joan of Arc, the Countess of Auvergne, Edmund Mortimer; it also combines other characters, for example, expanding Exeter's choric role with lines from

Bedford, Lucy, and Salisbury. It streamlines the plot by, for instance, reducing the proposed marriage of Henry to the daughter of the Earl of Armagnac to reported action immediately before Suffolk presents Margaret and eliminating scenes in which various retainers and servants loyally support their masters.

The seven scenes of the first act draw on fifteen scenes from *1 Henry VI* and six scenes from *2 Henry VI* to dramatize the quarrels between Winchester and Gloucester and between the Yorkists and Lancastrians; the deaths of Talbot and his son; Henry's marriage to Margaret; and the conspiracy of Suffolk and Margaret. The six scenes of act 2 carry the plot forward to Henry's flight from battle at St Alban's, where both Shakespeare's *2 Henry VI* and the first play of the adaptation finish. Scripted as twelve scenes and drawn from twenty-two scenes of *3 Henry VI*, the second part of *Rose Rage* opens with York's seizure of the throne and takes its interval after scene 19, in which Edward IV woos Lady Elizabeth Grey and sends Henry to the Tower and Richard eyes the throne.[6] The adaptation, which retains just over 30 percent (3100 lines) of Shakespeare's trilogy, introduces the lightest possible revision for bridging and clarity. Instead of writing new lines, the editors, Hall and Warren, select appropriate lines from another scene in the trilogy.[7] With three exceptions, *Rose Rage* has no interpolated lines. Henry V's will, as recorded in Edward Hall's *Chronicle*, opens the play.[8] Jack Cade's rap piece introduces his grievances. Richard closes the play with

> Now is the winter of our discontent
> Made glorious summer by this son of York;

and halts abruptly after the next word: "And."[9]

This brief overview of the script suggests what a careful comparison of the published script and the trilogy would reveal: losses that affect character and theme, losses that diminish the many parallels and juxtapositions, losses that exclude all but three of the eight women. My focus is, however, on the twenty-five scenes of *Rose Rage* and on Propeller's presentation of that script: on how twelve men in their thirties and early forties played twenty-eight men, three women, and the young Prince of Wales and Earl of Rutland; on how the company contributed music and sound effects, functioned as dressers and stage management, and played supporting roles—messengers, rebels, and soldiers; on influences upon and ramifications of the design, lighting, music, and sound; and on how an adaptation of early modern plays based on medieval English history worked in a nineteenth- and early twentieth-century setting for a twenty-first-century audience.

Setting the action in an abattoir signaled the centrality of the trilogy's imagery of slaughter and butchers. Hall credits Pavelka with the idea and explains that Propeller seeks for their productions of Shakespeare "an abstracted environment [in which] to find a more interesting metaphoric way of expressing the poetry of the drama."[10] The design, based on a Victorian slaughterhouse in Smithfield, London, added resonance to lines such as Warwick's response to the murder of Gloucester: "Who finds the heifer dead and bleeding fresh, / And sees fast by a butcher with an axe, / But will suspect 'twas he that made the slaughter?" (sc. 8; *2 Henry VI*, 3.2.187–89) and Margaret's lament that Henry's "realm [is] a slaughter-house" (sc. 23; *3 Henry VI*, 5.4.78). The abattoir, where slaughter is the occupation, worked as a visual metaphor for a period where, as Tony Bell points out, "hand-to-hand combat might have sanitized people to violence." So, too, from the deliberate violence one may infer parallels with numerous contemporary conflicts and television coverage of them.

The set was institutional and unwelcoming. Rows of numbered wire lockers outlined the three sides of the acting space and cast a weblike shadow on the floor. From the large meat hooks on the lockers hung costumes and industrial quality rubber gloves. Above, at center stage was suspended a tangled wire with red and white roses, visible in most scenes and lowered for the

Costumed as upper-class Victorian gentlemen, the court gathers around the casket of Henry V to mourn his death. Above them, center, one of the choric butchers watches the ceremony. On the wire cages that outline the acting space hang rubber gloves and white jackets worn whenever an actor assumes the role of a butcher. A Victorian abbatoir was the main influence on Michael Pavelka's set, but the lockers, rings, and box also suggest a school gymnasium. (The 2001/2002 Watermill Theatre production of *Rose Rage: The Henry VI plays in two parts*. Directed by Edward Hall. Photo by Michael Pavekla.)

Temple Garden scene. When York's sons took revenge on Young Clifford,
the barbed roses were flown out and a chain with hooks, to which they
attached their victim, dropped down. Four large metal rings hung before the
lockers upstage, and four industrial lamps were suspended over the acting
space. Set in various configurations, two low rectangular wooden boxes, the
only stage furniture, suggested a number of objects: for example, set on top
of each other, a tomb for Henry V; used singly, a throne for Henry VI and
Edward IV, a couch for Margaret and Suffolk, a platform for the butcher's
block, a table at which Rutland cut a chain of paper crowns with oversized
scissors; upturned, a cradle for Rutland. The English flag, with the cross of
its patron, Saint George, dressed the stage. Sometimes it lent authority, as the
drape for Henry V's casket or the throne; or it served as a symbol of patriotism, when Talbot carried it on the battlefield. At other times it was ironical,
as when it covered the couch where Margaret and Suffolk flirted; still other
times it alluded to contemporary England's rowdy football supporters, as
when the loutish Edward IV draped it around his bare shoulders.[11] In some
scenes, an oversized flag covered the stage floor. In a chilling image, what
appeared at first to be a bloody cloth concealing the dead body of Gloucester
was, in fact, the flag of St. George.

**Encouraged by Queen Margaret (Robert Hands), Prince Edward (Christian Myles),
costumed as a toy soldier, tortures the Duke of York (Guy Williams). Behind them, two
butchers are ready to hack at entrails—an act that will signify the death of York—and
two other butchers guard the proceedings with tools of their trade. (Photo by Alastair
Muir.)**

In addition to being a visual statement for a major motif of the trilogy, the abattoir offered a handy way to help Propeller achieve its performance goal of breaking down the actor-audience barrier. Costumed as butchers, in white hats, knee-length white coats, and with their black trousers stuffed into black boots and wearing protective masks that resembled animals' snouts, actors undertook duties normally performed by the stage management; dressers; music, sound, and lighting technicians. Before each act, the actors gradually gathered on the stage where they sharpened knives and cleavers against the faintest background of soothing symphonic music, mopped and swept the tiled floor, and stared vacantly at the audience. Throughout the plays those actors not required for the action provided an omnipresent chorus of butchers: they cut open the will of Henry V; they spoke lines, such as those scripted for messengers; they sang or hummed songs and hymns; they shone flashlights or spots; they sharpened knives or scraped or beat them against the wire cages; they helped each other into transforming costumes; and they watched ominously.

As Hall points out, Stanley Kubrick's *A Clockwork Orange* (1971) influenced the staging: "I wanted to make the violence in *Rose Rage* similarly beautiful to heighten our sense of revulsion and to express the lengths that the characters would go to in order to cause pain to one another."[12] In the film, based on Anthony Burgess's novel, a gang of four similarly clad adolescents entertain themselves. They beat an elderly, drunken beggar; terrorize traffic on a lonely country road; gang-rape women; indulge in sexual and violent fantasies; and inflict violence on each other to maintain or challenge authority within the gang. Classical music—including the overture to Rossini's *The Thieving Magpie*, Elgar's *Pomp and Circumstance,* nos. 1 and 4, and Beethoven's *Ninth Symphony*—intensify the brutality. Hall borrowed three traits from the film: uniform costumes for those inflicting the violence; a variety of kinds of violence; and music to heighten or comment ironically on the violence.[13] In *Rose Rage* the omnipresent butchers, who invited the audience into the performance, were the means through which Hall staged the numerous murders and battles in the trilogy.[14] Upstage of the twenty-two deaths by murder or in battle that the adaptation retains, butchers provided both aural—the sounds of steel upon steel—and visual effects (and, for those close to the stage, olfactory effects). They hacked at entrails—heart, spine, and lungs—on butcher's blocks. Sometimes they presented the meat in a tidy plastic bag such as one gets at the butchers. For some beheadings, they sliced cleanly through a red cabbage. A butcher presented Margaret (Robert Hands) with a red velvet bag containing the head of Suffolk (Vincent Leigh). Other beheadings were more brutal: butchers smashed a cabbage with a stave, splattering the stage with the remains.[15] When Cade's men murdered the Clerk of Chatham (Richard Clothier) and Sir Humphrey Stafford (Guy Williams), a butcher dropped meat into a bucket and another spread saw dust on the floor.

Blood dripping from a bladder to a bucket visualized the death of Warwick (Tony Bell) at the hands of Edward IV (Tim Treloar). By the close of part 1, meat and cabbage littered the floor; business before part 2 included butchers sweeping the debris from the floor.

A *Clockwork Orange* was not the only film to influence the production. As Pavelka points out, both Lindsay Anderson's *If . . . .* (1968) and Kubrick's film "depict brutal worlds involving power and social status."[16] The "world" of *If . . . .* is a repressive English boarding school, where a gang more privileged than the working-class lads in *A Clockwork Orange*, rebels against the strict discipline and the arrogant prefects who enforce it. Pavelka's set suggested a gymnasium, a recurring image in *If . . . .* and the place where the head prefect whips the offending trio and reserves the cruelest beating for the ring-leader. The *Rose Rage* set had lockers; its boxes could be a wooden horse; the rings, gymnasium exercise rings.[17]

Costumes identified the historical period. When Gloucester (Matthew Flynn), Winchester (Christian Myles), Exeter (Emilio Doorgasingh), and other mourners discarded their butchers' white coats for the funeral of Henry V, they replaced the working-class uniform with costumes proscribed for Victorian upper-class gentlemen, the formal uniforms of class, profession, and occupation. According to Pavelka, "the sharp tailoring of the men's fashion presented an interesting conflict with the brute force of the action both aesthetically and for the performers, physically."[18] The Victorian costumes and allusion to the public school suggested the privileged class from which the nineteenth century drew its political leaders and the long-ranging effects of their leadership.

The music was appropriate to both the period setting and the medieval world of the play, especially to Henry's faith. It was, explains Hall, "traditional English music—hymns and madrigals—which evoked strong feelings of an England based in the Victorian era when class and breeding were all-important."[19] However, the abattoir, the often ironic juxtaposition of music and action, and the chorus of singing or humming butchers lent to the music an emotional distancing, not the expected religious or sentimental or patriotic tone. Beneath the chilling sound of steel upon steel in the pre-show business of butchers sharpening knives and cleavers were the faintest strains of an Elgar symphony. "Abide with me," long associated with funerals, set the scene as formally dressed mourners gathered together around the flag-draped casket of Henry V but quickly broke into bickering factions. In the next scene (2; *1 Henry VI*, 2.4), set in the Temple Garden, the lively tempo of a nineteenth-century song with lyrics promising happiness in an English garden evoked a situation quite different from the quarreling noblemen plucking flowers from the tangled wire of the rose bush. In the Temple Garden and other scenes, Tony Bell observes, "the crisp and beautiful music, with traditional English chamber harmonies, heightened the roughness of the violence." While butchers sang a lullaby urging "sleep, my pretty baby, in your rest so warm and cosy," pyjama-clad Rutland (Simon Scardifield) cut out a paper crown with oversized scissors, then settled down to sleep with the flag of St. George as his blanket (sc. 15; *3 Henry VI*, 1.2; 1.3). Young Clifford (Flynn), his murderer, and two butchers waited nearby. As Bell points out, the "gentility" of the "'twee' Victorian song, masked the violence." Just as the adolescent gang in *Clockwork Orange* enjoyed beating, raping, and torturing, so Young Clifford murdered Rutland "with casual glee."[20]

Two hymns were used *passim* with ironic—and sacrilegious—effect. "O worship the King" welcomed Henry VI (Jonathan McGuinness) and Edward IV. It called attention to Henry's weak rule. In the third scene (*1 Henry VI*, 3.1) an anxious Henry VI sat like a schoolboy at his desk writing while Winchester and Gloucester argued before him. In the seventh scene (*2 Henry VI*, 1.3), Margaret spoke for him—"the King, forsooth, will have it so" and took decisions. In the thirteenth scene (*2 Henry VI*, 5.1) the hymn announced Henry's arrival, with Margaret, Somerset (Scardifield), and others, to challenge York (Williams), who proclaimed himself "great England's lawful king." When next the butchers sang "O, Worship the King," Henry had relinquished the crown and the hymn provided transition to Edward IV (sc. 19; *3 Henry VI*, 3.2), who seductively entertained the petitioner, Lady Elizabeth Grey (Scardifield), who, like Margaret with Suffolk, was witty, strong, and slow to yield. Even if "King" referred to an earthly monarch, neither of these English kings earned the accolade "glorious" or possessed "measureless Might" and "ineffable love" or was "girded with praise."

"He who would valiant be" was sung on battlefields in France and England. In scene 4 (*1 Henry VI*, 4.3), the hymn, which urges the would-be valiant "in constancy" to "follow the Master," was background for York's complaints that the handsomely dressed Somerset had failed to provide the promised horsemen and again for the battle in which Talbot (Treloar) and his son (McGuinness) lost their lives. In scene 22 (*3 Henry VI*, 5.2) it accompanied the slow motion death of Warwick, who died at the hands of Edward IV, whom he had deserted. It was the transition to the next scene (23; *3 Henry VI*, 5.4), in which Margaret appealed to the citizens of Tewkesbury and rallied her troops.

In business inspired by a scene from *A Clockwork Orange* in which "the protagonists sing blissfully while they beat up their victim," Margaret sang "a madrigal while she torture[d] the Duke of York."[21] The butchers contributed a hymn that yoked York's completed political pilgrimage with the spiritual one he embarked upon (sc. 16; *3 Henry VI*, 1.4). "Jerusalem," with patriotic—even chauvinistic—associations that now overshadow William Blake's "dark satanic mills," opened part 2 (sc. 14; *3 Henry VI*, 1.1). To prepare for York's ascent to Henry's throne, singing, jingoistic butchers covered the stage with a large flag of St George and the box, with a smaller one.

Marking the shift from English battles to the French court, a trio of butchers sang "Ce Mois de Mai," an upbeat madrigal, to entertain King Louis XI (Williams), resplendent in a handsome blue velvet dressing gown and satin night cap (sc. 20; *3 Henry VI*, 3.3). The production closed with a traditional English folk song associated with feasts, appropriate because a boar's head was carried on to celebrate Edward IV's victory. On a darker level, the boar's head both reminded that the cost of Edward's victory was butchery and anticipated actions of the family butcher Richard (Clothier), whose symbol was the boar.

In addition to these and other hymns, songs, and madrigals, medieval Christian music—a *Kyrie*, a *Sanctus*, and *Da pacem, Domine*—provided a *Leitmotif*. But the effect was quite different from, for example, Kenneth Branagh's use of *Non Nobis, Domine* in the film of *Henry V*. There, in a long sequence, battle-weary troops trudge through the muddy field at Agincourt, attributing their victory to God's intervention for the English. In *Rose Rage*, butchers singing a *Kyrie*, *Sanctus*, and *Da pacem, Domine* transformed music associated with Christian ritual into music for ritual slaughter. A *Kyrie* marked the bloody deaths of Suffolk (sc. 8), Winchester (9), Clifford and Somerset (13), York (16), Exeter (23) and *Da pacem, Domine*, the deaths of Gloucester (8) and Young Clifford (18).[22] The chants, Bell observes, introduced "Christianity at moments when the killings were most brutal."

The third and final category of music—Jack Cade's rap piece demanding "down with the government"—achieved two artistic goals. First, it drew upon Elizabethan and contemporary styles and addressed universal subjects. Bell, who wrote the piece and played Cade, points out that "it has the same kind of pulsing rhythm that Shakespeare uses for the witches' chants in *Macbeth*"[23] and employs a "bastardized court language." Bell sought a style that would "sit comfortably in the sixteenth century." Although it appeared to be improvised, it was not; nor did it include specific contemporary references, as does the Lord High Executioner's "little list" in *The Mikado*. But its rap form and timeless complaints—"corruption at the top," "up go the taxes never give a reason"—appealed also to contemporary audiences.[24] Spoken by and appealing to the working class, it fitted in with the motif of "rage" and echoed the rhythms of chants of street-market traders. Second, it was conceived as the "set piece" to contribute significantly to Propeller's goal of breaking down the barrier between audience and actor. There was a sharp shift in tone from a *Kyrie*, sung as Winchester's body was carried off, to the first Cade scene. The house lights came up, and butchers threw staves onto the stage. To the steady beat of a snare drum, Cade burst from the auditorium onto the stage addressing both audience and butchers, who dismantled some lockers as he rapped. Bell explains that his goal was "to beguile and threaten at the same time, like a charismatic peoples' champion, so that the audience felt both euphoric and fearful. I kept the vocal delivery conversational to draw them in and the movement a constant 'prowl' across the stage."[25]

Helped considerably by the rap piece, the breaking down of the set and his energetic engagement with the audience, Cade made an immediate impact. His costume—a woolly hat, casual jacket, with badge-laden lapel—helped to place him as working class or, perhaps, a prototype of the football hooligan or member of an extreme far right political group, such as the British National Party.[26] (In fact, photographs of dockers striking in the 1920s were the source for the costume.) Bell's goal (successfully achieved) was to chart the stages of Cade's journey—from charismatic leader of a united group to maniacal leader of a dissipated band—so that it would seem natural that they (not Iden, as in *2 Henry VI*) would kill their leader.

For actors playing other roles and, especially, for those playing the noblemen who lost lines in the early scenes, costumes, as well as casting and stage business assumed additional importance in establishing character. Gloucester's height gave him an unfair advantage over the young king and the petty, jealous Winchester, whose sarcastic "amen" answered the protector's prayer for the soul of Henry V. In evening dress and top hats, Somerset and Suffolk were more urbane than Warwick and York. Somerset, wearing evening dress—with a lovely white silk scarf at his neck—for his battlefield confrontation in scene 4 (*1 Henry VI*, 4.4), revealed his contempt for York, Talbot, bloodied by battle, and Exeter, who wore a military uniform.

Warwick's long black leather coat and gloves, which set him apart from the other peers, gave him a powerful presence, even in the opening scene, where he silently observed the bickering between Winchester and Gloucester, and in the third scene, where he supported Henry's inept attempts to play peacemaker. Especially in the first act, when Warwick has only forty-five lines to establish his motivation, Bell found the role difficult to play. In part 1, when he is in the court, Warwick is "quite still." It was easier in part 2, because there is a "dynamism," a "thrust to what he is doing." Nevertheless, in these scenes where York and others had longer speeches, Bell's stage presence spoke for Warwick. Warwick did, however, close part 1, with the final lines of *2 Henry VI*. He is the first speaker in *3 Henry VI* and part 2, but *Rose Rage* opens with his announcement that "This is the palace of the fearful King" and his encouragement of York to take the throne (sc. 14; *3 Henry VI*, 1.1.25–27). In each brief speech, Warwick the king-maker revealed his importance to York. Typically a few forceful words, not bloody or brutal actions, defined Warwick. He engaged in various verbal disputes, predicted the death of "a thousand souls" (sc. 2; *1 Henry VI*, 2.4.127), knew enough about strangling to identify its marks on the corpse of Gloucester, and cautioned Henry that he would "fill the house with armèd men" and in support of York "Write up his title with usurping blood" (sc. 14; *3 Henry VI*, 1.1.170–73). Warwick himself, however, stood apart from the carnage. Calmly smoking a cigarette, he watched York's sons capture and torture Young Clifford (sc. 18). The visualization of his death at Edward's hands—blood dripped slowly into a bucket—symbolized his complicity in the steady bleeding of the country (sc. 22).

In casting and costume, York, as Warwick, was a far sturdier figure than the slight, boyish Henry VI. Warwick's coat suggested wealth, self-confidence, and power. At first glance York's long black coat, with its fur collar and lapel and blood-red lining was elegant. By the close of part 1, however, it linked him with the imagery of the slaughterhouse. As the lights went down and Warwick, lit by a spot, urged York to take London, the Duke of York stood downstage center, triumphantly holding aloft two hands full of bloodied meat. With this one exception, only the butchers, not characters, handled the meat. Around York's feet lay evidence of the cost of his claim to the throne and his incitement of Cade: meat, cabbage, staves, Cade's knitted cap, and Lord Saye's judicial wig littered the floor. With Rutland (sc. 15), York displayed a gentle side. York helped his young son size the paper crown he had cut and kissed the boy goodnight. In interpolated stage business Rutland's ghost watched Margaret taunt and kill York and spoke York's last lines with him; in the next scene, Rutland's ghost was the messenger reporting the death of York.[27] Fittingly, at York's death, the butchers hacked at entrails, put some in a plastic bag, and hung them on a meat hook. Several scenes later (sc. 21; *3 Henry VI*, 4.1), Hall "pushed the boundaries further and further."[28] On a grill next to the throne, a butcher barbecued meat. As the meat sizzled, Richard and Clarence discussed their brother's hasty marriage; the newlyweds—Edward with unbuttoned shirt and open wine bottle—and Lord Rivers (Flynn) joined them; Rivers ate a sausage.

Henry's crown, the flag-covered throne and "O worship the King" announced his title; a prayer book and rosary signaled his faith. But McGuinness's Henry more closely resembled a schoolboy whom, Duke Humphrey claims, Winchester would "overawe." In scene 3, he slipped quietly on from inside one of the wire lockers and sat nervously at his paper-strewn desk while a metronome kept strict time and his "tutors," Gloucester and Winchester, argued before him. The adaptation juxtaposes the disagreement between Gloucester and Winchester, which Henry cannot resolve with "prayers . . . / To join [their] hearts in love and amity" and the quarrel between Vernon (Hands) and Basset (Clothier), which Henry ineptly resolves by choosing a red rose and declaring he loved both his kinsmen (sc. 3; *1 Henry VI*, 3.1.67–68; 4.1.152–55). In a military uniform in which he resembled a new recruit rather than an authoritative leader, Henry made the naïve decisions of accepting Margaret and creating a dukedom for Suffolk. Henry's astonishment when Margaret spoke for him—"The King, forsooth, will have it so"— and when Margaret and Suffolk demanded Gloucester's staff of office marked the beginning of Henry's independence from them. After butchers hustled the struggling Gloucester offstage, Henry's empathetic simile, delivered from downstage center, introduces the imagery—if not the tone—that inspired the set:

> And as the butcher takes away the calf,
> And binds the wretch, and beats it when it strains,
> Bearing it to the bloody slaughterhouse,
> Even so remorseless have they borne him hence
>
> (sc. 7; *2 Henry VI*, 3.1.210–13)

In Propeller's production, which stripped death of its pathos, it was significant that Henry fainted at the news of Gloucester's death. Once he revived, however, the murder emboldened Henry to confront Suffolk and Margaret. The defining trait of McGuinness's Henry was compassion: for Margaret, who grieved over Suffolk; for Winchester, who died without "mak[ing] a signal of [his] hope" of "heaven's bliss" (sc. 9, *2 Henry VI*, 3.3.27–29); for York, whose slain body Henry covered with his jacket.

On the one hand, it was not surprising when bold men such as York or Cade or Richard seized center stage and directed a speech or soliloquy to the audience. On the other hand, when Henry took center stage, it was a measure of the distance he had traveled from "effeminate prince." Sitting on the edge of the stage McGuinness delivered the "molehill" speech directly and thoughtfully, with a passionate calmness. A butcher at each side of the stage shone a spotlight on Henry, and *Da pacem, Domine* acted as a benediction to his discourse. From upstage Henry watched the next phases of the scene: the fathers and sons, the sons of York murdering Young Clifford. During this part of the scene Hall juxtaposed the pacifist Henry with Richard, downstage and gazing over the audience's head as though anticipating his bloody road to the throne.

In his final scene the omnipresent rosary and prayer book, incongruous to Henry's earlier images of schoolboy and military recruit, fitted the pilgrim, who wore a long grey shift and no shoes. Henry entered to the swelling strains of a *Sanctus* and to incense. The murder was brutal: Richard stabbed him with a switchblade, taunted him, and hung his body on the rings upstage. But butchers did not sing a jaunty tune or an ironic hymn; nor did they hack at entrails. The ethereal image—a single white spot shone on the slain king—signaled the defining difference between McGuinness's Henry and his adversaries: rage drove them; compassion comforted Henry. When butchers held entrails aloft, the image underscored Richard's determination to slay his way to the throne: "Clarence, thy turn is next, and then the rest" (sc. 24; *3 Henry VI*, 5. 6. 90)

As Margaret, Robert Hands wore a costume that suggested the femininity first attracting Suffolk. But it did not attempt as, for example, the all-male

productions at Shakespeare's Globe attempt, to disguise the male actor in
female garments. Hands wore a black headband, a white fluffy fur stole, a
filmy white scarf, a choker of many rows of pearls and earrings, which Margaret fiddled with, nervously, as when she met Suffolk, or seductively, in
later scenes with him.

Hands captured Margaret's various moods. Meeting Suffolk in France (sc.
5), she was witty, flirtatious, and quick to slap the earl when he kissed her.
In scenes 6 and 7 props suggested the degree to which Margaret was an unsuitable consort for Henry. When Henry greeted Margaret, he put his prayer
book on the throne. It was still there in next scene, when the flag-draped box
became a couch on which Suffolk reclined and enjoyed a post-coital cigar.
Next to him Margaret adjusted her earrings and freshened her makeup. With
a boldness astonishing—and silencing—Henry and the peers, Margaret
spoke for the king, took from Henry and read the accusation against the
Duchess of Gloucester, and picked up Gloucester's staff of office, which the
duke had laid at his nephew's feet. Four scenes later, she cradled the red
velvet bag containing Suffolk's head. In part 2 Margaret shrieked on from
the stalls to protest Henry's disinheriting the Prince of Wales (Myles), whom
she had suited in what looked like a toy soldier's uniform (sc. 14) and whose
knighthood she had engineered (sc. 18). Cruelly, she taunted York (sc. 16),
forcing him to wear the paper crown he had helped young Rutland to size.
Playing the betrayed woman, Margaret turned on the charm to seek assistance
from King Louis XI (sc. 20). She appealed forcefully to the audience—the
"Friends of Tewkesbury"—to join her in battle against the Yorkists (sc. 23).

Like others of his generation, York's sartorial taste displayed his wealth
and station. His three eldest sons, however, revealed both the passage of time
from the nineteenth century to pre–World War II and the gradual breaking
down of the dress code. Edward, George (Leigh), and Richard wore business
suits, played some scenes in shirt sleeves and waistcoats, and carried as weapons a knife, Edward; two meat hooks, George; a switchblade, Richard. Richard resembled a pre–World War II gangster and played one scene with a shirt
sleeve rolled up to reveal his deformed arm. As a trio, York's thuggish sons
quickly appeared to support their father's claim to the throne (sc. 13) and
ruthlessly avenged the murder of their brother Rutland by taunting, torturing,
and killing Young Clifford (sc. 18). Although Edward shed tears when he
reported York's death to Warwick (sc. 17), the dominant impression he
gave—that of a drunken lout—linked him with football hooligans or far right
groups that hijacked the flag of England in the late twentieth century. In the
final scene, Edward IV staggered on, bare-chested wrapped in the English
flag and clutching an open wine bottle.

Although carrying a meat hook in each hand suggests otherwise, George
was the most dapper and sensitive of the three. Slowly grasping the red rose
Warwick offered him, he revealed some reluctance to desert his family. A

cloth soaked with Rutland's blood drew him back. In scenes with the three sons, George was most often upstage, observing.

Richard's usual position, leaning against the proscenium arch at stage right, called attention to his role of outsider. Like the choric butchers, he watched events on stage or stared vacantly into space or gazed into the audience as though peering into the future. Although Edward and George participated in the brutal dispatch of Young Clifford, Richard enjoyed cold-blooded murder. He threw around the bag containing Somerset's severed head, he burned Young Clifford with Warwick's cigarette, he taunted and tortured Henry VI before murdering the deposed king. Without sentiment and with an apparent eye on their future usefulness, he picked up Rutland's paper crown and the cloth wet with his brother's blood and used the cloth to reclaim the deserter George for the family. Just as the Duke of York was the only character to handle the raw meat, so his son Richard, seeking entrance to Henry's prison cell, was the only character to disguise himself as a butcher.

*   *   *

In both published script and Propeller's production, the overall effect of the text for *Rose Rage* is of a swift, clear narrative. Reception of the adaptation from its opening at the Watermill through its UK and international tour dates to its final performance at the Theatre Royal Haymarket attests to its stage-worthiness. The *Guardian*'s Lyn Gardner observed that "Hall's achievement is to capture both the absurdity and full horror" of the War of the Roses. Paul Taylor, for the *Independent*, described *Rose Rage* as "a very shrewd and vivid piece of theatre." In the *Daily Telegraph* Charles Spencer wrote that it "works extraordinarily well. It's pacy, gripping, imaginative, chilling and blessedly short."[29] Hall achieved his goal of making the plays accessible to an audience that might not be willing or able to book tickets for the full trilogy.[30] Producing the trilogy is also risky box office, if the twenty-three years between the two Royal Shakespeare Company productions is any gauge.

The list of characters and stage directions in the script provide insight into distinguishing features of the production. The script lists thirty-three characters and, as so often in Shakespeare's histories, unnumbered and unnamed extras: messengers, rebels, and soldiers. So, too, it gives familiar stage directions. Scattered throughout the script are calls for alarums and excursions, entrances with soldiers, marches, flourishes, parleys, and sennets. Yet Hall and his ensemble transformed the script significantly. Doubling, by a cast of twelve men—no stars—was skillful. The butchers—an omnipresent chorus except when they all appeared as Cade's followers or, later, his opponents— represented the anonymous extras. The butchers also, perhaps, for those familiar with the trilogy, stood in for characters such as Thomas Horner and his apprentice, who demonstrate the widespread effects of wars on less-well-off subjects. But most crucially, the butchers gave *Rose Rage* its distinctive characteristic: ironic detachment. At first glance the title may seem facile or trendy, combining, as it does, an allusion to the Wars of the Roses with the contemporary incidence of road rage. But the contemporary allusion helps to underscore that civil wars still flare, wars that may blur the distinction between military science and spontaneous outbursts. Propeller's production reminds us that in the late twentieth and early twenty-first centuries butchers still slaughter opponents and civilians to gain or keep control.

Notes

1. *Rose Rage* opened at the Watermill on 3 February 2001, toured the UK and international venues, and played a six-week season at the Theatre Royal Haymarket, summer 2002. For reviews of the production at the Watermill, see *Theatre Record* 21, no. 3; 158–61; for reviews of the London production, see *Theatre Record* 22, no. 12, 799–803 and my review in *Shakespeare Bulletin* 21, no. 1: 25–26. This essay is based on the London production, and the cast is for that production.

The script with revisions introduced during rehearsals was published by Oberon Books, London, in 2002. All references are to this revised edition. All references to Shakespeare are to the Arden editions edited by Andrew S. Cairncross.

I am grateful to June Schlueter, editor, *Shakespeare Bulletin*, for permission to draw on my review of the production, published Winter 2003.

I wish also to record my debt to Tony Bell, a founding member of the company, for providing background on Propeller's philosophy, for discussing the production, and for lending materials. Unless otherwise noted, references to Bell are to this interview.

2. *The Wars of the Roses*, directed by Peter Hall, adapted by John Barton in collaboration with Hall and published, London, 1970. *The Plantagenets*, directed by Adrian Noble. The title page (London, 1989) attributes the script to William Shakespeare; Noble's introduction acknowledges that "the first stages of the adaptation were done in collaboration with Charles Wood" (xii). *The Wars of the Roses*, directed by Michael Bogdanov and adapted by Bogdanov and Michael Pennington. *Shakespearean Criticism*, vol. 24, ed. Joseph C. Tardiff (Detroit, 1994), excerpts reviews of Hall-Barton and Noble, as well other productions, including Terry Hands's 1977 trilogy for the Royal Shakespeare Company (RSC).

3. For Propeller Edward Hall has directed *Henry V* (1997), *A Comedy of Errors* (1998), *Twelfth Night* (1999) and *A Midsummer Night's Dream* (2003). His other credits include, for the RSC, *The Two Gentlemen of Verona* (1998), *Henry V* (2000), and *Julius Caesar* (2001).

4. Propeller's commitment to education reinforces their goal of revealing how the company creates a production. Propeller offers workshops, post-performance discussions, and educational materials. "Shakespeare in Action," prepared for *Rose Rage*, includes photographs of the production and interviews with the director, Edward Hall,

the designer, Michael Pavelka, and the actors who played Jack Cade (Tony Bell), Queen Margaret (Robert Hands), Gloucester and Young Clifford (Matt Flynn).

5. The performance time of both RSC adaptations was six hours. The running time of the most recent RSC trilogy, directed by Michael Boyd in 2000, was just under nine hours.

6. Part 1, act 1 (scenes 1–7), includes lines from *1 Henry VI*: 1.1, 2.4, 2.5, 3.1, 3.4, 4.1–7, 5.1, 5.3, 5.5; *2 Henry VI*: 1.1, 1.3, 2.1–3, 3.1. Part 1, act 2 (scenes 8–13), includes lines from *2 Henry VI*: 3.2–3, 4.2–4, 4.6–8, 5.1–3. Part 2, act 3 (scenes 14–19), includes lines from *3 Henry VI*: 1.1–3.2, omitting 2.3. Part 2, act 4 (scenes 20–25), includes lines from *3 Henry VI*: 3.3–5.7, omitting 4.3, 4.5–8.

Two years before it staged *Rose Rage* the company met to read through the trilogy. At a read-through after Hall and Warren adapted the script and during the seven weeks of rehearsal, the company suggested changes, such as restoring speeches, merging several scenes (Bell interview).

7. Of the more than 12,350 lines of the trilogy and *Richard III*, the Hall-Barton version of 1964 retained 6000 lines and introduced 1450 lines by Barton. Barton and Hall, xvi.

8. Hall and Barton's *The Wars of the Roses* opened with some of the same passages from Henry V's will, as recorded in Hall's *Chronicle*. A stage direction assigns the passage to "the voice of King Henry V" (3).

9. *King Richard III*, ed. Antony Hammond (London, 1981). The lines from *Richard III* are not in either of the printed editions of *Rose Rage*. The *Plantagenets* closes even more abruptly, with "Now."

10. "Butchers and Villains," an interview with Edward Hall, in "Shakespeare in Action" (4), published by the Watermill as part of Propeller's commitment to education.

11. In *The Wars of the Roses* Bogdanov made the reference to football hooligans unmistakably explicit in *Henry V*. When *Rose Rage* played in London, world-cup fever was at its height, flags of St. George were omnipresent on- and offstage, but football fans were on best behavior.

12. "Butchers," 4.

13. A fourth influence was the narrative device. In voice-over Alex dispassionately narrates the gang's escapades; his imprisonment, treatment, and release; and the reversal of the treatment. In *Rose Rage*, Pavelka points out, "the ensemble 'chorus' who manipulate the storytelling . . . would necessarily be dispassionate masked butcher boys." "O bloody spectacle!", an interview with Michael Pavelka, in "Shakespeare in Action," p. 6.

14. For the Hall-Barton solution see, for example, Peter Roberts, "History Revitalized," in *Plays and Players*, vol. 10, no. 12 (Sept. 1963): 42–43. For Noble's solutions, see, for example, Robert Smallwood, "Shakespeare at Stratford-upon-Avon, 1988," *SQ* 40:90. For Bogdanov's treatment of deaths, see, for example, Lois Potter, "Recycling the Early Histories: 'The Wars of the Roses,' and 'The Plantagenets,'" *SS* 43:175.

15. In "Butchers" Hall reports: "we discovered in rehearsals that red cabbages exploded very satisfactorily when hit by a club!" During the foot and mouth outbreak, the company had difficulty getting enough meat (interview with Hall, *The Chronicle*

[Mold] 7 September 2001). Yet another problem awaited them in Istanbul, where feral cats got into the meat. When they returned to the theater, the company found "blood and offal all over the set and a chorus of cats" *Whatsonstage*, 4.

16. Pavelka, 6.

17. Bell interview.

18. Pavelka, p. 6.

19. "Butchers," 4. Tony Bell, together with Vince Leigh and Dugald Bruce-Lockhart, devised and arranged the music. In *If* . . . . traditional English hymns were similarly evocative.

20. Bell observes that the child-murderer Myra Hindley, who listened to tape recordings of her victims' crying, practiced a similar brutality.

21. "Butchers," 4. The allusion is to the scene in which the gang tricks its way into an isolated house, binds the husband to his chair, tapes his mouth and forces him to watch them rape his wife. During the episode, the gang sings "Singing in the Rain." The husband later reveals that his wife died a month after the attack, a "victim of the modern age."

22. Preparing for the production, Pavelka and Hall "visited Westminster Abbey to absorb an explicit statement of our royal heritage. The business of the meat market and the atmosphere of the Abbey gave us exciting and contrasting components, for example; splitting meat and singing psalms." "O bloody spectacle!" (6).

23. Bell interview.

24. Bell cites Alison Weir's *Lancaster and York: The Wars of the Roses* (London, 1995) as his source for Cade's complaints. See 147–48.

25. "Down with the Government," an interview with Tony Bell, in "Shakespeare in Action," 9.

26. As Lois Potter (180) points out, the "ESC [English Shakespeare Company] played Cade's speeches as National Front propaganda."

27. When the dying Cardinal tried to pray, the ghost of Gloucester sat on his bed. The cardinal delivered the lines beginning "If thou beest death, I'll give thee England's treasure," to the ghost (sc. 9; *2 Henry VI*, 3.3.2–4).

28. Bell interview.

29. Reviews of the production at the Watermill, dated 10 Feb. (*Guardian*), 19 Feb. (*Independent*), and 12 Feb. 2001 (*Daily Telegraph*) and compiled in *Theatre Record* 21, no. 3: 160, 161, 159 respectively.

30. *The Chronicle*, [Mold], 7 September 2001.

Recovering a Black African's Voice in an English Lawsuit: Jacques Francis and the Salvage Operations of the *Mary Rose* and the *Sancta Maria and Sanctus Edwardus*, 1545–ca 1550

GUSTAV UNGERER

THE encounters between the English and the black Africans or Moors in Tudor England have remained an ill-mined territory despite a rich crop of Africanist studies released in the last three decades. The prevailing view that the uneven encounters set in rather late, that blacks in Tudor England were rarities bereft of their personal voices, that the English had no experience as slave traders in the first half of the sixteenth century, that the English slave trade was pioneered by John Hawkins, that no blacks were bought or sold in England until the seventeenth century, does no longer stand the test of historical examination.[1] The prominent Africanist historian James Walvin noted that the history of British involvement with black Africans did not begin with the first effective importation of black slaves into England. Thus he argued that it would be worthwhile investigating the earlier and wider history of European explorations and discoveries.[2] Spanish historians have followed his recommendation, establishing the undeniable fact that the English merchants stationed in Andalucía at the close of the fifteenth century kept African slaves, Moors, mulattoes, and Negroes as domestic servants and as indentured workers in their soap factories. What is more, the English merchants, in the wake of their Genoese partners and in emulation of their Spanish colleagues, became heavily enmeshed in the African slave trade as early as the 1480s when the trade was still in its infancy.[3]

The present article is meant to be a contribution to the understudied subject of the black presence in early modern England.[4] It draws on a set of interrogatories conducted by the High Court of Admiralty in London. What emerges from these state records is the story of Jacques Francis (Jaques Frauncys), a Guinea diver kept as a slave by the Venetian Piero Paolo Corsi who was hired, in July 1547, by a partnership of Italian merchants to recover goods from the

sunken trading vessel, the *Sancta Maria and Sanctus Edwardus,* owned by
Francesco Bernardi of Venice, and who, in 1546, had been commissioned by
the admiralty to participate in salvaging the wreck of the *Mary Rose.* Jacques
Francis is likely to have gone down in the annals of an English court of law
as the first black witness to give firsthand evidence in a hotly contested lawsuit. The court ignored the argument put forward by the Italian merchants,
who had lost their goods in the wrecked vessel, that the African diver had no
right to appear before a European court.

I will first dwell on the historical context, recording the salvage operations
in Southampton waters, and then I intend to address the cultural and legal
issues raised by the appearance of Jacques Francis as witness before the court
of admiralty in February 1548. A dispute over the legal and cultural status of
Jacques Francis arose in the courtroom. The admiralty judges were ready to
acknowledge the humanity and selfhood of the Guinea diver who had obviously salvaged some nautical gear from the *Mary Rose* whereas the Italian
witnesses denounced the black diver as an uncivilized man, a "slave," a
"morisco," a "Blacke more," a "bondeman," and an "infidell borne."
Therefore his testimony, they argued, was inadmissible.

The African witness summoned to be questioned by the court of admiralty
in London did not turn out to be a cultureless and savage figure unable to
respond in intelligible language. On the contrary, the civilized and highly
articulate Jacques Francis, who in Guinea is likely to have been trained as a
pearl diver and who in England had lived up to the potential of his qualities,
was aware of his outstanding record of underwater exploits as a skilled diver
and of the valuable service he had been performing the English state in recovering part of the expensive ordnance of the *Mary Rose* , the recovery of the
ship and her ordnance being a matter touching the fibers of national pride.
He stood his ground, seizing the opportunity offered him by an English law
court of making the best of the dispute over his humanity, his black identity,
and over the definition of his legal status and ethnic origin. The cultural objections raised against him by the Italian merchants and his master Piero
Paolo Corsi were symptomatic of the difficulties in coming to terms with the
racial ambiguities generated by the presence of black Africans and Moors in
early modern Europe and, in particular, in England. These ambiguities were
to be mirrored in Prospero's contradictory attitude toward indispensable Caliban, and European dependence on the specialist knowledge of Africans was
to be probed in the record of Othello's military prowess and the service he
has done to the Venetian state.

*   *   *

It was the dramatic loss of the *Mary Rose* on 19 July 1545 that launched
the spectacular career of Jacques Francis as a wreck diver and salvage opera-
tor whose services to the English government were considered indispensable

for recovering the wreck. The warship was ready to take action against the French invasion fleet commanded by admiral Claude d'Annebaut when she sank within a few minutes, engulfing about 400 seamen and soldiers before the very eyes of king Henry VIII. The disaster was definitely not caused by enemy gunfire; it was rather the result of the unfortunate conjunction of poor unprofessional crew discipline and incompetent seamanship. Overloading had obviously brought the lower gun deck too close to the waterline, and when the ship heeled over under the impact of a gust of wind, the water rushed in through the lower-deck gunports left open for action and the ship suddenly capsized.[5]

As the *Mary Rose* sank in six fathoms in low tide, the authorities expected that the ship and her ordnance would be salvaged by foreign specialists. Built in the first year of king Henry VIII's reign, she was one of the first English warships to mount heavy cannon, which was valued at over £1700. She was carrying some ninety-six guns, among them thirty-three serpentines, twenty-six stone guns, ten murderers, five brass curtals, five brass falcons, besides six guns in her tops.[6]

For John Dudley, Lord Lisle, the admiral of England, the disaster of the *Mary Rose* threatened to upset the naval campaign he was conducting in order to ward off a French invasion of the Isle of Wight. The immediate measures he took and the fleet orders he issued in mid-August show that he was an innovative naval commander at home with the latest tactics in naval warfare. His determined efforts to salvage the *Mary Rose* delayed his immediate pursuit of the French fleet, but as soon as he realized that the salvage operations were bound to fail, he resumed his task to prevent the imminent French attack, making contact with the enemy on 15 August.[7]

In the absence of a competent English salvage company, the admiralty entrusted the two (Venetians Piero de Andreasi [Petre de Andreas] and Simone de Marini of Southampton) with the salvage operations. Under their command thirty Venetian mariners and one Venetian carpenter, assisted by sixty English mariners, made two attempts to weigh the *Mary Rose*, the first on 5 August, the second four days later. The frantic efforts to raise the ship were abandoned after having recovered most of her rigging.[8] The two Venetians responsible for salvaging the ship were paid off on 8 December 1545, each receiving twenty "markes sterling . . . by waye of the Kinges Majesties rewarde for their paines taken aboute the wayeng of the Mary Rose."[9] The cost of the salvage operation including the heavy equipment amounted to £559.[10]

Although the English admiralty resigned itself to the loss of the *Mary Rose*, it never gave up hope of recovering at least some of her guns. For this purpose it engaged the services of the Venetian Piero Paolo Corsi (Peter Paule) and his team of salvage operators about July 1546. Its members, as appears from various records in the High Court of Admiralty (HCA), were Jacques Francis, John Ito, George Blake (Blacke), besides two unnamed teammates. Their activities can be reconstructed from the payments Corsi received under the administration of Sir Thomas Seymour, Lord Lisle's successor as admiral of England, and from the suit brought against Corsi by Domenico Erizzo and some other Italian merchants who appeared as witnesses before the HCA. Thus, on 17 May 1547, Sir John Williams, Treasurer of the Augmentations, received a warrant from the Privy Council to pay £20 to Corsi, "being a dyver, undertaking the recovery of th'ordenance of the Mary Rose."[11] Another payment of £57 11s 5d is recorded as having been delivered before 30 June 1547.[12] On 9 May 1549, Sir John Williams had another warrant for £20 to be handed out to "Peter Paule towardes recovering of th'ordynance."[13] The last disbursement granted by the Privy Council is dated 3 August 1549 when Sir Wymond Carew, Treasurer of Tenths and First Fruits, had a warrant for £50, "emprest of the Relief of Spiritualities," that is, money of ecclesiastical origin, "for recovering of certayn ordynance out of the Mary Rose."[14]

The continuous flow of money authorized by the Privy Council over several years can be interpreted as a sign that Corsi's team with Jacques Francis as head diver was successful in recovering some of the ordnance from the wrecked warship and that the English government appreciated the innovative services rendered by the salvage team that was unparalleled in England. Indeed, Domenico Erizzo, who sued Corsi for having stolen one or two of his blocks of tin from the wreck of the *Sancta Maria and Sanctus Edwardus* testified before the judges of the HCA that in 1546 Corsi "causyd certen Instrumentes to be made for th'only etente and purpose to wey certen gere owte of the Marye Rose lost at Portesmouth. Whiche he hathe sondrye tymes occupyed about the same."[15] It emerges from Erizzo's deposition that Corsi's commission must have been initiated by Lord Lisle in 1546 after Piero de Andreasi and Simone de Marini had been paid off in December 1545.

The historic deposition Jacques Francis made before the HCA on 8 February 1548 affords a rare insight into his proper work as a diver and leaves no doubt about the fact that the commission renewed under the administration of Sir Thomas Seymour in 1547 granted the salvage team the right to extend their field of operation and to explore other wrecks in Southampton waters. Grasping the opportunity to assert his competence as a diver and feeling free from an ingrained consciousness of inferiority, the unabashed Jacques Francis, a visible and audible black subject in a white court, testified before the judges of the admiralty that he and Corsi and "vij more men" about Easter 1547, "chauncyd to fynde in the see at the Needles," a notorious site of many shipwrecks on the west coast of the Isle of Wight, "CC blockes tynne, a Bell and certen ledde," which he "dyd handell and see vnder water beyng there peryshyde and forsakyn. And therevppon" Corsi "hauyng a Commission of my Lorde Admyrall for that purpose dyd prepare dyvers Instrumentes and thinges to his costes of CCC Crownes."[16]

The testimony produced by Jacques Francis revealed him to be a principal witness providing the key to unraveling the reason for the clash between his master and Domenico Erizzo over Erizzo's goods aboard the wreck of the *Sancta Maria and Sanctus Edwardus*. The salvage operations of the *Mary Rose* no doubt entailed unexpected logistical problems and great expenses that exceeded the two government payments made in May and June 1547. Corsi was notoriously short of cash, vociferously complaining that his work was underpaid. His lack of money was to cause some serious friction between him and his crew, Jacques Francis included. Unfortunately, he deceived himself into believing that as head of the salvage team he was somehow justified in improving his financial situation by appropriating salvaged gear to the detriment of the rightful owners, one of them being Domenico Erizzo.

As Jacques Francis argued in defense of his master before the judges of the court of admiralty, the very moment Corsi set about recovering two hundred blocks of tin and lead and a bell from a wreck, most likely from the *Sancta Maria and Sanctus Edwardus*, Erizzo had Corsi arrested in Southampton. "And by that meanes," the African witness pointed out to the judges, the complainant "kepte the sayd Peter that he could not vse his feate in takyng vppe thereof by the space of all the monethe of maye" 1547, that is during "the beste tyme that he shuld haue byn occupied. And by reason thereof his Instrumentes and vyttelles so preparyd were not occupyd [*sic*] and by that meanes loste the sayd Tynne, bell and ledde." He assessed the damage, the "hynderaunce" done to his master, at £700 (HCA 13/93/292v). Jacques Francis was, of course, not an impartial witness. His assessment of the damage may therefore be exaggerated. What he withheld from the court, but other witnesses repeatedly emphasized, is the fact that Corsi was detained for one day only.

Domenico Erizzo, a longtime resident in England, was a member of a partnership of Italian merchants who had laded the *Sancta Maria and Sanctus Edwardus* with goods for Leghorn and Messina. Fire broke out on board about St Martin's day (4 July 1546) and the ship was burned at her anchorage two miles from Southampton.[17] Erizzo and some of his partners took measures to recover some of their lost goods. Thus Erizzo hired the services of Corsi for the months of July, August, and September 1547, paying the "victeling and wages bothe for" Corsi "and iij other servants," one of them being Jacques Francis.[18] The Florentine Domenico Milanes, factor of Angelo Milanes, also relied on Corsi's expertise in dealing with shipwrecks. He testified that Corsi came up to him and other merchants in Southampton, offering his services; whereupon Milanes and "one John Cayne" on behalf of the merchants "dyd compounde and agree with" Corsi "for ijs iiijd euerye daye and meate and dryncke for hym and his ij seruantes," that is, Jacques Francis and John Ito, to recover the tin and lead from the wrecked ship. Although Corsi and his team were working for the whole month of October 1547, their per-

formance did not come up to the merchants' expectations. Corsi was therefore discharged by Angelo Milanes for failing to recover some gear.[19]

As a matter of fact, Corsi did surreptitiously salvage at least two blocks of
tin, one bearing the mark of Domenico Erizzo and the other of Bartolomeo
Fortini. Fortini, one of the most prominent merchants of the Florentine nation
residing in London, was making a fortune as royal purveyor of saltpeter and
brimstone.[20] In 1546, he had given orders to lade the *Sancta Maria and Sanctus Edwardus* with wool, cotton, cloth, leather, tin, and lead to the value of
£6000. Unlike Erizzo, he did not sue Corsi because his block of tin, valued
at £6 or £7, and though "falsely conveyed awey" by Corsi in a boat to Gos-
port, where it was hidden under a bed in one Pope's house, was eventually
delivered to Angelo Milanes's Southampton residence and finally restored to
Fortini by order of the mayor of Southampton.[21]

The unfortunate Erizzo, aware as he was of the fact that it was a difficult
undertaking to sue Corsi, considering that he enjoyed the protection of the
lord admiral Sir Thomas Seymour, ventured to take the case to the High
Court of Admiralty. Indeed, Corsi, sensing that he had maneuvered himself
into hot waters "for embeaceling of the ij pecys" of tin, had rushed up to
London in October 1547, breaking the contract he had just concluded with
Domenico Milanes, and secured from the lord admiral letters missives "directed to the mayor of Southampton that" he "shuld not be any tyme trublyd,
but permitted to passe quyetly withoute vexacion."[22] Corsi also had the backing of Thomas Beckingham, the mayor of Southampton, and of Angelo Milanes, who the same day Corsi was arrested in Southampton offered £7 as
surety. Thus Corsi "was fourthewith releasyd and dischargyd."[23] Erizzo lost
his suit in Southampton, but in London the court of admiralty ruled in his
favor. Corsi was sentenced to a term of imprisonment in the Tower sometime
after October 1549 and released on 26 March 1550.[24]

*   *   *

Jacques Francis, unlike the majority of black slaves in early modern England whose personal histories have been silenced and obliterated, did write
himself into the annals of Tudor naval history in presenting the judges of the
court of admiralty a personal account of his lived experience as a diver in
Southampton waters. Before giving evidence for the defense of his master
Corsi, he had to comply with the court rules, as had all the other witnesses,
of making a statement about his personal data. Thus instead of telling the
court that he was the "servus" of Piero Paolo Corsi, with whom he had been
staying for two years (ca. February 1546 to February 1548), he chose to in-
form the judges that he was his "Famulus," obviously giving preference to a
term that meant slave member of a household rather than enslaved captive.
He had been born in Guinea, was about twenty years old and swore he had
known his master for two years and Domenico Erizzo for seven months. His

statements, presumably made in Portuguese or in the "fala da Guiné," the nonstandard Africanized form of Portuguese spoken by most Africans in Portugal, were translated by the interpreter John Tyrart.[25]

The country of his origin, the "Jnsula de Gynney," can be identified as Arguin Island off the coast of Mauretania where the Portuguese had established their first trading post (feitoria) in 1445. Right from the very beginning of the island's integration into the nascent Portuguese empire, Arguin enjoyed the administrative status of a separate agency. This singularity would seem to rule out the islands of Sao Tomé and of Príncipe in the Gulf of Guinea.[26] No other contemporaries from Guinea can claim to have shared a public platform with white witnesses from England and Italy. The three Guineans dubbed Binne, Anthonie, and George, whom John Lok was to take with him to England on his return from his second voyage to Guinea early in 1555, were, in emulation of Portuguese practice initiated by Prince Henry, the Navigator, linguistically indoctrinated as interpreters whose task was to help open up new trading facilities in Africa.[27] They were given little chance of asserting their own personalities, but once groomed as commercial and cultural brokers may have been manumitted as was the custom in Portugal.[28]

Jacques Francis's statement that he had known the Venetian Piero Paolo Corsi for two years must be understood as meaning that the two had not met before Corsi was commissioned by the admiralty in 1546 to salvage the ordnance of the *Mary Rose*. It is, therefore, justifiable to speculate that Corsi, on receiving the commission in Southampton, increased the members of his salvage company, buying Francis from a local Italian merchant. He had obviously realized that without the performance of a first-class diver he would not be able to meet the requirements of his contract with the admiralty. Francis's leading position within the salvage company was uncontested. John Ito and George Blake were obviously less qualified and consequently were not singled out to give evidence in defense of their master.[29]

The current view that there were no sales of black Africans and Moors in England until the third decade of the seventeenth century is disproved by historical reality.[30] Jacques Francis is a case in point. The record of the commercial transaction between Corsi and Francis's former master as it must have been registered by a local notary of Southampton has not come down to us, but there is little doubt that it must have existed. In support of this assumption one can adduce as a former instance the case of Maria Moriana, the Moorish servant of the Italian merchant Filippo Cini who had hatched a base plot to sell the manumitted Maria in Southampton in the 1470s .[31]

There was, indeed, a great difference between the sales of black slaves in late medieval and early modern England and the sales in the Iberian Peninsula. While sales became an institutionalized custom in Portugal and Spain, where slaves were sold as mere chattels, as "things," at public auctions and often at cattle markets like livestock, the sales in Tudor England seem to have

been made on a much smaller scale and on a private basis. Thus the distinguished physician and merchant, Dr. Hector Nuñez, who was endenizened in
1579, bought an Ethiopian from an English mariner for £4 10s in 1587. He
also kept two black female servants in his household. [32]

Although the services Jacques Francis rendered his master were invaluable,
Corsi evinced little desire not to treat him as a depersonalized piece of property to be exploited and then to be disposed of. Corsi was clearly not an easy
person to get on with. Disillusioned and hampered by serious financial straits,
he could not afford to pay his workers adequately and thus fell to quarreling
with them over their accommodation and diet. Domenico Erizzo testified that
"beyng in Southampton" in October and November 1547, he saw Corsi
"walke vppe and downe the streetes in a longe gowne beyng in varyaunce
with a servante of his for that he denyed to paye his wages" (HCA 13/5/
192). Antonio de Nicolao, who had known the salvage team since 1546, gave
evidence that when he was in Southampton in August, September, and October 1547, Corsi and his men were staying "at the Dolphin," Corsi "payeng
for ther meate and dryncke." Nicolao met them "sondry tymes" at the inn
and there in his presence Corsi "offeryd" Jacques Francis "to sell to any that
wold haue bought hym"(HCA 13/93/275v). Had Corsi succeeded in finding
a buyer, he would have deprived himself of the opportunity of relying on his
African servant as a witness for his defense in the case brought against him
by Erizzo. Corsi and his salvage operators must have been quite a sight at
Southampton where Giacomo Ragazzoni in September 1547 saw Corsi
"evyry day or evyry other daye . . . at his fre libertye in the stretes" (HCA
13/93/304).

The lawsuit in London and the lawcourt's recognition of Jacques Francis's
legal status as a witness put Corsi to a great deal of unthought-of expenses.
As master of an enslaved servant, Corsi was obliged to foot the bill for the
journey from Southampton to London, for the accommodation and diet in the
city, and for the proper appearance of Francis before the court of admiralty.
Coercing Francis into paying for such unexpected extravagances was simply
out of the question, for Francis and his teammates, as Antonio de Nicolao
attested, were "all poore laboryng men and sekyng ther levyng abowte in
sondrye places where they maye gett hit [sic] hauyng but letle of ther owne"
(HCA 13/93/275v). The most expensive item, no doubt, turned out to be the
dress appropriate for the special circumstances and conforming to the legis-
lated dress codes of urban civility.[33]

The rare spectacle the Edwardian Londoners saw in the city and the High
Court of Admiralty on 8 February 1548 was the fashioning of a black African
witness dressed up in European clothes bought in Southampton. The unfamil-
iar sight the Londoners perceived was not the figure of a naked black man
just one degree removed from a monkey, as the merchant adventurer Robert
Baker was to describe a Guinea chief in 1563, but of a black African clad in

the garments of a white man.[34] The physical appearance of an athletic diver in excellent trim who, though black-skinned, exuded civility, must have surprised them and may have warned them against taking his alien body as a marker of cultural difference. To see in him an early instance of those slaves who, alienated from their cultural and ethnic origins, were to adopt new cultural identities and acquire new cultural skills would be to jump to the wrong conclusion.[35] What speaks against the possibility that Francis may have been a deculturated African seeking cultural integration into Western Europe is the defamation campaign launched against him by some of the Italian witnesses.

The Italian witnesses, coming from a country with a long tradition in dealing with black slaves and servants, were strongly prejudiced against his presence. They raised a number of controversial issues that may have surprised the English court: religious, ethnic, social, and legal ones. The religious issue was particularly charged with feelings of discrimination. Thus the forty-year-old Niccolo de Marini, who had been born in Southampton and had known Jacques Francis for three years, testified that Francis was "an infidell borne and so ys commonlye reputyd and taken of all men knowyng hym" (HCA 13/93/unfoliated). The thirty-two-year-old Venetian Antonio de Nicolao argued in the same vein. "Fraunces," he told the court, was "not christenyd. And therefore . . . he beleauyth that no credite nor faithe oughte to be geven to his Sayenges as in other Strange Christian cuntryes hit ys to no suche slave geven" (HCA 13/93/275v–276r). The thirty-year-old Domenico de Milanes, who had known Francis for two years, concurred that "James Ffrauncis" was born in Guinea "where they are not cristynyd. . . . Wherefore he thinckethe that no credyte shuld be geven vnto his sayenges or deposicions" (HCA 13/93/278).

For these witnesses the religious was inseparable from the ethnic issue. Their response to racial difference had been hardened by the religious divide. They unanimously believed that the blacks existed outside the boundaries of the Christian fold and hence remained exploitable objects even if they converted to Christianity. Thus Niccolo de Marini discredited Francis for being both "a morisco" and a "Blacke more"; Antonio de Nicolao for being a "morisco born"; and Domenico de Milanes for being "a gynno borne." In reducing Francis to the contradictory and ill-defined stereotype of a blackamore they adamantly refused to acknowledge the reality of his individual existence as a diver and witness.[36] They saw in him an uncultured black figure whom they wished to efface from the legal proceedings against his master Corsi.[37]

Fortunately, the strategy of silencing his African voice for being an alleged unbeliever misfired in the English courtroom. Jacques Francis was determined to stand his ground. As mentioned, he came to life in his own words when he introduced himself to the court in a self-confident manner not as a slave, that is a sold captive, but as a domestic slave working in company with the free servants. The appropriate Portuguese term he must have deliberately chosen was rendered into Latin by the translator or the clerk as "Famulus" (13/93/202v). Niccolo de Marini and Antonio de Nicolao, however, defined his status as that of a "slave," and Domenico de Milanes affirmed that he had been "slave and bondeman to the sayd Petur Paolo." All these objections were ultimately of no consequence, for the court of admiralty had made up its mind to grant Francis the status of a legal witness. It brushed aside all the attempts made by the Italians to denounce Francis as the religious and racial Other.

Foreign merchants residing in England were under the illusion that English legislation on black slaves was as far advanced as the highly developed legal codes in their own countries. In fact, no such specialized body of laws existed yet and was not to exist until well into the eighteenth century. Even the eminent physician Hector Nuñez, who had been pioneering English trade relations with Morocco and had joined the English intelligence service, was surprisingly under the misapprehension, when he bought an Ethiopian from an English mariner in 1587, that the laws in England provided a slave code capable of meeting the contingencies arising in a slave-owning society. When the Ethiopian revolted against the sale, refusing to stay with Dr Nuñez and serve in his household for the rest of "his liffe," his new master found out to his great dismay that his appeal to "the course of the comon Lawes" of England produced no results, no "ordinarye remedie." As he felt unfairly treated, he appealed to the ministers of queen Elizabeth administering law in the Court of Requests, a debt court, in order to reclaim the money he had paid for the slave.[38]

The Italian witnesses were not aware that the judges of the High Court of Admiralty were facing a historic case for which in terms of the common law there was no judicial precedent and no past decision to draw upon. In these special circumstances, the court felt authorized to make a bold decision. Despite the fact that white slaves and bondmen or villeins were still known to exist in Tudor England and that the Vagrancy Act of 1547 had imposed slavery as a punishment for refusal to work, the court ruled that the question of ethnic difference was irrelevant. Whether this historic decision made in February 1548 served as a precedent for the manumission of a Russian slave in 1569 cannot be proved. The Russian slave may have been freed on the ground frequently advanced by lawyers and writers that England's air was too pure for slaves to breathe in. In any case, the system of the common law with its hostility to the codifying nature of the continental Roman law tradition can be made partly responsible for the confusion over the legal status of black servants and Negroes that prevailed until the 1720s.[39]

The High Court of Admiralty's decision to admit a black witness has to be seen as an instance of pragmatic tolerance. It enabled Jacques Francis to achieve what promised to look like a legal recognition of the incipient black presence in early modern England. He succeeded in demonstrating that a black African was capable of articulation, of giving his views an individual voice, and of providing expert information on a series of salvage operations whose level of technological achievement the English do not seem to have attained to. He thus upset the white man's notion of the black man's inferiority and unteachability, giving eloquent proof that his skill in recovering some of the ordnance of the *Mary Rose* went uncontested and unchallenged by English competitors. The court's landmark decision, however, was of no consequence. It came far too early. As things turned out, the steadily increasing influx of black Africans after 1550 gave rise to the discourse of difference. It pervaded travel narratives and imaginative literature alike and contributed to spreading the belief in the natural depravity of the black man.[40] The discourse of inferiority was seized on by Shylock in self-defence. He reminded the original audiences of the shameful fact that a good many of their contemporaries indulged in keeping blackamoors as bondmen and purchased slaves.[41]

Appendix

Interrogation of and Deposition made by Jacques Francis on Tuesday, 8 February 1547 (O.S.), 18 February 1548 (N.S.). PRO, HCA 13/93/ 202v–203r.

mercurij viij° Ffebruarij Anno dicto secundum computacionem Anglicanam 1547 Regno supra dicto nostri Edwardi sexti Anno Secundo.

Jaques Ffrauncys

Famulus, vt asseruit, Petri Paolo, cum quo habitauit circiter duos annos, et antea in Jnsula de Gynney, vbi natus erat, etatis xx^ti Annorum aut circiter libere, vt dicit, condicionibus testis etc. dicit ad jnterpretacionem Johannis Tyrart in jnterpretem assumptum, et iurat etc. se nouisse prefectum duos annos et Dominicum Erizo circiter vij menses nouit, vt dicit.

Ad Primum, Secundum, tercium, quartum, quintum et sextum dicit That the sayd Peter Paulo and this deponent with vij more men abowte Ester laste chauncyd to fynde in the see at the Needles CC blockes tynne, a Bell and certen ledde which this deponent dyd handell and see vnder water beyng there peryshyde and forsakyn. And therevppon the same Peter hauyng a Commission of my Lorde Admyrall for that purpose dyd prepare dyuers Instrumentes and thinges to his costes of CCC Crownes and wold haue takyn and sauyd all the same Tynne, bell and ledde withowte dowte. And then the same beyng preparyd, the sayd Domynico did arreste and staye the sayd Peter at Hampton and sayd that he had robbyd hym. And by that meanes kepte the sayd Peter that he could not vse his feate in takyng vppe thereof by the space of all the monethe of maye and the beste tyme that he shuld haue byn occupyed. And by reason thereof his Instrumentes and vyttelles so preparyd were not occupyd and by that meanes loste the sayd Tynne, bell and ledde vt dicit. Et aliter noscit deponere.

Ad septimum, viij, ix, x, xj, xij, xiij, xiiij, xv, xvj, xvij, xviij, xix et xx dicit That the sayd Dominico Erizo dyd before take waye from the sayd Peter Paulo one pece of tynne which the same Peter founde ij myles from Hampton in the see and brought vpp the same and never payd for the takyng thereof. But sayd falsely that the same Peter had stollen hit [*sic*] to his hynderaunce of CCCCCCC[li] which the same Peter might haue gotten with the sayd Tynne, bell and ledde that he found vt dicit. Et aliter nescit deponere.

Ad xxj credit eundem esse verum.
Ad vltimum dicit quod praedeposita per eum sunt vera.
               Ad Posiciones Addicionales
Ad Primum, Secundum, tercium et quartum nescit aliter deponere quam
   supra deposuit.
               Ad Jnterrogacionem
Ad Primum responsum est supra.
Ad Secundum respondet vt supra.
Ad Tercium responsum est supra et aliter nescit.
Ad Quartum fauet partes indifferentes et vellet victoriam ius habenti.
Ad Quintum respondet quod venit rogatus per dictum Paulo et suis Sump-
   tibus.
Ad vj, vij, viij respondet negative.
Ad ix, x, xj, xij, xiij, xiv, xv, xvj, et xvij dicit quod nescit respondere eisdem
   aliter quam supra deposuit.
               Ad Jnterrogacionem Secundo loco data
Ad Primum respondet quod est seruus Petri Paulo.
Ad Secundum respondet negative.
Ad Tercium, quartum, v, vj, vij et viij nescit respondere aliter quam supra
   deposuit.

Notes

1. The following studies, though breaking new ground, are all silent on the period of apprenticeship of English merchants as slavers in Spain and Portugal: Kenneth Little, *Negroes in Britain. A Study of Racial Relations in English Society* (London: Routledge and Kegan Paul, 1972); James Walvin, *Black and White. The Negro and English Society 1555–1945* (London: Allen Lane, 1973); Nigel File and Chris Power, *Black Settlers in Britain 1555–1958* (London: Heinemann, 1981); Peter Fryer, *Staying Power: The History of the Black People in Britain* (London: Pluto Press, 1984, reprint 1992); Paul Edwards, "The Early African Presence in the British Isles," ed. Jagdish

S. Gundara and Ian Duffield, in *Essays on the History of the Blacks in Britain* (Aldershot: Avebury, 1992), 9–29; Gretchen Gerzina, *Black England: Life Before Emancipation* (London: J. Murray, 1995); Kim F. Hall, *Things of Darkness. Economics of Race and Gender in Early Modern England* (Ithaca and London: Cornell University Press, 1995).

2. James Walvin, "From the Fringes: the Emergence of British Black Historical Studies," ed. J. S. Gundara in *Essays*, chap. 10.

3. See Alfonso Franco Silva, *La esclavitud en Sevilla y su tierra a fines de la edad media* (Sevilla: Deputación Provincial, 1979); *La esclavitud en Andalucía, 1450–1550* (Universidad de Granada, 1992); Juan Gil, "Los armadores de Sebastián Caboto: un inglés entre italianos," *Anuario de Estudios Americanos* 45 (1988), 3–65; Consuelo Varela, *Ingleses en España y Portugal, 1480–1515. Aristócratas, mercaderes e impostores* (Lisbon: Colibri, 1998). I am currenty investigating to what extent Thomas Malliard, Robert Thorne, Roger Barlow and other English merchants were operating as slaveholders and slave dealers in Seville, Sanlúcar de Barrameda and Cádiz in the opening decades of the sixteenth century.

4. The temptation "to force some visibility on the obliterated black subject in the dawning moments of the English colonial experience" is understandable but not sensible. Thus Imtiaz Habib, whom I have been quoting and who wields an obtrusive postcolonial jargon, has been misled by Folarin O. Shyllon's study *Black People in Britain 1556–1833* (London: Oxford University Press, 1972) into overstating the case of a Spanish mercenary in the service of king Henry VIII. Their identification of Sir Peter Negro as a black officer does not take into account that the Negros were of Genoese descent. Dozens of them settled in Spain and Portugal in the course of the fourteenth and fifteenth centuries, far too many to be listed here. The factor Paolo di Negro, for whom Columbus was working on Madeira in 1479, may stand for the others. I have consulted all the available contemporary records in Spanish and English; none mentions that Sir Peter Negro was black. I therefore can't help concluding that the career of the Spanish mercenary Pedro Negro under king Henry VIII is quite irrelevant to the study of the ideological conception of Othello. See Imtiaz Habib, "*Othello*, Sir Peter Negro, and the Blacks of Early Modern England: Colonial Inscription and Postcolonial Excavation," *Literature Interpretation Theory* 9 (1998), 15–30, and *Shakespeare and Race: Postcolonial Praxis in the Early Modern Period* (Lanham: University Press of America, 1999). In like manner, Edward Scobie in *Black Britannia: A History of Blacks in Britain* (Chicago: Johnson Publishing Company, 1972), followed G. B. Harrison's line of argument in maintaining that the prostitute Lucy Negro "was in fact" a "black . . . African" and the Dark Lady of Shakespeare's Sonnets (5–6). In point of fact, the Black Luce of the 1570s was the notorious London bawd Mrs Baynam. See Ian W. Archer, *The Pursuit of Stability: Social Relations in Elizabethan London* (Cambridge: Cambridge University Press, 1991), 231; and the Lucy Negro of the 1580s was, before her fall, an attendant of Queen Elizabeth. See Leslie Hotson, *Mr. W.H.* (London, 1964), chap. 11.

5. See David Loades, *The Tudor Navy. Administrative, Political and Military History* (Aldershot: Scolar Press, 1992), 133–34; Michael Oppenheim, *A History of the Administration of the Royal Navy and of Merchant Shipping in Relation to the Navy from 1509 to 1660* (Aldershot: Gower Publishing, 1988), 66, 80, original ed. London,

1896. Recent underwater inspections have shown that the hull of the *Mary Rose* is not battle-damaged.

6. The number of the guns given by Loades is ninety-six (96), by Oppenheim eighty-five (p. 55); for their value see Loades, 138; for a contemporary description and list of the ship's guns made by Anthony Anthony, surveyor of the ordnance, and presented to Henry VIII in 1546 see C. S. Knighton and D. M. Loades (eds.), *The Anthony Roll of Henry VIII's Navy* (Aldershot: Ashgate, 2000).

7. David Loades, *John Dudley Duke of Northumberland 1504–1553* (Oxford: Oxford University Press, 1996), 68–72, 85. Oppenheim held the view that most lord admirals had "no experience whatever of the sea" and was also wrong in taking Lord Lisle to task for having failed to come "aux prises" with the French admiral (64–66).

8. For a more detailed account of the immediate operations see Oppenheim, 66–67, and for the recovery of the hull in 1982 and some of the guns see Margaret Rule, *The Mary Rose: The Excavation and Recovering of Henry VIII's Flagship* (London, 1983).

9. John Roche Dasent (ed.), *Acts of the Privy Council. N.S. Vol. I, 1542–1547* (London: HMSO, 1890), 285, henceforward *APC*.

10. Loades, *The Tudor Navy*, 138. Up to June 1547, the expenses amounted to £402 6s 8d according to the record consulted by Oppenheim (67).

11. Dasent, *APC, 1547–1550* (London, 1890), 92.

12. It is recorded in the Pipe Office Declared Accounts. See Oppenheim, 67.

13. Dasent, *APC, 1547–1550,* 282

14. Ibid., 308.

15. Deposition made by Domenico Erizzo on 14 December 1547. Public Record Office (PRO), HCA 13/5/191–95.

16. PRO, HCA 13/93/202v. For the identification of the Needles as a site of shipwrecks I am indebted to Vanessa J. A. Carr of the Research Department of the PRO.

17. The only naval historian to have drawn attention to the disaster and to the black Guinea diver is Alwyn A. Ruddock, *Italian Merchants and Shipping in Southampton 1270–1600* (Southampton: University College, 1951), 252–53.

18. Deposition made by Domenco Erizzo on 14 December 1547 (HCA 13/5/191–95).

19. Deposition made by Domenico Milanes on 18 July 1548 (HCA 13/93/242–43), and by Antonio de Nicolao on 23 May 1548 (HCA 13/93/275v).

20. Dasent, *APC ,1547–1550,* 123, 133, 176.

21. Depositions made by Bartolomeo Fortini on 11 September 1549 (HCA 13/93/294–95) and by Niccolo de Marini on 7 May 1549 (HCA 13/93/271).

22. Deposition made by Domenico Erizzo on 14 December 1547 (HCA 13/5/195).

23. Depositions made by Thomas Beckingham on 14 May 1549 (HCA 13/93/273v), by Domenico Milanes on 5 June 1549 (HCA 13/93/278); by Giacomo Ragazzoni (Jacobus Ragason) on 25 October 1549 (HCA 13/93/303v–304); and by Niccolo de Marini on 7 May 1549 (HCA 13/93/271) and 5 June 1549 (HCA 13/93, unfoliated).

24. The lieutenant of the Tower received the warrant from the Privy Council "t'enlarge Peter Paule, Italion, without paying any fees for his imprisonment" (Dasent, *APC,1547–1550,* 418.

25. See Appendix for the Latin text of the court minutes; I have added the punctua-

tion and expanded the scribal abbreviations. For the shades of meaning between "servus" and "famulus" see Steven A. Epstein, *Speaking of Slavery: Colour, Ethnicity, and Human Bondage in Italy* (Ithaca: Cornell University Press, 2001), 20. In medieval England, a "famulus" was a full-time-worker on a manor's demesne. See E. M. Postan, *The Famulus: The Estate Labourers in the 12th and 13th Centuries*, Economic History Review Supplement, no. 2 (Cambridge: Cambridge University Press, 1954). The "fala da Guiné" came into being in Portugal as a vehicle for communication between the slaves imported from Africa and the Portuguese population. What was originally the product of the slaves' response to the new realities was eventually appropriated by the Portuguese dramatists of the fifteenth century and by the Spanish playwrights of the sixteenth and seventeenth centuries as a sign of racial difference and cultural inferiority. The "lengua de negro" or "habla guinea" became a stock marker of inferiority in the Spanish drama of the Golden Age. See Baltasar Fra Molinero, *La imagen de los negros en el teatro del Siglo de Oro* (Madrid: Siglo XXI, 1995), 21–25, 161.

26. For a comprehensive account of the island's seizure by the Portuguese and its early history see Peter Russell, *Prince Henry "the Navigator". A Life* (New Haven: Yale University Press, 2000), 204–12. Arguin was the first center of the Portuguese slave trade, Sao Tomé became its new center in the course of the sixteenth century. See John William Blake, *West Africa: Quest for God and Gold 1454–1578* (London: Curzon Press, 1977), 86.

27. For John Lok's kidnapping of a group of Africans in 1554 see P. Fryer, 5–6; for an account of the development of English trade to Guinea after 1552 see chap. 5 in Kenneth R. Andrews, *Trade, Plunder and Settlement. Maritime Enterprise and the Genesis of the British Empire* (Cambridge: Cambridge University Press, 1984, repr. 1991).

28. For Africans groomed as commercial and cultural brokers and for the "fala da Guiné" as used in contemporary Portuguese and Spanish plays and poems see A. C. de C. M. Saunders, *A Social History of Black Slaves and Freedmen in Portugal 1441–1555* (Cambridge: Cambridge University Press, 1982), 12, 99, 168, 169; David Northrup, *Africa's Discovery of Europe 1450–1850* (Oxford: Oxford University Press, 2002), 59–63. For language as a vehicle of imperialism and marker of difference see Stephen Greenblatt, "Learning to Curse: Aspects of Linguistic Colonialism in the 16th Century" in *Learning to Curse: Essays in Early Modern Culture* (New York: Routledge, 1990), and "Kidnapping Language" in *Marvellous Possessions: The Wonder of the New World* (Oxford: Clarendon Press, 1991); Patricia Palmer, *Language and Conquest in Early Modern Ireland: English Renaissance Literature and Elizabethan Imperial Expansion* (Cambridge: Cambridge University Press, 2001), 20–24, 34.

29. The members of Corsi's company were known to several Italian merchants who resided in Southampton and appeared as witnesses before the admiralty: Domenico Erizzo (HCA 13/5/191); Anonio de Nicolao (HCA 13/93/275v); Niccolo de Marini (HCA 13/93 unfoliated), deposition made on 5 June 1549.

30. Peter Fryer in *Staying Power* holds the view that there is no evidence of black people being bought and sold in England until 1621 (8).

31. The case is well documented. Maria Moriana with the help of some Italian acquaintances appealed to the Lord Chancellor, lamenting her ignorance of English and

Latin and complaining about the ingratitude of her master. See Ruddock, 126–27. The only other case of a black servant freed in England known to me occurred in 1490, when king Henry VII manumitted the Portuguese "Pero Alvarez negro e forro." Alvarez returned to Portugal where king John II acknowledged his manumission, granting him the right to settle in his kingdom as a freedman. See Pedro A. d'Azevedo, "Os Escravos," *Archivo Historico Portuguez* 1 (1903): 289–307, doc. iii. The Portuguese court, I think, was the chief purveyor of black servants to the early Tudor royal household and possibly to the Scottish court.

32. For the physician's purchase of the Ethiopian see Rosalyn K. Knutson, "A Caliban in St. Mildred Poultry," ed. Tetsuo Kishi, Roger Pringle, Stanley Wells, *Shakespeare and Cultural Traditions. Selected Proceedings of the International Shakespeare Association World Congress, Tokyo, 1991* (Newark: University of Delaware Press, 1994), 110–26. The physician's name is spelt "Hector Novmieis," in the original document (PRO, REQ 2/164/117), as Vanessa J. A. Carr of the research department was kind enough to confirm. There is not the least doubt about the physician's identity. For documentary information on Dr. Hector Nuñez see Lucien Wolf, "Jews in Elizabethan England," *Transactions of the Jewish Historical Society of England* 11 (1926): 1–91.

33. Also theater owners and brothel-keepers of upper-class establishments had their largest investments in the wardrobes of their companies and of their prostitutes. See Gustav Ungerer, "Prostitution in Late Elizabethan London: The Case of Mary Newborough," *Medieval and Renaissance Drama in England* 15 (2003): 138–223.

34. For the atrocious verse account of Robert Baker's two Guinea voyages in 1562 and 1563 published in Richard Hakluyt's first edition of the *Principal Navigations* (1589), see Kenneth R. Andrews, 115.

35. The issue of the black slaves' adaptability, resilience, acculturation, and acquisition of new identities has been addressed by David Northrup.

36. For the imprecision and interchangeability of the derogatory stereotypes "Moor" and "blackamoor" as used in historical accounts and imaginative literature see Ania Loomba's excellent study *Shakespeare, Race and Colonialism* (Oxford: Oxford University Press, 2002), 46, 47. The term "Morisco" as applied to Jacques Francis is quite beside the point. It actually meant the converted Moors in Spain; in Tudor England, the "Morescoes," as Ania Loomba notes, were the blackfaced, often royal and aristocratic, actors in mummers' plays, miracle plays, morris dancing, and masques (28).

37. The denunciators did not account for the contradiction between their denigration of the Guinea diver as a heathen and his Christian names. There is no doubt about his non-Christian origin, but when captured by the Portuguese, he was obliged to convert, assuming a new identity. What the Italian merchants may have resented is that Francis on reaching manhood probably repented his conversion, openly flouting the observances of the Catholic faith.

38. The case of the Ethiopian has been uncovered by Rosalyn L. Knutson, 116; for the Portuguese legal code, the *Ordenaçoes Manuelinas* (1514, 1521) regulating the slave trade and the legal status of the African slaves see Saunders, 114–16; for Spain see William D. Phillips, Jr., *Slavery from Roman Times to the Early Transatlantic Trade* (Manchester: Manchester University Press, 1985), 111; for the cross-cultural

interactions between Elizabethan England and Morocco see Gustav Ungerer, "Portia and the Prince of Morocco," *Shakespeare Studies* 31 (2003): 78–112. There was no space in my above-mentioned essay on Morocco to address Dr Nuñez's pioneering involvement. As head of the Marrano community in London, he was running a syndicate of merchants linked by close family ties, whose policy was to open up trade with the Mediterranean countries. In the late 1560s, the syndicate was importing Moroccan sugar, melasses, paneles (brown unpurified sugar) and rameals (inferior sugar) via Antwerp in ships flying the Moroccan flag. See HCA 13/16/36v–37; 13/17/48–54; 13/17/54v–58v; 13/17/72–77; 13/17/77v–81v; 13/17/84v–86; 13/17/153–56.

39. For the case of the Russian slave see Folarin O. Shyllon, "Blacks in Britain: A Historical and Analytical Overview," ed. J.E. Harris, *Global Dimensions of the African Diaspora* (Washington, DC: Howard University Press, 1982), 175; for the unsettled legal status of the blacks in England of the eighteenth century see Kenneth Little, 192–95; for the survival of bondmen and villeins in Tudor England see Alexander Savine, "Bondmen under the Tudors," *Transcations of the Royal Historical Society,* second series, 17 (1903), 235–86; for the 1547 Bill for Vagabonds and Slaves introducing the concept of slavery as punishment see C. S. L., Davies, "Slavery and Protector Somerset: The Vagrancy Act of 1547," *Economic History Review,* second series, 19 (1966): 533–49.

40. For an analysis of the growing demand for publications on the African others see Alden T. Vaughan and Virginia Mason Vaughan, "Before *Othello*: Elizabethan Representations of Sub-Saharan Africans," *The William and Mary Quarterly,* 3rd series, 54 (1997): 19–44.

41. William Shakespeare, *The Merchant of Venice* , ed. M. M. Mahood (Cambridge: Cambridge University Press, 1987), 4.1.90–98.

A School for Girls in Windsor

LAETITIA YEANDLE

A letter written from Coventry by Anne Higginson to Lady Ferrers at Tamworth Castle, May 8 [temp. James I or Charles I], taken from the Ferrers collection at the Folger Shakespeare Library. Call no. L.e. [644].

By James I's reign, as the nobility, gentry, and well-to-do middle classes increasingly felt the need to educate their daughters in certain accomplishments of polite society, one begins to find references to schools established for this purpose, particularly in the neighborhood of London. One of the earliest references is to the Ladies' Hall at Deptford in 1617. These schools seem to have been often run by married women. The curriculum could include reading, writing, music, dancing, needlework, and, especially after Charles I's marriage to Princess Henrietta Maria, French. Other opportunities for female education among the upper classes existed as well. It was still customary for those of higher rank to educate their daughters at home or to place them in the households of other noble or well-connected families. If tutors were employed to teach the sons of the family, daughters might also benefit from their instruction. Before the dissolution of the monasteries, nuns had provided some education, and about the beginning of the seventeeth century a number of schools were founded by English nuns and monks in the Spanish Netherlands and France to educate the children of Catholic families that could afford to send their sons and daughters abroad. During the Civil War, some girls' schools in England faced difficult times.

While going through an uncataloged collection of manuscripts relating to the Ferrers family of Tamworth Castle in Warwickshire (Appendix 1), I chanced on a letter that piqued my curiosity. The writer strongly recommends a boarding and day school in Windsor run by a friend of hers for the daughters of ladies and gentlewomen. The letter has no year date, but from its general appearance was probably written in the first half of the seventeenth century. The general design of its watermark is more like that found in paper of the second rather than the first quarter of that century. Since there is not too much factual information on schools for girls at this time I thought the letter might be of interest to social historians and to Leeds Barroll, who has

272

long worked in the field of education and studied the rôle of women in this period.

The letter reads as follows:

[Address leaf]

> To my most Honnared
> and Worthie good Ladi
> the ladi fferrers att
> he<?>r Castell att Tamworth
> geue theese
>
> In

[Remainder of leaf is missing]

[fol. 1ʳ]

My verie good La: my humble Sarvis remembered vnto your
Worship with my due thanks for your great kindnes vnto mee when
I was att Tameworthe, good Madam I neauar was furthar
then Master Halls att Couentree sinc I was with you by the
reason I found Mistress Halls verie weake, and desiared my
company, but my husband went hom presently and according
to his promyse vnto your La: sent a letter vnto Windsore
the Answare hee sent mee yesterday, which is this the
Ientillwoman wee spake of doth contenew her course in
teacheing still, and shee sayth none more wellcom vnto her
then the shalbee of my motiing[*], and because I did writ your
ladiship was one of my best frends shee sayth her best
care shalbe for there good which shee maketh noe question of
but you will geue ther great thankes for ther good education
eueri waye, yf please you to place them with her
her rattes ar this syxteen pounds a yeare a peec, for dyett
lodging, washeing, and teacheing them to worke, reading,
writing, and danceing,) this cometh vnto xxxii^li a yeare, but
for musicke you must paye for besyds according as you will
haue them learn, shee hath teachers, for viall, Singing,
verginnolls, and lutte, which itt may bee will com neare to
the othar eight pound, soe as I told you the wold cost you
som twentie pounds a peece for all, shee saythe shee
hath now tweintie Ientillwe<e>men borders, and half as many
more ladis and Ientillwemens daughter com forth of the
town and Cloisters, for shee hath non but such for the

meannar' sort ar not abell to reache her ratte, shee dothe
protest shee hath tweintie pounds a yeare of som that bee
in her house besyds musicke, but shee sayth shee will sett
her loest ratts vnto mee, as I know shee hath of my own
kindred which I placed with her fowr years agoe, now
good Madam I desire to know your mynd before I goe hom
which wilbe by gods leue vppon frydaye,, and yf your la:
to purpose this Iornneye my husband and my self wilbee

[fol. 1ᵛ]

readi to waitt vppon you, and yf I ware worthie to counssell
you the should ^lose^ noe tim, for the house is larg, a dainttie aire
and Seewtt Walks which the vse to goe, besyds the will profitt
more in Sommar now days be long and lyghtsom, then in

From f.1ᵛ of Anne Higginson's letter to Lady Ferrers.

winter when days be coold and short, althoughe then the sett
in a warme parlor with a good fier, besyds your eldest
daughtter groweth talle and wilbe a woman quickely, and
I feare not but with her Meisters care in her teacheing
will soone return agayne, that your youngest may take
her place, this craueing pardon for being ouar bold to
trobell you this much, but good Madam itt is my loue
vnto your good Ladishep and yours, whom I pray god
to blesse with long, lyfe health, and happines, to his
glorie and your euar comfort, and euar rest your La:
to bee commanded in all loue and dutie

Anne Higginson

yf your Ladiship be not att hom att this tim, I desire
you to send me a Answare vnto couentree vnto Master Ball
and I know hee will send itt vnto Northhampton vnto mee
soe soone as hee receueth itt, for I thinke my husband
doth sett downe his rest to com lyue in couentree, hee
is perswaided by many of his good frends, and hath a
house vppon lykeing vntill mydsomar, to resolu vppon
I haue promysed this mesinger ii^s for bringing yor letter

Couentree this
<x>viiith of may

good Madam send mee word, wheathar Mistress fferrers
bee married or noe, and how shee dothe

The school mentioned in this letter is apparently not otherwise known. The
exact identity of the writer, Anne Higginson, and of the recipient, Lady Ferrers, is not clear. Since Anne Higginson refers to Lady Ferrers's eldest daughter and her youngest, I assume that Lady Ferrers had at least three daughters.
From the letter we learn that Lady Ferrers was looking for a school for two
of her daughters, to begin with her eldest and one other; later, when the eldest
had left, which would probably be after only a short stay, the youngest could
take her place. It so happens that family trees of the Ferrers family at the end
of the sixteenth and the first half of the seventeenth centuries show two members as having each three daughters: Sir John Ferrers (d. 1633) and his son,
Sir Humphrey Ferrers (ca. 1600–1633). If the daughters were the children of
Sir John Ferrers, then they were his daughters by his first wife, Dorothy, the

---

*The word "motiing" probably derives from the verb *to moot* meaning "to speak"
or "to say." *Mooting* can mean "pleading," usually in a legal sense.

daughter of Sir John Puckeringe, who died in 1616, and the stepdaughters of Lady Elizabeth Ferrers, their father's second wife. Their names, in the order in which they appear in family trees, were Frances, Anne, and Jane. Frances married (ca. 1619?) John Pakington (1600–1624, created a baronet in 1620) of Westwood Park in Worcestershire and had a son born in 1620. Anne married on 13 October 1614 the antiquary, Simon Archer (1581–1662, knighted in 1624) of Umberslade in Warwickshire. Jane (d. 1656) married sometime after her father's death in 1633 Thomas Rous (1608–1676, created a baronet in 1641) of Rouslench in Worcestershire and had a son who matriculated in 1654. If the letter was addressed to Lady Dorothy it would have to have been written before 1616 and probably before October 1614 when her daughter Anne was married. If the letter was addressed to Lady Elizabeth it presupposes the existence of a fourth daughter and would have been written ca. 1617 or 1618 after Lady Dorothy's death in 1616 and before Frances's marriage about 1619. In either case, whether the letter was addressed to Lady Dorothy or Lady Elizabeth, it would provide a fairly early reference to a school for the daughters of ladies and gentlewomen.

If the daughters were the children of Sir John's son, Sir Humphrey, the letter was addressed to Lady Anne Ferrers (d. 1667), the sister of Sir John Pakington, bart (1600–1624). She married Sir Humphrey in 1619 and had a son, John (1629–1680), who was never knighted, and three daughters, Lettice, Anne and Elizabeth, who might well have been of an age to be attending school in the 1630s. About 1637 Lady Anne remarried as his second wife, Philip Stanhope, earl of Chesterfield (1584–1656), widowed in 1636. They had a son Alexander (1638–1707) and in late 1641 her daughter Lettice married one of his sons by his first marriage, Ferdinando (ca. 1615–1643). Lettice's sister Anne married Walter Horton of Catton in Derbyshire (b. ca. 1626); her other sister Elizabeth married as his second wife John Hyde (b. before 1608), son of Sir George Hyde of Kingston Lisle in Berkshire (d. 1623) and Katherine, daughter of Sir Humphrey Ferrers, I presume the Sir Humphrey who died in 1608 and was Elizabeth's great grandfather.

The Mistress Ferrers mentioned in the letter, whose marriage was imminent or had just taken place, was probably not a daughter but some relation. Could she possibly be Sir John Ferrers's daughter Jane who married Thomas Rous after her father's death in 1633? If so, the letter would date from the mid-1630s and would have been written to Lady Anne Ferrers. It would then concern the education of Lettice, Anne and Elizabeth.

And who was Anne Higginson? The surname turns up in several Midland counties. John Bridges, for example, in his *History of Northamptonshire* refers to a Higginson family of Berkswell, Warwickshire, six miles west of Coventry. The only Anne Higginson about whom I could find substantive information was Anne (Herbert) Higginson (d. 1640), the wife of the Reverend Francis Higginson (d. 1630) who was chosen as "Teacher" at Salem,

Massachusetts. Both emigrated to New England in 1629. However, her basically secretary hand as seen in a letter at the Massachusetts Historical Society is not the same as the secretary hand of the Anne Higginson of the Ferrers letter. It is always possible that both letters were written by amanuenses.

Despite our not knowing exactly who wrote the letter, nor who received it, nor in what year it was written, I hope its contents will be of interest to historians of the seventeenth century. Perhaps when the Ferrers collection is fully cataloged in the not-too-distant future, pertinent information will come to light.

Like so many letters of the time the letter is written on a bifolium folded in half with a watermark of two posts or pillars and the initials D(?)LG in between them, not unlike the design of no. 3486, dated 1636, in Heawood. It measures approximately 307 by 202 mm. The left-hand margin is about 30 mm. wide; there is none on the right-hand side. The letter has the remains of a red circular seal, ca.10 mm. in diameter. The lower portion of the address leaf is missing. The letter and its signature are written in the secretary hand with few abbreviations or corrections. I have silently expanded common abbreviations. The last word on the address leaf, "In", is in another hand and may have been followed by "haste" when the leaf was intact.

The Ferrers collection was acquired at a sale of Sir Thomas Phillipps's manuscripts at Sotheby's on December 12, 1977. The letter was part of Phillipps MS 28688.

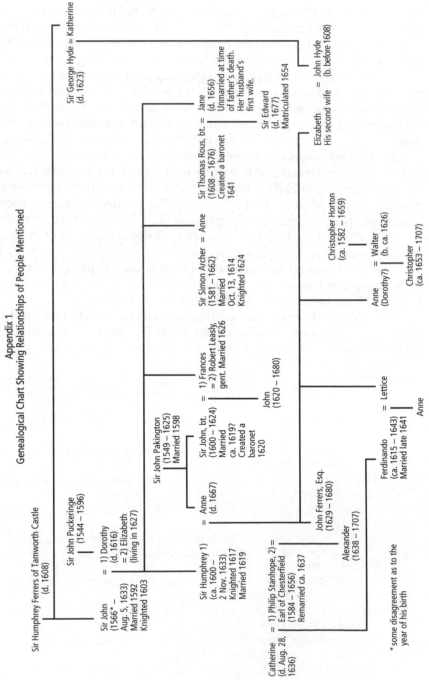

Appendix 1
Genealogical Chart Showing Relationships of People Mentioned

Sir Humphrey Ferrers of Tamworth Castle (d. 1608)

Sir John Puckeringe (1544 – 1596)

Sir George Hyde = Katherine (d. 1623)

Sir John (1566* – Aug. 5, 1633) Married 1592 Knighted 1603
= 1) Dorothy (d. 1616)
= 2) Elizabeth (living in 1627)

Sir John Pakington (1549 – 1625) Married 1598

Jane (d. 1656) Unmarried at time of father's death. Her husband's first wife.

Sir Edward (d. 1677) Matriculated 1654

Elizabeth = John Hyde
His second wife (b. before 1608)

Sir Humphrey 1) (ca. 1600 – 2 Nov. 1633) Knighted 1617 Married 1619
= Anne (d. 1667)

Sir John, bt. (1600 – 1624) Married ca. 1619? Created a baronet 1620
= 1) Frances = 2) Robert Leasly, gent. Married 1626

Sir Simon Archer (1581 – 1662) Married Oct. 13, 1614 Knighted 1624
= Anne

Sir Thomas Rous, bt. (1608 – 1676) Created a baronet 1641

Christopher Horton (ca. 1582 – 1659)

Catherine (d. Aug. 28, 1636)
= 1) Philip Stanhope, 2) = Earl of Chesterfield (1584 – 1656) Remarried ca. 1637

John Ferrers, Esq. (1629 – 1680)

John (1620 – 1680)

Anne (Dorothy?) = Walter (b. ca. 1626)

Christopher (ca. 1653 – 1707)

Alexander (1638 – 1707)

Ferdinando (ca. 1615 – 1643) Married late 1641
= Lettice

Anne

* some disagreement as to the year of his birth

Selected Bibliography

Alcock, N. W. "The Ferrers of Tamworth Collection." *Archives* 19, no. 86 (October 1991): 358–63.

Bridges, John. *The History and Antiquities of Northamptonshire. Compiled from the Manuscript Collections of . . . John Bridges, esq. By the Rev. Peter Whalley.* Oxford: Sold by T. Payne . . . , 1791.

Cokayne, George E., Complete Peerage of England, Scotland, Ireland, Great Britain and the United Kingdom . . . London: The St. Catherine Press, 1910–59.

———, ed. *Complete Barontage*: [1611–1800]. Exeter: W. Pollard & Co., 1900–09.

Collins, Arthur. *Collins's Peerage of England . . . greatly augmented . . . by Sir Egerton Brydges.* London: Printed for F.C. and J. Rivington [et al.], 1812.

Fraser, Antonia. *The Weaker Vessel. Woman's Lot in Seventeenth Century England.* London: Weidenfeld and Nicolson, 1984.

Gardiner, Dorothy. *English Girlhood at School.* London: Oxford University Press, 1929.

Heawood, Edward. *Watermarks, Mainly of the 17th and 18th Centuries.* Hilversum, Holland: The Paper publications society, 1950.

Henderson, Katherine U. *Half Humankind: Contexts and Texts of the Controversy about Women in England, 1540–1640 . . .* Urbana: University of Illinois Press, 1985.

The House of Commons, 1558–1603, ed. P. W. Hasler. London: Published for The History of Parliament Trust by H.M.S.O., 1981.

The House of Commons, 1660–1690, ed. B. D. Henning. London: Published for The History of Parliament Trust by Secker & Warburg, 1983.

Keeler, Mary Frear. *The Long Parliament, 1640–1641.* Philadelphia: American Philosophical Society, 1954.

Laurence, Anne. *Women in England, 1500–1760.* London: Weidenfeld and Nicolson, 1994.

Madan, Falconer. "The Gresleys of Drakelowe." Vol. I (n.s.) of *Collections for a History of Staffordshire,* ed. The William Salt Archaeological Society. London: Harrison and Sons, 1898.

Palmer, C. F. R. *The History of the Town and Castle of Tamworth.* Tamworth: J. Thompson; London: J. B. Nichols, 1845.

Thompson, Roger. *Women in Stuart England and America.* London, Boston: Routledge and K. Paul, 1974.

University of Cambridge. *Alumni cantabrigienses . . . ,* comp. John Venn and J. A. Venn. Cambridge: University Press, 1922–54.

The Victoria history of Berkshire, ed. P. H. Ditchfield et al. [London: A. Constable and Co.], 1906–24.

The Victoria History of the County of Stafford, ed. William Page et al. London: A. Constable, 1908–96.

The Victoria History of the County of Warwick, ed. H. A. Doubleday et al. [London: A. Constable], 1904–69.

The Visitation of the County of Warwick . . . 1682 . . . 1683, ed. W. H. Rylands. London: Harleian Society, 1911.

Wedgwood, Josiah C., "Staffordshire Parliamentary History." Vols. [20] and [22] of *Collections for a History of Staffordshire*, ed. The William Salt Archaeological Society. London: Harrison and Sons, 1919 [for 1917], and 1920–22.

Index

281